# LOCOMOTIVES OF THE PENNSYLVANIA RAILROAD
## Volume 1, THE EARLY YEARS, 1848-1874

By Richard D. Adams

*"If* [the Rev. Henry Ward] *Beecher should go to Altoona,*
*he would find himself without a subject,*
*unless he chose Motive Power."*

William Jackson Palmer to Isaac Clothier

A PUBLICATION OF THE PENNSYLVANIA RAILROAD TECHNICAL & HISTORICAL SOCIETY

ISBN Numbers
Hardbound edition 978-0-9821485-2-5
Softbound edition 978-0-9821485-3-2

A Publication of the Pennsylvania Railroad Technical & Historical Society

### Editor
Chuck Blardone
2886 Wimbledon Lane
Lancaster, PA 17601-1454
717.898.9057
cblardone@comcast.net

### Proofreader
George Pins

### Layout
Gail Gottlund

### Photo Enhancement and Graphics
Chuck Blardone

### Cover Design
Chuck Blardone

### Printed by
Kutztown Publishing Co., Inc., Kutztown, PA 19530

# LOCOMOTIVES OF THE PENNSYLVANIA RAILROAD
## Volume 1, THE EARLY YEARS, 1848-1874

### By Richard D. Adams

## The Pennsylvania Railroad Technical & Historical Society

The Pennsylvania Railroad Technical & Historical Society is an educational, Pennsylvania non-profit tax exempt 501(c)(3) corporation, incorporated in 1974. Our goals are to promote the preservation and recording of all information regarding the organization, operation, facilities and equipment of the PRR.

The Society has 3,000 members worldwide; many gather each year at our annual meeting, usually held in early May. Meetings are held in different cities to encourage maximum participation. Local chapters around the country provide members and invited guests with regular meetings throughout the year.

The Society's quarterly journal, *The Keystone* magazine, has been published continuously since 1968. The Society also publishes an online electronic monthly newsletter, *The Keystone e-NEWS*, and an online electronic monthly modeling magazine, *The Keystone Modeler*. The PRRT&HS also publishes books on PRR subjects. A complete listing of all available magazines, books and other items may be seen and purchased directly from the PRRT&HS, at our web site, *www.prrths.com*.

The former PRR passenger station in Lewistown, Pennsylvania, built in 1849, has been restored by the Society. It houses our extensive archive collection, which is currently being inventoried and organized. When complete, the collection will be available for research. Portions of the Mechanical Department files are now available, by appointment, to researchers.

Your participation and membership in the Society is solicited. Please write to PRRT&HS, P.O. Box 54, Bryn Mawr, PA 19010-0054, call 610-527-3565, or e-mail *ahartPRR137@aol.com* for further information.

# FOREWORD

## By Al Buchan, President, PRRT&HS

This book is the third in a series on PRR equipment published by the Pennsylvania Railroad Technical & Historical Society, begun in 2007 with *Pennsylvania Railroad Business & Special Cars – A Century of Tuscan Red Deluxe,* followed in 2008 by *Pennsylvania Railroad Flat Cars in Revenue and Work Service, 1881-1968.*

Although the late Dick Adams was an aficionado of PRR steam locomotives and had researched this area of interest during his entire life, one could probably say this book began in earnest on May 5, 1985, when Dick rode a replica of the *John Bull* at the Railroad Museum of Pennsylvania at Strasburg. In the ensuing years, Dick continued to toil on this project, unfortunately never getting it to a final stage ready for publication prior to his untimely death on December 9, 2005.

Luckily for us the project and all of the research did not also pass away, because one of Dick's long-time close friends, Gary Rauch, got involved at the request of another of Dick's good friends, Bob Johnson, who was aware of the Society's desire to publish this work. Because Gary was very much in favor of having Dick's scholarship made available, he agreed to help prepare the manuscript for publication, despite a lack of specific knowledge of the subject matter. Gary likes to tackle projects during which he learns something, such as the various presentations and articles that he has completed for the Society, and he tells us, "This was a monumental learning experience."

Most of the book's photos are from Dick's collection, which has been donated to the Society. Being unfamiliar with early steam locomotives, it was a major task in itself for Gary to identify them. He scanned them; they have subsequently been Photoshopped by Chuck Blardone.

Gary notes that although Dick did acknowledge some of the people who helped along the way, others may not have been recognized. If you worked with Dick on this project and have not been appropriately recognized, please accept our apologies; it is an unintentional oversight.

Special recognition goes to Chris Baer. After Gary had worked on Dick's manuscript to ensure correct language and adherence to the Society's style guidelines, Chris made many suggestions for corrections and clarifications.

We hope you enjoy this book.

## Front Cover:

**#422 (Baldwin, c/n 1658, September 1867).** #422 was one of the last non-standard 4-4-0's built for the PRR by Baldwin. On May 14, 1871, it came in for repairs at Altoona, having run 153,280 miles on the Middle Division. It was estimated that it would cost $1,262.73 to repair. *(Railroad Museum of Pennsylvania)*

## Rear Cover:

**#251 (Baldwin, c/n 1129, May 1863).** Originally built for branch line passenger service, #251 was frequently used on the official photographer's train. The locomotive was sold to E.H. Wilson & Co., a used equipment dealer, in March 1882. *(Author's collection)*

# PREFACE

On May 5, 1985, I was at the Railroad Museum of Pennsylvania in Strasburg, Pa., standing on the footplate of the replica of the *John Bull* with Russ Wilcox and Ben Kline. Ben hooked up the valve gear, opened the throttle, and the *John Bull* began to move. The ride was less than 200 feet, but nonetheless it was an unforgettable experience. I had been in the cab of a number of PRR steam locomotives, but had never experienced anything like this.

When I returned home I began to look through my collection of locomotive registers. On a handwritten register for January 1, 1874, I found the *John Bull* was still listed. I decided to add the photographs I had on hand and publish the register. The project turned out to be more complex than I envisioned.

Most of the information available was from secondary sources, and needed to be checked against a variety of both published and unpublished materials. In the course of my research I discovered a major discrepancy in the official PRR information. Several secondary sources raised significant questions about the identity of the locomotives built by the Lancaster Locomotive Works. In answering those questions I ended up with enough material for a small book. The Friends of the Railroad Museum of Pennsylvania graciously published my work, *The Lancaster Locomotive Works, 1853-1870*. This was the genesis of the larger work presented here.

I trust the following material will give the reader an insight into the initial development of the steam locomotive on the Pennsylvania Railroad, and the mechanical practices that were significant to that development. The roster is included to give a picture of the actual equipment in use.

A number of people contributed to this work and I am deeply indebted for their help and support. I especially want to thank Joe Acri, the late Harry Albrecht, Ian Fischer, Roger L. Keyser [now deceased], James J.D. Lynch, Jr. (deceased), Russell Wilcox (deceased), Robert Emerson (formerly of the Railroad Museum of Pennsylvania), and Dr. Robert Dructor, of the Pennsylvania Historical & Museum Commission.

I wish to give a special thanks to those who have reviewed this work, especially Chris Baer. I am especially indebted to my wife, Jan Alsever, who read the manuscript and offered corrections and suggestions.

I hope that those interested in the Pennsylvania Railroad will find this record both interesting and helpful.

*Richard D. Adams*
*July 6, 2005*

## ADDENDUM TO THE PREFACE

Dick Adams worked for many years on the manuscript for this book. He gathered information from a wide variety of sources, including private collections. At the time of his death, he had not quite completed the integration of these data, nor had he completed the work of creating archival citations for all of his sources. The notes he bequeathed to the PRRT&HS do not include all the sources, so I have tried to track down the proper references within the constraints of time and travel. The interested reader should be able to find most of the information which Dick used, using the citations in this book.

Because Dick addressed many aspects of the early history of PRR locomotives, there is some duplication in the presentation, to facilitate telling the complete story of each aspect. In some cases, the sources disagreed, as the reader will learn from Dick's scholarly exegesis of the information regarding which engine was really the first PRR locomotive. Dick was unable to resolve all of the inconsistencies before his death, and I have attempted to avoid such contradictions, in some cases by deleting confusing material.

There are terms used in this book to describe a variety of locomotive appliances that did not stand the test of time, and thus might be unfamiliar to students of latter-day steam power. An excellent and easily-available source describing these early inventions is John White's book, *American Locomotives, An Engineering History, 1830-1880*, which is included in the Bibliography. The reader interested in seeing illustrations of some of these features should refer to the Index of Figures.

Please note that as locomotives were removed from the roster, the numbers were used again, often multiple times, so that engine numbers are not unique to a particular locomotive. Finally, as the author points out, most of the available photos of the earliest PRR locomotives show the engines as rebuilt; please read the captions carefully.

I would like to thank Joe Acri, Rich Ader, Chris Baer, Kurt Bell, Robert L. Johnson, John Sanders, and of course our editor, Chuck Blardone, for their contributions to this effort.

*Gary C. Rauch*

## DEDICATION

This book is dedicated to the memory of Harvey C. Eldridge, who acquired from the PRR, over a period of years, many of the images in this book, and, before his death, gave them to the author. Harvey Eldridge was an engineman on the New York Division, interested in PRR locomotive history. Harvey proudly told the author, *"I ran the Nelly Bly."*

# TABLE OF CONTENTS

# LOCOMOTIVES OF THE PENNSYLVANIA RAILROAD
## Volume 1, THE EARLY YEARS, 1848-1874

### CHAPTER 1

#### THE PENNSYLVANIA RAILROAD IN 1874

On January 1, 1874, J. Edgar Thomson, president of the Pennsylvania Railroad, had only five months to live, dying on the night of May 27. Since the organization of the PRR in 1846, he had shaped the character and destiny of the railroad, first as Chief Engineer, and then in 1852 as the Company's third president. It would not be an overstatement to call the PRR "Mr. Thomson's Railroad."

The Pennsylvania Railroad was the child of Philadelphia commercial interests who sought reliable, year-round transportation to the expanding midwest. The Commonwealth of Pennsylvania had invested tremendous sums of money in the Main Line of Public Works, a system of railroads and canals between Philadelphia and Pittsburgh. The state system was plagued by difficult topography, low water, graft, blatant patronage, and selectively prohibitive tariffs. Philadelphia was losing out to the emerging transportation systems that fed the western trade to Baltimore and New York.

The Pennsylvania Railroad Company was formed by special act of the legislature, signed into law on April 13, 1846, to build a line of railroad from Harrisburg to Pittsburgh. After certain requirements of financing were achieved, letters patent were issued and portions of the line at the eastern and western termini were put under contract. With this action an attempt by the Baltimore & Ohio Railroad to build into Pennsylvania to Pittsburgh was disallowed and

Philadelphia's trade route was secure.

J. Edgar Thomson was hired as chief engineer by the Board and began construction of the railroad. Thomson gave major attention to building the line from the east. The railroad began at Harrisburg, crossed the Susquehanna River, and proceeded up the valley of the Juniata River toward the Allegheny Mountain. Revenue operation was officially begun on September 1, 1849, when *Mifflin* (**Fig. 95**) hauled

a passenger train from Harrisburg to Lewistown. The Company completed its line to McVeytown in the Juniata Valley by December 24, 1849, and reached Hollidaysburg, at the foot of the Allegheny Mountain, by September 16, 1850, where it connected with the Commonwealth's Allegheny Portage Railroad. The PRR used the Allegheny Portage until its own line over the mountain was completed in 1854 and the arching of the Gallitzin tunnel was

PASSENGER STATION, PHILADELPHIA—1876.

*Figure 1. The Centennial Station in Philadelphia was opened in 1876, replacing the original 30th Street Station that served the PRR from 1864-1876.*

(Author's collection)

completed in early 1855. The line from Harrisburg to Pittsburgh was declared complete.

The company began to expand, and on August 1, 1857, purchased the Main Line of Public Works from the Commonwealth, which included the Philadelphia & Columbia and Allegheny Portage Railroads, and the main line canal. This gave the PRR its own line from Philadelphia to Pittsburgh. Further expansion was achieved by supporting the construction of connecting lines and gaining control by stock ownership or lease. The PRR invested heavily in the Northern Central, gained control of the Cumberland Valley,

leased the Philadelphia & Erie in January 1862, and acquired control of the stock of the Allegheny Valley. The maneuvering of Jay Gould forced the PRR to tie down its western connections. The Company acquired the Pittsburgh, Ft. Wayne & Chicago by lease in June 1869, and had control of the Columbus, Chicago & Indiana Central and the Pittsburgh, Cincinnati & St. Louis Railway by stock purchase that same year. On April 1, 1870, the PRR caused the Pennsylvania Company to be formed to operate all lines west of Pittsburgh and Erie.

The PRR moved to acquire its own line to the New

York area with the lease of the United Canal & Railroad Companies of New Jersey (Camden & Amboy, New Jersey Railroad & Transportation Company and the Delaware & Raritan Canal Company) and the Philadelphia & Trenton in June 1871, which, due to a court case, did not take effect until December 1871. Through the Baltimore & Potomac, the PRR reached Washington from Baltimore in 1872, although through service was not possible until the B&P Tunnel opened in 1873. By January 1, 1874, the PRR extended from Jersey City to Chicago and through controlled connections reached St. Louis. The Philadelphia, Wilmington & Baltimore, Western New York & Pennsylvania and New York, Philadelphia & Norfolk were yet to come under PRR control to complete the system. In the previous year (1873) the PRR (Lines East) earned $39,983,000 in revenue while the Pennsylvania Company (Lines West) earned $30,720,000.

The interests of the management of the Pennsylvania Railroad extended far beyond the original vision of its incorporators and the expansionist impulse finally became an issue at the stockholders meetings. The management had not consulted the stockholders when they moved to acquire the lines to Chicago and St. Louis and the United Railways of New Jersey. A stockholder's investigating committee was appointed on March 10, 1874, which finally reported after Thomson's death.

J. Edgar Thomson had assumed tremendous control over the affairs of the Company. He virtually ran the PRR himself and developed a managerial structure that placed him at the apex of power. On the Board, Thomson and as many as four vice-presidents represented the management. (There was one V.P. on the Board in 1860-63, two in 1863-69, four in 1869-1873, three in 1874-80, two in 1880-82, and finally four again, after 1882). Thomson kept the stockholders in line by high profits, regular dividends that averaged between 6 and 7% per year

*Figure 2. The Harrisburg Station was built in 1857, and was used until 1887. The locomotive is presumed to be* Cambria *(#9), built by Norris Brothers in 1849.*

(Author's collection)

during his tenure, and a continual upgrading of their property. Ultimately the PRR's management never altered the Company's structure of accountability, as the stockholder's investigating committee report testifies. The PRR was owned by its stockholders. Thomson was first and foremost a servant of the Company. His biographer, James A Ward, summed up the PRR President's drive: J. Edgar Thomson used all his considerable talents to complete *a transportation empire linking the Atlantic with important Midwestern river cities, and to erect unassailable defenses about it.*[1]

Thomson's concern to protect and extend the influence of the PRR led him and the friends of the PRR to assemble a railroad empire that ultimately controlled almost 10% of the nation's railways. This effort began rather modestly as the President and a few PRR insiders invested small sums in the resources along the line. The most conspicuous member was Thomas A. Scott, Thomson's successor as PRR president. The group initially included Andrew Carnegie, William Jackson Palmer, Herman Haupt, Matthias Baldwin and various PRR Board members. The financial associations were later expanded to include Simon Cameron, George Pullman, George Washington Cass, and Jay Cooke. This group invested in every transcontinental line being built in the 1870's except the Central Pacific, and for a short time controlled the Union Pacific.

The panic of 1873 ended all this. Jay Cooke's Northern Pacific defaulted and broke these arrangements. Thomas A. Scott was deeply involved in building the Texas & Pacific, and the panic forced

▶

*Figure 4. Looking west at Lewistown Junction, the hotel served as the PRR's passenger station. The woodshed blocks the view of the freight warehouse, which later became the passenger station, and now houses the PRRT&HS archives. The locomotive is the* Clarion *(#12), a Baldwin 4-4-0.* (Author's collection)

*Figure 3. The McVeytown Station in the Juniata Valley, as it appeared in the 1870's.* (Robert L. Johnson collection)

him to make arrangements with his creditors to extend the payments of some debts, to avoid making an assignment in default of his obligations. The rest of the Philadelphia group also had to scramble to meet their obligations. For a season, the PRR's inner circle and friends controlled a rail empire that stretched from New York City to Promontory Point, Utah, and through the Southern Railway Security Company from Philadelphia to Memphis and Mobile.

**◄ Figure 5.** *The Official Photographer's train, with a Baldwin 4-4-0 (the Clarion?), is on the eastbound track in Jack's Narrows, west of Mount Union. The canal still has water in it.* (Author's collection)

## PENNSYLVANIA RAILROAD COMPANY
### January 1, 1874

**PENNSYLVANIA RAILROAD COMPANY:**

A. J. Cassatt, General Manager

**PENNSYLVANIA RAILROAD GRAND DIVISION:**

G. Clinton Gardner, General Superintendent

J. Reilly, Superintendent of Transportation

**Philadelphia Division:**

Wm. F. Lockard, Superintendent

| | |
|---|---|
| Philadelphia to Harrisburg | 105.3 miles |
| Delaware Extension | 9.8 |
| Downingtown to Waynesburg | 18.0 |
| Pomoroy to Delaware City | 38.7 |
| Dillerville Intersection to Columbia | 29.5 |
| Columbia to York | 13.5 |
| Philadelphia Division | 214.8 miles |

**Middle Division:** S. A. Black, Superintendent

| | |
|---|---|
| Harrisburg to Altoona | 131.6 miles |
| Middle Division | 131.6 miles |

**Pittsburgh Division:** Robert Pitcairn, Superintendent

| | |
|---|---|
| Altoona to Pittsburg | 116.7 miles |
| Altoona to Henrietta | 27.6 |
| Y Switches to Newry | 3.0 |
| Williamsburg Jct. to Williamsburg | 13.5 |
| Springfield Jct. to Mines | 8.9 |
| Roaring Springs to Ore Hill | 3.0 |
| Martinsburg Jct. to Martinsburg | 0.7 |
| Cresson to Ebensburg | 11.0 |
| Greensburg to Connellsville | 24.3 |
| Pittsburgh Division | 208.7 miles |

**Lewistown Division:** Persifer F. Smith, Superintendent

| | |
|---|---|
| Lewistown Jct. to Milroy | 12.3 miles |
| Lewistown to Selinsgrove | 43.9 |
| Lewistown Division | 56.2 miles |

**Bedford Division:** William H. Brown, Superintendent

| | |
|---|---|
| Mt. Dallas to State Line | 38.7 miles |
| Dunnings Creek Jct. to Holderbaum | 10.5 |
| Bedford Division | 49.2 miles |

**Tyrone Division:** S. S. Blair, Superintendent

| | |
|---|---|
| Tyrone to Lock Haven | 54.3 miles |
| Milesburg to Bellefonte | 2.5 |
| Tyrone Intersection to Curwensville | 44.0 |
| Osceola Jct. to Houtzdale | 6.0 |
| Dunbar Jct. to Colliers | 1.9 |
| Philipsburg to Morrisdale | 3.7 |
| Tyrone Division | 112.4 miles |

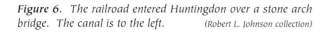

*Figure 6. The railroad entered Huntingdon over a stone arch bridge. The canal is to the left.* (Robert L. Johnson collection)

**Western Pennsylvania Division:**

Robert Neilson, Superintendent

| | |
|---|---|
| Blairsville to Allegheny City | 63.5 miles |
| Blairsville Intersection to Indiana | 19.0 |
| Butler Branch Intersection to Butler | 21.0 |
| Western Pennsylvania Division | 103.5 miles |
| **Total PRR Grand Division** | **876.4 miles** |

**UNITED RAILROADS OF NEW JERSEY**
**GRAND DIVISION:**

F. Wolcott Jackson, General Superintendent

**New York Division:** Geo. W. Barker, Superintendent

| | |
|---|---|
| New York to West Philadelphia | 90.0 miles |
| Harsimus Jct. to Harsimus Cove | 1.5 |
| Rahway to Perth Amboy | 7.9 |
| New Brunswick to East Millstone | 8.3 |
| Monmouth Jct. to Rocky Hill | 6.5 |
| Princeton Jct. to Princeton | 3.0 |
| Holmesburg Jct. to Buselton | 4.2 |
| N.Y. Division | 121.4 miles |

**Belvidere Division:** J. A. Anderson, Superintendent

| | |
|---|---|
| Trenton to Manunka Chunk | 67.9 miles |
| Somerset Jct. to East Milstone | 22.6 |
| Lambertville to Flemington | 12.0 |
| Belvidere Division | 102.5 miles |

**Amboy Division:** I. S. Bucklew, Superintendent

| | |
|---|---|
| New York to Philadelphia | 92.2 miles |
| (*via* boat New York to South Amboy) | |
| Jamesburg to Monmouth Jct. | 5.5 |
| Bordentown to Trenton | 6.1 |
| Kinkora to New Lisbon | 14.2 |
| Florence to Foundry | 2.2 |

*Figure 7. Clarion poses on bridge #10 over the Little Juniata River, east of Tyrone. The lettering on the tender dates the photograph between 1863 and 1867.* (Author's collection)

**Figure 8.** *The main line heads west out of Altoona toward the Horseshoe Curve. The line to the left goes to Hollidaysburg.* (Robert L. Johnson collection)

**Figure 10.** *A passenger train at the same spot as* **Fig. 9.** *The date is probably between 1865 and 1870.* (Author's collection)

**Figure 9.** *A 4-6-0 drifts downgrade near the Horseshoe Curve at Kittanning Point, followed by a freight train. Note the cabin car on the freight, which appears to be a box car fitted with windows.* (Robert L. Johnson collection)

**Figure 12.** *A mail train heads east at Pack Saddle on the Western Division.* (Author's collection)

| | |
|---|---|
| Burlington to Hightstown (*via* Pemberton) | 50.8 |
| Mt. Holly to Medford | 8.5 |
| Evanstown to Vincentown | 2.8 |
| Amboy Division | 187.8 miles |
| **Total United Railroads of New Jersey Grand Division** | |
| | **411.7 miles** |

### PHILADELPHIA & ERIE GRAND DIVISION:
W.A. Baldwin, General Superintendent
**Eastern Division**, T. Gucker, Superintendent

| | |
|---|---|
| Sunbury to Renovo | 92.4 miles |
| Montandon to Laurelton | 18.6 |
| Eastern Division | 111.0 miles |

**Middle Division**, E.L. Tyler, Superintendent

| | |
|---|---|
| Renovo to Kane | 100.7 |
| Middle Division | 100.7 miles |

**Western Division**, J. W. Reynolds, Superintendent

| | |
|---|---|
| Kane to Erie | 94.5 |
| Western Division | 94.5 miles |

**Danville, Hazelton & Wilkes-Barre Division**

| | |
|---|---|
| Sunbury to Tomhicken | 45.2 |
| DH&W Division | 45.2 miles |
| **Total P&E Grand Division** | **351.4 miles** |

### RAILROADS CONTROLLED BY THE PENNSYLVANIA RAILROAD COMPANY

| | |
|---|---|
| West Jersey RR | 129.2 miles |
| Cumberland Valley RR | 125.0 |
| Pittsburgh, Virginia & Charleston RR | 31.0 |
| Allegheny Valley RR | 258.9 |
| Oil Creek & Allegheny RR | 121.0 |
| Buffalo, Corey & Pittsburg RR | 42.2 |
| Northern Central Ry | 319.8 |
| Baltimore & Potomac RR | 91.3 |
| Alexandria & Fredericksburg Ry | 34.4 |
| **Total Controlled Roads** | **1,152.8 miles** |

### RAILROADS CONTROLLED BY THE PENNSYLVANIA COMPANY

| | |
|---|---|
| Pittsburg, Ft. Wayne & Chicago Ry | 468.3 miles |
| Cleveland & Pittsburg RR | 199.6 |
| New Castle & Beaver Valley RR | 14.9 |

**Figure 11.** *Looking east at Conemaugh, the shop and enginehouse are just beyond the tree in the center of the photograph. The Little Conemaugh River runs along the hillside behind the engine-house.*

(Author's collection)

▶

*Figure 13. Looking east at Greensburg.*
(Author's collection)

| | |
|---|---|
| Erie & Pittsburg RR | 82.5 |
| Lawrence RR | 17.4 |
| Ashtabula, Youngstown & Pittsburg RR | 63.5 |
| Mansfield, Coldwater & Lake Michigan RR | 61.2 |
| Toledo, Tiffin & Eastern RR | 42.4 |
| Cleveland, Mt. Vernon & Columbus RR | 157.5 |
| Jeffersonville, Madison & Indianapolis RR | 226.0 |
| Indianapolis & Vincennes RR | 117.0 |
| Indianapolis & St. Louis RR[2] | 265.1 |

**Total Roads Controlled by the Penna. Company**

**1,715.4 miles**

### RAILROADS CONTROLLED BY THE PITTSBURG, CINCINNATI & St. LOUIS RY

| | |
|---|---|
| Pittsburg, Cincinnati & St. Louis Ry | 201.1 miles |
| Cincinnati & Muskingum Valley Ry | 148.4 |
| Little Miami RR | 196.1 |
| Columbus, Chicago & Indiana Central Ry | 582.3 |

**Total Roads controlled by the PC&St.L Ry 1,150.7 miles**

St Louis, Vandalia, Terre Haute & Indianapolis RR

**238.0 miles**

▶

*Figure 14. The Pittsburgh Union Station and hotel, built in the 1860's, was destroyed by fire during the riots of 1877.*
(Author's collection)

# CHAPTER 2
## THE LOCOMOTIVES OF PRR PREDECESSOR LINES

## THE PHILADELPHIA & COLUMBIA
### The Steam Railway Comes to America

The world's first successful commercial railway, England's Stockton & Darlington, opened on September 27, 1825, and was soon followed by the Liverpool & Manchester in 1830. The winner of the L&M's Rainhill trials to determine the best locomotive type, Stephenson's *Rocket*, set the basic style for the locomotive engine until the end of steam. The *Rocket* combined a self-contained firebox at the rear of the locomotive, a multiple fire tube boiler, a blast pipe to produce the necessary draft to keep the fire burning, and cylinders transmitting their power to the drive wheels by simple directly-connected rods.

The commercial steam railway was less than five years old when it came to America. It is rather amazing that it took so short a time for this radically new technology to cross the Atlantic and produce our first railways, actually between the opening of the Stockton & Darlington and the Liverpool & Manchester. The American development of the commercial steam railway turned out to be atypical in several respects, when compared to the British model. American railways were constructed through open country rather than through the already heavily populated English landscape, and the distances between population centers were much greater here than in England. Second, American railways followed the land rather than relying on expensive works such as cuts, fills, tunnels, and stone viaducts. American railways were lightly built and had an up and down profile. Finally, there was limited capital in America to produce gigantic works and the light traffic was insufficient to produce enough dividends to cover grand improvements once the infant companies started running. Most of our early railway engineers made their obligatory trip to England to examine the railways there. This included the PRR's own J. Edgar Thomson.

### The Threat From the North and the South

During the early years of the republic the three major middle-Atlantic cities, New York, Philadelphia and Baltimore, were in competition. With the construction of the Erie Canal, New York City vastly extended its area of commercial dominance and surpassed the other two. Ground was broken for "Clinton's Ditch," as the Erie Canal was known, on July 4, 1817, and the canal was opened throughout on October 26, 1825. The National Road and the Chesapeake & Ohio canal, which terminated in Georgetown outside Washington, both primarily Federal projects, somewhat benefited Baltimore. The city finally took a radical step in promoting the Baltimore & Ohio Railroad, which was chartered by the Maryland Legislature on February 28, 1827. The first stone was laid on July 4, 1828 and the line was opened through to Frederick, Md. on December 1, 1831.

### The Main Line

Philadelphia's hinterland was particularly vulnerable. The Susquehanna River, which drained the central part of the state, emptied into the Chesapeake Bay not far from Baltimore. The way west from Philadelphia was blocked by a series of mountain ridges that extended westward for approximately 140 miles, ending at Chestnut Ridge just east of Greensburg. Pittsburgh was located on the Ohio River, which flowed west to the Mississippi. To remedy the threat to Philadelphia, the Pennsylvania Legislature appointed a three-man Commission for Promoting the Internal Improvement of the State on March 27, 1824, to explore routes for a canal between the Susquehanna and Allegheny Rivers. The initial report was not well received, and on April 11, 1825, another act was passed which created a five-man Board of Canal Commissioners, charged with examining seven routes to the west. The final plan was adopted on February 25, 1826, when the Public Works was authorized by the Legislature, which approved construction at each end but did not provide a route for the middle part. On July 4, 1826, Governor George Shulze turned the first spade of earth at Harrisburg.

John Wilson was appointed by the Canal Commissioners to make surveys for a canal or railroad between Philadelphia and the Susquehanna River. Wilson was born near Stirling, Scotland, March 19, 1789. For a time, he was a major in the Corps of U.S. Topographical Engineers, resigning his commission in 1818. He died on board ship February 27, 1833 at Matanzas, Cuba, while about to sail for the U.S. His health had been ruined by exposure to malaria and other subtropical diseases while working in South Carolina.

Wilson began at Valley Forge on the Schuylkill, about 24 miles above Philadelphia, and moved westward along the "Great Valley" of Chester County. The engineer corps under Wilson's supervision consisted, in addition to Wilson, of a surveyor, a leveler, a rodman, two chainmen, and one or two axmen. One of the chainmen was J. Edgar Thomson. John Wilson's son, William Hassel Wilson, was employed by his father and recorded his recollections of the early days of the Philadelphia & Columbia rail line.[3] The survey team proceeded up the Chester Valley to Mine Ridge. Because of the scarcity of water along the projected route, the Chief Engineer decided against the adoption of a canal and made his report to the Board of Canal Commissioners. The party then made their way to Middletown and made a survey for the extension of the canal then under construction to Columbia. The Susquehanna was unusually low and the party was exposed to malaria. After reaching Columbia the survey team proceeded eastward to connect with their previous work, but was felled by the fever. They resumed after some weeks and completed their work. John Wilson's report on the canal survey is dated December 14, 1827, and the railroad report, December 17, 1827. Both were presented to the Canal Commissioners on December 25, 1827.

The Board of Canal Commissioners reported to the Legislature that *a navigable communication between eastern and western waters of Pennsylvania is wholly impracticable.* The governor then approved an Act on March 24, 1828 and the entire length of the Main Line was officially located, except for the Portage, which was left open, including whether it should be a road or railroad. The Main Line was to consist of five sections: a 103-mile Western Division canal from Pittsburgh to Johnstown, a 36-mile portage across the Allegheny Mountain, a 127-mile Juniata Division canal from Hollidaysburg to Duncan's Island, a 43-mile Eastern Division canal from Duncan's Island to Columbia, and an 82-mile railroad from Columbia to Philadelphia.

## THE PHILADELPHIA & COLUMBIA RAILROAD

The location of the railroad from Philadelphia to Columbia was started during the summer of 1828, when the grading and bridging of 20 miles of road at each end were authorized and put under contract. The contracts were a right of patronage and were dispensed with an eye toward buying votes and paying off supporters. No consistent plan was followed to locate and complete one section of railroad or canal before moving on to the next. The contracts were let all along the Main Line, where friends needed to be rewarded and enemies silenced. The general sentiment of the residents of Lancaster County was that if the railroad should ever be completed, which they doubted, it would ruin the County, as the Philadelphia market would be overstocked with the products of farms from a distance where land was cheaper and the expenses less. They also worried that the railroad would need fewer horses than the Conestoga wagons using the Lancaster-Philadelphia Pike. They certainly did not consider that the railroad might use locomotive engines.

The work of grading and bridging began in 1829 under the guidance of Major John Wilson. J. Edgar Thomson, who had been promoted to Principal Assistant Engineer, took charge of the eastern division. William H. Wilson was the Sub-Assistant Engineer of the western division. Although the Commission was willing to let contracts, the Legislature was slow in appropriating money. The survey work was more or less complete and money was so slow in coming that, with the consent of the Canal Commissioners, Major John Wilson and his corps, including J. Edgar Thomson, began a location of the Camden & Amboy Railroad. William H. Wilson was left in charge of the unfinished work on the eastern 20 miles.

The line as finally located passed north of the city of Lancaster, touching the northeast corner. The roadbed was graded, but nothing more was done.

An Act was approved by the governor on March 21, 1831 to complete the first 20 miles of the Philadelphia & Columbia, and also the Portage Railroad over the Allegheny Mountain. The citizens of Lancaster successfully petitioned the Legislature in 1832 to have the road run through the central business district of their city. Finally, in 1831-1832 the Legislature made a large appropriation and the work was again vigorously undertaken.

In the early part of 1830, William H. Wilson accompanied his father to observe the track laying on the Baltimore & Ohio Railroad in the vicinity of Ellicott's Mills, Md. He writes that *the track then in progress of construction was formed of granite sills about eight by fifteen inches square, in various lengths from six feet upwards, bedded on broken stone trenches. Upon the sills were placed flat iron bars, two and a half inches wide by five-eighths of an inch in thickness, which were secured by spikes driven into wooden plugs inserted into holes drilled into the stone sills.*[4] The B&O had sent some of their engineers to England to observe the railroads there, and after their return this track construction was adopted.

In April 1831, two Divisions of the P&C were organized, of about 40 miles each. William H. Wilson was placed as Principal Assistant Engineer on the eastern end, which extended from Broad Street in Philadelphia to Coatesville. In June the grading and bridging of the middle section was placed under contract, construction was started on the Schuylkill bridge, and the grading of the three-mile section to Broad Street was started.

The P&C had a variety of track construction methods: granite or wooden sills on which were secured flat rails, and "rolled iron edge" rails held by chairs to stone blocks with locust sills. Six miles of line were laid with granite sills, like the B&O, as an experiment 18 miles were laid with wooden sills and flat rails, and the rest was laid with stone blocks and "rolled iron edge" rails. The stone blocks were placed three feet apart. The iron rails, secured from the Ebbw Vale Iron Works in Wales, were of the Wigan pattern, with top and bottom surfaces parallel, and weighed 41¼ lbs. to the yard. The rails originally came in two lengths, 9' and 15'. The 15' rails were used on curves, but it was soon found that longer lengths could be more easily bent. Eighteen-foot lengths came into use. The rails were placed so that joints were alternated, and every nine feet a wooden cross tie was substituted for the two stone blocks. In typical English fashion the rails were secured in chairs by iron and later wooden wedges. When renewals became necessary, the edge rails were replaced by "T" rails and wooden crossties. It became apparent that the granite blocks were too rigid.

The first 20 miles of line from the head of the inclined plane above the Schuylkill River westward was opened for travel on October 18, 1832. When the line was completed from Philadelphia via Lancaster to Columbia (one track), and equipment had been tested on the Columbia-to-Lancaster segment, through operation began on April 16, 1834. As finally located, the railroad began at the corner of Broad and Vine Streets in Philadelphia, ran for a short distance north on Broad, then west on Pennsylvania Avenue to 21st Street, and thence northwest to a crossing of the Schuylkill River below Peters Island. On the west bank of the river was an inclined plane 2,805' in length, with a rise of 187' (7%), called the Belmont Plane. From the top of the plane, the line kept to high ground, climbing to Paoli. It then followed along a low range of hills, which formed the southern boundary of the Chester Valley, crossing the Brandywine Creek at Downingtown and the West Branch of the Brandywine at Coatesville. The line crossed from the Schuylkill watershed to the Susquehanna watershed over Mine Ridge at Gap, the highest point on the line. To reach Lancaster, it crossed Pequea Creek at Leaman Place and

then Conestoga Creek on a 1,412'-long viaduct just east of town. It then followed the Conestoga Valley south of a line of low hills between Dillerville and the Susquehanna, and then descended an 1,800' inclined plane with a 90' drop to reach the canal basin at Columbia. Knight and Latrobe commented that *the curves upon this road are very numerous, and of short radii, frequently 600 feet, and in some cases even less; whilst the grades are often at the rate of 30, and in places 45 feet to the mile.*[5] When completed, the cost of the road, as reported to the Auditor General of the Commonwealth in 1843, was $4,204,969.96.

On October 7, 1834 the line was formally opened with double track (81.8 miles). The tracks were 9'-9" center to center. Like most early railroad ventures, the P&C was originally to operate like a turnpike. The road was constructed to accommodate horse drawn vehicles, and the track layout and switches were constructed with this in mind. Crossovers between the double tracks were placed at intervals and side tracks of about 200 feet in length were constructed 1½ miles apart for the whole distance of the road. Individual transporters would haul their goods in their own conveyances, and the railroad would charge a toll for use of its tracks. Passengers were handled in stagecoach-like conveyances with center doors and the driver perched in his elevated seat at the front. A trip from Philadelphia to Columbia took about nine hours, and the horses were changed every 12 miles. Private transporters using their own four-wheeled wagons and teams handled freight. These cars could carry about three to four tons. The cars ran individually, and when a passenger car overtook a freight car, the freight was to turn out onto the first siding to let the passenger car pass. The toll for use of the road varied from six mills to 4¢ per ton depending on what was carried, and 1¢ a mile for each passenger. In addition there was a tax of 1¢ per mile for a freight car, 2¢ per mile for a baggage car, and 1¢ per mile

for each set of wheels on a passenger car.

In April 1834 the Legislature gave the Canal Commissioners permission to let contracts for a number of locomotives, but there was considerable opposition to their use by persons using the road or residing near it. They feared that the engines would destroy the value of their horses, and that the sparks from the locomotives would destroy their houses and barns. Edward F. Gay, then chief engineer of the road, strongly urged the exclusive use of locomotives in several of his reports. Finally, on April 1, 1844, the Canal Commissioners acted to prohibit private horse-drawn conveyances on the P&C west of the head of Belmont Plane.

## The Delaware & Hudson Canal Company Has For Sale

It is not surprising to learn that the first locomotive engines for our railways were imported from England. The earliest English locomotives to arrive were the four single-flue colliery-type engines purchased by the Delaware & Hudson in 1829. Due to inadequate trackage they barely operated. The next locomotives imported were in 1831, and were of the revised plan of Stephenson's *Rocket*. One of the first of these was the Camden & Amboy's *John Bull*.

Before the Legislature had given permission to proceed in procuring locomotives for the P&C, the Board of Canal Commissioners received a letter:[6]

*Phila'd., Feb'y 7th 1834*

*Gentlemen:*

*Understanding it is contemplated to use Locomotive engines upon the Columbia Rail Road, I take the liberty to inform the Board of Commissioners, that the Delaware & Hudson Canal Company a few years since imported four engines of the best construction and workmanship to run upon their road. These engines were found on trial to answer all the purposes of the Company; but it was thought they were too heavy for the elevated parts of the road and the use of them on that account discontinued.*

*They are now for sale and could no doubt be purchased for much less than the original cost. Not knowing with whom the negotiation should be opened and being desirous that the Engines should be sold; I take the liberty of making communication hoping it may be thought in ..... to purchase them for the Columbia road.*

*Very respectfully*
*Your Obd. Servt.*
*Chas. S. Wurts*

*P.S. The locomotives are I am informed calculated for heavy draought (sic) and could be placed on the road immediately after the opening of navigation in the spring.*

Three of the locomotives the D&H had for sale were built by Foster, Rastrick & Company, and the fourth was built by Robert Stephenson & Company. All were single-flue, vertical-cylinder engines with walking beams. The Canal Commissioners were interested enough in the offer to look further into the matter:

*Lancaster, March 13th 1834*
*Board of Canal Commissioners*
*Gentlemen:*

*I have had an interview with John Wurts, Esq. President of the Carbondale Railroad Company, who informs me that they have imported four Locomotive Engines of the best English construction for their Railroad but when they came to try them it was found that their road was too weak to admit the use of them. The company are therefore desirous of selling them... these Engines cost in England £750 and can now be purchased at a sum considerably less than $3,000 .... each. Two other engines can be procured immediately, so that six engines can be put upon the road as soon as ordered.....*

*A. Snyder, Esq. informs us that he can procure two more in England at any time he may receive an order and that Engines can be constructed there on eight weeks notice.... If any objections should be made to the use of steam on account of the delay in procuring Engines, you can furnish the above information ... The Engines at the*

*Carbondale road are 6½ tons and otherwise adapted to our road ....*

*Very respectively yours*
*W.B. Mitchell*

Two months later Mr. Mitchell continued to follow up on the D&H offer, but with a significant announcement at the end of his letter:

*Lancaster, March 18th 1834*
*Dear Sir,*

*I have been so much from home lately that I have not answered your several letters with the promptness, which I should have done... I returned from Phila. day before yesterday and have made an arrangement with M.W. Baldwin to go with me to Raundet [sic] on the Hudson river, to examine the Carbondale Engines... Mr. Baldwin, although an Engine builder himself, is of the opinion that those Engines, though not calculated for those high velocities which had latterly been the go in England, are well adapted for the Columbia road when we don't desire a greater speed than from 12 to 16 miles per hour... I take him along for the purpose of making a careful examination of their workmanship and material, ... if their performance turns out satisfactory I think we had better buy them ... Baldwin's new Engine will be ready for trial in less than three weeks and Long's small one will go on trial tomorrow a week ...*

*Respectively yours*
*W.B. Mitchell*

### The Locomotive Engine Arrives

Long's "small one," *Black Hawk* (built May 1833), was the first steam locomotive to be tested on the Philadelphia & Columbia between Lancaster and Columbia, as early as April 2, 1834. It was tested only. The Canal Commissioners allowed public demonstrations of Long's locomotives but never bought them. Stephen H. Long (1784-1864) was a graduate of Dartmouth who then taught math at West Point. He went west as a part of the Army Engineers

to explore the Spanish Borderlands, and then was assigned by the War Department to survey the newly-organized B&O railroad in 1828. He was thereafter appointed chief engineer of the proposed railroad. Colonel Long had his own independent ideas about motive power. He proposed light coal burning locomotives as suitably fitted for American railroads, with approximately six tons as the maximum weight. In conjunction with William Norris of Philadelphia, Long formed the American Steam Carriage Company and began building locomotive engines to his design. Sipes reports that:

*... as the eastern end of the road was not then completed, this engine was hauled over the turnpike to Lancaster, where her trips were to commence, and she was to be used between that city and Columbia. The day for her trial-trip was a beautiful one, and thousands of people had gathered from the surrounding county to witness the novel performance. Governor Wolf and the State officials were all in Lancaster to participate, and excitement ran high. Men were stationed along the track to keep the too-venturesome boys out of danger, and among these guardians was an Irishman, who made himself particularly officious. Armed with a club, he paraded along the road, shouting to the eager urchins, "Get out of the track! When she starts, she'll go like a bird, and ye'll all be kilt." The important moment came, - the engineman pulled the lever, but the locomotive would not go. At length, by pushing, the train got underway; but the wonderful machine did not "go like a bird." [7]*

The first successful engine on the P&C was Matthias Baldwin's third locomotive, *Lancaster* (**Fig. 109**). This was the first locomotive actually bought for the roster. Originally ordered by the Philadelphia & Trenton, it was delivered to the P&C at a cost of $5,580, and put on the road on June 28, 1834. The *Lancaster* was a "Jervis" type single-driver engine. John B. Jervis of the Mohawk & Hudson Railroad added a four-wheel truck to the front of the locomotive to guide it over America's rough track, creating a 4-2-0. This type was almost the universal American type of locomotive through the 1840's. Baldwin's *Lancaster* had a "D"-shaped Bury firebox with inside connection and Baldwin's own half-crank axle.

The initial motive power roster of the Philadelphia & Columbia totaled about 40 locomotives to handle the traffic on 82 miles of railroad. Most of them were "bread and butter" 4-2-0's. Initially several were imported from England by the P&C; six from Robert Stephenson, Newcastle on Tyne, and two from Tayleur & Company, Newton-le-Willows, but they did not work out as well as the local product. After the failure of Long's "small one," William Norris turned to the well-accepted 4-2-0. William Norris was a dry goods merchant with an eye to the profits that could be made in the emerging market of steam railways. In 1834 he hired Joseph Harrison. Although Harrison's time at Norris was brief, he introduced the first of what was to become the standard product, with the Philadelphia & Columbia's *William Penn*. The locomotive had the driving axle placed in front of the Bury firebox, steeply-inclined cylinders with a long stroke-to-bore ratio, and outside valves driven by inside motion. The locomotive was inside-connected with a half-crank axle.

Another of the P&C's locomotives built by Norris, *George Washington*, created quite the controversy. On July 10, 1836, it ascended the grade of the Belmont incline hauling a load of ten tons. Nine days later the locomotive did itself one better when she hauled a train of two cars with 53 passengers, weighing 31,270 lbs., up the Belmont incline in two minutes, 24 seconds. The results were widely publicized and widely questioned. With a steam pressure of between 60 and 80 psig it would have been impossible for an engine of 14,930 lbs., of which 8,700 lbs. were on the drivers, to haul such a load. It has been suggested that Frederick DeSanno, Norris' works manager, modified the drawbar so that

the tender weight was thrown upon the locomotive and also had two or three men on the engine and two or three more on the tender. This would give a weight on drivers of perhaps 11,500 lbs. With the spring safety valve adjusted, from 90 to 100 psig then could have been carried in the boiler.

*Washington County Farmer* represented a further development of the "Jervis type" built by Norris. This locomotive weighed 18,170 lbs. In October 1836 she hauled a train weighing 30,116 lbs. up the Belmont incline from a standing start at the bottom. It had the usual Norris placement of the driving axle in front of the Bury firebox, steeply-inclined cylinders with a long stroke-to-bore ratio and outside valves driven by inside motion. This locomotive was outside-connected.

As more locomotives were added from local builders, the Canal Commissioners felt that they had to support the Commonwealth's local manufactories, and additional locomotives were purchased from a variety of small machine shops that built from one to several engines: the Bridgewater Iron Works of Philadelphia, Coleman Sellers & Sons of Philadelphia, Davis H. Dotterer of Reading, Garrett & Eastwick of Philadelphia, and Pennel, Lenher & Hume of Lancaster. There were even several engines built by McClurg, Wade & Company of Pittsburgh. The only out-of-state builders were the New Castle Manufacturing Company of New Castle, Del. and Ross Winans of Baltimore, Md. The early builder of choice was M. Baldwin of Philadelphia, closely followed by William Norris of Philadelphia, later operating as Norris Brothers.

The road located its shops at Parkesburg. The foreman of the shops was John Brandt. Brandt was born at Lancaster in 1781 or 1782 and trained as a blacksmith. He moved to Philadelphia in 1828 to work with Coleman Sellers & Sons. Brandt returned to Lancaster to resume his trade as a blacksmith, but was soon employed by the P&C. He organized the

Parkesburg Shops and served as foreman from 1833 to 1838. (Brandt was sacked by the Democratic administration of Gov. David R. Porter in early 1839 because he had served under the previous Antimasonic regime.) Brandt is known to have been on the Georgia RR in 1839-40, and on the New York & Erie in 1842-1851. Brandt later served as Superintendent of the New Jersey Locomotive & Machine Company of Paterson, N.J., and then the Lancaster Locomotive Works of Lancaster, Pa. At both establishments he built engines for the P&C.

During 1837, two engineers from the Baltimore & Ohio, Jonathan Knight and Benjamin Latrobe, made an examination for the principal railroads of the Northern and Middle States. They visited the P&C on the 1st of December, and rode from Philadelphia to Parkesburg, where instead of meeting with the Superintendent of Motive Power, Alexander Mehaffy, they encountered Brandt, the Superintendent of the Parkesburg Shop. Brandt told Knight and Latrobe that the engines of Baldwin were preferred by the P&C. Baldwin had stated and Brandt then confirmed that the *Paoli* had made 175 trips in as many successive days between the inclined planes at the Schuylkill and the Susquehanna without receiving or needing any repairs. The engine ended this service because it was found that the journal boxes had worn out. Baldwin also said that he had met but with a single instance of a fractured crank axle, out of 100 that he made.

The tenders on the P&C locomotives were made so that some of their weight could be transferred to the locomotive by means of a screw. Two kinds of spark arrestors were used, one placed at the top of the smokestack and the other at the base. Brandt considered that the spark arrestor at the top of the stack interfered least with the draft. The wire netting on the top burned out in about three or four weeks, while the netting on the sides lasted about six months. The spark arrestor at the base of the stack burned out quickly, but while intact was the most effective in reducing sparks.

**Chart 1** shows the locomotives on the road, on October 31, 1837, as listed by Knight and Latrobe. The remarks were prepared by John Brandt.[8]

A number of the early locomotives of the P&C were subsequently transferred to the Allegheny Portage. It would appear that there was quite an exchange between the two state roads. A list of the location of the P&C's locomotives for November 30, 1846 shows *Conestoga* at Clarke's Ferry, Pa., known today as Clarks Ferry. There it was clearly being used as a boat engine, the same as *Wisconsin,* shown in **Chart 1**. The Clarke's Ferry road and towpath bridge, which was essential to tow canal boats from the east to the west side of the river, was partially washed out in a flood on March 15, 1846, and not restored until December 1846.

## Politics and Coal [9]

Knight and Latrobe noted in their report that the P&C used any kind of wood in any stage of seasoning, which was then supplemented with bituminous coal to ensure free combustion and rapid generation of steam. The early engines on the P&C were designed to burn wood, and considerably more money was spent on wood than on coal. Brandt reported to Baldwin that he had run one of his engines, hauling 35 cars, from Columbia to Philadelphia to determine the cost of fuel. The locomotive, unnamed in the report, consumed two cords of wood at $4 per cord for a total of $8, and 15 bushels of bituminous coal

▶

Key

| | |
|---|---|
| BLW | M. Baldwin, Philadelphia, Pa. |
| CS&S | Coleman Sellers & Sons, Philadelphia, Pa. |
| G&E | Garrett & Eastwick, Philadelphia, Pa. |
| McCW | McClurg, Wade & Company, Pittsburgh, Pa. |
| NCMfg | New Castle Manufacturing Co., New Castle, Del. |
| Wm N | William Norris, Philadelphia, Pa. |

Chart 1

**Philadelphia & Columbia Engines on the Road as of October 31, 1837**

| Name | Type | Builder | c/n | Date Built | Date Placed on Road | Remarks |
|---|---|---|---|---|---|---|
| Backwoodsman | | McCW | | 11/1836 | 11/18/1836 | |
| Bald Eagle | 4-2-0 | G&E | | 3/1837 | 3/3/1837 | |
| Brandywine | 4-2-0 | BLW | 18 | 10/1835 | 10/25/1835 | 2nd class, in running order, outside connection. |
| Bush Hill | 4-2-0 | Wm N | | 4/1837 | 4/13/1937 | |
| Columbia | 4-2-0 | BLW | 4 | 7/1834 | 5/18/1835 | 2nd class, now in running order, intended for 4 wheels and made 6-wheeled engine. Not a good machine. |
| Conestoga | 4-2-0 | BLW | 67 | 2/1837 | 2/22/1837 | After 35 trips, taken to the Portage Road, 1st class. |
| Constitution | 4-2-0 | Wm N | | 6/1837 | 6/19/1837 | |
| Delaware | 4-2-0 | BLW | 8 | 2/1835 | 5/18/1835 | 2nd class, wants repair, out of use. |
| Downingtown * | 4-2-0 | BLW | 88 | 8/1837 | 4/16/1837 | 1st class, at work. |
| Enterprise | 4-2-0 | G&E | | 5/1837 | 5/23/1837 | |
| Farmer, Wash. Co., | 4-2-0 | Wm N | | 10/1836 | 10/18/1836 | Runs between Phila. and Schuylkill, repaired by maker. |
| Franklin, Ben. | 4-2-0 | Wm N | | 8/1836 | 8/18/1836 | |
| Gay, Edw. F. * | 4-2-0 | BLW | 68 | 3/1837 | 3/14/1837 | 1st class, at work. |
| Indiana * | 4-2-0 | BLW | 75 | 5/1837 | 5/1/1837 | 1st class, on Columbia Rail Road. |
| Independence | 4-2-0 | Wm N | | 4/1837 | 4/4/1837 | |
| Juniata | 4-2-0 | BLW | 15 | 9/1835 | 7/7/1835 | 2nd class, outside connection, encountered Susquehanna at Cotesville bridge, repairs of accident cost $695. |
| Kentucky | 4-2-0 | BLW | 14 | 7/1835 | 7/23/1835 | 2nd class, went to Harrisburg R Road, was run off that road. |
| Lafayette | 4-2-0 | Wm N | | 3/1837 | 3/21/1837 | |
| Lancaster | 4-2-0 | BLW | 3 | 6/1834 | 5/18/1835 | 2nd class, charged with $440, for new tender used by other engine, oldest engine on road. |
| Madison, Jas. | 4-2-0 | Wm N | | 3/1837 | 3/21/1837 | |
| Mississippi * | 4-2-0 | BLW | 78 | 5/1837 | 5/9/1837 | Ran off road while road was repairing, cost of repairs $133, accident not included, will cost $400. |
| Montgomery* | 4-2-0 | BLW | 79 | 5/1837 | 5/15/1837 | 1st class, on Columbia Rail Road. |
| Morris, Rbt. | 4-2-0 | Wm N | | 5/1836 | 5/12/1836 | Met with accident. |
| Octorara | 4-2-0 | BLW | 69 | 4/1837 | 4/7/1837 | 1st class, repairing at Baldwin's expense, firebox gave way |
| Ohio | 4-2-0 | BLW | 22 | 2/1835 | 5/18/1835 | 2nd class, ran against a car on siding, accident cost $300. |
| Paoli * | 4-2-0 | BLW | 65 | 2/1837 | 2/22/1837 | 2nd class, running. |
| Parkesburg * | 4-2-0 | BLW | 72a | 3/1837 | 4/2/1837 | 1st class, on Columbia Rail Road. |
| Pennsylvania | 4-2-0 | BLW | 7 | 2/1835 | 5/19/1835 | 2nd class, ran off track and shattered to pieces. Repairs of accident $1,307. |
| Pequa * | 4-2-0 | BLW | 74 | 4/1837 | 4/23/1837 | 1st class, running. |
| Philadelphia | 4-2-0 | BLW | 6 | 11/1834 | 5/18/1835 | 2nd class, wants repairs, run down. |
| Pittsburger | 4-2-0 | McCW | | 3/1837 | 3/29/1837 | |
| Planet | 4-2-0 | NCMfg | | ? | 5/28/1836 | |
| Sampson | 4-2-0 | CS&S | | 9/1836 | 9/1/1836 | |
| Schuylkill | 4-2-0 | BLW | 10 | 4/1835 | 5/18/1835 | 2nd class, ran off road, almost rebuilt, ran 16,000 or 17,000 miles without losing a trip. |
| Susquehanna | 4-2-0 | BLW | 9 | 3/1835 | 5/18/1835 | 2nd class, encountered Juniata not yet repaired, will cost $1,500. |
| Telegraph | 4-2-0 | G&E | | 4/1837 | 4/16/1837 | |
| United States | 4-2-0 | Wm N | | 5/1837 | 5/22/1837 | |
| Virginia | 4-2-0 | BLW | 66 | 2/1837 | 2/22/1837 | |
| West Chester * | 4-2-0 | BLW | 63 | 2/37 | 1/19/1837 | 2nd class, in shop, dome gave way. |
| Wisconsin * | 4-2-0 | BLW | 81 | 5/1837 | 5/28/1837 | 1st class, turned into ferry-boat engine at Clarke's Ferry on Susquehanna. |

* Have done nearly all the work on the road for the last six months.

costing $4.20. The coal interests in the Legislature were puzzled by the road's dependence on wood. An investigation was launched, followed by resolutions professing concern for the public welfare. Since the inception of the road, the farmers along the route had complained about the wood sparks from the locomotives, which had set fields and barns afire. The Senate resolution ended by asserting that:

*Whereas, the use of wood for fuel on the Railroads of this Commonwealth is productive of danger, and occasions much apprehension to the owners of property through which such railroads pass, which might be avoided by the use of mineral coal;*

*Therefore,*

*Resolved, that the committee of Roads, Bridges and Inland Navigation inquire into the practicability and expedience of using mineral coal, exclusively, as fuel for locomotives on the railroads of this Commonwealth, and of prohibiting by law, the use of any other fuel for such purpose.*[10]

The resolution was adopted after a second reading on December 18, 1837. Since the only railroads over which the Legislature had direct control were the two roads of the Main Line, the Philadelphia & Columbia and the Allegheny Portage, they would be directly implicated in the legislative resolution. Governor Joseph Ritner took a stand against the experiments with mineral (anthracite) coal on the state roads. In a typical election-year move, the Governor claimed that the impact of the financial depression of 1837 made the experiments much too expensive for the Commonwealth to undertake. The resolution was passed anyway and the Board of Canal Commissioners was directed to carry out fuel experiments on the Philadelphia & Columbia.

A direct result of this resolution was the purchase of one of Ross Winans' "Grasshopper" type 0-4-0 locomotives, *Baltimore*, in February 1837, which was specifically designed to use anthracite coal. The Winans "Grasshopper" was a continuation of

Phineas Davis' design for the B&O. They had an upright boiler and a walking beam drive. A locomotive called *Anthracite*, built by Garrett and Eastwick, was also tried out and ran about seven trips. The report of the Motive Power department to the Canal Commissioners stated that...

*The experiments, which the board directed to be made, have established the fact that anthracite coal can be successfully used as fuel in propelling, at any required speed, the locomotive engine, while its use will add to the security of passengers, and the safety of the property of persons bordering upon the road.*[11]

Governor Ritner shifted positions and in his last annual message announced that the P&C had complete success in using anthracite. The newly-elected Porter administration continued to make every effort to popularize the use of mineral coal in locomotives. The Porter faction felt that the expense of new equipment and experimentation was secondary to the possibility of showing the superiority of Pennsylvania coal. Success meant an extension of the Porter Democrats' power, prestige for Pennsylvania and profits for the mine operators. Two coal-burning locomotives were purchased from William Norris of Philadelphia in March 1839, *Simon Cameron* and *Simon Snyder*. The next coal burner was purchased from Ross Winans, an improved "Grasshopper" with horizontal cylinders replacing the vertical cylinders and walking beams, aptly named *W.F. Packer*. Packer was one of the three Canal Commissioners appointed by Porter when he took office, and was later governor. The State road also purchased five locomotives from D.H. Dotterer & Company of Reading, who made claims that his engines could burn either anthracite or wood. Of the 42 locomotives on the P&C on November 30, 1841, only one burned wood exclusively, 30 burned bituminous coal and wood, nine burned both bituminous and anthracite coal and wood, and two burned anthracite. An attempt was made to convert a wood-burning

Baldwin locomotive to coal-burning by using Eastwick & Harrison's wrought-iron grate, designed specifically for coal burning. In this arrangement a "U"-shaped slot in the top of each grate bar was filled with clay. The draft of the locomotives was found insufficient to keep the anthracite burning properly. James Cameron, Superintendent of Motive Power, added a small steam driven blower to provide the draft. He felt that Winans' blower used on the "Crab" type locomotive was superior and urged the State to buy the patent and apply it to the road's locomotives. Regardless of the still-unresolved problems with burned-out grates, clogged tubes and short firebox life, Cameron reported that the practicability of using Pennsylvania coal had been firmly established.

The next report issued by Cameron's successor was less enthusiastic. Winans' vertical boiler locomotive was considered barely satisfactory using anthracite. The majority of locomotives could not be made to burn anthracite at all, and could only be made to burn bituminous with the addition of a blower. The Commonwealth decided not to spend further money on Winans' locomotives and to economize on fuel. Wood mixed with bituminous was again the norm. Unfortunately the sparks from bituminous coal held their heat longer than wood sparks. The hazard of fire prompted the Legislature to pass a law on February 3, 1846, which provided compensation to those who had suffered fire loss caused by the sparks thrown out by the State's locomotives.

## Changes

The first branch off the Philadelphia & Columbia was the West Chester Railroad, built in 1832 to form a connection between the P&C near Frazier and the town of West Chester, about nine miles distant. It was also in 1832, on June 9, that the Pennsylvania Legislature approved an Act to construct the Portsmouth & Lancaster rail-road from Portsmouth (Middletown) and later Harrisburg to Lancaster to connect with the State road.

The P&C replaced its Columbia Plane on March 4, 1840 with a new 6.5-mile line. Things were about to change radically. On April 13, 1846 the Pennsylvania Railroad was chartered. The major effort of construction of the new road was concentrated on its eastern end, building up the Susquehanna to a crossing of the river at Rockville, proceeding up the west bank to the Juniata River, and then on to the west. On August 29, 1848, the Harrisburg, Portsmouth, Mountjoy & Lancaster railroad Company applied to the PRR board for a switch to connect it to the PRR. (Incorporated June 9,1832, as the "Portsmouth and Lancaster rail-road Company," this line was renamed "Harrisburg, Portsmouth, Mountjoy & Lancaster railroad Company" on March 11, 1835.) After long negotiations, on April 21, 1849 the PRR entered into a contract with the HPM&L to conduct operations over the line and to purchase all its equipment, effective with the opening of the PRR's line to Lewistown.

The new railroad to the west threw a great deal of traffic onto the P&C and during the next ten years it replaced its entire locomotive fleet. In April 1845 the P&C bought a flexible-beam-truck 0-6-0 from Baldwin, and added two more in 1847. Developed by Baldwin in 1842, these locomotives were intended for heavy service on the poor trackage of America's emerging railway system. They were equipped with a flexible front truck carrying two axles, which were fixed to slide laterally, while remaining parallel to the rigid rear axles. Baldwin patented this arrangement on August 25, 1842 (#2759). J. Edgar Thomson, while chief engineer of the Georgia Railroad, bought the first Baldwin flexible-beam-truck 0-6-0 in 1842.

The P&C bought its first 4-4-0 in May 1848, and through May 1851 the road acquired a total of 15 of these rather primitive 4-4-0's from Norris Brothers. The locomotives continued the typical Norris construction pattern and appear to be a lengthened 4-2-0, with the addition of a set of drivers behind the Bury firebox. The first few were built without cabs, which were later added by the P&C. The P&C eventually settled on 54" drivers for freight and 60" drivers for passenger locomotives.

The P&C then turned to its former Parkesburg Shop foreman, John Brandt, now at the New Jersey Locomotive & Machine Company of Paterson, N.J., for eight passenger 4-4-0's with 60" drivers and 16" x 22" cylinders. The locomotives had the typical Brandt sloping cylinders. The valve covers sloped down from the connection with the smokebox to the outside, a peculiar arrangement that was Brandt's signature. The road purchased two Baldwin 4-4-0's from the PRR, *Lehigh* and *Luzerne*, with 54" drivers, and another 4-4-0 from Baldwin with 60" drivers. Although the P&C purchased only one more Baldwin 4-4-0 and several 4-4-0's

from Richard Norris & Son of Philadelphia, and the New Jersey Locomotive & Machine Company, it became the major customer of the on-line Lancaster Locomotive Works. Brandt had moved from Paterson to Lancaster in 1854 and built 15 4-4-0's for the P&C. Over a period of ten years, the P&C changed from a road operated by 4-2-0's to a road operated by 4-4-0's. Three flexible-beam-truck

### Chart 2

### Philadelphia & Columbia All-Time Register of Locomotives

| Name | Type | Builder | c/n | Built Date | Drivers, in. | Cylinders, in. | Date In Service | Note |
|------|------|---------|-----|-----------|-------------|---------------|----------------|------|
| Green Hawk | 2-2-0 | Long | | 10/1832 | | | | Ret'd to Boston & Prov. |
| Black Hawk | 2-2-0 | Long | | 5/1833 | 54 | | | Ret'd to Boston & Prov. |
| ? | 2-2-0 | Long | | 5/1833 | | | | Ret'd to Boston & Prov.? |
| The first three locomotives were demonstrated only, and were not part of the official roster. | | | | | | | | |
| Firefly | | Tylr | 4 | 7/1833 | 54 | 9x14 | 7/24/1835 | Sold, 1836 or 1837 to C&W |
| Red Rover | | Tylr | 5 | 7/1833 | 54 | 9x14 | 7/27/1835 | Sold, 1836 or 1837 to C&W |
| Lancaster | 4-2-0 | BLW | 3 | 6/1834 | 54 | 10x16 | 5/18/1835 | To AP, 3/11/1847 |
| Columbia | 4-2-0 | BLW | 4 | 7/1834 | 54 | 10-1/2x16 | 5/18/1835 | To AP, 3/11/1847 |
| Pennsylvania | 2-2-0 | Stph | 104 | 1834 | 54 | 10x15 | | Rblt NCMfg, 1836, *Comet*, to AP |
| Philadelphia | 2-2-0 | Stph | 105 | 1835 | 54 | 10x15 | | Rblt NCMfg, 5/28/1836, *Planet*. |
| Kentucky | 2-2-0 | Stph | 110 | 1835 | 60 | 10x16 | | Rblt NCMfg, 7/22/1836, *Columbus*. |
| Philadelphia | 4-2-0 | BLW | 6 | 11/1834 | 54 | 11x22 | 5/18/1835 | |
| Pennsylvania | 4-2-0 | BLW | 7 | 2/1835 | 54 | 10-1/2x16 | 5/18/1835 | |
| Delaware | 4-2-0 | BLW | 8 | 2/1835 | 54 | 10-1/2x16 | 5/18/1835 | |
| Susquehanna | 4-2-0 | BLW | 9 | 3/1835 | 54 | 10-1/2x16 | 5/18/1835 | |
| Schuylkill | 4-2-0 | BLW | 10 | 4/1835 | 54 | 10-1/2x16 | 5/18/1835 | |
| John Bull | 2-2-0 | Stph | 112 | 1835 | 60 | 10x16 | 5/18/1835 | Rebuilt? |
| Ohio | 4-2-0 | BLW | 22 | 2/1835 | | | 5/18/1835 | Io AP, c.1845. |
| Atlantic | 2-2-0 | Stph | 113 | 1835 | 60 | 10x16 | 6/19/1835 | Condemned 11/30/1841. |
| Albion | 2-2-0 | Stph | 117 | 1835 | 60 | 10x16 | 7/7/1835 | Rebuilt NCMfg to 4-2-0. |
| Juniata | 4-2-0 | BLW | 15 | 9/1835 | | 10x18 | 7/7/1835 | To PRR, 8/1857. |
| Kentucky | 4-2-0 | BLW | 14 | 7/1835 | | 10x18 | 7/23/1835 | To AP, c.1841. |
| Wm. Penn | 4-2-0 | L&N | | 10/1835 | | | 10/14/1835 | To Strasburg RR, c.1854. To PRR. |
| Brandywine | 4-2-0 | BLW | 18 | 10/1835 | | 10x18 | 10/22/1835 | Rblt. to 4-4-0. To PRR #141, 8/1857. |
| Rbt. Morris | 4-2-0 | Wm N | | 5/1836 | | | 5/12/1836 | To AP, 1837 or 1838. |
| Planet | 4-2-0 | NCMfg | | | | | 5/28/1836 | Rblt. Ex-*Philadelphia*. |
| Geo. Washington | 4-2-0 | Wm N | | 7/1836 | 48 | 10x17 | 7/13/1836 | To AP, 1837 or 1838. |
| Columbus | 4-2-0 | NCMfg | | | | | 7/22/1836 | Rblt. Ex-*Kentucky*. |
| Comet | 4-2-0 | NCMfg | | | | | 7/26/1836 | Rblt. Ex-*Pennsylvania*. To AP. |
| Ben. Franklin | 4-2-0 | Wm N | | 8/1836 | | | 8/19/1836 | To AP, 1837 or 1838. |
| America | 4-2-0 | CS&S | | 9/1836 | | | 9/1/1836 | |
| Sampson | 4-2-0 | CS&S | | 9/1836 | | | 9/1/1836 | Rblt. Wm N, 1841 - *Delaware* |
| Wash. Co. Farmer | 4-2-0 | Wm N | | 10/1836 | | | 10/18/1836 | To PRR, 8/1857. |
| Backwoodsman | | McCW | | 11/1836 | | | 11/18/1836 | To AP, 1837 or 1838. |
| Paoli | 4-2-0 | BLW | 65 | 2/1837 | | | 2/22/1837 | To AP, 1845. |
| Virginia | 4-2-0 | BLW | 66 | 2/1837 | | | 2/22/1837 | |
| Conestoga | 4-2-0 | BLW | 67 | 2/1837 | | 12x16 | 2/22/1837 | |
| Bald Eagle | 4-2-0 | G&E | | 3/1837 | | | 3/3/1837 | |
| Baltimore | 0-4-0 | Win | | 2/1837 | | | 3/10/1837 | |
| Edw. F. Gay | 4-2-0 | BLW | 68 | 3/1837 | | | 3/14/1837 | |
| Lafayette | 4-2-0 | Wm N | | 3/1837 | | | 3/21/1837 | To AP, 1837 or 1838. |
| Jas. Madison | 4-2-0 | Wm N | | 3/1837 | | | 3/21/1837 | To AP, 1837 or 1838. |
| Pittsburger | | McCW | | 3/1837 | | | 3/29/1837 | To AP, renamed *Mountaineer*. |
| Parkesburg | 4-2-0 | BLW | 72a | 3/1837 | | | 4/2/1837 | |
| Independence | 4-2-0 | Wm N | | 4/1837 | | | 4/4/1837 | To AP, 1837 or 1838. |
| Octorara | 4-2-0 | BLW | 69 | 4/1837 | | | 4/7/1837 | |

0-6-0's were the only other type of engine to operate.

Although the P&C had the power of the public treasury behind it, things didn't always go as well as they could. The problem, of course, was politics, partisan politics. The prominent role of the State Treasurer in the problem sounds familiar to present-day citizens of the Commonwealth of Pennsylvania. On February 5, 1850, the Treasurer, Gideon J. Ball, published an open letter to the Senate:

*… as regards the allegations of the Canal Commissioners, and the complaint of Messrs. Norris Brothers inquired of your resolution. I have to reply as follows:*

**Chart 2**
**Philadelphia & Columbia All-Time Register of Locomotives (continued)**

| Name | Type | Builder | No. | Date | Drv | Cyl | Date2 | Notes |
|---|---|---|---|---|---|---|---|---|
| Telegraph | 4-2-0 | G&E | | 4/1837 | | | 4/16/1837 | To AP. |
| Downingtown | 4-2-0 | BLW | 88 | 8/1837 | | | 4/16/1837 | |
| Bush Hill | 4-2-0 | Wm N | | 4/1837 | | | 4/17/1837 | To AP, 1837 or 1838. |
| Pequa | 4-2-0 | BLW | 74 | 4/1837 | | | 4/24/1837 | |
| Indiana | 4-2-0 | BLW | 75 | 5/1837 | | | 5/1/1837 | |
| Mississippi | 4-2-0 | BLW | 78 | 5/1837 | | | 5/9/1837 | Sold to Mine Hill & Schuylkill. |
| Montgomery | 4-2-0 | BLW | 79 | 5/1837 | | | 5/15/1837 | Sold to Montgomery Coal Company. |
| United States | 4-2-0 | Wm N | | 5/1837 | | | 5/22/1837 | To AP, 1837 or 1838. |
| Enterprise | 4-2-0 | G&E | | 5/1837 | | | 5/23/1837 | |
| Wisconsin | 4-2-0 | BLW | 81 | 5/1837 | | | 5/28/1837 | |
| Constitution | 4-2-0 | Wm N | | 6/1837 | | | 6/12/1837 | To AP, 1837 or 1838. |
| West Chester | 4-2-0 | BLW | 63 | 2/1837 | | 10-1/2x16 | 7/19/1837 | |
| G.P. Porter | 4-2-0 | J Bks | | 3/1839 | | | 3/1/1839 | To PRR, 8/1857. |
| Andrew Jackson | 4-2-0 | J Bks | | 3/1839 | | | 3/1/1839 | |
| Simon Cameron | 4-2-0 | Wm N | | 3/1839 | | | 3/15/1839 | |
| Simon Snyder | 4-2-0 | Wm N | | 3/1839 | | | 3/15/1839 | |
| James Buchanan | 4-2-0 | J Bks | | 3/1839 | | | 4/1/1839 | |
| Edw. B. Hubley | 4-2-0 | BLW | 123 | 4/1839 | | | 4/15/1839 | |
| Martin Van Buren | 4-2-0 | BLW | 125 | 4/1839 | | | 4/18/1839 | Renamed *James Clark*. |
| Old Berks | 4-2-0 | DHD | | 7/1839 | | | 7/1/1839 | |
| H.A. Muhlenburg | 4-2-0 | DHD | | 11/1839 | | | 8/8/1839 | |
| W.F. Packer | 0-4-0 | Win | | 3/1840 | | | 3/1/1840 | C.1845 exchanged for materials. |
| Hugh Keys | | PL&H | | 5/1840 | | | 5/15/1840 | |
| G.H. Keim | | DHD | | 4/1840 | | | 4/1/1840 | |
| Delaware | 4-2-0 | | | | | | | Ex-*Sampson*. Rblt. WmN 5/1841. |
| Iron Gray | | DHD | | 9/1841 | | | 9/30/1841 | |
| Westmoreland | | DHD | | 11/1841 | | | 11/20/1841 | |
| Atlas | 0-6-0 | BLW | 232 | 4/1845 | 42 | 14x19 | 5/1/1845 | To PRR #142. |
| Lehigh | 0-6-0 | BLW | 291 | 1/1847 | 42 | 13-1/2x18 | 3/1/1847 | Renamed *Lewistown*. To PRR #143* |
| Chester | 0-6-0 | BLW | 292 | 3/1847 | 42 | 13-1/2x18 | 4/1/1847 | To PRR, 8/1857. |
| Tioga | 4-4-0 | NB | | 5/1848 | 48 | 12-1/2x22 | | To PRR #144. |
| Venango | 4-4-0 | NB | | 6/1848 | 48 | 12-1/2x22 | | To PRR #145. |
| Francis R. Shunk | 4-4-0 | NB | | 1849 | 54 | 12-1/2x24 | | To PRR #146. |
| Wyoming | 4-4-0 | NB | | 5/1849 | 60 | 11x26 | | To PRR #147. |
| Wissahicken | 4-4-0 | NB | | 5/1849 | 60 | 11x26 | | To PRR #148. |
| Clarion | 4-4-0 | NB | | 10/1849 | 54 | 12-1/2x24 | | To PRR #149. |
| Shawnee | 4-4-0 | NB | | 11/1849 | 54 | 12-1/2x24 | | To PRR #150. |
| Swartara | 4-4-0 | NB | | 12/1849 | 54 | 12-1/2x24 | | To PRR #151. |
| Wyalusing | 4-4-0 | NB | | 3/1850 | 60 | 11x26 | | To PRR #152. |
| Tuscarora | 4-4-0 | NB | | 4/1850 | 60 | 11x26 | | To PRR #153. |
| Constitution | 4-4-0 | NB | | 1/1851 | 60 | 11x26 | | To PRR #154. |
| Union | 4-4-0 | NB | | 2/1851 | 60 | 11x26 | | To PRR #155. |
| Jesse Miller | 4-4-0 | NB | | 4/1851 | 54 | 12-1/2x24 | | To PRR #158. |
| Lancaster | 4-4-0 | NB | | 5/1851 | 54 | 12-1/2x24 | | To PRR #157. |
| Columbia | 4-4-0 | NB | | 5/1851 | 54 | 12-1/2x24 | | To PRR #156. |
| Keystone | 4-4-0 | NJL&M | | 6/1853 | 60 | 16x22 | | To PRR #159 |
| Conowingo | 4-4-0 | NJL&M | | 6/1853 | 60 | 16x22 | | To PRR #160 |
| Utah | 4-4-0 | NJL&M | | 7/1853 | 60 | 16x22 | | To PRR #161. |
| Minnesota | 4-4-0 | NJL&M | | 7/1853 | 60 | 16x22 | | To PRR #162. |
| Clearfield | 4-4-0 | NJL&M | | 9/1853 | 60 | 16x22 | | To PRR #163. |
| Clinton | 4-4-0 | NJL&M | | 9/1853 | 60 | 16x22 | | To PRR #164 |
| Atlanta | 4-4-0 | NJL&M | | 9/1853 | 60 | 16x22 | | To PRR #165 |
| Wheatland | 4-4-0 | NJL&M | | 10/1853 | 60 | 16x22 | | To PRR #166 |
| Lehigh | 4-4-0 | BLW | 566 | 1/1854 | 54 | 17x22 | | Ex-PRR *Lehigh*. To P&C 3/1854. To PRR 167 8/1857. |

(The *Lehigh* (renamed *Lewistown*) was rebuilt by the P&C as a 4-4-0 with four 48" drivers and 13-1/2" x 18" cylinders.)

| Name | Type | Builder | No. | Date | Drv | Cyl | | Notes |
|---|---|---|---|---|---|---|---|---|
| Luzerne | 4-4-0 | BLW | 565 | 1/1854 | 54 | 17x22 | | Ex-PRR *Luzerne*. To P&C 3/1854. To PRR 168 8/1857. |
| Kansas | 4-4-0 | BLW | 588 | 4/1854 | 60 | 16x22 | | To PRR #171. |
| President | 4-4-0 | RN&S | | 4/1854 | 60 | 16x22 | | To PRR #169. |
| Governor | 4-4-0 | RN&S | | 4/1854 | 60 | 16x22 | | To PRR #170. |
| Shanghai | 4-4-0 | NJL&M | | 5/1854 | 66 | 16x20 | | To PRR #172. |
| Old Hickory | 4-4-0 | RN&S | | 5/1854 | 60 | 16x22 | | To PRR #174. |
| Nebraska | 4-4-0 | BLW | 590 | 6/1854 | 60 | 16x22 | | To PRR #173. |
| John Gilpin | 4-4-0 | NJL&M | | 6/1854 | 66 | 16x22 | | To PRR #175. |
| Tam O' Shanter | 4-4-0 | LLW | | 12/1854 | 60 | 16x22 | | To PRR #176. |
| Uncle Toby | 4-4-0 | LLW | | 1/1854 | 60 | 16x22 | | To PRR #177. |
| Bardolph | 4-4-0 | LLW | | 5/1855 | 60 | 16x22 | | To PRR #178. |
| Old Fogy | 4-4-0 | LLW | | 5/1855 | 60 | 16x22 | | To PRR #179. |
| Young America | 4-4-0 | LLW | | 10/1855 | 60 | 16-1/2x22 | | To PRR #180. |
| Attila | 4-4-0 | LLW | | 12/1855 | 66 | 17x20 | | To PRR #181. |
| Alaric | 4-4-0 | LLW | | 2/1856 | 60 | 17x22 | | To PRR #182. |
| Tony Weller | 4-4-0 | LLW | | 2/1856 | 60 | 16-1/2x22 | | To PRR #183. |
| Yorick | 4-4-0 | NJL&M | | 3/1856 | 54 | 16x22 | | To PRR #185. |
| Alert | 4-4-0 | LLW | | 4/1856 | 60 | 18x22 | | To PRR #186. |
| Corporal Trim | 4-4-0 | NJL&M | | 5/1856 | 54 | 16x22 | | To PRR #187. |
| My Son Samuel | 4-4-0 | LLW | | 5/1856 | 60 | 16-1/2x22 | | To PRR #184. |
| Fingal's Baby | 4-4-0 | LLW | | 6/1856 | 60 | 16x22 | | To PRR #188. |
| Fallstaff | 4-4-0 | LLW | | 6/1856 | 60 | 18x22 | | To PRR #189. |
| Old Dominion | 4-4-0 | RN&S | | 6/1856 | 60 | 18x22 | | To PRR #190. |
| Hoosier State | 4-4-0 | RN&S | | 7/1856 | 60 | 18x22 | | To PRR #191. |
| Geo. Washington | 4-4-0 | RN&S | | 7/1856 | 54 | 18x22 | | To PRR #192. |
| Jas. Buchanan | 4-4-0 | LLW | | 8/1856 | 60 | 18x22 | | To PRR #193. |
| Hiawatha | 4-4-0 | LLW | | 2/1857 | 60 | 16x22 | | To PRR #194. |
| Jn. Breckenridge | 4-4-0 | LLW | | 2/1857 | 60 | 16x22 | | To PRR #195. |

| | |
|---|---|
| BLW | M. Baldwin, Philadelphia, Pa. |
| CS&S | Coleman Sellers & Sons, Philadelphia, Pa. |
| DHD | Davis H. Dotterer, Reading, Pa. |
| G&E | Garrett & Eastwick, Philadelphia, Pa. |
| J Bks | James Brooks (Bridgewater Iron Works), Philadelphia, Pa. |
| L&N | Long & Norris (American Steam Carriage Company), Philadelphia, Pa. |
| LLW | Lancaster Locomotive Works, Lancaster, Pa. |
| Long | Stephen H. Long, Philadelphia, Pa. |
| McCW | McClurg, Wade & Company, Pittsburgh, Pa. |
| NB | Norris Brothers, Philadelphia, Pa. |
| NCMfg | New Castle Manufacturing Company, New Castle, De. |
| NJL&M | New Jersey Locomotive & Machine Company, Paterson, N.J. |
| PL&H | Pennel, Lenher & Humes, Lancaster, Pa. |
| RN&S | Richard Norris & Son, Philadelphia, Pa. |
| Stph | Robert Stephenson, Newcastle on Tyne, England |
| Tylr | Tayleur & Company, Newton-le-Willows, England |
| Win | Ross Winans, Baltimore, Md. |
| Wm N | William Norris, Philadelphia, Pa. |

*Messrs. Norris Brothers, never personally presented at the Treasury for payment, nor did any person for them, an order from the Canal Commissioners for the amount they claim; nor have I as yet official notice that the State owes them. In default of such notice, duty required that I should refrain from paying away the public money.*

*Had those gentlemen presented such an order, I would have been justified in withholding payment, the evidence being that Messrs. Norris Brothers, charged seven hundred dollars more for each locomotive furnished the State than they charged the Pennsylvania Railroad Company - or, in other words, they furnished that Company with a more expensive article for seven hundred dollars less, and received one thousand five hundred dollars in trade - so large a profit would seem to justify a liberal credit.*

*The engines referred to were purchased, it seems, under the authority given in the sixteenth section of the last appropriation bill. This being true, it scarcely justified the sale by the Canal Commissioners of five locomotives worth at least TWENTY-FIVE THOUSAND DOLLARS, for the paltry sum of THIRTY-THREE HUNDRED AND NINETY DOLLARS, thereby SACRIFICING UPWARDS OF TWENTY-ONE THOUSAND DOLLARS, which evidences gross ignorance of the value of property, or a criminal neglect of duty. Perhaps these facts would not have justified me in hesitating to pay Messrs. Norris Brothers had I been drawn on for the money.*[12]

During the previous year, 1849, Norris Brothers supplied six 4-4-0's to the P&C. The interesting thing in Mr. Ball's letter is the sale of five locomotives by the Canal Commissioners. They were obviously some of the aging 4-2-0's built in the 1830's, and would scarcely be worth $25,000, except to the public treasury.

## William Penn Goes West

One of the P&C's earliest locomotives, *William Penn*, put on the road on October 14, 1835, had a long and amazing history. *William Penn* was built by Long & Norris of Philadelphia in 1835 as construc-

tion number 9. It was rebuilt with outside cylinders by the P&C and later sold to the Strasburg Rail Road in 1854. Ten years later, this outdated machine was brought to the Lancaster Locomotive Works, then under the direction of Edward Norris, and rebuilt as a tank locomotive. A new firebox replaced the original Bury firebox, and solid drivers were purchased from A. Whitney & Sons of Philadelphia. Sold to the original Western Pacific, the *William Penn* was shipped around the Horn and operated as WP "J." It became Central Pacific #175 in 1870. Rebuilt for yard service in 1877, the locomotive was sold in 1885 for $1,000 to the Pacific Iron & Nail Company The engine was photographed in an Alameda, Ca. junkyard in 1898; there is some evidence that it may have lasted until 1921.[13]

## Sold At Auction

On October 15, 1850, a new 7½-mile line replaced the Belmont Plane, providing service to West Philadelphia. However, there was no direct connection with the City RR until December 25, so that all freight bound for city warehouses continued to use the old road via the Belmont Plane until then. Out west, the PRR continued construction and completed its own line from Harrisburg through to Pittsburgh on February 15, 1854, although it had used the Allegheny Portage to bridge the gap from September 1850. The PRR could not long operate its railroad without a connection to Philadelphia, and on June 25, 1857 (to be effective August 1) the Pennsylvania Railroad purchased the "Public Works," which included the Philadelphia & Columbia, the Allegheny Portage and the Main Line canal. During the latter part of 1857 the PRR incorporated the locomotives of the Philadelphia & Columbia and Allegheny Portage Railroads into their stock, which added 71 locomotives to the roster.

# THE ALLEGHENY PORTAGE RAILROAD

After the "Public Works" was authorized by the Legislature on February 25, 1826, it was another two years before an Act was approved by the governor to locate a railroad across the Allegheny Mountain, and a railroad from Philadelphia via Lancaster to Columbia. In the autumn of 1829, Sylvester Welch was employed by the State of Pennsylvania as principal engineer of the Western Division of the Pennsylvania Canal, and moved to Blairsville, on the Conemaugh River, accompanied by Solomon W. Roberts. The canal was then nearly completed from Pittsburgh to Blairsville, and was in progress from Blairsville to Johnstown. Roberts records that much of the work was badly done, and it was not strong enough to withstand the occasional floods to which it was exposed. *We struggled on with the work, and the canal was opened to Johnstown, at the western base of the Allegheny Mountain, in December 1830.*[14] On Roberts' division, there was an aqueduct across the Conemaugh River at Lockport, having five arches, each of 60-foot span, built of cut stone.

## Locating The Railroad

Navigation began when the Western Division of the canal (Pittsburgh - Johnstown) was opened. On March 21, 1831, the Board of Canal Commissioners was authorized by an act of the Legislature to build a portage railroad over the Allegheny Mountain. The Board appointed Sylvester Welch, the principal engineer of the western division of the Pennsylvania Canal, to the same position in the building of the Portage Railroad, and he nominated Solomon Roberts as his assistant. On April 8, 1831, they began explorations near the summit of the mountain. On April 12, the party of 16 persons went into camp near the head of the mountain branch of the Conemaugh River, and began to locate the railroad. Roberts records that the country was very rough, and the running of the line was obstructed by fallen timber.

The crossing of the Allegheny Mountain was to be overcome by inclined planes on an average of about a half-mile long, with an angle of elevation of about five degrees. The average height overcome by each plane was to be about 200 feet, and they were to be worked by stationary steam engines and endless ropes.

W. Milnor Roberts joined the engineer corps in the month of May as the principal assistant, and located the eastern portion of the Portage Railroad, from the summit of the Allegheny Mountain down to Hollidaysburg, a distance of about 16 miles, which included the steep eastern slope of the mountain.

The contracts were let for construction between Johnstown and Summit on May 25, and between Hollidaysburg and Summit on July 29, 1831. It was on November 29 of the same year that the first packet boat arrived at Hollidaysburg from the east. As ultimately laid out and built the Portage Railroad (36.69 miles) consisted of ten inclined planes (numbered from the west) and 11 levels. The principal office was established at Ebensburg, although it was several miles from the railroad, but because it was on the turnpike it was readily accessible.

A large part of the line ran through a heavy forest of spruce and hemlock, and many of the trees were over 100 feet high. A right-of-way 120 feet wide was cleared. Immense fires were made, but the green timber did not burn well, and many of the trees were rolled down the mountain slopes and left to decay.

After the grading and masonry of the Portage Railroad were put under contract the line was divided, the western half being in charge of Solomon Roberts, and the eastern in charge of W. Milnor Roberts. About 2,000 men were employed in construction.

The rails were laid to a width of 4' - 9". On the Planes flat iron strips were laid on wooden stringers with wooden crossties holding the stringers to gauge. On the Levels "edge rails" 18 feet in length were used. The track was carried on iron chairs with wooden sills fastened to wooden crossties on fills and embankments. On solid ground the track was laid on stone blocks. The blocks had two holes drilled in them and oak plugs put in the holes. Cast iron chairs were fastened to the blocks, with the spikes driven into the oak plugs. The rail, imported from England, was "double headed" and held in place in the chairs by wooden wedges. To maintain gauge it was necessary to substitute wooden crossties for each alternating stone block.

At the head of each incline was the engine-house, with two stationary engines of about 35-horespower each. The engines in Planes 1, 3, 4, 6, 7 and 8 had cylinders with a 14" bore and 5' stroke. The engines on Planes 2, 5, 9, and 10 had cylinders of 13" bore. The "endless" rope passed through a series of vertical sheaves then a large horizontal sheave and around another vertical sheave before descending down the Plane. To maintain tension there was a carriage attached to a weight that could move 50' in the winding pit to take up the slack.

The endless rope was originally of hemp, with a life of about 16 months. In 1842, at the suggestion of John A. Roebling, the Canal Commissioners ordered a wire rope for Plane 3. On account of the winding machinery then in use, the experiment was a failure. After some improvement of the machinery, in 1843 the wire rope proved successful. A wire rope was installed on Plane 10 in 1844 and by 1849 all Planes were equipped with Roebling's wire rope.[16]

## Opening The Line

The first car was taken over the road on November 26, 1833, and the line was opened as a public highway (single track) with the opening of navigation on the canal on March 18, 1834. A month later the Board of Canal Commissioners authorized the purchase of five locomotives, and the second track was completed. On May 10, 1835 the *Boston* made the first run of a locomotive engine on the line; it was used on the "Long Level" between Plane #1 and Plane #2. The next day the operation of the road as a public highway was discontinued.

Roberts recalled that *The experiment of working the road as a public highway was very unsatisfactory. Individuals and firms employed their own drivers, with their own horses and cars. The cars were small, had four wheels, and each one would carry about 7,000 pounds of freight. Usually four cars made up a train, and that number could be taken up, and as many let down an inclined plane, at one time, and from six to ten such trips could be made in an hour. The drivers were a rough set of fellows, and sometimes very stubborn and unmanageable. It was not practicable to make them work by a timetable, and the officers of the road had no power to discharge them. My memory recalls the case of one fellow, who would not go backward, and could not go forward, and so obstructed the road for a considerable time. It resembled the case of two wild wagoners of the Alleghenies, meeting in a narrow mountain pass, and both refusing to give way. Our nominal remedy was to have the men arrested and taken before a magistrate, perhaps many miles off, to have him fined according to the law, a copy of which I used to carry in my pocket.*

*When the road had but a single track between the turnouts, a large post, called a center post, was set up half-way between two turnouts, and the rule was made that when two drivers met on the single track, with their cars, the one that had gone beyond the center post had the right of way, and the other that had not reached it*

### Chart 3

### Planes and Grades of the Portage Railroad[15]

**From West to East - Johnstown to Hollidaysburg**

| Planes and Levels | Length, in Miles | Elevation Overcome, in Feet |
|---|---|---|
| Johnstown to Plane 1 | 4.13 | 101.46 |
| Plane 1 | 0.30 | 150.00 |
| Level - Plane 1 to Plane 2 | 13.06 | 189.58 |
| Plane 2 | 0.33 | 132.40 |
| Level - Plane 2 to Plane 3 | 1.49 | 14.50 |
| Plane 3 | 0.28 | 130.50 |
| Level - Plane 3 to Plane 4 | 1.90 | 18.80 |
| Plane 4 | 0.42 | 187.86 |
| Level - Plane 4 to Plane 5 | 2.56 | 25.80 |
| Plane 5 | 0.49 | 201.64 |
| Summit Level | 1.62 | 19.04 |
| Plane 6 | 0.51 | 266.50 |
| Level - Plane 6 to Plane 7 | 0.15 | 0.00 |
| Plane 7 | 0.51 | 260.50 |
| Level - Plane 7 to Plane 8 | 0.63 | 5.40 |
| Plane 8 | 0.58 | 308.00 |
| Level - Plane 8 to Plane 9 | 1.25 | 12.00 |
| Plane 9 | 0.51 | 189.50 |
| Level - Plane 9 to Plane 10 | 1.76 | 29.58 |
| Plane 10 | 0.43 | 180.52 |
| Level - Plane 10 to Hollidaysburg | 3.75 | 146.77 |
| | 36.65 | 2,570.29 |

*must go back to the turnout which he had left. The road was, in many places very crooked, and a man could not see far ahead. The way the rule worked was this: when a man left a turnout he would drive very slowly, fearing that he might have to turn back; and, as he approached the center post, he would drive faster and faster, to try to get beyond it, and thus in this way drive back any cars that he might meet, and in this way cars have been driven together, and a man killed by being crushed between them.*[17]

Apart from the inclined planes the Allegheny Portage Railroad had two other unique features. The first was the Staple Bend Tunnel, four miles east of Johnstown. The tunnel, 901' in length, 20' wide and 19' high, was the first railroad tunnel to be built in the United States. Just to the east of Plane #1, the tunnel cut off a loop in the Little Conemaugh River. The second feature was the single-stone-arch Conemaugh Viaduct, built in 1832-33, which cut off an-

other loop in the river, saving two miles. The arch of the viaduct had a span of 80' and was 78½' above the foundation and 28' wide. Subsequently used by both the New Portage Railroad and the PRR, it was destroyed in the Johnstown Flood of May 31, 1889.

During the operation of the inclined planes on the Portage Railroad, it was necessary to change power 24 times in 36 miles. To move a sectional canal boat over the line from Johnstown to Hollidaysburg involved 12 stationary engines, ten on the planes and one at each basin to pull the car with the sections of the boat up out of the basin. On the levels and at the basins there were 12 teams of horses and nine locomotives used. Altogether this meant that the number of men necessary to move a boat from Johnstown to Hollidaysburg was 12 enginemen and 12 firemen at the stationary engines, nine enginemen and firemen for the locomotives, and 12 teamsters, 54 men in all.

### The New Portage Railroad

Between September 1850 and February 15, 1854, the Pennsylvania Railroad used the Allegheny Portage to connect its two sections of railroad, until its own line over the mountain was completed. During this time (1851-1856) the Commonwealth reconstructed the Allegheny Portage, eliminating the planes, at a cost of $2,500,000. The new line was 41 miles long. The New Portage Railroad turned south at Duncansville toward Newry to avoid Plane #10, and followed Blairs Run Gap past Plane #9 to Plane #8, where the line curved across the stream on the Mule Shoe Curve to the north side of Blairs Run Gap, and continued across the face of the mountain to the valley of Sugar Run, thence heading up the opposite side of the valley (southern side) from the PRR. At the summit at Gallitzin the New Portage pierced the mountain by a tunnel of its own and paralleled the PRR to Ben's Creek; it then occupied the roadbed of the old Portage Railroad using the Conemaugh

Viaduct and Staple Bend tunnel.

On June 25, 1857, the PRR purchased the "Public Works" for $7,500,000, and took possession on August 1, 1857. On November 1, 1857, the PRR discontinued operation over the New Portage and the next year removed the rails and shipped them west for use on the PFt.W&C.

## THE HARRISBURG, PORTSMOUTH, MOUNTJOY & LANCASTER

On June 9, 1832, an Act was approved by the Pennsylvania legislature to construct the Portsmouth & Lancaster rail-road from Portsmouth (Middletown) to Lancaster to connect with the State road. The organization was completed on July 19, 1834, and the stockholders met and elected a board of directors, which included James Buchanan and Simon Cameron. The next year the charter was amended to permit extending the line from Portsmouth to Harrisburg, and to change the name to the Harrisburg, Portsmouth, Mountjoy & Lancaster railroad.

In August construction was started, but was impeded by political difficulties initiated by the interests in Columbia. On September 16, 1836, the first locomotive and train arrived in Harrisburg. The *John Bull* (Stephenson #112, built in 1835) was borrowed from the State Road, brought by canal boat from Columbia, and pulled a train from Harrisburg to Portsmouth (Middletown) and return. By December the 15 miles westward from Lancaster to Rheems was completed. The road was operated from each end, with a stagecoach connection between. In October 1837 the line was completed, except for the Elizabethtown Tunnel. The tunnel opened on August 18, 1838. In 1839 a connection was made with the Cumberland Valley Railroad at Harrisburg.

As noted previously, with the beginning of the Pennsylvania Railroad, the HPM&L line applied to the PRR's Board on August 29, 1848, for a switch to

## Chart 4

### Allegheny Portage All-Time Register of Locomotives

| Name | Type | Bldr. | c/n | Date | Driv., in. | Cyl., in. | In Service | Notes |
|---|---|---|---|---|---|---|---|---|
| Delaware | 4-2-0 | NCMfg | | 5/1833 | | | 5/10/1833 | B; renamed *Tennessee*. |
| Allegheny | 4-2-0 | NCMfg | | 5/1833 | | | 5/10/1835 | C |
| Boston | 4-2-0 | MDF | | 5/1833 | | | 5/10/1835 | B |
| Pittsburgh | 4-2-0 | McCW | | 9/1835 | | | 9/3/1835 | A |
| Conemaugh | 4-2-0 | McCW | | 9/1835 | | | | B; renamed *Pennsylvania*. |
| Rbt. Morris | 4-2-0 | Wm N | | 5/1836 | | | 5/12/1836 | Ex-P&C. |
| Geo. Washington | 4-2-0 | Wm N | | 7/1836 | 48 | 10x17 | | |
| Comet | 4-2-0 | NCMfg | | 7/1836 | | | 7/18/1836 | Ex-P&C. |
| B. Franklin | 4-2-0 | Wm N | | 8/1836 | | | 8/19/1836 | B; ex-P&C.* |
| Backwoodsman | 4-2-0 | McCW | | 11/1836 | | | 11/18/1836 | Ex-P&C. |
| James Madison | 4-2-0 | Wm N | | 3/1837 | | | 3/21/1837 | Ex-P&C. |
| Lafayette | 4-2-0 | NB | | 3/1837 | | | 3/21/1837 | Ex-P&C. |
| Mountaineer | 4-2-0 | McCW | | 3/1837 | | | 3/29/1837 | B; ex-P&C.** |
| Bush Hill | 4-2-0 | Wm N | | 4/1837 | | | 4/17/1837 | Ex-P&C. |
| United States | 4-2-0 | Wm N | | 5/1837 | | | 5/22/1837 | Ex-P&C. |
| Constitution | 4-2-0 | Wm N | | 6/1837 | | | 6/12/1837 | Ex-P&C. |
| Independence | 4-2-0 | Wm N | | 7/1837 | | | 7/4/1837 | Ex-P&C. |
| David R. Porter | 4-2-0 | DHD | | 6/1840 | | | 6/12/1840 | |
| Paoli | 4-2-0 | BLW | 65 | 2/1837 | | | 1845 | Ex-P&C. |
| James Clarke | 4-2-0 | DHD | | 7/1840 | | | 7/10/1840 | |
| Kentucky | 4-2-0 | BLW | 14 | 10/1835 | 54 | 11x16 | 1845 | Ex-P&C. |
| Ohio | 4-2-0 | BLW | 22 | 2/1836 | | | 1845 | Ex-P&C. |
| Lancaster | 4-2-0 | BLW | 3 | 6/1834 | 54 | 10x16 | | Ex-P&C. |
| Columbia | 4-2-0 | BLW | 4 | 7/1834 | 54 | 10½x16 | | Ex-P&C. |
| Francis R. Shunk | 4-4-0 | NB | | 1849 | 54 | 12½x24 | | Ex-P&C, returned. |
| Lycoming | 4-4-0 | NB | | 1850 | 54 | 12x24 | | To PRR 210. |
| Cherokee | 4-4-0 | NB | | 8/1851 | 54 | 11x24 | | To PRR 197. |
| Juniata | 4-4-0 | NB | | 8/1851 | 54 | 10½x20 | | To PRR 199. |
| Cambria | 4-4-0 | NB | | 8/1851 | 54 | 11x24 | | To PRR 196. |
| Westmoreland | 4-4-0 | NB | | 11/1851 | 54 | 11x24 | | To PRR 198. |
| Montgomery | 4-4-0 | NB | | 6/1852 | 54 | 12x24 | | To PRR 203. |
| Pittsburgh | 2-6-0 | S&P | | 3/1853 | 44 | 17x22 | | To PRR 200. |
| Philadelphia | 2-6-0 | S&P | | 3/1853 | 44 | 17x22 | 3/1853 | To PRR 201. |
| Bedford | 4-6-0 | BLW | 487 | 8/1852 | 44 | 18x22 | | Ex-PRR *Bedford*, 202. |
| W.T. Morrison | 4-6-0 | RN&S | | 4/1854 | 48 | 17x24 | | To PRR 209. |
| Hercules | 4-6-0 | RN&S | | 4/1854 | 48 | 17x24 | | To PRR 205. |
| Blair | 4-6-0 | RN&S | | 4/1854 | 48 | 17x24 | | To PRR 208. |
| Jupiter | 4-6-0 | RN&S | | 6/1854 | 48 | 17x24 | | To PRR 204. |
| T.N. Forsythe | 4-6-0 | BLW | 640 | 3/1855 | 48 | 19x22 | | To PRR 207. |
| Wm. Hopkins | 4-6-0 | BLW | 688 | 3/1856 | 48 | 19x22 | | To PRR 206. |

\* - Originally P&C *Pennsylvania*, Stephenson #104 /1834, rebuilt NCMfg 1836.
\*\* - Ex-P&C *Pittsburger*.
A - Only boiler remains 12/1/1845.
B - Only boiler and flues remain 12/1/1845.
C - Used as shop engine at Hollidaysburg shop 12/01/1845.

| | |
|---|---|
| BLW | Baldwin Locomotive Works, Philadelphia, Pa. |
| DHD | Davis H. Dotterer, Reading, Pa. |
| MDF | Mill Dam Foundry, Boston, Mass. (R.M. Houton) |
| McCW | McClurg, Wade & Company, Pittsburgh, Pa. |
| NB | Norris Bros., Philadelphia, Pa. |
| NCMfg | New Castle Manufacturing Company, New Castle, Del. |
| RN&S | Richard Norris & Son, Philadelphia, Pa. |
| S&P | Smith & Perkins, Alexandria, Va. |
| Wm N | William Norris, Philadelphia, Pa. |

connect it to the PRR. After protracted negotiation the PRR entered into a contract with the HPM&L on April 21, 1849, to conduct operations over the line and purchase all its equipment, effective with the opening of the PRR's line to Lewistown. The HPM&L owned and maintained track and facilities and was to be reimbursed by stated tolls. On October 16, 1849 the HPM&L equipment was taken into the PRR stock. On January 1, 1861, the PRR leased the HPM&L for 999 years.

## Chart 5

### HPM&L All-Time Register of Locomotives

| No. | Name | Type | Bldr | Date | c/n | Driv., in. | Cyl., in. | Notes | To |
|---|---|---|---|---|---|---|---|---|---|
| | Middletown | 4-2-0 | BLW | 11/4/1836 | 57 | | | | |
| | Mt. Joy | 4-2-0 | BLW | 11/6/1836 | 59 | | | | |
| | Flying Dutchman | 4-2-0 | BLW | 1/20/1837 | 62 | | 10-1/2x16 | #3 crank | |
| | Harrisburg | 4-2-0 | BLW | 2/18/1837 | 64 | 54 | 10-1/2x16 | #3 crank | PRR. |
| | Conewago | 4-2-0 | BLW | 6/1/1837 | 82 | ? | 10-1/2x16 | #3 crank | |
| | C.B. Penrose | 4-2-0 | BLW | 6/29/1837 | 84 | 54 | 11-1/2x16 | #3 crank | PRR. |
| 1 | Henry Clay | 4-2-0 | Wm N | 1838 | | 48 | 10x20 | | PRR 1. |
| 2 | David R. Porter | 4-2-0 | Wm N | 1839 | | 48 | 10x20 | | PRR 2. |
| 3 | Franklin x | 4-4-0 | BLW | 8/24/1847 | 306 | 54 | 11-3/8x8 | 15 ton 8-whl C | PRR 3. |
| 4 | Washington | 0-6-0 | BLW | 2/15/1847 | 293 | 42 | 13-1/2x18 | 15 ton 6-whl D | PRR 4. |

The *David R. Porter* "has run off track & been considerably damaged" (11/1849). The loco was rebuilt by the PRR as a 4-4-0 at Harrisburg (8/1851) and renamed "Heisley," after the civil engineer killed in the accident.

\* Made from Campbell's boiler.

# CHAPTER 3
## MEN, SHOPS, AND MACHINERY
### MOTIVE POWER DEVELOPMENT ON THE PRR

### J. Edgar Thomson, Chief Engineer & General Superintendent: 1847-1852

During the Pennsylvania Railroad Company's beginning years the purchase and maintenance of locomotives was the concern of the Chief Engineer and General Superintendent, J. Edgar Thomson. Thomson was born February 10, 1808, in Delaware County, Pennsylvania and began his professional career in 1827 in the engineering corps employed on the original survey of the Philadelphia & Columbia Railroad. In 1830, he entered the service of the Camden & Amboy as Assistant Engineer of the Eastern Division. He left the C&A and traveled in Europe to examine the railways there. Shortly after his return in 1832, he was appointed Chief Engineer of the Georgia Railroad. On April 9, 1847, he joined the PRR as Chief Engineer.[18] His initial task for his new employers was to establish an operating railroad where there had been none; the purchase of the first locomotive in 1848 was part of getting the initial segment of line into operation. Regular service was inaugurated on September 1, 1849, when the first revenue train was operated between Harrisburg and Lewistown.

Before Thomson was hired the Board divided the road into three divisions, Eastern, Middle and Western. W.B. Foster was assigned the Eastern Division, while Edward Miller, associate engineer, was assigned the Western Division.[19] The initial location of the railroad began in early 1847, before Thomson arrived. One of his first acts was to abolish the Middle Division and extend the Eastern and Western Divisions to the summit of the Allegheny Mountain.

He then began a reconnaissance, and of the several proposed routes he determined that the line should follow the valley of the Juniata River to the Allegheny front at Robinson's Summit (later Altoona), then climb directly up the mountain to Sugar Run Gap. Here a tunnel would take the line under the summit. The road was then projected by several routes to Pittsburgh. Although the route via the Conemaugh, Kiskiminetas and Allegheny Rivers seemed the easiest, it was rejected due to its length. Another projected line left the valley of the Conemaugh at Torrance after passing though Pack Saddle Gap, and headed across some very broken country via Greensburg to Turtle Creek, thence to Pittsburgh by climbing up to East Liberty and downgrade into town. This is basically the route Thomson proposed in his First Annual Report. The grading of the 18 sections west of Harrisburg was let on July 15, 1847, and on November 26 the next 40 miles of the eastern end of the line was let to Lewistown.[20]

An uneasy working relationship soon developed between the Chief Engineer and the PRR's first president, Samuel V. Merrick. The differences in personality and perspective were not helped by the management structure of the Company. Thomson felt that he was elected by the Board and was responsible to that body. Obviously, Merrick felt differently. James A. Ward notes in his biography of J. Edgar Thomson that *the basic issue appeared to be who was going to run the company*.[21] Thomson had built and operated the Georgia Railroad and had a better understanding of what it took to construct a line of railroad, and operate it with an eye to potential prof-

its, than Merrick, who, with his friends on the Board, represented the Philadelphia mercantile class.

Before the first section was opened, Thomson sent Herman Haupt to visit the railroads of New England to investigate their operating practices. On March 27, 1849, he submitted a plan of organization to the Road Committee, who referred it to the Board.[22] Thomson suggested that Haupt be appointed as General Superintendent. This triggered a Board fight. The Merrick party saw an opportunity to curb Thomson's authority. Since the General Superintendent would control appointments for employment on the new road, the issue was critical. Merrick, allied with William Patterson and several other directors, tried to discredit Haupt. Thomson withdrew Haupt's name and had himself appointed General Superintendent. Haupt and Thomson revised the organizational plan and submitted it to the Board for approval. There were to be four departments: Conducting Transportation, Maintenance of Way, Motive Power, and Maintenance of Cars. All were under the Superintendent of Transportation. By the summer of 1849, Herman Haupt was appointed to that office, and reported to Thomson as General Superintendent.[23]

The history of the PRR's motive power began almost a year before the "official" opening of the first portion of the line.[24] On Tuesday, October 3, 1848, Thomson sent a letter to the Road Committee, which interestingly was chaired by Merrick, concerning the purchase of locomotives.[25] Since Thomson was on site in Harrisburg overseeing the construction plans and estimates, or out along the road with the survey teams, much of his input to the Board was by correspondence. The Road Committee referred the letter to the Board meeting held the next day. The letter stated that Baldwin had on hand and offered the Company two or three locomotives, and Thomson desired the Board's action.[26]

Baldwin had built three 21-ton, eight-wheel E class locomotives for the B&O.[27] When completed they weighed about 2½ tons more than specified in their contract, and the B&O refused to accept them. Baldwin contacted Thomson and offered the locomotives, intending to fill the contract with the B&O by the construction of three lighter machines. Under the terms of the original contract, the B&O was to pay $9,300 cash for each locomotive. Baldwin was willing to sell to the PRR for the same amount, but payable by the balance due the Company on the PRR stock Baldwin had acquired, the remainder of the price to be paid in Philadelphia bonds. Baldwin did not expect payment until the locomotives were required for use.[28]

The locomotives Baldwin was offering the PRR were flexible-beam-truck 0-8-0's. The first locomotives of this type were 0-6-0's. *Atlas*, built in 1846 for the Philadelphia & Reading, was the first flexible-beam-truck 0-8-0. Thomson was quite familiar with Baldwin's locomotives. While on the Georgia Railroad, he equipped the line with the Philadelphia builder's products, first ordering 4-2-0's, then buying the first Baldwin flexible-beam-truck 0-6-0 in 1842, and by 1846 ordering the line's first 4-4-0's.

Although the three locomotives were heavier than

Thomson preferred, the weight was distributed over eight wheels and the price was right. Thomson hinted to the Board that Baldwin might be induced to take rather more in Company stock than in Philadelphia bonds. The Board authorized Merrick and Thomson to examine the locomotives, and, if found suitable, to purchase them from Baldwin. Merrick reported to the Board on October 18, 1848 that he had arranged for the purchase of all three locomotives for $27,900.[29]

On November 22, 1848 an order was drawn for $19,200, payable to Baldwin, for the locomotives.[30] Two of the three, subsequently named *Dauphin* and *Perry*, **(Fig. 93)** left the Baldwin works shortly after November 17 and were shipped west. They were put to use in the construction of the road to Lewistown. After a short period of service on the PRR they were sold to the Philadelphia & Reading. The third locomotive was *Westmoreland*, which Baldwin held until the Company needed it. Put on the road in

▶

*Figure 15. #9 (Norris Brothers, 1849).* Cambria *was the first Norris locomotive purchased by the PRR and was "Put on the Road" in January 1850. J. Edgar Thomson commented that it was "highly finished but not a good proportioned machine."* (Author's collection)

September 1850, *Westmoreland* remained in service until 1866.

These three were typical of Baldwin's #2 type eight-wheeled, E flexible-beam-truck locomotives. All eight coupled wheels were placed in front of the firebox, rather than placing the firebox between the third and fourth set of drivers. The boiler was 8' - 4" in length and 38½" in diameter. The firebox was the quite popular Bury design. A number of early American locomotives were equipped with this hemispherical firebox. Developed by Edward Bury in England in 1830, it carried a large steam space above the water. Although complicated to fabricate, the Bury dome was attractive to American railroads, with their bad water. The firebox was 42" long and 34" wide. The dome over the firebox was 38" in diameter and rose 26" above the top of the boiler. The Bury dome was fitted with a whistle and safety valve. There was another safety valve located near the front of the boiler barrel, on an auxiliary dome which was 18" in diameter and 30" high. The cylinders had a 17" diameter and 22" stroke, and were pitched at an angle of 22½" in ten feet. Equipped with Baldwin's half-stroke-cutoff valve gear, the locomotives had two full-stroke pumps to supply the boiler with water. The main rods were connected to the crank pins on the rear set of drivers. There was a 1" x 4" auxiliary frame, and the total weight of each locomotive was 50,975 lbs. The engines were painted green and did not have the road name painted on the tender.[31]

A new railroad, chartered to cover the distance the PRR had outlined in its initial plans, offered a ready market for locomotive builders. Norris Brothers of Philadelphia offered the Board a locomotive for trial [32] and another brother, Edward S. Norris, who was attempting to build locomotives in Schenectady, N.Y., offered to take 20% off the price of locomotives in stock.[33] With the imminent opening

of the first portion of the road, Thomson approached the Board for more locomotives. On April 18, 1849, the Board authorized the Chief Engineer to have two passenger cars, one baggage car, and two passenger locomotives built.[34] In November, Thomson requested three more locomotives, which he felt would be required on the opening of the road to Huntingdon in the spring.[35]

The third locomotive acquired by the Company was *Mifflin*. Built by Baldwin in September 1849, and placed in passenger service, *Mifflin* was the first PRR locomotive to operate in revenue service. Two similar models followed, *Blair* later in September 1849, and *Indiana* in January 1850. *Mifflin* (**Fig. 95**), *Blair* (**Fig. 97**), and *Indiana* (**Fig. 99**) present a puzzle of their own. The class A in the Baldwin classification system were special locomotives. Baldwin built only five class A, and the PRR got three of them.

Governor Paine, president of the Central Vermont, offered a premium of $10,000 to anyone who could build a locomotive that could reach a speed of 60 mph. Matthias Baldwin wrote to inform him that he would be willing to build such a locomotive, and included drawings.[36] He proposed a 22½-ton machine with a single pair of 72" driving wheels and a boiler with 970 sq. ft. of fire surface, and he was willing to guarantee the speed.[37] Although Baldwin was uneasy about the terms of payment, 12-month notes of the Central Vermont, he went ahead and built the locomotive, named *Governor Paine* (Baldwin c/n 343), with a date of September 7, 1849. Baldwin was willing to incur the cost of designing a custom locomotive and risk the questionable financing because he wanted to introduce his products to New England.[38] The Baldwin class A locomotives had a very large single driver, actually 78" for *Governor Paine* and 72" for the rest.[39] They were similar in many ways to the English Crampton-type, which were intended for fast passenger service.

On June 16, 1848, Thomson asked Baldwin to work up an eight-wheel locomotive for the PRR.[40] Baldwin responded by offering several options: a freight eight-wheeler, "your" passenger engine, or the single driver class A passenger engine he designed for the Central Vermont.[41] Baldwin had previously shown Thomson the drawings for the class A engine and suggested that if Thomson would take one of these there would be a saving.[42]

Thomson did acquire the *passenger engine*, and on July 17, 1849, wrote to Baldwin that the locomotive (*Mifflin*) had arrived, had been tested on the road for about five miles, and appeared to operate beautifully. He was a little put out that it weighed 2½ tons more than he wanted.[43] Thomson's tune soon changed and he complained that the engine didn't seem to have much power. He credited this to the small height of the dome, which was causing the engine to work wet steam. He asked Baldwin to send Pettit up to Harrisburg to make a drawing of the additions he felt would be necessary.[44] Thomson also wanted a drawing of the Reading's "cow-catcher" so that he could have one put on the engine.[45]

The PRR's class A locomotives had 14" x 20" cylinders, a single pair of 72" drivers inside-connected with a half-crank axle, and a four-wheel engine truck with 33" wheels. They had Bury fireboxes 44" in diameter and 58" from the grate to the crown sheet. The dome on the firebox carried a safety valve and whistle. The cylinders were located at the middle of the boiler, and the steam was fed to the cylinders by an outside dry pipe. The valve gear was the Baldwin full-stroke type, worked with "D" hooks. There was a pair of carrying wheels 46" in diameter located in front of the drivers and ahead of the firebox, so arranged that a lever located in the cab might be thrown to transfer some of the load normally supported by these wheels to the drivers for starting. The lever could be thrown off when sufficient headway was attained. The wheel arrangement of these locomotives, according to the later Whyte system, would have been 4-2-2-0.[46]

Why would the PRR buy such specialized locomotives with such limited potential use? One can only surmise, but Baldwin went ahead and built several on speculation to amortize the cost of new drawings and patterns, and again had two or three he wanted to dispose of on the cheap. Thomson's letter to Baldwin supports this bit of conjecture, *You can sell at cost and interest to us two of the engines we purchased of you, one of them I would prefer keeping .... if you sell them [we will] take others in their place.*[47]

After acquiring *Mifflin*, *Blair* and *Indiana* were added later.[48] *Mifflin*, *Blair* and *Indiana* all ran between 28,500 and 31,000 miles during 1850. The next year (1851) they ran only 13,200, 4,206, and 8,760 miles, respectively. *Mifflin* was rebuilt by Baldwin in 1853 for $2,697.48 and was then changed to a 4-4-0 by the PRR in 1855 and 1856. The locomotive received a new wagon-top boiler, relocated cylinders and four 66" drivers. The *Annual Report* shows no mileage for *Mifflin* during these two years. In 1860 *Mifflin's* mileage picked up with 27,004 run in passenger service and 234 on freight. *Blair* was rebuilt in the Mifflin Shop as a 4-4-0 with 72" drivers. 1859 was *Blair's* best year after rebuilding, when she turned in 10,680 miles. *Indiana* remained a 4-2-0 but had new 60" drivers with chilled tires installed in 1853. *Indiana* plodded along in freight service, turning in about 10,000 to 15,000 miles per year. There was no mileage recorded for 1858 when the engine was in the shop. Both *Indiana* and *Blair* were scrapped by November 1864, and, in that year *Mifflin* was transferred to the Philadelphia & Erie.

The first train, a lumber train, arrived at Lewistown on August 23, 1849. On August 30, a special with a large party came up from Harrisburg. Herman Haupt reported that the train (from Philadelphia) was halted at Harrisburg. Upon investigation

it turned out that Colonel Patterson had ordered the stop. If the halt had not been carried out there would have been a head-on collision. Since there was no telegraph, Haupt sent an engine up the line in advance of the special train to "give notice." Haupt wryly remarked that *Colonel Patterson did not know enough not to interfere with a schedule that had been arranged by the Superintendent.*[49] For our interest this reveals that there were at least three locomotives on the road that day.

On September 1 train service began, but no advertisement concerning the schedules appeared in the Lewistown *Gazette* until November 3. The paper then announced that freight trains would run between Lewistown and Philadelphia (via the State Road), leaving Lewistown on Wednesdays and Saturdays and returning from Philadelphia on Mondays and Thursdays.[50] No passenger trains were mentioned in the paper until Monday, December 24, when it was announced that the passenger train would leave Lewistown at 15 minutes to ten daily.

The PRR's next locomotives came from the Harrisburg, Portsmouth, Mountjoy & Lancaster rail-road Company, a road running from Harrisburg to a connection with the state owned Philadelphia & Columbia at Lancaster. The PRR began negotiations with the Harrisburg & Lancaster, as the road was known, on April 5, 1848.[51] On April 21, 1849 the PRR leased the H&L and purchased its equipment. The Company acquired three 4-2-0's, a 4-4-0, and a Baldwin flexible-beam-truck 0-6-0. Due to a conflict about the terms of the lease, the H&L did not release the locomotives until October 16, 1849.

Early in the negotiation process Thomson wrote to Baldwin about the "soon to be acquired" H&L locomotives. *We have agreed upon a basis of settlement with the Hbg. RR Company by which we control their motive power — we shall want to get rid of their small engines in some way — if not disposed of we must lengthen out their boilers — get new cylinders & iron frames —*

*possibly larger drivers also. What could you [do] then for each?*[52] Baldwin responded, *These old engines that are too small, and too weak and good for [nothing?]. What should I say about them? I should say don't alter them but sell them, this is the best you can do with them. To alter it will cost about as much as to make new ones...*[53] The PRR, hard pressed for funds, continued to operate the H&L engines as built, only rebuilding one when it ran off the road soon after the railroad was opened to Lewistown.[54]

## Herman Haupt, Superintendent of Transportation: 1849-1850 General Superintendent: 1851-1852

In the *Second Annual Report* (November 15, 1849), Chief Engineer Thomson noted that the responsibility for conducting transportation on the road was given to Herman Haupt in his position as Superintendent, which placed him in charge of all motive-power matters. (There was no General Superintendent of Motive Power until the 1880's). In the latter part of 1847, Thomson hired Haupt to work on the location of a section of the Eastern Division.[55] Haupt was born in Philadelphia on March 26, 1817. He graduated from the U.S. Military Academy in June 1835, but resigned his commission to become assistant engineer under Henry R. Campbell on the survey for a railroad between Norristown and Allentown. Haupt then joined the survey for the State Works in 1836 to locate a projected railroad between Gettysburg and Hagerstown. Between 1845 and 1847, he taught at Pennsylvania College (Gettysburg) and wrote his *General Theory of Bridge Construction*, published in 1851. By the spring of 1848 Haupt was promoted to Assistant to the Chief Engineer. On September 1, 1849, he became Superintendent of Transportation, and from January 1851 to November 1852 was General Superintendent of the PRR. He resigned to survey a railroad in Mississippi, but in April 1853 was elected Chief Engineer of the PRR, with responsibility for finishing the road from Altoona to Pittsburgh. Haupt was appointed to supervise the Hoosac Tunnel project for the Troy & Greenfield in 1856, which, due to construction difficulties and political opposition, turned out to be a disaster. During the Civil War, he was Superintendent of Construction and Transportation for the U.S. Military Railroads, and became a Brigadier General. During the 1870's, he managed some of the PRR-controlled roads in the south. In 1878-1879, he designed and built the first long distance pipeline for transporting crude oil for the Tide-Water Pipe Company, Ltd. Haupt was the General Superintendent of the Northern Pacific from 1881-1884 and saw its completion to the Pacific. He served as president of the Dakota & Great Southern from 1886-1888. Haupt died on December 14, 1905 on a PRR train, while returning from New York to his home in Washington, D.C.

Haupt reported that for the first two months of revenue operation (September - October 1849) the PRR's locomotives burned 348 cords of wood. On April 5, 1850, there were two daily trains from Harrisburg to Lewistown and a freight train that operated every day except Sunday. By June the passenger trains began to run though to Huntingdon, where they connected with the packet boats and stage lines for travel further west.[56] By September 17, 1850, the Eastern Division (later Middle Division) was opened to the Portage Intersection, near Hollidaysburg. No sooner had the PRR made connection with the Allegheny Portage at Portage Intersection than the Canal Commissioners closed it on December 7, 1850 for repairs. This episode began a long struggle with the State Works over a variety of issues, until the PRR finally purchased the Commonwealth's railroads and canals in 1857. As the construction progressed, the Company began to operate the completed trackage for local service. The freight revenue for 1850 was $42,084.04. As the demands on the Superintendent of Transportation increased, the Motive Power Department was put in charge of the foreman of the Harrisburg Shops (the

◄ *Figure 16. #? (Baldwin). Of the 26 locomotives reported at the end of 1851, ten were Baldwin "C" 4-4-0's with 15" x 20" cylinders and 54" drivers. This has been identified as either the* Wyoming *(#20), which had 60" drivers, or the* Somerset *(#27), which had 54" drivers; the latter is the more likely. It has a Bury firebox with one safety valve on the "Bury dome" and another along with the whistle on the column directly behind the smokestack. The engine had half-stroke cutoff worked by drop-hook motion.* (Author's collection)

old H&L Shops). The acquisition of locomotives was clearly in Thomson's hands.

The first locomotive put into service which operated successfully, and also set a pattern for further additions to the roster, was *Juniata* **(Fig. 98)**, placed on the road on November 2, 1849. It had four 54" drivers, a Bury firebox, 14" x 20" cylinders, and weighed 45,275 lbs. Suitable for either freight of passenger service, *Juniata* was the first of several thousand 4-4-0's operated by the PRR.

Beginning on November 30, 1848, Thomson and Baldwin carried on an extensive correspondence, as they worked out the dimensions and characteristics for a locomotive that would suit Thomson's requirements. The major issue was the fire surface necessary to insure the capacity of the machine that Thomson wanted.[57] Thomson also had his own ideas on how Baldwin might make improvements to his designs.

*Mr. Pettit has almost persuaded me to adopt the outside connected engine for [the] second class machine. I might change my mind if you could show a better plan of attaching cylinders to your boiler than you have. Norris' method, I think preferable to yours if it were not for the objection to the weight of his cast iron bed plates and the risk of failure. If you could make something like it of wrought iron properly stayed, it would answer the purpose probably. The bearings of the inside connection, to insure steadiness, ought to be made longer than it has been customary to make them, say 9 inches.*[58]

(This is probably Robert Pettit (1804-1874), who was a civil engineer on the Public Works and the father of Robert Ellmaker Pettit (1846-1894), a PRR General Superintendent.)

Thomson finally decided, with some persuasion by Pettit, on an outside-connected locomotive and told Baldwin to go ahead and build them. He also told his friend Matthias Baldwin that next fall he would have to try a Norris machine — *and you must do your best to beat him.*[59] When the *Juniata* and *Huntingdon* arrived in October and November of 1849, Thomson wrote to Baldwin that he *did not look for the passenger locomotive until spring when we are opened to Huntingdon — you must take your time — as we have not the funds to pay in advance.*[60]

On January 9, 1850, Thomson wrote to the Board recommending the purchase of ten locomotives.[61] There were several different types and two builders, M.W. Baldwin and the Norris Brothers, represented in the PRR's locomotive stock after four months of operation. The matter was referred to the Road Committee. The Board then took action discharging the Road Committee from any further consideration of recommendations of the Chief Engineer on the subject of additional freight cars and locomotives.[62] This resolution placed the authority to order locomotives entirely in Thomson's hands and allowed him to pass the majority of the road's business to Baldwin. By specifying what he wanted, Thomson effectively cut out other producers.

In a letter to the Board meeting of January 23, 1850, Thomson assured that he intended to give Norris a fair chance for locomotives, but felt that his price was too high.[63] Thomson solicited bids from both Norris and Baldwin for the new locomotives. Norris had produced only one locomotive for the PRR so far, *Cambria* **(Figs. 2 and 15)**, a 4-4-0 with 54" drivers and 13" x 22" cylinders. There was some disagreement between the Company and the Norris Brothers over the cost of *Cambria*.[64] The Norris' bid $8,000 each for locomotives built to the specifications of *Cambria*, but without vibrating boxes.[65] The "vibrating boxes," which offered a certain amount of lateral motion, were made on a plan patented by Septimus Norris and James Tull on July 3, 1847 (#5180). This added an additional $250 to the cost of each locomotive. Norris Brothers also bid $7,500 for locomotives built to the plan of *Juni-*

*ata* and *Huntingdon*.[66] Some insight into the competitive nature of locomotive building can be gained by quoting Thomson's letter to the Board on February 20, 1850: *Mr. Baldwin offers to make eight locomotives similar to the* Cambria *for $6,750 cash. Messrs. Norris & Bros. price is $8,000 and will take ⅓ in stock. Mr. Baldwin offers for engines similar to the* Juniatta *(sic) to take $7,000 for cash or $7100 for ¼ stock. Norris Bros. price is $7,500, ⅓ stock or 1 ⅖% off for cash.*[67]

At the meeting held the next week (January 30, 1850) the Board authorized the General Superintendent to contract for 250 freight cars and 10 locomotives. Thomson's correspondence reveals his dislike for the products of the Norris Works in Philadelphia. He cites their "humbuggery" about the value of their engines and comments that *Cambria* (a Norris product) *is highly finished but not a good proportioned machine.*[68] The fascinating phrase in his letter to the Board is Thomson's statement that *the general plan of the Juniata & Huntingdon having been arranged by myself is of course preferred to the Cambria …*[69] A letter read at the same Board meeting stated that Thomson had *of course* allotted the contract for eight locomotives to Baldwin, reserving the remaining two for further consideration.[70]

Thomson's reaction to *Cambria* is somewhat more complex than his correspondence with the Board might indicate. Although Baldwin got the order for new locomotives, the letters that Thomson wrote Baldwin show a rather interesting side to their business relationship. Almost immediately after *Cambria* arrived on the PRR, Thomson wrote to Baldwin describing the new locomotive. Although the fire surface was similar in both *Cambria* and *Juniata*, *Juniata* weighed 2½ tons (5,200 lbs.) more than the engine furnished by Norris. The weight on drivers was only 600 lbs. more for *Juniata* than for *Cambria*. Thomson also noted that *Cambria* was a very highly finished machine.[71] Another letter followed in a few days:

*I intend having all parts of the Cambria [checked over], she is a machine of higher finish than yours, but I do not like her form—portions, particularly the location of the truck, which is thrown in advance of the machine to increase the weight on the drivers. By this means he gains the same amount of adhesion as yours do and saves the two tons in the weight of the machine at the expense of future repairs—the question is whether the transportation of its additional 2-tons of dead weight will pay for the extra repairs, which must be the consequence of a deficiency of material.*[72]

Thomson, always concerned with locomotive weight, was letting Baldwin know that Norris had saved approximately two tons of weight by the arrangement of the engine truck on *Cambria*. He raised the question with Baldwin about the extra weight of his locomotive. At this point Thomson was not sure that the extra weight of Baldwin's locomotives, and thus the extra cost, would be offset by the repair cost that ultimately would be incurred by Norris' use of lighter materials. Thomson added that: *We shall want a number of machines to be delivered next summer and fall of similar class to the Juniata and Huntingdon for which we ask for your proposal.*[73]

Thomson soon changed his mind in regard to the dimensions and began to increase the cylinder size. *In our new engines I propose to bring the stroke to 22-inches—I think that this, all things considered, is far affordable to increase the diameter of the cylinder. Norris engine has about 7 per cent larger capacity in cylinders than yours & in consequence draws better in a dead pull. Our folks generally like the arrangement of the valves and cut-off of the Cambria better than those of the Juniata.*[74]

The fascinating element in this correspondence is that Thomson kept feeding Baldwin information and suggestions to improve his locomotives. Baldwin had a standard line of locomotives that he was offering for sale. Thomson, who was operating these locomotives, was continually trying to influence

Baldwin to make them stronger, and thus cheaper to operate.[75]

*Juniata* and *Huntingdon*, and a subsequent 21 others built between October 1849 and May 1852, were Baldwin's eight-wheel class C. The boiler, 17' - 4" long, had a Bury firebox 44" long, 36" wide and 54" high. There was one safety valve on the Bury dome and another safety valve and the whistle on a column toward the front of the boiler. The cylinders had a 14" bore and a 20" stroke. In later machines, the bore was increased to 14½" and then to 15". Five of these locos were equipped with 60" drivers. All had the usual Baldwin half-stroke-cutoff valve gear. Two full-stroke pumps were connected to the crossheads on either side, which supplied water to the boiler. The four drivers were 54" in diameter on locomotives used in both freight and passenger service, and 60" on those intended solely for passenger service. The engine truck wheels were 37" in diameter. The first of these engines were equipped with six-wheel tenders, but later double-truck tenders were supplied.[76]

The *Fourth Annual Report* for 1850 shows that *Juniata* ran 31,999 miles in passenger service and 6,744 in freight service, for a total of 38,773.[77] By 1853, *Juniata*, with its 54" drivers, was used principally in freight service, running between 18,000 and 20,000 miles per year. It was in the Altoona Shop for general repairs in 1860 and then ran approximately 11,000 miles per year in freight service in 1861 and 1862, the last two years the *Annual Reports* included locomotive statistics. *Juniata* was finally cut up in March 1872, after 23 years of service; *Huntingdon* was not cut up until February 1876.

A revealing aspect of the Baldwin–Thomson correspondence was their "other" business arrangements. After Thomson informed him about the arrival of the new locomotives, Baldwin wrote, *I am endeavoring to buy the stock you wanted but couldn't find*

*any in the market...*[78] Thomson was purchasing locomotives from Baldwin for both the Pennsylvania and the Georgia Rail Road & Banking Company, and Baldwin was buying stock for Thomson's private account on the Philadelphia market.

The Board's concerns extended not only to the purchase of locomotives but to the wood supply necessary to operate them. On July 10, 1850, the Board instructed Thomson to examine a tract of woodland offered by a Mr. Miller, and, if he found it desirable, to purchase the parcel for a price not exceeding $800, payable in stock.[79]

A revealing minute recorded by the Board is in their record of the meeting held on April 30, 1851.[80] Thomson requested that the Board pay for ten locomotives; $6,750 for locomotives of 19 tons and $7,000 for locomotives of 20 tons. Thomson had made a verbal contract for the locomotives during a visit to the seashore the previous summer. He reported to the Board that he did not think that it was necessary to enter into a written contract since the needs of the Company might change as the business of the road developed. Thomson concluded that such an agreement was desirable even though the Board had not authorized him to enter into any contract. Since the locomotives were already on the property, the Board without further question authorized payment. The other visitor at the Jersey shore that previous summer was Matthias Baldwin. Twenty-six locomotives were in service at the end of 1851. There were 13 different types, eight of which were represented singly, three "classes" which had two each, another three, and another made up of nine Baldwin 4-4-0's similar to *Juniata* for freight service.

In 1851, Enoch Lewis, Master Mechanic of the Mifflin Shops, conducted a series of tests with wood, coke, and Pittsburgh and Allegheny coals in order to determine which fuel would be most economical and satisfactory. *Clearfield*, a Baldwin 4-4-0 (54", 15" x 20") built in April 1851, was used for the tests, which were held between Johnstown and Lockport. The line from Conemaugh to Lockport was opened on August 25, 1851, and the extension from Lockport to Beatty's was put in operation on December 10, 1851.

*Clearfield* ran 22 trips, for 522 miles, averaging 13 cars per trip using wood, consuming 14.78 cords. Twenty-six trips were run (590 miles) averaging 11½ cars per trip using a mixture of coal and wood, consuming 11.15 cords of wood and 63 bushels of Allegheny coal. When Pittsburgh coal was used the results were inconclusive. It was noted, however, that Pittsburgh coal burned better, with less ash, and did not produce intense heat upon the grates. A test was made using Ligonier Valley coke, but they could not succeed in burning it. When using bituminous coal alone the Company had to contend with burned-out grates and damaged fireboxes. Lewis figured that one ton of coal was equal to 2½ cords of wood. The result favored soft coal, especially when mixed with wood. This, Lewis thought, would result in a saving of 33%.[81] The Company purchased 20,463 cords of wood in 1851 at a cost of $43,971.95, and only 8,029 bushels of coal at $571.85. In 1854, the Company purchased 35 new locomotives, 21 of which were coal-burners. Two years later the costs of wood and coal on the Main Line were $49,000 and $52,000, respectively. Conclusive fuel tests were not completed until 1859.

At the far western end of the proposed railroad, after the initial construction to secure the charter, work on Section #1 was begun in the spring of 1850.[82] The rails came to the city by canal and were delivered to the tracklayers on small cars hauled by horses. In the autumn of 1851 the first locomotive arrived. A flat [canal boat] came into the canal basin at Pittsburgh with the *Heisley* [83] on board, in charge

*Figure 17.* #27 (Baldwin, c/n 464, February 1852). Identified as Somerset, this may be one the earliest photographs of a PRR locomotive. It appears as built, with the auxiliary frame. The dome on the Bury firebox is clearly visible. Note the "round" main rod and connecting rod. Between October 1849 and May 1852, 17 of these locomotives were built for passenger and freight service.
(Author's collection)

of Major Charles Cheney. A few days later, *Indiana* **(Fig. 99)**, arrived, in charge of Edward Boyle. *Heisley* was unloaded successfully and put on the track, but in unloading *Indiana*, the front of the flat gave way and sank, with the engine resting on the bottom. After several days of hard work the recovery operation was suspended and a contract was made with Messrs. Knapp and Totter, who succeeded in getting the engine out of the canal basin. Three passenger cars, three platform cars and one small

freight car came soon after and were safely put on the track.

An enginehouse was built on the hillside opposite Lumber (now 22nd) St., into which both engines were put and fitted up. *Heisley* was used to haul iron from the yard to the tracklayers, who by this time had reached East Liberty, and when the work was completed to Wilkinsburg the ties were hauled from that point. On Wednesday, December 10, 1851, an excursion train left the Pittsburgh station on the corner of Liberty Avenue and O'Hara (now 12th) St., and ran only as far as Brinton's station,[84] where a connection was made with stage coaches that conveyed the passengers to end of track at Beatty's,[85] a distance of 28 miles. The train returned from Brinton's at 9 a.m., stopping at Wilkinsburg and East Liberty, arriving at Pittsburgh at 10 a.m. A second run was made leaving Pittsburgh at 3 p.m., stopping at all stations; it left Brinton's to return to Pittsburgh before midnight. The train was hauled by *Heisley*.

The stagecoaches failed to make "anything like close connections" on account of the delay of trains on the mountain, all freight and passengers being brought over the mountain by way of the Portage Inclines. There was little effort by the Allegheny Portage to get them through on time except on Sunday, when the freight was stopped and a clear track was given to passengers. The stagecoaches also made bad time on account of the deep snow and the severity of the cold.

In his record of the early days on the Western Division, Tibby notes that Al Pancake was sent to the Blairsville Branch to run the engine *Henry Clay*.[86] The branch from Blairsville Intersection (Torrance) to Blairsville was the only branch line authorized in the PRR's charter. As the trains became heavier it was found that *Heisley* was not able to haul them, due to its light weight and chilled driving wheels. *Indiana* was put to work. *It had only one pair of driving wheels six feet in diameter and when given a chance could do some fast running.*[87]

A timetable in the *Pittsburgh Gazette* shows the opening to Radebaugh's as July 15, at about which time the stables of the stage company were removed to Rhodebaugh's (*sic*)[88], which was then made the terminus of the road from Pittsburgh. This still left ten miles of staging between Radebaugh's and Beatty's. During the summer several passenger and one baggage car were received, and also two engines from Baldwin named *Pike* and *Union*. *Pike* was put in charge of Joshua Donneley, with Richard Allen as fireman. A new schedule was put into effect, with two express trains and one accommodation train each way.

The date had been set a number of times for the train to come through on the PRR's own rails, but was postponed on account of the heavy work on the embankment at Greensburg, and the slips in the embankment. Finally on the afternoon of Friday, November 26, 1852, *Wyoming* (**Fig. 16**), with William Williams at the throttle, came through to Pittsburgh amid much rejoicing. (The exact date is unclear; the *Pittsburgh Gazette* shows the first train arriving in the evening of November 29.) *There is a difference of opinion about the engine that Williams came through with. He was running the Clearfield regularly, but a few days before an accident occurred by which the Clearfield was disabled, and he was so anxious to make the run through that he took the Wyoming and made it. The run was continued on the old schedule a while on account of the insecurity of the embankment at Greensburg.*[89]

The enginehouse and car shops at the "outer depot" were far enough advanced during the summer that early in the autumn engines were put into the enginehouse, and a small space was occupied in the car shop by some machinists, with a few lathes that were run by a large hand-turned wheel. Mr. Glasgow was the foreman in charge of the shops. He remained only a short time, and Mr. Stamp was appointed in his place. Stamp met with an accident and lost one of his legs, being run over by an engine at the passenger station. He performed the duties for a short time after his recovery; when he resigned, the position was given to George Greer (*sic*).[90] Ambrose Ward was foreman of the car shops. During the summer of 1852, the work on the Mountain Division had fallen behind on account of a scarcity of labor, as the work on the New Portage Railroad was undertaken at the same time. A great many men were induced to leave the employ of the Company and go to the Portage road.

There were 43 locomotives in service; an additional eleven 4-4-0's and seven six-drivered freight locomotives were acquired. The latter are of particular interest. Between August 1852 and January 1853, Baldwin built 12 of these locomotives, divided between 4-6-0's (25-ton, 10-wheel D) with center-bearing swiveling trucks (also called vibrating trucks) and 2-6-0's (25-ton, 8-wheel D) with the 30" leading truck set in rigid pedestal jaws ahead of the cylinders. Designed as coal burners, they all had 18" x 22" cylinders, 44" drivers, and wagon-top boilers 42" in diameter. The fireboxes were 60" x 36". In 1854 the PRR equipped the Baldwin 2-6-0's with center-bearing swiveling four-wheeled engine trucks, making them 4-6-0's.[91] Most of the 4-4-0's built in 1852 were for freight service, but in August Baldwin built a "heavy passenger" locomotive for the PRR, *True American*. It had 66" drivers and 16" x 22" cylinders. A total of five of this type, Baldwin 23-ton, eight-wheel C, were built.

Smith & Perkins of Alexandria, Va. built one of the six-drivered freight locomotives. The design was similar to the *Pawnee* class built by James Millholland for the Philadelphia & Reading. The locomotive was a pseudo-Mogul. The engine truck was behind the cylinders and held in rigid pedestals on the main frame. There were no flanges on the first and second pairs of 44" drivers. The first two (and two built for the Allegheny Portage) had wagon-top boilers, with a column on the roof sheet with a safety valve. A dome near the front of the boiler waist held the whistle. The inclined cylinders were 17" x 22" and were bolted to the frame and the side of the smokebox. Steam was admitted to the cylinders by full- or half-stroke valves operated by drop hooks.[92]

For the first few years of its existence the Pennsylvania Railroad struggled to complete its Main Line from Harrisburg to Pittsburgh. All too often the projected construction was postponed with a note to the Board that the *means of the Company was insufficient to justify the extension.* Despite the financial difficulties which delayed the work between Tyrone Forge and Altoona, the Main Line was opened and in operation from Harrisburg to Portage Intersection by September 17, 1850.

The Company found it difficult to operate 193 miles of road and maintain the growing fleet of motive power from the former H&L shop at Harrisburg. The PRR established its own first shops at Mifflin, which were completed in 1851, and construction of the Company's main shop was begun at Altoona.[93] The property that would become the Altoona Shops was purchased by Archibald Wright, thought to be an agent of the Company, from David Robeson. The deed transfer concluded on April 24, 1849, and ceded 224 acres to Mr. Wright of Philadelphia for $10,000. He then transferred the property to his son, John A. Wright, who laid out the town lots.

The name "Altoona" has several possible derivations. Robert Steele, who ran the first train into Altoona in 1851, reported that Colonel Beverly Mayer, of Columbia, Pa., who was employed as a civil engineer laying out the yard tracks, named the place Altoona after the city of Altona in Schleswig-Holstein, Germany, west of Hamburg on the Elbe River. Popular tradition claims that the name is a corruption of the Cherokee word meaning "high lands of great worth." The younger Wright had spent some time in the Cherokee country of Georgia, where he had been attracted by the name Allatoona.[94] Allatoona was the name given to the summit on the Western & Atlantic Railroad between Atlanta and Dalton/Chattanooga. However, it was Thomson, not Wright, who was involved in the W&A, since it was an ex-

tension of the Georgia Railroad. It is supposed that Thomson may have chosen the name. There is little hard evidence for either derivation.

The Company began construction of its shops in Altoona in 1851, when Wright conveyed the deed of the property to the PRR.[95] Initial construction included an eight-stall enginehouse, which also doubled for freight car repairs, and a paint shop. A long, one-story building housed a machine shop, woodworking shop, blacksmith shop, and foundry.[96]

By the beginning of 1852, the railroad was complete except for 28 miles on the Western Division between Beatty's Station and Turtle Creek, and the gap bridged by the Allegheny Portage Railroad over the Allegheny Mountain.

The line west from Harrisburg was completed as follows:

Harrisburg to Lewistown, 61 miles    September 1, 1849
Lewistown to McVeytown, 11 miles   December 24, 1849
McVeytown to Shaffer's Aqueduct, 13 miles

April 1, 1850
Shaffer's Aqueduct to Huntingdon, 12 miles

June 10, 1850
Huntingdon to Portage Intersection, 40 miles

September 16, 1850
The line west from Conemaugh was completed as follows:

Conemaugh to Lockport, 21 miles    August 25, 1851
Lockport to Beatty's, 20 miles    December 10, 1851

The connection with the Allegheny Portage was extended from Conemaugh to the Big Viaduct at the Ox Bow, avoiding Plane #1, on April 1, 1852.

The line east from Pittsburgh was completed as follows:

Pittsburgh to Brinton's, 11 miles    December 10, 1851;
revenue service began December 11
Brinton's to Carpenter's, 8 miles    July 15, 1852
Carpenter's to Radebaugh's, 10 miles    July 15, 1852
Radebaugh's to Beatty's, 9 miles,    December 1, 1852

## Enoch Lewis, Second Assistant Superintendent: 1852-1857

On February 3, 1852, J. Edgar Thomson was elected as the president of the Company. A revised organizational scheme went into effect on December 1, 1852; Enoch Lewis became the Second Assistant Superintendent and was given responsibility for motive power, in addition to his primary task of managing the Eastern Division. (The Divisions at this time were not the familiar ones. The Eastern Division ran from Dillerville to Mifflintown, the Middle Division from Mifflintown to Conemaugh, and the Western Division from Conemaugh to Pittsburgh. The more familiar divisions were established in February 1863, by combining parts of the Eastern and Philadelphia Divisions.) Lewis was born in Wilmington, Del. in 1821 and entered an apprenticeship with Eastwick & Harrison, the Philadelphia locomotive builders, in 1836. Eight years later he went with Eastwick & Harrison to Russia, where they set up the locomotive shop at Alexandroffsky. Lewis returned to the U.S. in 1846 and worked at various machine shops before joining the PRR in 1850. He was in charge of the Mifflin shop before his promotion to Second Assistant Superintendent on December 1, 1852. Lewis resigned in 1857 to join John A. Witney & Sons, car wheel manufacturers, but returned to the PRR to become General Superintendent until resigning on December 31, 1865. Lewis again returned to the PRR employ, becoming Purchasing Agent, on May 1, 1866. He retired on December 1, 1893 and lived until November 15, 1902.

Seventeen new locomotives were added in 1852 and the locomotive stock had increased to 78 by the end of Lewis' first year (1853) as Second Assistant Superintendent. The majority of those in operation (49) were 4-4-0's. There were two classes of 4-4-0's for freight service, the Baldwin with 54" drivers and 15" x 20" cylinders, and additional Baldwin freight 4-4-0's with 54" drivers and 17" x 22" cylinders equipped with wagon-top boilers. Between September 1853 and March 1856, Baldwin built 22 of these locomotive for the PRR. They were employed in freight service between Altoona and Pittsburgh. The Company added three passenger 4-4-0's from Seth Wilmarth, and its first large order for locomotives from Richard Norris & Son of Philadelphia, eleven 4-4-0 passenger locos. There were eleven Baldwin and Smith & Perkins 2-6-0s

and five Baldwin 4-6-0's for freight service, in addition to four Winans Camels. Even though the locomotive policy was in Lewis' hands, Thomson took a consuming interest in everything mechanical that related to "his" railroad, and was always on the lookout for new ideas and improvements.

The first new 17" x 22" cylinder freight 4-4-0 from Baldwin was *Adams* **(Fig. 114)**. The major change from the earlier Baldwin eight-wheeled C's was the replacement of the Bury firebox with a

"small" wagon-top boiler with a barrel 44" in diameter and a firebox 78" in length. There was a standpipe (column) with one safety valve on the roof sheet and a small dome on the waist with another safety valve and whistle. It had variable-cutoff valve gear and auxiliary frames.[97]

The arrival of three 4-4-0's from Seth Wilmarth is somewhat of a surprise, since Thomson had previously informed the Board of his objections to Boston locomotives.[98] Wilmarth operated the Union Iron

*Figure 18.* #42 (Baldwin, c/n 505, December 1852). Cumberland *is pictured sometime in the 1860's with the number on the valve chamber, typical of Laird rebuilds. Originally built with a rigid single leading wheel, all six of these pseudo-Moguls had four-wheel vibrating trucks added in 1854. #42 has a new boiler, Stephenson valve gear, an injector, and a Laird stack.*
(PRR photo; author's collection)

Works on Foundry Street in South Boston, and started producing locomotives in 1848. A large contract from the Erie in 1854 proved his undoing. Of the three locomotives he built for the PRR, *Antelope* and *Atlanta* **(Fig. 20)** had 78" drivers and *Eagle* had 66" drivers. They had 16" x 22" cylinders and wagon-top boilers. There was a safety valve on the dome over the firebox and another safety valve and whistle on a column on the boiler waist. The engines had auxiliary frames and were wood burners. *Ante-lope* was scrapped in December 1869 and the other two were transferred to the Philadelphia & Erie in 1865.[99] C.H. Caruthers reported that since boyhood he had heard vague statements of some older men on the PRR that a fourth Wilmarth engine was built for the PRR but was lost on its ocean passage from Boston to Philadelphia. Caruthers recalled that an extra tender used on the Pittsburgh Division between 1853 and 1869 was often referred to in his presence as belonging to an engine that was lost at sea.[100]

The eleven 4-4-0's received from Richard Norris & Son were the first locomotives that this builder supplied since the initial purchase of *Cambria* in 1850. All had straight boilers with 30" domes on the roof sheet and deep fireboxes for burning wood. Four had 72" drivers, while the rest were equipped with 60" drivers. All had 16" x 24" cylinders set horizontally. The large-drivered engines had slab frames, while the others had slab frames from the pilot beam to the pedestals of the forward driving

*Figure 19. #43 (Smith & Perkins, December 1852). Smith & Perkins of Alexandria, Va., built 12 2-6-0's with rigid leading wheels for the PRR, and two for the Allegheny Portage. They were limited to slow speed due to their tendency to derail and turn over. Before rebuilding, several enginemen lost their lives on these engines. #43, the Altoona, was rebuilt as a 4-6-0. The loco retained its drop hook valve gear, which had separate eccentrics for front gear, back gear and cutoff.*

*(PRR photo; author's collection)*

*Figure 20.* #40 (Seth Wilmarth, March 1852). *The PRR purchased three 4-4-0's with 16" x 22" cylinders, 78" drivers and hook-motion valve gear with independent variable cutoff from Seth Wilmarth of Boston in 1852-53.* Atlanta *is shown after rebuilding at Altoona with 60" drivers and Stephenson valve gear, in March 1866. Note the injector just in front of the cab.* Atlanta *was somewhat of a jinx. She struck a tree on Christmas day of 1854, overturned and was "completely wrecked." Rebuilt and placed back on the road in March 1855,* Atlanta *was in service only two weeks before she struck a rock and was "broken worse than before."*

(PRR photo 1248; author's collection)

boxes, and bar type from that point back. The locomotives were equipped with large springs between the drivers that extended almost to the top of the boiler.[101] Within two years, two had to be rebuilt because the cylinders were inadequately fastened and the frames were too light.

The additional Smith & Perkins pseudo-Moguls differed from the first two in that they had straight boilers and copper fireboxes. The safety valves were in a "buck horn" (**Figs. 113, 115 and 139**), which extended though the sand box on the boiler waist, with the whistle on the middle branch of the buck horn. An interesting feature was the water space on each side of the smokebox. Although strengthened with stay bolts, this arrangement proved troublesome. Ultimately ten of this type were acquired.[102]

Ross Winans of Baltimore pursued an independent course in locomotive design, and his Camel-type locomotives, the first coal-burning locomotives built in large numbers, were like no other American engines. Thomson, on a visit to Baltimore in January 1849, saw one of Winans' new engines. Although he didn't buy one immediately, he did write to Baldwin that: *You had better turn your attention to this matter [of burning coal], as we shall not in a few years burn anything else on the Penna. RR.*[103] It took quite a while to finally burn coal successfully, but Thomson did

◄ *Figure 21.* #57 (Richard Norris & Son, May 1853). *The PRR was not an enthusiastic Norris customer. Aside from* Cambria, *acquired in January 1850,* Kiskiminetas *and three similar engines purchased in March of 1853 were the next Norris locomotives put on the road. Originally built with 16" x 24" cylinders and 72" drivers,* #57 *is shown as rebuilt by Altoona in April 1862. In the 1854 Annual Report, Enoch Lewis notes that he had entirely rebuilt two Norris locomotives, due to lightness of frame, narrowness of main bearings, and inadequate fastening of cylinders. Laird was not impressed with the stability of the crossheads. Note the stiffening bar attached to the cylinders.* #57 *still retains the old hook motion.*

(PRR photo ME1260A; author's collection)

acquire some Winans Camels **(Figs. 39, 40, 78, 110 and 122)**. These locomotives, medium-furnace Camels, had sloping fireboxes suspended behind plate frames, with two firing chutes on the firebox to reach the front area of the grate. The cylinders, 19" x 22", were level and were worked by drop hook valve motion with a cam-drive cutoff. There were eight 44" drivers connected by solid-end rods. The boiler had a gigantic dome on the waist, and the cab was perched on top of the boiler, which prompted the name "Camel." [104]

The entire line of the PRR from Harrisburg to Pittsburgh was opened for business on February 15, 1854, although the arching of the tunnel at Gallitzin and the grading at the summit were not completed until June 1855. Herman Haupt had returned as Chief Engineer in 1853, and completed the mountain section, including the tunnel at Gallitzin. The PRR shifted all traffic to its own line and discontinued using the rebuilt Allegheny Portage from Johnstown to Hollidaysburg. This reduced considerably the tolls the Company had to pay the State. The tonnage on the PRR increased to 171,972 tons of through freight and 193,034 tons of local freight in 1855, an increase of 128,282 tons over the previous year. The decided increase in the local traffic in coal and lumber was due to the removal of the state tax on those items.

The costs for locomotive repair escalated in 1854. Lewis had the furnace ends of the Winans engines closed in, put new four-wheel trucks under the six Baldwin D class locomotives (#'s 42, 44-47, and 49) to improve their operation on curves, and rebuilt two Norris passenger locomotives because of lightness of frame, narrowness of the main bearings, and inadequate fastening of the cylinders.

Six "assistant freight engines," or pushers, were purchased, along with four Winans Camels and two Baldwin flexible-beam-truck 0-8-0's. Thirteen freight 4-4-0's from Baldwin and eight from Norris

*Figure 22.* #106 (Baldwin, c/n 587, April 1854). Potter *was typical of a large class of Baldwin freight 4-4-0's with 17" x 22" cylinders and 54" drivers. By the end of 1854 twenty were in service. The boiler was of wagon-top type, with a rather ornate "stand pipe" with a safety valve placed at about the center of the wagon top. A small dome on the boiler waist contained the throttle valve and had an opening for the whistle. Perhaps pictured after receiving a new firebox (August 1862), the locomotive retained many of its original fittings, with hook-motion valve gear, short-wheelbase vibrating truck and inclined cylinders.*
(PRR photo ME1300A; author's collection)

were also added. Two 2-6-0's came from Norris and six from Smith & Perkins. Baldwin supplied five passenger 4-4-0's with 66" drivers, and one with 72" drivers.

The eight Norris 4-4-0's added in 1854 were intended for freight service and had 16" x 24" inclined cylinders, 54" drivers and round instead of square sandboxes.[105] The two six-drivered engines from Norris were pseudo-Moguls with 44" drivers and a 30" wheel held in rigid jaws behind 17" x 22" cylinders. Designed to burn coal, they had sloping fireboxes 5' - 6" long by 2' - 9" wide which extended back into the cab. The boilers were straight and 44" in diameter. The valve gear was operated by "V" hooks, single on full stroke and double on cutoff.

The water pump was worked off the rear driver with a wrist attached to the rod pin.[106] One of these Norris 2-6-0's, Allegrippus [107] **(Fig. 118)**, was involved in the first accident of note after the mountain section was opened. About three miles above the Horseshoe Curve, the new embankment gave way and *Allegrippus* fell about 40 feet down the side of the mountain. The engineman, Thomas Ridley, was badly injured. The scene of the accident has been known as Allegrippus since that time. Mountain railroading not only included accidents but also necessitated being ready for heavy snow along the Allegheny range. The Company reported one "snow plough" on wheels and 12 pilot plows ready to be attached to engines.[108]

The locomotives of the PRR had a variety of different valve gears — in fact there were 12 in use by 1857.[109] These were usually some form of hook motion promoted by the individual builders. The first locomotives employing Stephenson link motion were purchased in 1856 from Richard Norris & Son: *Wyalusing* and *Shamokin*.[110] Baldwin was slow in accepting the link motion and promoted their own hook motion with Baldwin's special design of variable cutoff. The first Baldwin locomotive built for the PRR with link motion was *Tiger* (#134, **Fig. 125**), delivered January 1857. The Stephenson link motion came into general use and was practically the standard gear for many years. By 1874 only two Smith & Perkins locos retained the old hook motion.

During the early years of operation, the question of chilled-tread cast-iron drivers *versus* cast-iron centers and wrought-iron tires was being debated by practical motive power superintendents. In 1854 the PRR determined that the latter were better, and in 1864 adopted these wheels as standard, although the cast-iron wheel with chilled tread was used for engine trucks.

The early braking system was a major factor in limiting train speed and train length. At first, the locomotives had no brakes and each car was equipped with a brake operated by a hand wheel. When approaching a station the engineman would whistle for the brakes and the train crew would take their assigned positions and apply the brakes on each car. The PRR assigned one brakeman for each six eight-wheel cars or 12 "single" (four-wheel) cars.[111] The first improvement was the application of the Cramer brake system, perfected in 1853, to passenger cars. This consisted of a strong spiral spring attached to the brake staff at the end of each car; this spring was wound up by the brakeman immediately after leaving a station. Attached to the mechanism was a cord running through the train to the engine cab. The brake was so designed that when the engineman

pulled the cord, the coil spring on each car was released, winding up the chain leading to the brake mechanism, thus forcing the brake shoes against the wheels.

The shops at Altoona were progressing. During 1854 the enginehouse and machine shop were completed.[112] In 1855, Lewis noted in his report (December 31, 1855) that the boiler of *Cumberland* (#42, a Baldwin D Class, built in December 1852, **Fig. 18**) had been rebuilt to a plan furnished by his former employer, James Harrison, to improve the combustion of bituminous coal. He also altered *True American* (#64, a Baldwin 4-4-0, built in September 1853) to test the advantage of burning coke. The test was limited due to failure in procuring good coke. Only

three new locomotives were added during 1855.[113]

The Company had 118 locomotives at the end of 1855 to handle traffic. The majority were Baldwin 4-4-0's, of several designs. The mountain division from Altoona to Johnstown demanded heavier power than the lines east or west of the Allegheny Summit. For this service the PRR purchased a variety of six- and eight-drivered locomotives from Baldwin and from Ross Winans. The helper locomotives assigned to the eastern slope were the Baldwin flexible-beam 0-8-0's, the Ross Winans Camels, and the six-drivered Baldwin Class D's. The Smith & Perkins and Norris pseudo-Moguls, along with the Baldwin 4-4-0's, handled the through freight assignments. Because of their instability, the Smith and Perkins

*Figure 23.* #118 (Baldwin, c/n 670, November 1855). Black Oak (#117), Aughwick (#118) and Blue Ridge (#120) were the second group of ten-wheelers purchased by the PRR. Aughwick (#118), built by Baldwin in November 1855, originally had hook-motion valve gear with variable cutoff. Shown here as rebuilt at Altoona in 1867, #118 has Stephenson valve gear and a balloon stack. The PRR moved to make the 4-6-0 standard for freight service, and acquired ever larger and more modern machines.
(PRR photo ME1261A; author's collection)

pseudo-Moguls were soon relegated to shifting service.

The first of the three locomotives acquired in 1855 was *Flirt*, built by Baldwin in December 1854 but not put on the road until January 1855. *Flirt* had 72" drivers and 16" x 22" cylinders. The other two were 4-6-0's, *Black Oak* and *Aughwick* (Fig. 23). They were equipped with 48" drivers and 19" x 22" cylinders, and were the second group of 4-6-0's acquired by the PRR.

Lewis' report for 1856 (December 31, 1856) focused on the cost of firebox renewal. Iron fireboxes were becoming a source of great expense and were lasting from 6 to 12 months before renewal was necessary. Copper lasted from two to three times longer than iron. Lewis noted that the Smith & Perkins freight locomotives were built with copper fireboxes and had given no trouble during their two years of service.[114] The Company was now putting in several new copper fireboxes. Fifteen new locomotives were purchased during 1856, including five more Camels from Ross Winans, another 4-6-0 from Baldwin (*Blue Ridge*, Figs. 26 and 27), four more 25-ton C 4-4-0's for freight, and the two previously-mentioned Norris 4-4-0's with Stephenson valve gear, *Wyalusing* and *Shamokin*. The PRR also added its last Smith & Perkins locomotives in 1856, three 4-6-0's. They had wagon-top boilers with a substantial steam dome having two safety valves on the center waist sheet of the boiler. The whistle was on a column that went through the sand box. The valve gear was suspended-link, or the Gooch type. The water pumps were operated by a return crank from the main (second) driving pin. The four-wheel truck was the Bissell type with a spring equalizer above the truck frame. All three were soon leased to the Panhandle.[115]

The shop complex at Altoona continued to expand. A new enginehouse with 26 stalls was added, along with a new smithy with 18 forges, and a new foundry extension was added to the machine shop. It was projected that by early spring (of 1855) the new erecting shop would be ready. The officers reported to the Board that there was also a need for employee housing.[116] Over 1,000 men were working at the Altoona Shops in 1855. The population of Altoona would rise from about 2,000 in 1854 to 3,591 in 1860. The PRR was also giving attention to other repair facilities. The Mifflin Shops handled repairs on locomotives running between Mifflin and Harrisburg and Columbia. There were also shops at Conemaugh and Pittsburgh. The lack of space in enginehouses for the shelter of engines and running repairs was a continuing problem.[117]

## Alexander McCausland, Master of Machinery: 1857 - 1858

In 1857, Thomson instituted an entirely new organizational structure to operate the PRR. The railroad was divided into three divisions, Eastern (later Philadelphia), Middle, and Western (later Pittsburgh), each under a division superintendent. The division boundaries were still the same as in 1852. Now the head of each was a division superintendent rather than an assistant superintendent. The division superintendents reported to the General Superintendent based at Altoona. The general staff, located in Philadelphia, was made up of the president, vice presidents, general superintendent, controller, auditor and treasurer. Motive Power, Maintenance of Way and Accounting were included in the chain of command. The position of Master of Machinery was established and Alexander McCausland was appointed to the post.

That same year (1857), the PRR acquired the State Works, which included the Philadelphia & Columbia and Allegheny Portage Railroads and the Main Line canal; this added more locomotives to the roster and gave the PRR its own line to Philadelphia. The PRR received these locos from the Commonwealth:[118]

| | |
|---|---|
| 8 | 27 ton, First Class Passenger |
| 11 | 25-ton, Second Class Passenger |
| 16 | 32 ton, First Class Freight |
| 11 | 26-ton, Second Class Freight |
| 16 | 20 ton, Third Class Freight |
| 6 | 18-ton, Third Class Passenger & Freight |
| 5 | Condemned |

The Company began to bring the Philadelphia & Columbia up to PRR standards, but service on the Allegheny Portage was suspended and the rail removed and shipped west for use on the PRR-controlled Pittsburgh, Ft. Wayne & Chicago. Thomson noted that a number of the locomotives received from the State Works were worth only the material of which they were built.[119] Since several of the locomotive names were duplicated, the Company assigned numbers to all its locomotives, from 1 to 210. The names were removed and by the middle of 1858 all were gone except for two, which were cast on the side of the sandbox.

The Company also purchased 14 new locomotives from Baldwin: four 26-ton C 4-4-0's for passenger service, four flexible-beam-truck 0-8-0's, and four more 27-ton C's for freight service with 56" drivers and 17" x 22" cylinders. The *Eleventh Annual Report* (1857) shows that two 20½ ton shifting locomotives were purchased in 1857, *Consolidation* (#140) and *C.E. Spangler* (#211).[120] Baldwin lists these as 17-ton, six-wheel D's. A sketch of #140 (Fig. 127) by C.H. Caruthers reveals a Baldwin flexible-beam-truck 0-6-0 with a wagon-top boiler, the firebox between the second and third set of drivers, and an eight-wheel tender.[121]

McCausland was charged with repairing the locomotives received from the Commonwealth. These required renewal of flues and brasses. Between August and December, 14,929 lbs. of brass and 1,955 iron flues had been sent to the old P&C repair shops at Parkesburg. McCausland expected that another

*Figure 24. #166 (New Jersey Locomotive & Machine, November 1853). The PRR added 55 locomotives from the Philadelphia & Columbia in 1857. #166, former P&C Wheatland, was built by the New Jersey Locomotive & Machine Company to the peculiar style of John Brandt, Superintendent of the NJL&M and later Superintendent of the Lancaster Locomotive Works. Brandt's engines had cylinders with sloping valve chests. Rebuilt at Altoona, #166 had a Gill & Company firebox. Note the long wagon top and short slope to the boiler barrel. The plate on the bell stand has the name "J.P. Laird" on it, but unfortunately the handrail hides most of it.* (PRR photo; author's collection)

2,936 flues would be needed. He noted that the scrapping of the present copper flues used in the P&C locomotives would pay for the expense.

Firebox replacement continued to be a problem on coal-burning locomotives. During 1857, 18 new copper fireboxes were put in. *York* (**Fig. III**, #49, a D class Baldwin, built in January 1853) had an iron firebox put in, designed for difficult use. It lasted only 12 months and was frequently patched with copper. McCausland noted that copper was most economical unless iron could be produced of a different quality than then available. Although locomotives were being built to burn coal, the results were mixed at best, as the firebox problem indicates. McCausland had *Blue Ridge* #120 (**Figs. 26 and 27**), a Baldwin 4-6-0, built in January 1856) altered so that the boiler had a combustion chamber to increase the consumption of gas. The stack had no cone or spark arrestor. McCausland noted that the

*Figure 25. #174 (Richard Norris & Son, May 1854). Old Hickory was built for the P&C as a 4-4-0, and was rebuilt at Altoona into a 4-6-0 in March 1864. The P&C liked the Brandt arrangement of cylinders, and several locomotives ordered from Norris also had them. The photograph represents Laird's attempt to rebuild older power into a "modern" locomotive. The difficulty in picturing the early locomotives of the PRR is that most were photographed in the mid 1860's after they were rebuilt.* (PRR photo ME1267A; author's collection)

combustion was almost perfect.

1857 brought one of the periodic depressions in the country's economy, and although traffic continued to increase, the Company managed to handle it with its existing roster. The PRR purchased a new locomotive from Baldwin in November 1857 (#129, BLW, c/n 794). In October 1858 a 4-6-0 (#210, c/n 912, **Fig. 32**) with an experimental boiler designed by Leonard Phleger was purchased from Norris of Philadelphia. A 4-4-0, #156 (**Figs. 30 and 31**), with a Smith boiler, was purchased from Baldwin in May 1859. The Company did not purchase another new locomotive until it acquired three more 4-6-0's from Norris in November 1860 (#'s 146, 152 & 153). Locomotives #152 and #153 were equipped with Phleger boilers and had Norris construction numbers #903 and #904, respectively. It would appear from the construction number sequence that these were built before #210 and remained unsold until the PRR purchased them in 1860. These locos were rebuilt with conventional boilers in 1861 (#210) and 1864.[122] The Company reported 216 locomotives and 216 tenders at the end of 1857.

At the end of 1858 the locomotives of the Company were assigned as follows:[123]

**Chart 6**

**Division Assignment of Locomotives, 1858**

| Type | Division | | | | | |
|------|----------|--------|----------|---------|--------------|-------|
|      | Eastern | Middle | Mountain | Western | Philadelphia | Total |
| 0-6-0 |  | 1 |  | 1 | 1 | *3 |
| 0-8-0 |  | 2 | 19 |  |  | 21 |
| 2-6-0 |  |  |  | 16 |  | 16 |
| 4-2-0 |  |  |  | 1 |  | 1 |
| 4-4-0 | 33 | 22 | 3 | 28 | 59 | 145 |
| 4-6-0 |  | 2 | 7 | 6 | 4 | 19 |
| **Total** | **33** | **27** | **29** | **52** | **64** | **205** |

* #142, an 0-6-0, was omitted in this list, but was included in subsequent listings in the *Annual Reports*. This listing does not include "out of use" engines.

1857 represents a watershed in the development of the locomotive engine on the PRR. As just mentioned, the railroad did not purchase any new locomotives, with the exception of #'s 210 and 156, until 1860. The new locomotives added to the roster after that date were modern. Gone were the individual builders' hook valve gear, outside frames, sloping cylinders and old-style engine truck. All locomotives numbered above #211 and locomotives built to replace vacated locomotives numbered below #211 had link valve gear, horizontal cylinders (with the exception of some shifters), casings over the cylinder heads, injectors, and the wide-spread engine truck. During McCausland's tenure the PRR began to de-

velop its locomotive stock around two basic types of "modern" locomotive, the 4-4-0 for passenger service and the 4-6-0 for freight. On May 10, 1858, McCausland was succeeded by George W. Grier as Master of Machinery. No biographical information is available for McCausland or his successor.

## George W. Grier, Master of Machinery, 1858-1862

Grier took over the motive power of the PRR during a severe depression in the national economy. Twenty-two new copper fireboxes had been put in during 1857. The ten Smith & Perkins locomotives built between December 1852 and April 1854 were originally equipped with copper fireboxes. They were in constant use during that time and some were coming up for renewal during the next year. Grier projected that a copper firebox, burning Pittsburgh coal, would last five years, while an iron firebox would last from 18 to 22 months. An iron firebox was $479, while a copper one cost $680. Although the first cost of a copper firebox was higher, the value of the scrap copper reduced the actual cost.

Only one new locomotive was added to the equipment in 1858, #210 from Richard Norris & Son equipped with Phleger's patent boiler. Locomotive #190 (*Old Dominion*, RN&S, June 1896) was rebuilt with a Dimpfel boiler by Baldwin and #206 was being equipped with a Gill & Company patent firebox. When Baldwin rebuilt *Old Dominion* it received a new boiler construction number, 829, on November 4, 1858. In some records the engine is shown as Norris 1856 and in others as Baldwin 1858. The drivers were reduced to 54" in 1859 and the locomotive was in the shop for a new firebox in 1862. It received a new, normal style of copper firebox and was rebuilt as a 2-6-0 at Altoona in November of 1863; #190 was scrapped in October 1869. Caruthers noted that: *the large manhole in the back-head remained, and became a puzzle to the younger men who handled it in later years after its running gear had been remodeled in Mogul style and it became a helper on the Allegheny mountains.*[124]

Grier conducted a five-month series of fuel tests in 1859 using bituminous coal.[125] The chief problem, after the fireboxes and grates were modified to handle the more intense heat from coal, was the smoke, which was much more bothersome than from wood. William Jackson Palmer supervised the test. When he was 19, Palmer traveled to England, paying part of his expenses by writing articles on English coal mining for the *Miners' Journal*. These articles came to the attention of Thomson, and he contacted Palmer while he (Thomson) was in England, asking him to find out as much as he could about the British methods of burning coal in locomotives. Palmer did not supply any new information. He affirmed that the British handled the smoke problem by shifting to coke or by using smoke-consuming devices. After returning home he became secretary of the Westmoreland Coal Company and helped to introduce this fine Western Penn-

*Figure 26.* #120 *(Baldwin, c/n 679, January 1856).* Blue Ridge *was rebuilt at Altoona in 1857 with a slightly sloping firebox with a firebrick arch.* #120 *was "second best" in the lack of annoying smoke emission in the fuel tests of 1859. After another rebuilding at Altoona (in 1867?),* #120 *retained her original drivers and rods.*   (PRR photo ME1320A; author's collection)

sylvania gas coal to the cities on the east coast. On June 1, 1857, Palmer, whose first love was railroads, became Thomson's confidential secretary. Thomson paid Palmer's $900 annual salary out of his own pocket. In the spring of 1859, Palmer found himself entrusted with the job of conducting the test on smoke consumption on the Pennsylvania Railroad for his chief. Later on, Palmer, a native of Delaware, attained the rank of general in the Civil War and then moved west, becoming the president of the narrow-gauge Denver & Rio Grande.[126]

The fuel tests were conducted from April 1859 until August of the same year, and were made using Pittsburgh and Broad Top coals. The tests were conducted on two different portions of the railroad: between Altoona and Gallitzin on the Pittsburgh Division, 12 miles, with a grade of 95 feet to the mile, and between Altoona and Mifflin on the Middle Division, 82 miles, in which the heaviest grade was 21 feet to the mile. The train hauled on the mountain, between Altoona and Gallitzin, consisted of eight box cars, all loaded, weighing 138⅜ tons. The train used between Altoona and Mifflin consisted of 20 loaded box cars weighing 347.4 tons. All details pertaining to the coal and water used were attended with the utmost care. The coal was weighed, and each locomotive charged with the amount used beginning with the lighting of the fires. The boiler was washed out and refilled with cold water before each test. This water was as of uniform a temperature as possible and all measurements of water in the tender were taken on the level. When water was supplied at points where the track was on a grade the tender was leveled by the use of screw jacks.[127]

The trials were made with six freight locomotives taken from regular service **(Chart 7)**.

The least successful locomotive was 4-4-0 #139 **(Fig. 29)**, taken from service without any alteration. It had a long, deep firebox and a "balloon" stack. The firebox door had only one opening in it. This locomotive emitted the most smoke, especially when Pittsburgh bituminous was used. When running with the firebox door open the smoke was greatly diminished. It is interesting to note that although giving the poorest results of the six in smoke consumption, #139 was the most economical in the consumption of fuel.

The next most successful was #51 **(Fig. 28)**, a Ross Winans Camel unchanged except for the removal of the forward firing chutes. The firebox had three large doors and the loco retained the Winans variable exhaust. #51's long firebox subjected the gasses to the action of the fire longer and showed less smoke than #139. With Pittsburgh coal the smoke dis-

**Chart 7**

### Locomotives Used in Fuel Tests

| # | Type | Builder | c/n | Date Built | Drivers, in. | Cylinders, in. | Notes |
|---|------|---------|-----|------------|--------------|----------------|-------|
| 51 | 0-8-0 | Winans | | 2/1853 | 42 | 19x22 | |
| 120 | 4-6-0 | Baldwin | 679 | 1/1856 | 48 | 19x22 | Brick arch. |
| 139 | 4-4-0 | Baldwin | 770 | 8/1857 | 54 | 17x22 | |
| 190 | 4-4-0 | Norris | | 6/1856 | 54 | 18x22 | Dimpfel boiler. |
| 206 | 4-6-0 | Baldwin | 688 | 3/1856 | 48 | 19x22 | Gill & Company firebox. |
| 210 | 4-6-0 | Norris | 912 | 10/1858 | 49 | 16x24 | Phleger boiler. |

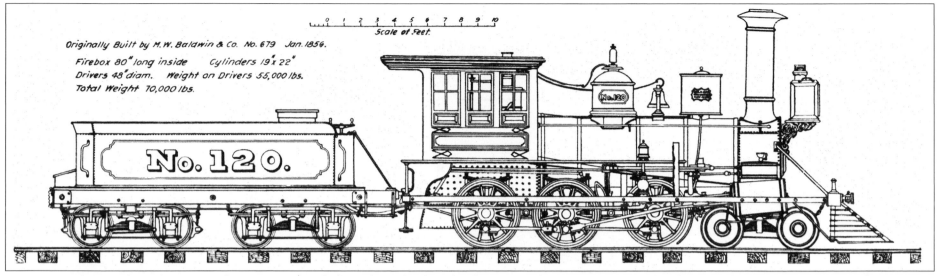

Originally Built by M.W. Baldwin & Co. No. 679 Jan. 1856.

Firebox 80" long inside     Cylinders 19" x 22"
Drivers 48" diam.   Weight on Drivers 55,000 lbs.
Total Weight 70,000 lbs.

Scale of Feet.

**Figure 27.** PRR #120, Blue Ridge, six 48" drivers, 19" x 22" cylinders. Blue Ridge *figured in the PRR's smoke consuming tests, conducted from April through August of 1859. The locomotive was rebuilt at Altoona in 1857 with a firebrick arch supported by water tubes, which formed a combustion chamber of approximately 21" between the water tubes and the flue sheet. Water grates were also used. There were four firing doors set one beside the other, in two tiers.*
*(C.H. Caruthers drawing; author's collection)*

charge ceased before the next fire was put in. With Broad Top coal the results were much better. #51 showed the extent to which smoke consumption could be carried on in locomotives with the largest practical admission of air through the firebox doors and without a combustion chamber or deflector.

The next locomotive, #190, had a Dimpfel boiler. The Dimpfel boiler had a concave crown sheet riveted to the usual side sheets and back sheet. The crown sheet was attached at the front to a slightly curved sheet with a concave side underneath. This sheet extended forward to a position usually occupied by the front tube sheet. At its sides it was riveted to curved sheets that formed a barrel within the

boiler barrel with about 4" less radius. This formed a semi-circular combustion chamber, which was attached to the outer shell of the barrel with radial stays. This chamber was closed except in the center, where an opening about 6" wide extended from the top to the bottom. There were numerous openings in the bottom of the boiler barrel to admit air. From the front of the sheets of the combustion

chamber 186 water tubes, 1¼" outside diameter, extended backward and upward from the front of the firebox, where they curved upward and entered the crown sheet. This expensive and cumbersome boiler steamed well, but it was next to impossible to keep the tubes from leaking. The arrangement made maintenance difficult and expensive. For all of this, #190 emitted only a little less smoke than #51; the

▶

**Figure 28.** *Fireboxes of #51 and #120. The firebox of #51, a Winans Camel, was modified by closing off the two firing chutes on the firebox roof and putting 360 ³⁄₁₆"-diameter holes in the firebox doors. The firebox of #120 shows the slight slope, brick arch supported by water tubes, and the combustion chamber.*
*(C.H. Caruthers drawing; author's collection)*

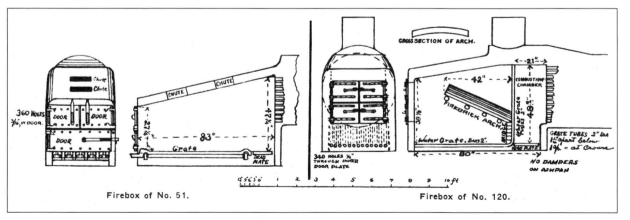

Firebox of No. 51.

Firebox of No. 120.

difference was hardly discernible.

#210 **(Fig. 32)**, a relatively new locomotive from Richard Norris & Son, was equipped with a Phleger boiler. The barrel of this boiler was filled with 2" flues, and had an inverted semi-circular section attached to the top of the barrel extending from the front of the wagon top to within 10" of the smokebox. This "tube" was opened to the interior of the barrel and contained a dry-pipe, which terminated on the outside of this structure in the usual "T." The firebox was shallow and set above the drivers, with two water bridges in horizontal position. One extended up from the grate at the front, and the other extended down from the crown sheet. In front of this baffle-like arrangement there was a combustion chamber 30" long. The only air which entered the firebox, aside from that through the grate, was

through a few small holes in the firebox door. This unique boiler showed even greater improvement in smoke consumption, especially on runs up the mountain to Gallitzin. On the Mifflin runs the results were not as good since the locomotive was not worked as hard.

Locomotive #120 **(Figs. 26, 27 and 28)** was rebuilt at Altoona with a slightly sloping firebox containing a firebrick arch extending from the front of the firebox for a distance of 3½ feet toward the doors. The arch was supported by eight hollow water plugs, while the grate was composed of water tubes extending from the back to about 18" from the front, where they curved up and entered the crown sheet. This formed a combustion chamber 21" long. The firebox doors had 340 holes of ¼" diameter in their inner plates. A blower and an unobstructed

straight stack were used. #120 did much better than the two preceding locomotives. The adequate admission of air, and the high temperature which the firebrick arch reached and maintained, ensured a more thorough consumption of gasses. The loco showed no smoke with Broad Top coal and only a slight amount with Pittsburgh coal.

The most successful locomotive in the test was #206, originally built by Baldwin for the Allegheny Portage. It had been rebuilt a short time before at Altoona with a Gill & Company coal-burning firebox. The device consisted of a water space forming a deflector, extending with an upward slope from the front of the firebox to within 16" of the firebox door, and thus forming an air chamber under the crown sheet. The deflector was formed of two copper sheets 4" apart, stayed with 600 hollow tube stays

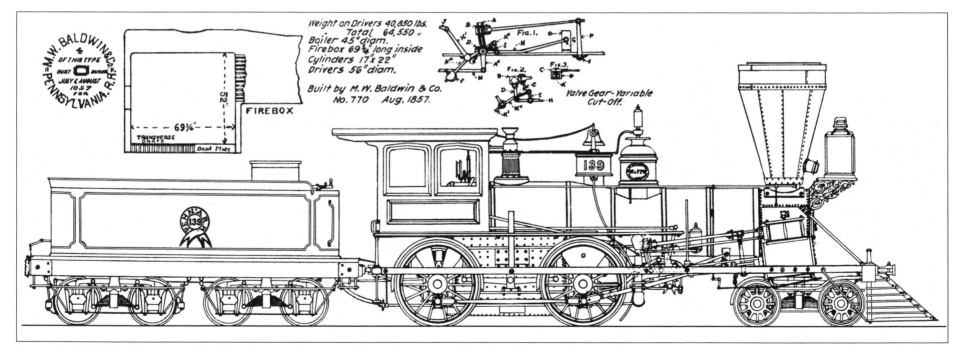

*Figure 29.* PRR #139, 56" drivers, 17" x 22" cylinders. #139 was built by Baldwin (c/n 770) in July 1857 as a coal burner. The locomotive was taken from regular service and not modified in any way before being tested. It had a long (69¾") deep firebox suitable for burning bituminous coal. The firebox door had only one air opening. #139 emitted the most smoke, but showed the greatest fuel efficiency of the six locomotives tested.

(C.H. Caruthers drawing; author's collection)

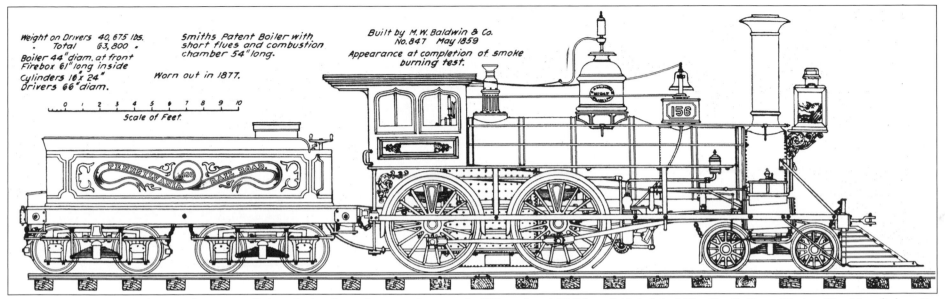

Weight on Drivers 40,675 lbs.
   ․   Total    63,800 ․
Boiler 44" diam. at front
Firebox 61" long inside
Cylinders 16"x 24"
Drivers 66" diam.

Smiths Patent Boiler with
short flues and combustion
chamber 54" long.

Worn out in 1877.

0 1 2 3 4 5 6 7 8 9 10
Scale of Feet.

Built by M.W. Baldwin & Co.
No.847   May 1859
Appearance at completion of smoke
burning test.

**Figure 30.** *PRR #156, 66" drivers, 16¼" x 24" cylinders. During the smoke-consuming tests, the PRR purchased #156 from Baldwin (c/n 847) with a Smith, or "Hudson River" type firebox. Because the feasibility of using bituminous coal was amply demonstrated, the Company wanted to gather figures on the cost of both wood and coal. #156 was used in these tests. As originally equipped, it had a deep firebox, a combustion chamber, and air admission through 24 hollow staybolts in the back leg of the firebox and about 100 ½" dia. perforations in the door. There were also 10 ⅜" dia. openings on each side of the door. The combustion chamber was divided for half its length by a midfeather 6" wide. The engine had shown itself to be an excellent wood burner in previous service on the Philadelphia Division. During these tests from Altoona to Gallitzin there were problems in burning coal. The firebox was modified.* (C.H. Caruthers drawing; author's collection)

and a firebrick roof 2" above it. In front of this was a 30" combustion chamber extending into the boiler barrel, with a water bridge extending to within 10" of the top of the chamber. Two 8" bridges also surmounted the diaphragm. The double fire door contained 333 ¼"-diameter holes in the inner plate and a number of larger holes on the outer plate. The Gill device proved to be most efficient of all, with hardly any smoke to annoy passengers at any time. With Broad Top coal only a tinge of smoke was visible, and with Pittsburgh coal very little more was noted.

The tests showed that bituminous coal could be used in passenger service without objectionable smoke, provided the fireboxes had ample combustion space. The admission of air for the proper combustion of the gasses must enter above the fire through small holes, at a great velocity. This mixture of air and gas should be allowed the longest run

possible before passing through the flues. The general results of the tests showed that, in order of comparative freedom from smoke, the locomotives ranked as follows: #'s 206, 210, 120, 190, 51, and 139. The Company felt that the first four, with some modification to #210, could be used in passenger service with Broad Top coal. Only #206, with the Gill & Co. "improvements," could be used with Pittsburgh coal.

To determine the cost differential between Broad Top and Pittsburgh coals, a test of eight days was conducted between Altoona and Mifflin. Locomotives #'s 206 and 139, used previously for the smoke-consuming tests, were fired with Broad Top and Pittsburgh coal on alternate days. The result was 39.43 lbs. of Pittsburgh coal consumed to the mile, and 39.19 lbs. of Broad Top. The Pittsburgh coal used in these tests was taken from the Com-

pany's storage bins, but the Broad Top coal, on account of its greater susceptibility to deterioration under lengthened exposure, was mined for the experiments.

A final series of tests was held to ascertain the comparative economy in the use of wood and coal. The Company wished to determine the relative heating value of a ton of coal and a cord of wood, the relative cost of wood and coal delivered to the tender, and the anticipated increase in cost of repairs due to the substitution of coal for wood. The locomotive selected for testing was #156 **(Figs. 30 and 31)**, built during May 1859 by Baldwin (c/n 847) with a Smith boiler having a deep firebox, a long combustion chamber, and short flues. This was the only new locomotive added to the equipment in 1859. Air was admitted through about 24 hollow staybolts in the back leg of the firebox and about 100

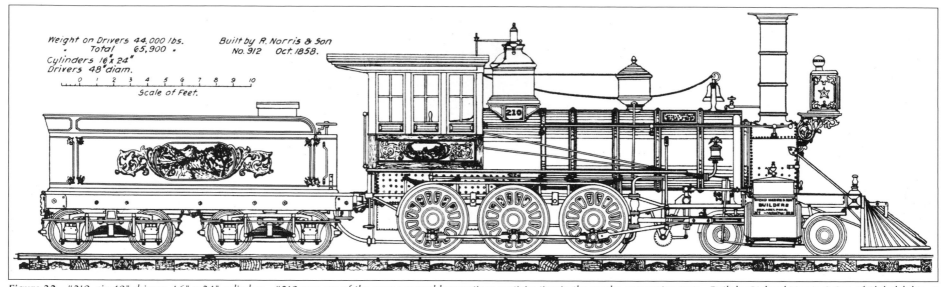

Weight on Drivers 44,000 lbs.
Total 65,900
Cylinders 16" x 24"
Drivers 48" diam.

Built by R. Norris & Son
No. 912   Oct. 1858.

Scale of Feet.

*Figure 32.* *#210, six 49" drivers, 16" x 24" cylinders. #210 was one of the more unusual locomotives participating in the smoke-consuming tests. Built by Richard Norris & Son of Philadelphia, it was equipped with a Phleger boiler. The boiler was filled with 2" dia. flues, and a semi-circular sheet formed a "hollow" above the flues which contained the dry pipe. The shallow firebox, set above the drivers, contained two transverse water bridges. One rose from the grate and the other was suspended from the crown sheet.* (C.H. Caruthers drawing; author's collection)

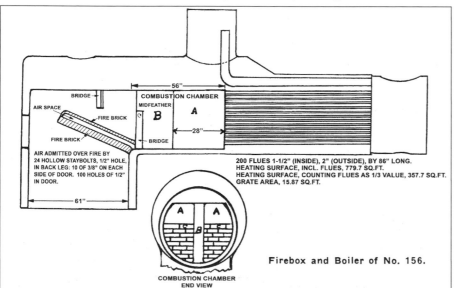

*Figure 31.* *Firebox of #156. The arrangement shows the modified Smith firebox, with the addition of a firebrick arch, a deflector, and a "wall" at the firebox end of the combustion chamber. With these alterations the Smith firebox performed admirably, but was in practicality the Gill arrangement.* (C.H. Caruthers drawing; author's collection)

small openings in the door. There were also ten air openings on each side of the door. The combustion chamber was divided in half for half its length by a "midfeather" 6" wide, beginning at the firebox end of the chamber.

The tests were run between Altoona and Gallitzin with four loaded eight-wheel box cars. The engine had shown itself as an excellent wood burner during a brief period of service on the Eastern (later Philadelphia) Division. When coal was tried it was unsatisfactory until a brick arch was installed and a smaller bridge of brick was added at the firebox end of the combustion chamber. With these alterations the locomotive was similar to the Gill arrangement. It consumed 84.92 lbs. of Pittsburgh coal per mile, against an average of 206.92 lbs. of hard wood. The Company estimated that one lb. of coal was equal to 2.31 lbs. of wood, or one net ton of coal was equivalent to 1.27 cords of wood. The report noted that the comparative value of good hard wood in connection with experiments on other railroads had been underrated. This was perhaps due to using different locomotives for each fuel. The cost of wood and coal varied on the various divisions of the PRR but was averaged at $3 per cord delivered on the tender, $2.22 per ton for Broad Top coal and $1.79 per ton for Pittsburgh coal.

In connection with the smoke-consuming tests, a straight stack with a neat cast iron top was developed and applied to all new locomotives and many old ones until 1862. The stack was entirely open and often large coals were thrown

▶

*Figure 33.* *#145 (Lancaster Locomotive Works, December 1860). The "Panic of 1857" not only slowed down the additions to PRR's locomotive stock; it also closed a number of locomotive builders. #145 was purchased by the PRR in 1860 from the trustees of the Lancaster Locomotive Works. Lancaster stopped production in October 1857 with approximately six locomotive on the erecting floor, some only partially completed. #145 is pure Brandt, with sloping valve chambers and twin steam domes. During Lancaster's period of production under John Brandt (December 1854 - October 1857) the locomotives had "LAN. LOCOMOTIVE WORKS, Lancaster, PA, Jn. Brandt, Jr., Supt." on the hub plates. #145's hub plates are blank.* (PRR photo ME1318A; author's collection)

out. To resolve this problem a number of locomotives were equipped with Laird or balloon stacks.

One more locomotive was equipped with a Gill & Co. firebox, #207 **(Fig. 79)**, and, along with #206, was run on the Middle Division. Locomotive #210 with the Phleger firebox continued to run on the Western Division. Grier noted that he was now satisfied that coal could be used with great economy and that smoke and gasses could be consumed. The Gill & Company plan included a combustion chamber, which would involve a considerable change in the boilers then being used. If the modified Gill arrangement used on #156 was installed it could be applied for $660 if the locomotive was taken out of service to make the change, or for $500 if deferred until coming in for a new firebox. Grier was still seeking a way to burn coal without the cost of major

▶

*Figure 34.* *#212 (Baldwin, c/n 1000, April 1861). When the Company purchased the State Works in 1857 (railroads and canals) from the Commonwealth of Pennsylvania, part of the terms of sale were that the Commonwealth would commute the tonnage tax, and the PRR would use these freed-up funds to finance branch lines, which as a result became known as commutation lines. During 1861 the PRR purchased two small tank locomotives, #212 and #217, for branch line passenger service. Engine #212 was the 1,000 th locomotive built by Baldwin. It is fitted with an injector.* (PRR photo ME1306A; author's collection)

*Figure 35. #217 (Baldwin, c/n 1005, July 1861). #217 differed from #212 in having a four-wheel engine truck.*
(BLW photo 13154-15; author's collection)

boiler renewals. At the suggestion of William Jackson Palmer, the Company began to experiment with a firebrick deflector.[128] While the smoke-consuming tests were going on, the Company installed another 19 new copper fireboxes in 1859.

The Loughridge chain brake **(Figs. 46 and 157)** came into use in 1859, and was a decided improvement on the previous braking systems. The device consisted of a system of rods and chains continuously connected throughout the train and leading to a drum on the engine where it was attached, by a worm gear, to a small friction wheel. On pulling a lever extending up through the footplate into the cab, this friction wheel, 16" in diameter, located behind the rear right driver, was brought into contact with the driving wheel, causing the drum to revolve and take up the length of the chain throughout the train, thus applying the brake shoes to the wheels. Another lever controlled retention in braking or release positions, by means of a pawl and ratchet. The Loughridge chain brake was very efficient on the tender and first car, but the power gradually diminished until at the fourth or fifth car it was negligible. On accommodation trains the use was most severe and required frequent renewal of wheels under the tender and baggage car. These early brake systems were used only on passenger cars and locomotives;

*Figure 36. #216 (Baldwin, c/n 1008, August 1861). 1861 brought another new type of locomotive, the "shifter." The PRR had been using older freight locomotives, such as the Smith & Perkins engines, as shifters. With the purchase of #215 and #216 it acquired its first locomotives built for distributing cars in yards. #216 is really a Baldwin flexible-beam-truck 0-6-0, with a saddle tank added. The PRR had a total of 15 of them.*
(BLW photo 13154-17; author's collection)

the freight trains were controlled and stopped by in-dividually-applied hand brakes. No further improvements were made until George Westinghouse, in 1869, perfected the idea of using compressed air for braking trains.

In 1860, four freight locos were added; two Norris engines with Phleger boilers and a 4-4-0 from the Lancaster Locomotive Works were purchased, and #190 was rebuilt. The Company also purchased the steam car *Novelty*, built by Kimball & Gorton and equipped with an engine built by Baldwin (c/n 912, 02/60), which was tried on several lines by the PRR and then sold to the Pittsburgh, Ft. Wayne & Chicago.[129] The Company shops continued their firebox replacement program and equipped a further 23 locomotives with copper fireboxes.

Locomotives #'s 116, 156, and 166 were fitted with the Gill & Company "improvement." #166 was not equipped with a combustion chamber and did not fully consume its smoke. Further tests were held using #'s 165 and 166 (both built by the New Jersey Locomotive & Machine Co. for the P&C), running on the same train on the same division. #165 burned wood and cost $8.13 per 100 miles to operate. #166, fitted with a Gill & Co. firebox, burned coal and cost $2.25 per 100 miles. Grier was now satisfied that bituminous coal was suitable for all freight and passenger locomotives.

The experiments with the brick arch continued. Alexander McCausland equipped #120, used in the smoke consuming tests, with a firebrick deflector, which had to be renewed four times during the year. The cost of fuel was $6.59 per 100 miles run. The firebrick deflector had some problems. The bricks melted and broke into pieces with only one month's use. These pieces blocked the air holes and prevented the free admission of air. #207 (**Fig. 79**, BLW, March 1855), equipped with a Gill & Co. firebox, was used for 14 months without repair and cost $4.59 per 100 miles to operate. Grier suggested to the Board that

the Company put the Gill & Co. "improvement" into their engines as fast as they could.

The economy began to slowly recover after the effects of the 1857 depression. By 1860, the tonnage on the road had increased to 1,346,525; much of this was due to the development of coal properties in the Broad Top and Pittsburgh coalfields. The PRR carried 296,855 tons of coal in its own cars and 226,338 tons in private cars. There were 208 locomotives on the roster. The economy was finally in full swing during 1861, aided by the Civil War; the Company added 18 Baldwin 4-6-0's, another Norris 4-6-0 with a Phleger boiler, and a Lancaster 4-4-0 intended for freight

service. Two small Baldwin tank locomotives, #'s 212 and 217 (**Figs. 34, 35 and 48**), were purchased for branch-line passenger service. In August the PRR purchased two locomotives from Baldwin, intended for service on the Delaware Extension.[130] The first, #215 (c/n 1006), was an 0-6-0 built with no tender and a square water tank placed over the boiler. It had sloping cylinders and was actually a Baldwin flexible-beam-truck 0-6-0 fitted with a saddle tank. #215 and sister #216 (**Figs. 36 and 37**) were the first locomotives that were built exclusively for shifting service. Between 1861 and 1867 the PRR purchased 15.

In 1861 the PRR began to use injectors. The Gif-

*Figure 37.* *#215 and #216 were first used on the PRR's Delaware Extension in Philadelphia. This view shows one of them with a train of early hopper cars.*                                  *(Author's collection)*

fard type was first installed under the footplate, usually on the engineman's side of the firebox. The check valve was let into the water space at the back of the firebox above the mud ring. This caused leaks and was replaced by a check valve on the side of the boiler barrel. At first only one injector was installed and the pumps taken off. The early injectors were "quirky" things and often failed. The railroad moved quickly to install two injectors or one injector and one non-adjustable injector, or "squirt." In 1864 the standard practice was to equip a locomotive with an injector on the left side and a pump on the right. After 1878 all locomotives were equipped with two Sellers injectors of the 1876 type.[131]

During 1861 the firebox replacement program continued and another 15 new copper fireboxes were installed. The situation changed as improvements in the manufacture of steel permitted its substitution for copper. Thomson was vitally interested in steel. He had kept up with European experiments testing steel rails and directed that experiments be made with steel fireboxes on the PRR. The Master of Machinery reported in 1861 that a firebox made of English homogenous cast steel plates was in the course of trial on one of the Company's engines (#122, *Lehigh*, built by Baldwin in January 1856).[132] The first two locomotives to be built new for the PRR with American-made steel fireboxes were #'s 231 and 232, two Baldwin 4-6-0's, turned out during January 1862.

The shops at Altoona continued to expand. In 1859 gas lighting was installed and the next year a new Sellers & Company cast-iron turntable was installed. Thomson reported that a new enginehouse and shops, able to accommodate 44 locomotives, would be opened on April 1 (1862).[133] In 1862 the smith shop was enlarged, and a new brass foundry was built the following year.

During Grier's tenure the locomotive stock continued to increase, with the major gain the addition of over 50 4-6-0 freight locomotives with cylinders from 16" x 22" to 18" x 22" and drivers from 48 to 54". The position of Master of Machinery became vacant on January 1, 1862.

### John P. Laird, Master of Machinery, 1862-1863 and Superintendent of Motive Power & Machinery, 1863-1866

With the appointment of John P. Laird as Master of Machinery on June 15, 1862, the PRR got an able and practical engineer. Laird was born at Houston-by-Paisley, Renfrewshire, Scotland on August 13, 1826. After training as a machinist in Glasgow, he came to the United States in 1845. His first job was at the Rogers Locomotive Works in Paterson, N.J. He then left for the Ballardvale Machine Shop in Massachusetts, where he stayed for two years before joining the Northern Railroad of New Hampshire. He was a locomotive engineman on this road and then on the Vermont Central until 1851, when he went to the Michigan Central. He ran locomotives

▶

*Figure 38.* #234 (Rogers Loco. & Mach., c/n 1011, March 1862). With the advent of the Civil War, the motive power situation on the PRR became critical. Orders were placed with Baldwin, Norris, and Rogers for new power. John Laird had worked for Rogers in the 1840's. #234 was one of four tenwheelers ordered from Rogers, the only Rogers engines purchased by the PRR. The locomotive is equipped with an injector. (PRR photo; author's collection)

on the MC until he was placed in charge of the Michigan City Shops in 1852. In 1853, Laird joined A. Latham & Co. of White River Junction, Vt., where he designed the locomotives constructed by this firm. After Latham failed in the panic of 1857, Laird worked for the Marietta & Cincinnati, where he designed a two-wheel equalizer leading truck, for which he received a patent. From there he went to the Indiana & St. Louis, before joining the PRR.

Laird came to the PRR at a critical time. The locomotive stock totaled 230 at the beginning of 1862. With the advent of the Civil War in 1861, Confederate pressure on the B&O main line shifted a great deal of traffic to the PRR, which taxed the existing fleet. New motive power was difficult to acquire and terribly inflated in price. A Baldwin 4-6-0 increased from $10,235 in 1862 to $17,624 in 1864 to a high of $30,900 in 1865. The PRR had leased four Winans Camels and four *Pawnee*-class 2-6-0's from the Philadelphia & Reading during 1861 and 1862.[134] To meet the increased motive power needs, Laird placed orders with Baldwin, Norris, and his old employer Rogers. The four 4-6-0's from Rogers were the only new locomotives that the PRR ever bought from this builder. By the end of 1862 there were 32 new locomotives on the roster, mostly 4-6-0's; 31 first class freight locomotives and one Second Class freight locomotive,[135] with Rogers building four, Norris nine, and Baldwin 19.

Laird began a program of rebuilding older power that had been in service from 10 to 15 years. For about $10,000 the shops at Altoona could turn out a locomotive "modernized" to current practice. At first the program was modest: a new firebox with water tubes supporting the brick arch, the addition of Laird's design of balloon stack, and two-bar crosshead guide. It is worth quoting Laird at length on his ideas about locomotive improvements:

*The use of new engines, with modern improvements, has demonstrated practically, by the amount of service rendered at a given cost, the importance of those improvements, among which may be mentioned ...*

*A wheelbase which will secure the easiest and best riding machine, at the same time diminish wear and tear on the engine and the road.*

*The proper counter balancing of the reciprocating parts, the momentum of which are known to be most destructive of machinery.*

*A valve motion which, while it is simple and durable in its parts, is the most economical and effective in operation.*[136]

▶

*Figure 40. #48 (Ross Winans, January 1853). Laird's second attempt at "modernizing" the Winans Camels took a more conventional turn. All that remained of the old Camel was the dome, throttle and three rings of the boiler barrel. #48 was rebuilt at Altoona in 1867. Compare this with Carruthers' drawing of #48,* Pluto, *shown in* **Fig. 110.** *(Author's collection)*

*Figure 39. #131 (Ross Winans, 1856). Concurrent with the purchase of new power, Laird began a program of rebuilding older power. The cost of a new locomotive tripled during the war to about $34,000 for a ten-wheeler, but the rebuilding program could turn out a "modern" locomotive for about $10,000. As many of the older parts were utilized as possible. The first attempt at "modernizing" a Winans Camel was #131 in 1862. The typical Winans sloping coal burning firebox was replaced, Stephenson valve gear added, the second driver removed, and Laird's own design of engine truck put on. #131 operated until late 1870, when a broken main driver axle severely damaged it.* (PRR photo ME1295A; author's collection)

*Figure 41.* #45 (Baldwin, c/n 789, October 1857). #45 had its front driver replaced with a 30" wheel. One benefit of the change is that we can see the partially exposed Baldwin flexible-beam truck.

(PRR photo ME1257A; author's collection)

Laird noted that no good material had been laid aside to make any changes, but where the opportunity had presented itself, improvements had been made with great success.

As time went on, the rebuilding process became more extensive, with new boilers, removal of the old hook motion, and the substitution of the new link motion. Frequently the wheel arrangement was changed; older 4-4-0's became 0-4-0's and the Winans Camels were rebuilt into 2-6-0's. Some of Laird's rebuilds were innovative. He tried several different approaches to rebuilding the Baldwin flexible-beam 0-8-0's. Two, #'s 97 and 98, **(Fig. 42)** became saddle tank 2-8-0's, and one (#45, **Figs. 41 and 108**) was equipped with 30" wheels in place of the original lead drivers. Another (#44) had 48" wheels added. #129 **(Fig. 43)** had a new frame, which spread the drivers as far apart as possible. The lead driver was between the pilot beam and the smokebox, and the rear driver was behind the firebox under the cab. #129 would appear to have been a real curve straightener. Most of Laird's rebuilds were on the more practical side. This was especially true of his rebuilds of earlier Norris 4-4-0's.

Laird noted in his report for 1862 that all locomotives in freight service were burning coal.[137] Ten in passenger service were also burning coal with success. One of the ten passenger engines was fitted for burning anthracite, to test the merits of the two kinds of coal. No further mention was made of anthracite until the United Railroads of New Jersey were leased. Several steel fireboxes were in service

◄

*Figure 42.* #98 (Baldwin, c/n 577, February 1854). #'s 97 and 98 were rebuilt with Laird's engine truck and saddle tanks, becoming 2-8-0T's. Although predating Alexander Mitchell's 2-8-0 for the Lehigh & Mahanoy, built by Baldwin in 1866, #98 cannot claim the title of the "first" 2-8-0, since it had Laird's engine truck rather than the Bissel truck, and was a rebuild, whereas Mitchell's locomotive was a new design, duplicated in the thousands.

(PRR photo; author's collection)

and were wearing well. The Master of Machinery suggested that steel was promising to be the best material for fireboxes.

By 1863 the problems with the firebrick deflector or arch had been sufficiently overcome, so it was being applied as fast as the locomotives could be spared for installation. Laird noted in his report that the firebrick deflector allowed the Company to go back to the plain firebox, as the best calculated for the perfect combustion of bituminous coal. The various expensive and complicated solutions were abandoned for the simple brick deflector, which was able to convert old wood-burners into "our best coal-burners," at a price not exceeding $50. The added benefit of retaining the simple form of firebox was that it was accessible for thorough inspection and repair. This was important since Laird lamented that it was almost impossible to get good iron. Several more steel fireboxes were installed and the results in service were quite satisfactory.

To handle the increased war traffic, the PRR added 44 freight locomotives, all 4-6-0's, with Norris building 21 and Baldwin 23, five passenger locomotives, with Norris building two and Baldwin three, two tank shifters, and one passenger tank locomotive (#251, **Fig. 146**) from Baldwin in 1863. During 1863 and 1864 a number of new Norris 4-6-0's were transferred to the Philadelphia & Erie and were immediately replaced on the PRR by newly-built Baldwin engines. At first the PRR transferred a few old locomotives to the P&E, then in 1862 four were sent north, and in 1863, 13, with 12 more, including two

▶

*Figure 43.* #129 (Baldwin, c/n 794, November 1857). One can only wonder at #129. It was rebuilt with a new firebox, frame and spread wheels. The elimination of the Baldwin flexible-beam-truck and lengthening of the wheelbase guaranteed that the locomotive spent most of its time on the ground. *(PRR photo ME1264A; author's collection)*

*Figure 44.* #94 (Baldwin c/n, 573, February 1854). #94 presents a more conventional appearance after her rebuilding. Built as Quaker City by Baldwin in February 1854, it was rebuilt in December 1865 as a 2-6-0, with a new frame, 48" drivers, larger cylinders and link motion, for a cost of $7,468. After some initial success with the Giffard "squirt," built by Sellers, the PRR returned to a pump and an injector. Note the pump connected to the rear driver. *(PRR photo ME1262A; author's collection)*

M.E.1262A

▶

*Figure 45.* *#237 presents something of an anomaly. This number was first held by a 4-6-0 built by Richard Norris & Son in February 1862. In the 1868 Register of Engines, #237 is listed as having four 44" drivers and 11" x 20" cylinders, the locomotive shown here, and noted as "rebuilt" by the Company in July 1867. It is unlikely that 0-4-0T #237 was rebuilt from 4-6-0 #237, because the loco pictured above has a Bury firebox. Norris stopped using the Bury firebox well before 1862.*
(PRR photo ME1271A; author's collection)

old Perkins freight locomotives, in 1864.

A rather interesting explanation appears in Laird's report for 1863:

*In the months of June and July the operations of this department were seriously interrupted by the invasion of Pennsylvania. At Columbia, Harrisburg, Mifflin, and Altoona all labor was suspended and our whole attention turned to the protection of property, a large portion of which was loaded up and moved to a place of safety.*[138]

Here we have the Master of Machinery's view on General Lee's incursion into Pennsylvania, which resulted in the Battle of Gettysburg.

Laird was able to announce in the 1864 *Annual Report* that all the Company's wood-burners had been changed to burn coal.[139] Laird did for $50 a locomotive what Mr. Grier had suggested would cost about $500 per engine.

Another element in successful coal burning was the care of the fireman. By 1864 the firemen had developed some skill in stoking a coal-burning locomotive. In January 1866, Enoch Lewis, the General Superintendent, requested that the Board grant

▶

*Figure 46.* *#209 (Richard Norris & Son, April 1854). #209 represents a more conventional rebuild. Built as a 4-6-0, W.T. Morrison, for the Allegheny Portage, #209 was rebuilt at Altoona. Note the Altoona plate with the rebuilding date of January 1864, between the drivers. The plate on the steam dome indicates one of Laird's patents. The locomotive is equipped with a Loughridge chain brake.*
(PRR photo ME1268A; author's collection)

*Figure 47.* #278 (Richard Norris & Son, c/n 1067, April 1863). A contemporary Norris 4-4-0, the locomotive shows some work has been done on it, since it has the typical Altoona number plate on the side of the valve chest. Note the ornate headlight bracket and bell stand. #278 is equipped with an injector.

*(PRR photo ME1274A; author's collection)*

Laird an allowance for his improvements in the fire-boxes of the locomotives used upon the road. In March the Board compensated Laird with $3,000 in bonds of the Bald Eagle Valley RR.

During 1864 the first steel tires were installed on a PRR locomotive. Forty-one new locomotives were added to the equipment: 26 freight (most replacing equipment transferred to the P&E), nine passenger, and six tank shifters. Norris built only two of the freight locos (4-6-0's). The cost of new locomotives

acquired to replace older equipment condemned or transferred to other roads was charged to repairs. Of the new locomotives acquired in 1864, 21 replaced former equipment. An addition to the machine shop at Altoona was built in 1864.

In 1865 the PRR's tonnage had doubled since 1860, with 2,798,810 tons carried. The roster now had 352 locomotives. While the number of 4-4-0's operated held at around 150, the major increase was the addition of over 100 ten-wheeled freight loco-

motives. The PRR had purchased its first shifting locomotives in 1861 and had begun to develop its roster around three basic types by 1865: 0-6-0 tank locomotives for shifting service, 4-4-0's for passenger, and 4-6-0's for freight. Baldwin was still the supplier of choice. 1865 is significant in that the PRR bought its last locomotive from Richard Norris & Son of Philadelphia, a 4-4-0, #348 (**Fig. 157**), built in February (c/n 1178). It was at about this time that Norris closed their Bush Hill works in Philadelphia and exited the locomotive business. Another brother, Edward Norris, continued to build locomotives at Lancaster for a few more years.

Laird rebuilt 36 locomotives in 1865. There were now 23 steel fireboxes in successful operation and 12 sets of steel tires in use. The steel fireboxes were most economical when special care was taken when working with the steel.

Laird left the Company service on July 15, 1866, became the Superintendent of the North Missouri, and then entered the service of the Oregon & California. In 1878 he became Superintendent of the Jacksonville, Pensacola & Mobile and was retained in that position when the road merged with the Florida Central.

While Laird was in Oregon, he purchased a locomotive from his former employer for service on the Oregon & California. In June 1871, he personally contracted to purchase PRR #76 (the former *Greensburg*), built by Smith & Perkins in November 1853. Originally a 2-6-0 with a rigid front truck, the loco was converted to a 4-6-0 by the Altoona Machine Shop. It became Oregon & California #13, the *John H. Couch*. When the Southern Pacific obtained control of the O&C, the old *Greensburg* was numbered SP #1508. Some records suggest that the loco was sold in 1892, while others hint at a date of 1902. The evidence points to the possibility that a former PRR loco built by Smith & Perkins was operating somewhere in the Pacific Northwest on a lumber road in the early 1900's.

John P. Laird died from inflammation of the brain in Tallahassee, Fla., on July 28, 1882, while still in the service of the Florida Central.

▶

*Figure 49.* #85 (*Richard Norris & Son, January 1854*). Nescopeck *was rebuilt at Altoona in 1865 and is at Andersonville Water Station. Note the typical Norris "D"-shaped smokebox.* (Railroad Museum of Pennsylvania collection)

*Figure 48.* #217, pictured earlier in Figure 35, operated for a time with the "officer's car" attached. The Laird stack dates the photo to Laird's tenure or later. In a letter home to England, T.W. Worsdell mentioned that he was "designing a small engine and car for the directors to inspect the line in." Worsdell joined the PRR in the second half of 1865 and became Master Mechanic at Altoona in 1868. (BLW photo 13154-16; PRR photo ME1299A; author's collection)

*Figure 50.* #347 (Richard Norris & Son, c/n 1177, February 1865). Ricker continued the Laird rebuilding program. The most notable rebuilds were the "passenger helper" 2-6-0's. Built by Norris as a 4-4-0 in February 1865, #347 blew up at Duncannon, Pa. on September 5, 1865, and was rebuilt at Altoona into a 2-6-0 for $13,849.     (PRR photo ME1287A; author's collection)

### Robert E. Ricker, Superintendent of Motive Power & Machinery, 1866-1867

On July 16, 1866, Robert E. Ricker was appointed Superintendent of Motive Power & Machinery. Born at Portland, Maine on March 17, 1828, Ricker held civil engineering positions on several roads starting with the Atlantic & St. Lawrence in 1844. He went to the Essex Railroad in June 1846, the Portsmouth & Concord in March 1850, the White Mountain carriage road in the fall of 1853, the Calais & Barring in 1854, the Detroit, Monroe & Toledo in April 1856, the New Albany & Salem in June 1856 and the Terre Haute & Indianapolis in September 1861. During the Civil War, Ricker was Superintendent of Military Transportation for Indiana.

An important development in 1866 was the establishment of the office of Mechanical Engineer, which was responsible for the design of locomotives, freight cars, and other machinery. The PRR's first Mechanical Engineer was John B. Collin. Collin was born at Malius (Malmö), Sweden on September 26, 1828, and after graduating from Gothenborg in 1848, was employed at the machine shops of Messrs. Nydquist & Holm of Trolhatten, Sweden, from 1848 to 1850. On July 31, 1850, Collin came to America and found employment with the Lowell Machine Shop of Lowell, Mass. in September 1851. During July 1852, he moved to the Lawrence Machine Shop at Lawrence, Mass., where he remained until May 1858. He then entered the employment of the PRR at the Altoona Machine Shop. Collin returned in January 1859 to the Lowell Machine Shop, until he took a po-

◄ *Figure 51.* #142 (Altoona, c/n 1, January 1867). #142 has been identified for many years as the first locomotive to be constructed new at Altoona. Note the eagle on the boiler check valve. The loco was built with 60" drivers and 16" x 14" cylinders, and equipped with a crosshead pump. Note the operating lever for the cylinder cocks, which runs through the handrail and is connected by a rod running from the handrail to the cylinders, just behind the smokebox.
(BLW photo 13154-19; author's collection)

61

◄ *Figure 52.* #148 (Altoona, c/n 2, June 1867). *Traditionally designated as the second locomotive to be built new at Altoona, #148 has a cylinder bore one-inch larger than #142 (17" x 24"). The sandbox has the "Altoona" look that was to follow on the standard design locomotives. It appears as if the photograph was taken before the windows were installed in the cab.* (PRR photo; author's collection)

sition with the Atlantic Works of Boston in August 1860. He came back to the PRR in February 1863 to work in the office of the Engineer of Bridges at Altoona. He returned to the Atlantic Works of Boston in October 1863, but was back with the PRR in October 1864 as the General Foreman of the Altoona Shops, until April 1866. After traveling in the west from April to July 1866, he returned to Altoona to take up his responsibility as Mechanical Engineer in August 1866. It was Collin who drafted the designs for the first standard classes of locomotives when standardization was implemented in 1867. John Collin was still Mechanical Engineer when he died from a liver infection at his home in Altoona on March 20, 1886. During the period of active design and production of steam locomotives on the PRR, only three men served as Mechanical Engineer, if one discounts the one-year term of John W. Cloud.

The physical property at Altoona continued to expand. A new 14-stall enginehouse was built in 1867 and the brass foundry was enlarged.

Ricker continued the Laird rebuilding program. The last of the Winans Camels were converted to 2-6-0's, with new boilers and fireboxes. The only recognizable feature of the old Camel configuration was the large steam dome, which was moved to the rear of the boiler **(Fig. 40)**. Several old 4-4-0's were converted to 2-6-0's with 60" drivers for service as passenger helpers on the Eastern Slope. Twenty-one locomotives were rebuilt with new boilers in 1866, 31 received new fireboxes, and 23 received new half-fireboxes.

*Figure 53.* #108 (Baldwin, c/n 1409, September 1865, six 44" drivers, 15" x 18" cylinders) was one of 14 locos built to this design for the PRR.
(BLW photo 13154-34; author's collection)

*Continued on page 64*

*Figure 54.* #421 *(Baldwin, c/n 1657, September 1867, four 66" drivers, 17" x 24" cylinders) had a Laird stack, and the sandbox and dome covers are similar in style to those used on Collin's standard designs.* (PRR photo ME1284A; author's collection)

#'s 108 **(Fig. 53)**, 421, and 383 represent the three types of locomotives the PRR had settled upon to operate the railroad, the 0-6-0 for shifting, the 4-4-0 for passenger, and the 4-6-0 for freight. They also represent Baldwin's most "modern" designs on the eve of the PRR standardization program. American railways typically purchased locomotives offered by the commercial builders, leaving the design and development up to the builders themselves.

*Figure 55.* #383 *(Baldwin c/n 1555, December 1866, six 54" drivers, 18" x 22" cylinders) had a steel firebox and a 24¾"-long combustion chamber.*
(PRR photo ME1304A; author's collection)

*Continued from page 62*

In 1866 the Company had 76 steel fireboxes in service. Ricker noted that none had failed and gave no trouble from cracking, leaking at seams, or drawing of staybolts. He considered the steel firebox a complete success. There were now 62 sets of steel tires in use. They showed remarkably less wear, compared to iron. Ricker proceeded to have them installed on all freight locomotives.

During 1866, the PRR received three old freight locomotives returned from the Philadelphia & Erie,[140] and Baldwin added 18 ten-wheel freight locomotives, seven eight-wheel passenger locomotives, and ten shifters. The annual report shows one "rebuilding" to fill a vacant number. This was PRR #142 (**Fig. 51**), the first locomotive to be built new at Altoona.[141] A 4-4-0 with 61" drivers and 16" x 24" cylinders, it was the first of 2,289 to be built at the Altoona Machine Shop. A Baldwin 4-4-0 cost about $15,000 in 1866, while Altoona was able to complete #142 for $11,726. Three more 4-4-0's were built at Altoona during Ricker's term, #'s 148 (**Fig. 52**), 127, and 239. A note in the *Annual Report* for 1867 states that the woodsheds at Thompsontown, Black Leg, Andersons, and Mapleton were removed. The railroad still burned 249,746 cords of wood that year (even though all engines had been converted to be capable of burning coal).[142]

In the development of the locomotive, as the rigid wheelbase increased, difficulty was experienced in negotiating curves. Engineers worked on various designs to overcome this difficulty, and in 1867 the swing-bolster four-wheel engine truck was developed. This allowed a side motion of the truck with respect to the line of the engine frame, which facilitated operation on curves, contributed to easier riding, and reduced both locomotive and track maintenance costs. The first PRR locomotive to be equipped with the swing-bolster engine truck was #419, a Baldwin 4-4-0 built in October 1867.

Ricker served as Master of Machinery until October 15, 1867. He left to become Superintendent and Engineer of the Central Railroad of New Jersey. In October 1878 he became General Manager of the New York Elevated Railroad, and left that post on January 1, 1880, to become General Manager of Gilbert & Bush Car Works at Troy, N.Y. On March 1, 1884, he became General Superintendent of the Denver & Rio Grande and later of the St. Louis, Iron Mountain & Southern. He died on May 17, 1894, in Weeping Water, Nebraska.[143] Ricker was the last person from outside the PRR family to hold a PRR senior motive power post during the steam era.

## Alexander J. Cassatt, Superintendent of Motive Power & Machinery, 1867-1870

Alexander J. Cassatt was born on December 8, 1839 in Pittsburgh. The son of wealthy parents, he spent most of his childhood in Europe, attending Darmstadt University before returning to America, where he graduated from Rennselaer Polytechnic Institute in 1859. He joined the Georgia Railroad as a civil engineer but left for a similar position on the PRR when the Civil War broke out in 1861. He was an able administrator and served in several managerial positions, including Superintendent of Motive Power and Machinery from November 16, 1867, until April 1, 1870. Cassatt continued to advance through the ranks, becoming First vice-president in 1880. Miffed that George Roberts had become PRR president rather than he, Cassatt resigned in 1882 at the age of 42. Following his resignation, he bred racehorses and established the New York, Philadelphia & Norfolk Railroad on the Eastern Shore of Maryland and Virginia. He did not really retire from the PRR, although he was no longer part of the management. He was re-elected to the Board of Direc-

*Figure 56.* #14 (Norris-Lancaster, February 1867). The PRR was not averse to spending money for research and development, and #14 represents such an investment. It was designed by James Millholland of the Philadelphia & Reading. Millholland took an independent course in his locomotive design and one result was his "Gunboats." A development of the Pawnee Class, they were introduced in 1863 and named after the gunboats of the Union Navy. The most interesting feature, aside from their iron cabs, was the sloping firebox Millholland employed for coal burning. (PRR photo 1246; author's collection)

tors on September 12, 1883, after an absence of only 11 months, and was on the same day made chairman of the Road Committee, which was the equivalent of an executive committee. As a result, he had considerable say in company affairs.

In 1899 Cassatt got his chance to become the PRR president, and served until his death in Philadelphia on December 28, 1906. His administration was marked by an aggressive improvement of the road. Steel freight cars, larger locomotives to haul them, replacement of steel truss with masonry arch bridges, elimination of grade crossings in many towns, the Brilliant Cut-off, the Trenton Cut-off, and six-tracking a portion of the New York Division were

▶

*Figure 57.* #24 (Baldwin, c/n 1631, May 1867). #'s 23 and 24 were identical 0-4-0 tank locomotives with 48" drivers and 14" x 22" cylinders. (Thomas Norrell collection; author's collection)

*Figure 58.* #489 (Altoona, c/n 104, November 1871), Class D. The first class of standard locomotives designed by John B. Collin to be introduced on the road was the Class D 4-6-0, in August 1868. (PRR photo ME1008A; author's collection)

▼

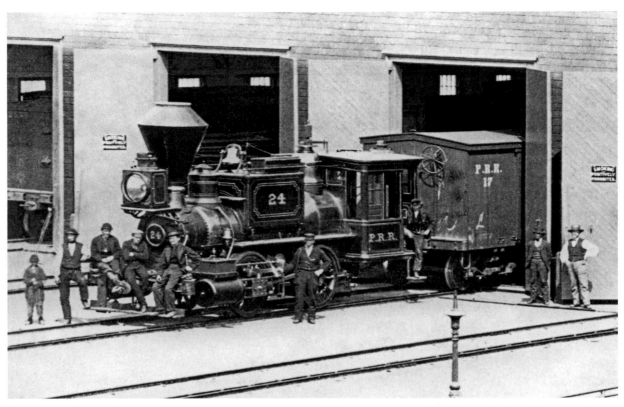

*Figure 59. #75 (Altoona, c/n 15, March 1869), Class D. Shown in service, #75 has been equipped with an air brake and the brace from the top of the smokebox to the pilot has been removed. A "collar" has been placed on top of the steam dome.*
(Railroad Museum of Pennsylvania)

some of Cassatt's projects. The most important was the Pennsylvania Station on Manhattan Island, which contributed to the development of subaqueous tunnels, electric locomotives, and steel passenger cars.

Cassatt reported for 1867 that the steel firebox was a great success and was being applied to the Company's locomotives.[144] He also intended to put steel tires on the road's mountain pushers and shifters. The Company added 66 locomotives to the equipment, which included one "special," a 4-6-0 built by the Norris Locomotive Works of Lancaster, Pa. to the design of James Millholland's "Gunboat" class in use on the Philadelphia & Reading. The Company bought 16 4-4-0's from Baldwin, but in an unusual move went to Norris-Lancaster for 12 4-6-0's and one 4-4-0, and to the New Jersey Locomotive & Machine Company for another ten 4-6-0's. There were also three 4-4-0's built at Altoona.

*Figure 60. #13 (Altoona, c/n 16, April 1869), Class A. The second class of standard locomotives to be introduced was the A in September 1868. #13 had 68" drivers and a wagon top boiler. A variant of the A had 60" drivers and a straight boiler. #13 was the third locomotive to be fitted with Westinghouse air brakes. The air pump is visible between the drivers. The locomotive itself is not fitted with brakes. In addition to our typical enhancing of photos, this one had been retouched by the PRR; our work retained the spirit of the PRR's efforts.*
(PRR photo; author's collection)

During 1868, Cassatt devised a plan to reduce the consumption of fuel and stores by the Company's locomotives. The usual practice was to fix certain quantities as standard by division, and pay a premium to the individual enginemen who ran below the standard. This was tried and failed, due to the many different types of locomotives used in a wide variety of services. Cassatt offered a reward on a standard set collectively for the railroad, derived from a system-wide average of consumption of fuel and stores per mile run. The bases were the figures for 1867: 67.0 lbs. of coal per mile, 4.01 quarts of oil, 2.47 lbs. of waste, and 4.48 lbs. of tallow per 100 miles. Any reduction in these figures was shared equally between the Company and the engine crews. The system was instituted late in the year and the savings amounted to $25,965.36, one half of which went to the men.[145]

The *Register of Engines for February of 1868* listed 416 locomotives of 11 different types from 11 builders operating on the Pennsylvania Railroad. Three major types predominated; 30 0-6-0 tank locos for shifting, 155 4-4-0's for passenger service, and 171 4-6-0's for freight service. The oldest on the line was #7, the former *Juniata* **(Fig. 98)**, a Baldwin-built 4-4-0 "arranged" by J. Edger Thomson and put on the road in November 1849. The newest were some Baldwin 4-4-0's with 66" drivers and 17" x 24" cylinders built for passenger service in September 1867. The PRR's locomotives were built in lots of from 2 to 12. Even though these lots were built at the same time by the same builder, the parts were not interchangeable between locomotives, and certainly were not interchangeable between locos of other lots and other builders.

*Figure 61.* #925 (Altoona, c/n 213, September 1873), Class B. *The third class of standard locomotives to be introduced was the B "mountain passenger helper." Only a few B locomotives were built. Note the air pump under the cab.*
(PRR photo ME1018A; author's collection)

*Figure 62.* #19 (Altoona, c/n 127, April 1872), Class E. *The fourth class of standard locomotives to be introduced was the E "mountain freight" locomotive in June 1869, built with 50" drivers.*
(PRR photo ME1009A; author's collection)

The PRR was facing a motive power problem. It wasn't that the railroad didn't have enough, it was that too many were out of service for repairs. At the end of 1867 the PRR reported 428 locomotives in the *Twenty-First Annual Report*. The difference between this number and the total listed in the *Register of Engines, corrected to February 1868* may be attributed to the accounting procedures used for the locomotives leased or transferred to connecting lines. Thirteen were in use (leased) on connecting roads, 86 were in the shops or awaiting repairs, and 329 were in service. At the end of 1868, with 434 locomotives reported, 320, eight less than the same time the year

before, were in service. Twenty-two required repairs. Nineteen were in the shops "rebuilding," which probably refers to new construction to fill vacant numbers; 37 had general repairs, and 36 had light repairs. In 1867, 20% were out of service, and by 1868 the figure had jumped to 26%. This means that the railroad had to roster approximately 100 locomotives to keep 75 on the road. The cost was substantially increased because each part had to be manufactured to suit the particular locomotive.

The performance record for the Philadelphia Division for March 1869, with no standard locos assigned, provides an interesting contrast. The

Division continued to operate a number of former Philadelphia & Columbia locomotives (35). The remainder of the 120 assigned consisted of some older power reassigned, with the majority relatively-new power built after the acquisition of the P&C.

Of the 120 locomotives, 25 were used exclusively in passenger service, seven in distributing service, 75 in freight service, and one was used in both freight and passenger service. Twelve showed no mileage at all. The highest mileage locomotive was #142 (**Fig. 51**, the first locomotive built at Altoona?), with 4,335 miles, or approximately 41 trips between Philadelphia and Harrisburg. Eighteen locomotives each ran 2,943 miles in freight service, or approximately 27 trips between Philadelphia and Harrisburg. With a day figured as the 106-mile run between Philadelphia and Harrisburg, these 18 freight locomotives piled up a record of 27 days in service and four days out of service during the month. The least amount of mileage, only 218, was put on by #194, a Lancaster 4-4-0 built in 1857. Interestingly, two of the high-mileage freight locos were built in 1856.

In looking at the repair costs, the 12 locomotives that showed no mileage had the highest cost figures or no cost at all. One can assume that they were in the shop under repair or awaiting repair (thus no cost figure). Ten percent of those assigned were not available for service because of repairs or awaiting repair. Eleven other assigned locomotives averaged less than 1,000 miles per month, but this low may be due to traffic demands and not mechanical problems. The Philadelphia Division shows a better average than the system with only 10% of its power unavailable, at least for the month of March. That

*Figure 63.* #238 (Altoona, c/n 38, September 1869), Class C. *The fifth class of standard locomotive to be introduced was the C. Designed for either freight or passenger, the C became the "best passenger locomotive on the road." #238 was one of the C locos built with a straight boiler; most of the class had wagon-top boilers. The engine has a Laird stack.*   (PRR photo; author's collection)

◀ *Figure 64.* #653 (Altoona, c/n 158, December 1872). *#653 is typical of most of the Class C locomotives with a wagon top boiler. The engine has a diamond stack.*
(PRR photo; author's collection)

**Chart 8**

**March 1869, Philadelphia Division: Quantity and Type**

| Type | 0-4-0 | 0-4-0T | 0-6-0T | 4-4-0T | 4-4-0 | 4-6-0 | Total |
|------|-------|--------|--------|--------|-------|-------|-------|
| Quantity | 1 | 4 | 12 | 1 | 58 | 47 | 120 |

The build dates of the locomotives were as follows:

| Type | 1848-49 | 1850-54 | 1855-59 | 1860-64 | 1865-68 | Total |
|------|---------|---------|---------|---------|---------|-------|
| Quantity | 4 | 18 | 17 | 35 | 46 | 120 |

still means the Company had to purchase ten locomotives to have nine available for service.

When Cassatt became Superintendent of Motive Power & Machinery in November 1867, he moved to institute a system of uniformity in plans and patterns for locomotives. In his annual report for January 1, 1869, he commented upon this matter:

*During the past year the importance of arriving as soon as possible, at a system of perfect uniformity in plans and patterns, the first decided effort in which direction was made by my predecessor, was kept steadily in view. The importance of this subject, both as a measure of efficiency, cannot be too highly estimated, for with such a system only can the cost of repairs of locomotives, and the proportion of engines out of service be reduced to a minimum. During the past year complete detailed drawings were prepared for all standard locomotives, and in all those purchased or built at the Company's shops, these plans have been closely adhered to.*[146]

An interesting element in this discussion is that Cassatt attributes the original impulse toward standardization to his predecessor, Robert E. Ricker. It was John B. Collin, the Company's Mechanical Engineer, who designed seven classes of standard locomotives for freight, passenger, and shifting service, identified by the first seven letters of the alphabet. In weight and power these locomotives did not differ remarkably from the designs of the commercial builders that preceded them. The uniqueness of the plan was that they were designed to meet the particular conditions of the various sections of the railroad, and they used interchangeable details as far as possible to reduce the stock of repair parts and reduce maintenance costs. The most radical departure from accustomed practice was that steel was specified for the boilers.

By 1865 the Company had achieved a certain level of standardization under the direction of Laird. The PRR locomotives of this era followed standard designs; the Company had settled on 4-4-0's with 60" drivers for locomotives used in both passenger and freight service; 4-4-0's with 66" drivers for passenger

*Figure 65.* #274 (Altoona, c/n 287, September 1875), Class C, is equipped with a Smith stack. When the "Pacific Railway" was being projected across Canada, a report was prepared for Sanford Fleming, Engineer in Chief of Construction, recommending one locomotive for both freight and passenger service. The report, prepared by Charles Blackwell, mentioned the PRR Class C and acknowledged the cooperation of Theodore N. Ely in making tracings available. 122 new locomotives were delivered to the Canadian Pacific Railway by the end of June 1882. Most of these were 4-4-0's for mixed traffic with 17" x 24" cylinders and 62" drivers, obviously influenced by the PRR Class C. Two are still in existence, CPR #136, retired in 1960 and in possession of the Ontario Rail Association, and Winnipeg Hydro #3 (ex-CPR #86), which is in service on the Prairie Dog Central Railway, a tourist operation. *(Railroad Museum of Pennsylvania collection)*

service; and 4-6-0's with 50" or 54" drivers for freight. All were equipped with spread engine trucks, level cylinders, wagon-top boilers, and Stephenson valve gear. Cassatt's proposal of inter-changeability of parts would save the Company money by reducing out-of-service time; with more locomotives available for service, fewer would be needed to cover the traffic. Eliminating special man-ufacturing work and reducing the variety of parts needed, a substantial savings could be realized on repair costs. As one can imagine, the research and development time needed to implement this new policy was considerable. The standardization pro-gram involved preparing drawings for the new loco-motives and making patterns, jigs, and so forth for the forgings, castings, and other parts that were to be interchangeable.

Initially seven standard classes were proposed, of only three wheel arrangements; the eight-wheeler, the ten-wheeler and the six-wheel shifter. The first seven letters of the alphabet designated the various classes, as follows:

**Class A - 8-wheeler** (a 4-4-0, with 66" drivers, 17" x 24" cylinders, 35" x 66⅞" grate and 143 tubes @ 2¼" O.D.), for express passenger service.

**Class B - 8- wheeler** (4-4-0, 60", 18" x 24", 35" x 72¾", 155 @ 2¼"), for mountain passenger helper service.

**Class C - 8-wheeler** (4-4-0, 60", 17" x 24", 35" x 72½", 151@2¼"), for general passenger service.

**Class D - 10-wheeler** (4-6-0, 56", 18 x 22", 35" x 60", 119@?), for general freight service.

**Class E - 10-wheeler** (4-6-0, 50" 18" x 22", 35" x 67¼", 123@2½"), for mountain freight service.

**Class F - six-coupled tank** (0-6-0T, 44", 15" x 18", 35" x 44¼", 89@2¼"), for switching service.

**Class G - 8-wheeler** (4-4-0, 56", 15" x 22", 35" x 55", 130@2"), for branch passenger service.

Some of these specifications were later changed, as shown in the summary of specifications for the

*Figure 66.* #48 (Altoona, c/n 47, December 1869), Class F. The sixth class of standard locomotives to be introduced was the F "shifter." When first built all standard classes were equipped with one pump and one injector. The passenger locomotives had the Smith stack (with exceptions), while the freight and shifting locomotives were equipped with diamond stacks. The first few D and E locomotives built had Laird stacks.

*(PRR photo ME43A; author's collection)*

standard classes in Appendix G.

The last locomotive added to the PRR roster in 1867 from an outside builder was 4-4-0 #422 **(Fig. 164)**, turned out by Baldwin on August 24.[147] This does not include #'s 127 and 238, which were either built new at Altoona or rebuilt and must be treated separately. The next new locomotive to arrive on PRR rails was the first standard loco to be built, class D #154, turned out by Baldwin on July 27, 1868. Al-toona finished its first standard loco, class D #79, on August 10, 1868. It took the best part of a year for the PRR to develop plans and begin construction of the standard classes. It is important to note that this development occurred over an extended period of time. There was the initial research and development time of approximately one year, then a period of im-

plementation and continued development, as the dates of introduction of the new classes illustrate.

The first seven class of standard locomotives were introduced over a period of two years and three months as follows:

| | | |
|---|---|---|
| August 1868 [148] | **Class D,** #154 | (BLW, c/n 1744) |
| September 1868 | **Class A,** #54 | (AMS, c/n 7) |
| April 1869 | **Class B,** #136 | (AMS, c//n 18) |
| May 1869 | **Class E,** #123 | (AMS, c/n 22) |
| June 1869 | **Class C,** #106 | (AMS, c/n 28) |
| November 1869 | **Class F,** #129 | (AMS, c/n 40) |
| November 1870 | **Class G,** #89 | **(Fig. 71,** AMS, c/n 68) |

The standard locomotives were designed to use as many interchangeable parts as possible. The av-erage number of forgings used in each locomotive was 245, and with very few exceptions these were

◄ *Figure 67.* *#168 (Altoona, c/n 13, December 1868), Class D. A standard D, #168, with a train of coal, is stopped for a picture on the high bridge at Saltsburg, Pa., on the West Penn. (Author's collection)*

was placed 90 degrees in front of the crank on the right-side main driver. The Pennsylvania was unique among American railroads in specifying a left-hand lead. Why this was first adopted is not certain.

All the standard classes were equipped with short smoke boxes. Several different types of stacks were used. The first classes D and E built had Laird stacks, but later production had diamond stacks, as well as some Smith stacks. The passenger locomotives were equipped with Smith stacks. (See **Index of Figures**, near the end of this book). James Smith, a Company employee, developed a spark arrestor covered by two patents. A screen extended from above the blast pipe upward into the stack. The stack itself had an attractive cast iron base and "capped" top. The class F shifting engines were equipped with diamond stacks **(Fig. 66)**. None of the first standard classes were originally fitted with driver brakes. The passenger locomotives had wooden pilots with vertical slats, while the freight locomotives were equipped with iron-strap "hen coop" pilots.

Two types of tenders were employed. Classes A through E had two-truck tenders with "U"-shaped iron tanks mounted on wooden frames. They had a capacity of 2,400 gallons of water and 8,000 lbs. of coal. The G class had a smaller tender with a capacity of 1,600 gallons of water. The F class shifters were equipped with a saddle tank of 820 gallons capacity.

As noted, the first standard locomotive to be constructed was #154, a class D, built by Baldwin in July 1868. The Altoona Machine Shop built its first standard loco, #79, also a class D, on August 10 of the same year. The person who actually supervised the construction of #79 on the erecting shop floor

identical in classes A, B, C & D. Classes A through E had wagon-top boilers with the steam dome over the firebox. The exceptions were the variant of class A and the original design of the C.[149] The original design of the C had both passenger and freight versions, which differed slightly in the boiler and firebox and were equipped with straight boilers. The design was modified (by March 28, 1873[150]), the passenger and freight variations were eliminated, and the C engines were equipped with a wagon-top boiler. Classes F and G also had straight boilers. All had steel fireboxes placed between the main and rear driver axle. The crown sheets were flat and were supported by crown bars. Brick arches supported by water tubes were used on all the passenger engines. Water was supplied by a full-stroke

pump worked off the right crosshead and a Sellers non-lifting injector on the left side of the engine.

The valves were of the plain "D" type, actuated by Stephenson valve gear, standard on all classes. On the ten-wheeled freight locomotives, classes D and E, the rockers were placed in front of the leading drivers, and the eccentrics were bent to clear the axle. The crossheads were cast iron with the four-bar-type guide, except for the Class F, which had an early type of alligator crosshead. The connecting and coupling rods had strap stubs, with the exception of the front connecting rod stub, which had a solid end with an adjusting wedge for the brass.

The specifications in the *Master Mechanic's Notebooks* indicate that all the standard classes had left-hand lead. The crank on the left-side main driver

was Thomas W. Worsdell. Worsdell was born in Liverpool, England, on January 14, 1838. Educated at the Quaker School at Akworth and Queenswood College, he entered railway service on the London & North Western Railway at Crewe. He was then apprenticed under his uncle but returned to Crewe in 1858, working in the drawing office under John Ramsbottom. In 1860 he left to manage an engineering works in Birmingham. In 1865, Worsdell came to America and joined the PRR. He was soon appointed Master Mechanic at the Altoona Machine Shop, where he put in the PRR's first steel firebox, and supervised the construction of the first locomotive built at Altoona, as well as building the first standard locomotive constructed there. His younger brother, Wilson, joined him as an apprentice in July 1867. The Worsdells returned to England in August 1871 and Thomas was appointed works manager at Crewe under Francis Webb. In February 1882 he became locomotive superintendent of the Great Eastern Railway, and on April 17, 1882 was appointed locomotive superintendent of the North Eastern Railway. Worsdell's use of two-window cabs was attributed to his time on the PRR. He resigned in September 1890 from the NER and was succeeded by his brother Wilson.

At the Altoona Machine Shop, George W. Stratton was appointed to fill the vacancy caused by Worsdell's departure. He was born in Philadelphia in January 1836 and began work in the Altoona Machine Shops on March 14, 1861. On January 28, 1863, he resigned and moved to Freedom in the Kishacoquillas Valley, where he was employed by the Freedom

▶

*Figure 69.* #360 (Baldwin, c/n 1546, November1866). The first PRR locomotive to be equipped with Westinghouse air brakes. Tests were run between Pittsburgh and Wall. This photo was heavily (and crudely) retouched at some point. Note the "artist's" addition of the air cylinder between the drivers. (Author's collection)

*Figure 68.* #434 (Baldwin, c/n 1805, January 1869), Class D. #434 has received a capped stack and is lacking her cylinder head covers. The train is headed west at Milesburg, Pa. with the regular work train, in charge of Conductor John Woodring (in the middle on the pilot). The track at the right is the branch to Bellefonte. (Author's collection)

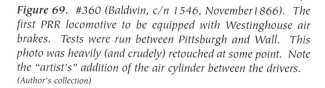

Iron Works, making loco tires from charcoal blooms. He remained there until September 22, 1864, when he returned to the PRR. He served as a machinist in the erecting shop and was promoted to gang foreman in February 1865. He became Assistant Master Mechanic on March 3, 1867 and was appointed Master Mechanic on October 1, 1871.

A new oil house was added to the Altoona Shop complex in 1868. These facilities, along with the previously-mentioned 14-stall enginehouse and the enlargement to the brass foundry, both built in 1867, were located between 9th and 10th Avenues (running north and south) and between 6th and 13th Streets (running east and west) on the south side of the main tracks, opposite the station. In 1870 the original location was dedicated solely to locomotive work and was referred to as the Altoona Machine Shops.

Twenty-five locomotives were added to the equipment in 1868. The Altoona Machine Shop reported that they had built 14, and installed 31 steel fireboxes. Altoona also built eight new steel boilers. Most of the locomotives were class D 4-6-0's, with Baldwin building the majority of them. Baldwin also built a non-standard 4-4-0, #30, and three non-standard 0-6-0's, #'s 435-437. The introduction of the standard designs heralded a major change in the motive power stock. Older locomotives were retired and either scrapped or sold. Newer non-standard locomotives were transferred (sold) to leased and controlled lines, with the new standard locomotives receiving the vacated numbers. By 1868 the PRR had the experience, resources and facilities to design and build their own locomotives, and the financial power to impose their own designs on the commercial builders. Ultimately the D and E locomotives were built in larger numbers than any of the other original standard classes.

Standardization was a process that was implemented slowly and continued to develop. The initial designs were continually refined and modified as time went on. The *Master Mechanic's Notebooks* are full of "approved" changes in the original designs as the operation of the equipment in service turned up problems and as the products of the suppliers and contractors did not meet standards. The *Notebooks* contain numerous mentions of Baldwin not building to standard and the Company's own shops not meeting Altoona's specifications.

For 1869 Cassatt reported that the Company added 53 locomotives to the equipment. Thirty-eight were constructed at Altoona, all with steel boilers, and 64 steel fireboxes were installed. The plan to economize on fuel and stores was progressing and a saving of $57,707 was noted. Baldwin turned out five 0-6-0's, #'s 438-442 (**Fig. 86**), the last non-standard locomotives to be built, except for experimental designs.

One of the most significant improvements in the safety of railway operation was the development of the air brake, which happened during Cassatt's tenure. In 1869, George Westinghouse conceived the idea of using compressed air for braking trains. In his first design, each car was equipped with a pneumatic cylinder whose piston was connected to the brake rigging. A pipe running the length of the train with flexible connections between the cars was supplied with compressed air from a steam-driven compressor on the locomotive. By allowing the compressed air to enter the train line through a brake valve operated by the engineman, the cylinders on each car forced the brake shoes against the wheels. To release the brake the engineman exhausted the train line into the atmosphere. While this was a great advance in braking, the length and speed of the trains were still limited because the brakes were applied to the cars serially, beginning with the car next to the engine. This, of course, allowed the slack between the rear cars to run in with serious results, particularly in long trains, and a rupture in the train line rendered the brakes inoperative.

In 1872 these shortcomings were overcome by the perfection of the Westinghouse "Plain Automatic" air brake. An auxiliary reservoir was added to each car together with a device known as a "triple valve." The equipment operated in exactly the opposite manner to the original system, in that the brakes were applied when the air pressure in the train line, running from end-to-end of the train, was reduced. As the train line was pumped up, the auxiliary reservoir on each car was charged with air at train-line pressure. A reduction in the train-line pressure caused the triple valve to admit air from the auxiliary reservoir to the brake cylinder to apply the brakes; the greater the reduction in train-line pressure, the greater the brakeshoe pressure. With this system, the time between the application of the brakes on the first and last cars was minimized, permitting trains of greater length to be operated with safety. Furthermore, any rupture of the train line applied the brakes on the locomotive and cars.

The first straight air-brake equipment was installed in April 1869 on the locomotive and cars of the Steubenville accommodation, which made a daily round trip of 86 miles on the Pittsburgh Division of the PC&St.L (Pan Handle). The train began its initial trip from the Pittsburgh Union Station. Once, when it emerged from the Grant's Hill tunnel and began to gather speed, a wagon drawn by two horses started to cross immediately in front of the locomotive. The horses became frightened and the driver lost control. The engineman closed the throttle and made a full brake application; the train stopped safely, just missing the wagon. The PRR officials watched the trials for several months and on September 18, 1870, an air brake was installed on locomotive #360 (**Fig. 69**) of the Pittsburgh Division (PRR). The device was removed and rebuilt and installed on locomotive #45. Six passenger cars were equipped with air brakes and tests were conducted between Pittsburgh and Altoona during November.

The straight air brake was made standard in 1870; the first automatic air-brake equipment was installed in 1875, and made standard in 1878.

### Isaac L. Dripps, Superintendent of Motive Power & Machinery, 1870-1872

On April 1, 1870, Cassatt was promoted and the office of Superintendent of Motive Power & Machinery became vacant. Isaac L. Dripps was immediately appointed to the position. Dripps was born in Belfast, Ireland, in 1810 and was brought to America as an infant. He joined the Camden & Amboy Railroad in 1831 and was present at the assembly of their first locomotive, *John Bull*. He advanced to take charge of the C&A motive power and worked with C&A President Robert L. Stevens to develop the cowcatcher and bonnet spark arrestor. Dripps was involved in the design of the 0-8-0 "Monster" coal-burning freight locomotives and the 6-2-0 Crampton passenger locomotives. During his tenure

with the C&A, he developed the sloping firebox. In 1854 he left the C&A for the Trenton Locomotive & Machine Manufacturing Company, where he was a partner until the company failed in 1858. Dripps built the first arch-bar trucks while at Trenton. After the closure of the Trenton Works, he was appointed Superintendent of Motive Power & Machinery of the Pittsburgh, Ft. Wayne & Chicago. During the next ten years he completely rebuilt the mechanical department, making the Ft. Wayne Shops one of the most modern establishments in the country. On April 1, 1870, Dripps became Superintendent of Motive Power & Machinery of the PRR. Forced to relinquish his position on March 31, 1872 due to ill health, he continued to serve the PRR as a consultant until he retired in 1878. Isaac Dripps died on December 12, 1892, at Altoona.

The freight tonnage doubled between 1865 and 1870, although there was a decrease in freight income. Thomson complained that there was a reduc-

tion of freight charges without any legitimate object by the New York lines, to a point below the cost of transportation. Even with this decrease in freight revenue, the health of the PRR was indicated by the cost of operation, which was 59.15 % of receipts. From a high of 5,402,911 tons in 1869, the PRR hauled only 2,550,389 tons of coal in 1870. The companies that owned their own cars and operated them regularly on the PRR were Penn Gas Coal, Westmoreland Coal, Powelton Coal & Iron, Philadelphia & Reading, Kittanning Coal, Union Line, Allentown Line, and National Line.

As the Company increased its stock of standard locomotives, the cost of repair per mile run was reduced. Cassatt, as the newly-appointed General Superintendent, noted that the cost of repairs had decreased from 13.75¢ per mile run in 1867 to 9.13¢ in 1870. Dripps reported that 22 new locomotives were built at Altoona in 1870 but only 18 were built with steel boilers. An additional eight

*Figure 70.* #930 (Altoona, c/n 218, October 1873), Class G. *The seventh class of standard locomotives to be introduced was the G, in November 1870. Used initially on branch lines, the class later saw service pulling official trains. #930 was assigned to the General Supt. at Altoona, until replaced in May 1891 by Class C #937.*  (PRR photo ME1003A; author's collection)

◀ *Figure 71.* #89 (Altoona, c/n 68, November 1870), Class G. #89 has received a "tall" capped stack and is in local service. *(Railroad Museum of Pennsylvania collection)*

charged to Motive Power was reduced by $195,212.45. The following table gives an accounting of the progress: [152]

| Year | Cost of Repair, ¢ per mile run | New standard locos built to replace those worn out |
|------|------|------|
| 1867 | 13.75 | 8 |
| 1868 | 12.08 | 12 |
| 1869 | 11.00 | 38 |
| 1870 | 9.13 | 22 |

The advertising hype of the 1870's put it this way:

*The Pennsylvania Railroad Company has abandoned, for several years, the very general practice of "rebuilding" locomotives; that is, of reconstructing them on an altered plan, retaining a portion of the old boiler and machinery, and replacing the worn-out parts with new. Since the practice was abandoned, and the old engines thrown bodily into the scrap-heap — new ones, built on uniform plans, taking their places and numbers — the cost of repairs per mile run has decreased from twelve and twenty-one one hundredths cents in 1866 to eight and sixteen one hundredths cents in 1872, and this not withstanding the fact that the load of engines has, during this same time, been very much increased. The result is the more remarkable, as all the new engines built to replace the old ones have been charged to repairs.*[153]

By 1873 the cost of repairs per mile, on the PRR Divisions, was 4.9¢.

When the PRR leased the United Railroads and Canal Co. of New Jersey (known as the "Joint Companies") effective December 1, 1871, giving the Company a through line to Jersey City, across the Hudson from New York City, the lease included the Camden & Amboy, and brought many more locomotives into the PRR stock, including *John Bull*, which Dripps had helped to assemble for the C&A in 1831.

Sixty-four locomotives were built by contract (Baldwin) in 1872; six to replace locomotives worn

steel boilers were built for existing equipment. The plan for encouraging enginemen and firemen to economize on fuel and stores showed a saving of $63,576.44.

By 1871 the cost of repairs had dropped to 6.81 ¢ per mile run. Thirty-three new locomotives were built at the Company shops and added to the equipment and two former Company locomotives were received back from the Philadelphia & Erie. [151]

The Altoona Machine Shops reported the following work:

| Locomotives | rebuilt entirely new | 38 |
|---|---|---|
| " | had general repairs | 196 |
| " | had ordinary repairs | 556 |
| " | new with steel fire-box | 38 |
| " | had steel fire-box built | 20 |
| " | had copper half fire box built | 1 |
| " | new with steel boilers | 38 |
| " | ad new iron boilers built | 8 |

One of the difficulties with the *Annual Reports* is reconciling the new locomotives reported by the General Superintendent as built at the shops (32 for 1871) with the number reported by the Superintendent of Motive Power & Machinery (33), and with the number shown built new in the report of the Altoona Machine Shops (38). To further confuse the issue, the consecutive list of Altoona Machine Shop numbers also shows 38 locomotives built with an 1871 date. Part of this can be resolved by noting how a locomotive is reported, either as built new, as an addition to the equipment, or built to replace sold or condemned equipment. The term "rebuilding" is frequently used in PRR records. This usually refers to new construction of replacement engines.

The new standard locomotives reduced expenses and increased availability; fewer were needed to handle the traffic. In 1871, Dripps reported that in the face of a tonnage increase the cost of repairs

out or destroyed, two to replace locomotives sold, and 56 for use on the PRR and the URR of NJ Division. Sixty-two new locomotives were constructed at the Company shops; one to replace a locomotive sold, 30 to replace worn out or destroyed equipment, and 31 additions with new numbers.

The addition of the URR of NJ locomotives escalated the cost of repairs. While only 339 were reported as having general repairs, there were 1,214 instances of ordinary repairs. Four of the 62 new locomotives built at Altoona during 1872 received iron boilers; the rest were built with steel boilers. During his tenure at Altoona, Dripps continued to turn out the standard locomotives designed by Collin. The Altoona Machine Shop built class E locomotives along with a few A, C, D and G, while Baldwin built D's. Between 1868 and 1873 Baldwin built 241 D locomotives for the PRR.

## G. Clinton Gardner, Superintendent of Motive Power – PRR, 1872-1873

When Dripps resigned on March 31, 1872 on account of failing health, George Clinton Gardner, formerly Assistant Superintendent of Motive Power, succeeded him on April 1, 1872.

Gardner was born in Washington, D.C., in 1834, the son of Adjutant-General Charles K. Gardner. He studied surveying and engineering and at the age of 16 secured a position in the Army Engineer Corps surveying the U.S.-Mexican boundary. He later served on the team locating the U.S.-Canadian border in the Oregon Territory. He resigned this post upon completion of work in 1869 and took a position as Assistant Engineer of the Philadelphia & Erie Railroad Company, a PRR subsidiary. In 1870 he was transferred to the PRR's Motive Power Department as Assistant Superintendent of Motive Power and was placed in charge of reorganizing the shops of the "Joint Companies" after lease by the PRR in 1871.

On February 28, 1873 he was promoted to become first General Superintendent of the Pennsylvania Railroad Grand Division. As General Superintendent, Gardner helped establish the company's school for special apprentices and the Railroad Association and Reading Rooms at Altoona. During the Strike of 1877, Gardner was on the ground on the first day of the riots at Pittsburgh, after which he was ordered by President Thomas A. Scott to return to Altoona to prevent similar outbreaks there. Gardner resigned effective April 1, 1879, because of the strain on his health. He took over the management of the Troy & Greenfield Railroad and the Hoosac Tunnel. He was subsequently engaged as an engineer and manager for a number of small and medium-sized railroads in the U.S. and Latin America. He died at his home in Richmond Hill, N.Y., in August 1904.

Gardner wrote a letter to *Van Nostrand's Eclectic Engineering Magazine*, published in March 1872 under the title *The Rolling Stock of the Pennsylvania Railroad*, describing the first seven classes of standard locomotives and the various practices of the Motive Power Department. A portion is reproduced here:

*There are seven classes of locomotives designated by the first letters of the alphabet, each having a large portion of their parts interchangeable one class with another - and, in fact, they are really only varieties of three well defined types of engines, known respectively as the 8-wheeler, 10-wheeler, and shifter.*

*The A engine, which is the leading engine over the Middle and Philadelphia Divisions of the road, that is between Altoona and Philadelphia, is an 8-wheeler with 17" x 24" cylinders and 5½ ft. drivers, and of this class there are two varieties, the one different somewhat in plan of boiler and the other having 5 ft. instead of 5½ ft. driving wheels. The distribution of the weight in this engine is as follows:*

| | |
|---|---|
| On forward drivers | 23,400 lbs. |
| On back drivers | 22,000 lbs. |
| On truck | 26,500 lbs. |
| Total | 71,900 lbs. |
| Area of grate | 35 x 66⅞" |
| Number of flues | 143 |
| Length of flues | 11' - 0½" |
| Outside diameter of flues | 2¼" |

*The B engine is a modification of class A, having cylinders 18" by 24", and 5 ft. drivers, with a larger boiler. These are called the "Mountain Passenger Helpers," and are used on the eastern slope of the Allegheny Mountains. One of these engines, assisting a C engine, takes the regular passenger train, usually of 7 cars, of a total weight of 370,000 lbs., from Altoona to the top of the mountain in 24 min., a distance of nearly 12 miles, making an ascent of about 1,000 ft. Weight of B engine, in working order, is distributed as follows:*

| | |
|---|---|
| On forward drivers | 24,800 lbs. |
| On back drivers | 22,900 lbs. |
| On truck | 25,400 lbs |
| Total | 73,100 lbs. |
| Area of grate | 35" x 72¾" |
| Number of flues | 155 |
| Length of flues | 10' - 8" |
| Outside diameter of flues | 2¼" |

*The C engine is almost identical with the B engine, differing in the size of cylinders, plan of the boiler and weight of frames, being also another modification of the A engine. They were designed for mixed trains to be used for local and fast freight, but have proved to be the most efficient passenger locomotives on the road, and are now in constant use for that purpose on the Pittsburgh division, that is between Altoona and Pittsburgh. An idea of the power of these engines may be formed from the fact that in ascending the western slope of the mountain on an average grade of 45 ft. to the mile, with a train of 9 cars, weighing about 487,000 lbs. it has frequently evaporated 24 hundred gallons of water in less than one hour. The weight of the C class is distributed as follows:*

| | |
|---|---|
| On forward drivers | 23,200 lbs. |
| On back drivers | 22,600 lbs. |
| On truck | 25,500 lbs. |

| | |
|---|---|
| Total weight | 71,300 lbs. |
| Area of grate | 35" x 72½" |
| Number of flues | 151 |
| Length of flues | 11' -0¾" |
| Diameter of flues | 2¼" |

The **D** engine is the standard ten-wheel freight engine, having cylinders of 18" by 22" with 4½ ft. drivers. These engines are used on all portions of the road except the mountain. The total weight of the **D** engine, in working order, is as follows:

| | |
|---|---|
| On forward drivers | 18,000 lbs. |
| On main | 18,300 lbs. |
| On back | 18,200 lbs. |
| On truck | 20,800 lbs. |
| Total weight | 75,300 lbs. |
| Area of grate | 35" x 60" |
| Number of flues | 119 |

The **E** engine is the standard "Mountain Freight," being a modification of the **D** engine, differing only in the drivers, and boiler. The drivers are 4 ft. instead of 4½ ft., and the boiler is larger. These engines are chiefly in use on the mountain; upon the trial of one of them she took a train weighing (exclusive of engine and tender) 500,000 lbs. from Altoona to Gallibzen [sic], a distance of 11.8 miles, in 35 min., ascending a maximum grade of 96 ft. to the mile, making a total ascent of 983 ft. The regular load over this part of the road is 418,000 lbs. The weight is distributed thus:

| | |
|---|---|
| On forward drivers | 19,200 lbs. |
| On main drivers | 19,400 lbs. |
| On back drivers | 18,000 lbs. |
| On truck | 19,000 lbs. |
| Total weight | 75,600 lbs. |
| Area of grate | 35" x 67¼" |

| | |
|---|---|
| Number of flues | 123 |
| Length of flues | 12' - 3¾" |
| Outside Diameter | 2½" |

The **F** engine is a six-wheel shifter with cylinders 15" by 18" and 44" drivers. These engines are used in making up, assorting and distributing the trains at the different yards. Its weight, in working order, is 63,500 lbs., distributed as follows:

| | |
|---|---|
| On forward drivers | 19,350 lbs. |
| On main drivers | 22,450 lbs. |
| On back drivers | 21,700 lbs. |
| Total weight | 63,500 lbs. |
| Area of grate | 35" x 44¼" |
| Number of flues | 89 |
| Length of flues | 12' - 6" |
| Diameter | 2¼" |

The **G** engine is a small class designed for construc-

*Figure 72.* #949 (Altoona, c/n 237, December 1873), Class H. *The first addition to the seven standard classes was the H "shifter," introduced in December 1872. Equipped with an enclosed cab and the PRR's first sloping tender, #949 is fitted with air brakes. The application of the air brake to a shifting locomotive gives an idea of how quickly and how widespread the PRR's adoption of the air brake was. The loco has a water pump operating off the crosshead. The stakes on the pilot beam and the tender sill are for use with the PRR's special method of poling cars, in which chains from the top of a stake were used to support the outer end of an auxiliary beam, the other end of which fit over the base of the stake. The pole used in poling cars on adjacent tracks was hung by two chains from the auxiliary beam.*

*(PRR photo 991; author's collection)*

tion trains and styled "Light Passenger or Ballast Engine." It has cylinders 15" by 22", with 55" drivers, and is mostly used for passenger and mixed service on accommodation trains or branch roads. Its weight is:

| | |
|---|---|
| On forward drivers | 19,400 lbs. |
| On back drivers | 19,800 lbs. |
| On truck | 20,800 lbs. |
| Total | 60,000 lbs. |
| Area of grate | 35" x 55" |
| Number of flues | 130 |
| Length of flues | 9' - 8" |
| Diameter | 2" |

With all these classes of locomotives the principal castings, such as driving boxes, eccentric straps, etc., etc. are common, and to give an idea of their uniformity it is only necessary to state the fact that the number of patterns required for one engine is 112, while the total number required for the seven classes is only 187; this is exclusive of the tender, which is alike for all. This, the present system of plans and classification has been followed since 1867, and the necessity for establishing some standards became apparent from the fact that five years ago the total number of 380 engines comprised 52 kinds, of which there were two or more of each and 71 odd engines; that is engines peculiar in some particular; whereas at the present time, when the engines number 496, there are but 38 kinds differing from the seven classes (with many of these varieties of the seven classes), and but 13 odd engines.

The trucks of these locomotives are of a variety known as the "swing centre" - the socket in which the centre pin or pivot of the engine rests has a lateral motion instead of being rigid as in the old-fashioned truck, and is suspended on links so that in passing around a curve of 350 ft. radius, which they readily do without straining either the engine or the truck, the centre line of the engine lies outside the centre of the truck. The lateral motion also reduces the severity of a blow from guard rails, frogs, etc., upon the flange of the wheels. Chilled wheels only are used under all trucks, as it was found upon trial of steel wheels, they would not stand the severe labor of guiding

the locomotives over our crooked roads. One chilled wheel proved equal in wear to three steel wheels, and as the breakage of a truck wheel is very rare, the chilled wheels in use were thought to be the safest. The flanges of chilled wheels are soon worn smooth and highly polished, whereas those of steel wheels become rough and torn, wearing in a short time too thin and sharp for safety.

The driving wheels of the standard engines are of cast iron centres, with hollow spokes, counter balanced with lead, and have steel tires, with the exception of those of the shifting engine, class F. It was found necessary to use chilled tires with these, for the same reason that chilled wheels were required for the trucks. In designing these engines, the steel tire being held in high estimation, the desire to use them whenever possible has been a controlling influence in determining the character of the engine. Having established the fact that an engine could not be guided by steel flanges, it became necessary to place the driving wheels far enough back from the cylinders to allow the entire duty of guiding the engine to be performed by the truck. Numerous efforts have been made to utilize the weight over the trucks for tractive purposes, but without success, except in connection with chilled tires, and they, being a great source of trouble, have been avoided as much as possible, not on account of breaking, but because they became loose and flat.

The locomotive boilers are made of soft crucible steel, the shell of the larger ones being $\frac{3}{8}$" and the other $\frac{5}{16}$" thick. The fire-box or furnace sheets are also of steel $\frac{1}{4}$" thick, with the exception of the tube or fire sheet, which has a thickness of $\frac{1}{2}$" and the tubes or flues are invariably of number 11 iron; sometimes the flue sheets are made of copper, $\frac{3}{4}$" thick, and the majority of the boilers have a combustion chamber from 4 to 6" long, to avoid exposing the thick metal of the flue sheet to the direct action of the fire.

In the construction of these boilers there are no braces between the crown of the furnace and the roof of the boiler, the entire strain on the top of the firebox being borne by the crown bars and thence transmitted by the sides to the

bottom ring. This practice, in use here several years, is believed to be stronger than the old custom of connecting the crown of the firebox with the roof of the boiler, as it is a fact that no boilers have exploded on this road in which these braces have been left out, whereas the explosions we have had were with those boilers having these braces. This practice, however, would not be safe for copper fireboxes, as they become very weak when old. The old-fashioned method of putting in fire-box stays is used, and the stay bolts are of $\frac{7}{8}$ iron spaced $4\frac{1}{2}$" by $4\frac{1}{2}$", or less, screwed through the sides and headed over, the screws having 12 threads to the inch. The furnace is supplied with water-grates, being tubes of $1\frac{7}{8}$" outside diameter, placed $3\frac{1}{20}$" from centre to centre. This kind of grate has been in use for a long time, and will outlast the furnace if kept free from mud, and the grate being very open, it is rarely necessary for the fireman to touch the fire with a poker. Opposite each tube there are screw-plugs for washing out the watergrates and removing all scale or mud that they may accumulate, which is done at intervals at from one to four weeks, depending on the water-station from which the supply of water is obtained. The feed water is supplied by one pump and one injector.

The steel of which these boilers are made is tested by having a sample from each sheet heated to redness, then plunged into cold water; after which, the same piece, while cold, is bent double and hammered flat. This steel does not acquire any temper whatever by being heated to redness and dipped in cold water, but will bend double afterwards just as well as before. It is not necessary, however, to have the steel so soft, for if it works well and can be shaped without cracking, that is all that should be required. The flanging of our steel sheets is mostly done by a charcoal fire, and, after flanging, the entire sheet is heated for the purpose of straightening it and relieving the strains. This is important, as the sheets are liable to break if hammered cold without having had the strains taken out by heating. The tensile strength of the steel used is about 90,000 lbs. per sq. in. In addition to the tires and boilers, much steel is used in the other parts of the engines, such as guides, connecting rods, crank pins, axles, etc., all of which, including the tires, are of crucible steel.

With regard to the service of these engines the question has been asked, "what is the life or mileage of a steel fire-box?" This as yet can receive no definite answer. The old fashioned steel fire-boxes, such as were built from 1861 to the spring of 1867, lasted somewhat longer than those made of copper, and upon examination of the furnace of an engine which had a new fire-box of English steel in December, 1861, and was run until March, 1871, it was found in quite good condition, and far better than the shell of the boiler, which was 17 years old. There was only one small patch on the left hand edge of the crown sheet, a piece of the flange being cut off and replaced by copper. The steel in this furnace is so hard as to be difficult if not impossible to drill, and although hard to begin with, it is safe to say that use has not made it any softer. The flue sheet is perfectly good, but that is probably owing to its being set in a combustion chamber of about 2 ft. in length. The total mileage of this furnace was 202,852 miles, and the engine (a small freight engine of Baldwin build, cylinder 17" by 22", with 4½ ft. drivers) being worn out, having been on the road since February 1856, was cut up to be replaced by one of standard build.

Several steel fire-boxes built since 1861 have, however, been taken out, and one great trouble has been the cracking of the sheets around the fire door, in the flanges of the throat sheet, and sometimes the flanges of the door and crown sheets. By the change, which was made in the spring of 1867, it is thought that the trouble with the door sheet has been overcome. The solid ring was abandoned, and since that time more than 100 locomotives have been built without the slightest sign of failure being perceptible about the door. With the solid ring a crack would show itself in about two years, when it became necessary to cut out a piece around the door and replace it with copper. The cracking of the flanges of the throat sheet has also doubtless been done away with by placing the flange on the water side. The intense fire striking the edge of the flange was perhaps the cause of the cracking;

the metal evidently becomes highly heated, it may be to redness, and this constant over-heating appears to contract the steel until it cracks, usually from the edge to the rivet hole; and if the crack passes beyond the caulking on the water side, it produces a leak that can only be stopped by a patch. The life of a steel fire-box built on our present plan will without doubt be not less than 7 years.

When steel fire-boxes first came in vogue it was the practice of some builders to still use an iron tube plate or flue sheet, and the cracking of these has sometimes been charged to steel. This, perhaps, gave rise to the question as to whether iron tube plates crack between the tube-holes the same as steel. There has not been a single flue sheet made since 1867 that has cracked between the flues, and the reason for substituting copper for steel was mainly the leakage of the flues, particularly of engines having the large and long flue, which are 2½" outside diameter and 14 ft. long. This leakage was attributed to insufficient surface of the thin ³⁄₈" steel flue sheet, and whatever the real cause was, it is certain that tubes of the same dimension are perfectly tight in copper sheets of ³⁄₄" thickness. The space between the tubes is usually ⁵⁄₈".

The fuel used upon this road is bituminous coal, mostly of the variety known as "Pittsburgh coal," which is excellent and makes an open dry fire, producing hardly any clinkers. It is reported as producing 8.2 lbs. of steam from water at 212 deg. to the lb. of coal, but the result on the road in practice has been found to be about 6½ lbs. of water to the lb. of coal. The maximum pressure carried is never over 130 psig.

All passenger engines have the atmospheric brake attachment, which consists of an upright direct-acting air pump placed on the right side of the locomotive, partly under the running board. It is worked by steam from the boiler and pumps air into a receiver placed under the footboard. The pump is automatic, and as the pressure of air in the receiver is reduced by the application of the brakes its stroke is more rapid - thus the pressure is restored in a very few moments as indicated to the engineman by a gauge in the cab placed just above the steam gauge; with

this appliance the stops at stations are more quickly made, thus saving much time. On the Pittsburgh Division the passenger engines take their water from water-troughs while running, which also reduces the delays, giving quicker time without increase of speed. These troughs are 18" wide and 4" deep, placed between the rails of both tracks at two convenient points, and in running over any one of the four, they being from 1,200 to 1,500 ft. in length, sufficient water to fill the tank is taken.

In 1872 a new locomotive was introduced, a six-wheel shifting locomotive with a tender. The new design was given the next letter, "H." The first class H was #781, built by the Altoona Machine Shop in October 1872. The design incorporated the standard features of Collin's locomotives. The H had an enclosed cab and sloping tender. During Gardner's term as Superintendent of Motive Power, 30 E locomotives were built at Altoona, along with 12 C, 1 A, and 6 of the new H shifters.

## Frank Thomson, Superintendent of Motive Power, PRR Grand Division,1873-1874

On March 1, 1873, after Gardner was appointed General Superintendent of the PRR Grand Division, Frank Thomson succeeded him. He was born in Chambersburg, Pennsylvania on July 5, 1841, and entered the Altoona Machine Shop as an apprentice in 1858. Between 1861 and 1864, Thomson assisted Colonel Thomas Scott, a future PRR president, in managing railroad operations for the U.S. Military Railroads. In June 1864, he rejoined the PRR as Superintendent of the Eastern Division of the Philadelphia & Erie. Between March 1873 and June 1874, Thomson served as Superintendent of Motive Power, PRR Grand Division. From there he was promoted to General Manager of Lines East. Thomson became Second Vice-President in 1888, and President of the Pennsylvania Railroad Company on February 3, 1897. His term was cut short by his unexpected death on June 5, 1899.

Thomson played an important and often-overlooked role in developing standardization on the PRR. He devised the first standard track section while on the P&E, and started the first regular system of awarding prizes for the best-maintained sections of track, which expanded into the annual fall track inspections. He sponsored the formation of the Association of Transportation Officers, which met twice a year to discuss engineering and operating matters and develop standards.

When 1873 ended, the PRR could report earnings of $24,886,008.90 and operating expenses of $15,440,305.16. The lease in 1871 of the "Joint Companies" had given the PRR its own line to Jersey City, across the Hudson from New York City, local lines in New Jersey, and a share via the Bel Del in the anthracite traffic coming off the Lehigh Valley. This lease added a tremendous volume of passenger traffic in the New York - Philadelphia corridor. The Company carried 8,003,043 passengers on its URRofNJ lines and only 5,879,684 on the PRR itself.

Between 1855 and 1873, freight traffic on the PRR increased from 365,006 tons to 14,494,444 (including URRofNJ and Bel Del). Early passenger figures are unknown, but in the eight years between 1865 and 1873 the number of passengers the PRR carried rose from 2,861,836 to 14,279,880. In 1850 there were 24 locomotives in service. At the end of December 1873 there were 662 on the PRR, 259 on the URRofNJ (this is one more locomotive on the PRR and URRofNJ than can be accounted for on the 1874 roster) and 150 on the Philadelphia & Erie.

An example of the conditions of engine service at this time can be had from contemporary tests of the load for a class E engine. [154] The following table is a statement of the number of cars weighing about nine tons each, seven of which were loaded with 11 tons each, which such an engine, weighing 122,700 lbs. (including tender and supply of coal and water), could haul as an ordinary rule and on an ordinary rail, between the indicated points. Presumably all six cars westbound from Conemaugh to Derry were loaded.

| Between | Miles | Cars East | Cars West |
| --- | --- | --- | --- |
| Pittsburgh & Derry | 45 | 18 | 18 |
| Derry & Conemaugh | 35 | 36 | 6 |
| Conemaugh & Gallitzin | 25 | 18 | — |
| Gallitzin & Altoona | 12 | — | 11 |
| Altoona & Columbia | 162 | 45 | 30 |
| Columbia & Philadelphia | 90 | 22 | 22 |

The demands on the passenger locomotives operating between Jersey City and Philadelphia severely taxed them, most of which were former Camden & Amboy and New Jersey Railroad & Transportation Company machines. Collin proceeded to design a locomotive specifically for the New York Division. Using plans for the C, he added a long firebox suited for anthracite coal. The firebox on the C was placed between the frames and the driver axles. On the new design the firebox was

between the frames, but extended toward the rear over the rear driving axle, providing a grate ten feet long, with an area of 28.7 sq. ft. The first of these were built at the Altoona Machine Shop in June 1873, numbered 912 – 923 **(Figs. 73 and 74)**. They were equipped with diamond stacks. Because of the similarity to the original Class C, with 62" drivers and 17" x 24" cylinders, the new locomotives were assigned Class C anth. – "C Anthracite."

155 new locomotives were added to the equipment in 1873, 93 built by con-

*Figure 73. #912 (Altoona, c/n 190, May 1873), the first Class C anth. Equipped with a diamond stack and long firebox extending back over the rear axle, it had a grate area of 28.7 sq. ft. The C anth. locomotives, designed to burn anthracite coal, were built for passenger service between Jersey City and Philadelphia.* (Roger L. Keyser collection)

*Figure 74. #923 (Altoona, c/n 201, July 1873), Class C anth. You can see the slope on the firebox (between the drivers). The locomotive still has a crosshead pump on the engineman's side.* (Railroad Museum of Pennsylvania collection)

tract, 57 by Altoona Machine Shop, and five at the Philadelphia & Erie's shop at Renovo, Pa. Perhaps the most interesting additions were the four non-standard Baldwin built 2-8-0's, #'s 950-953 **(Fig. 75)**, nicknamed the "Modoc Warriors," or "Modocs," from the contemporary Modoc War. The Modoc Indians of northern California were offering stiff resistance and were considered tough adversaries. The term "Modoc" may have been extended to other 2-8-0's. (One can find accounts of this terminology in the *U.S. Railroad & Mining Register*.) The first 2-8-0 on the Pennsylvania system was ordered for the subsidiary Philadelphia & Erie from Baldwin in June 1868 (BLW #1729, a 34-ton ten-wheel class E) with 20" x 24" cylinders and 49" drivers. The P&E ordered four more in 1870 and an additional five in 1873. The four 2-8-0's built by Baldwin for the PRR had wagon-top iron boilers, steel fireboxes, 49" drivers and 20" x 24" cylinders. Two years later the PRR had designed their own standard 2-8-0, nicknamed the Pennsylvania "Jack."

There continued to be a problem with the amount of cinders put out of the locomotive stacks. In 1873 some freight locomotives had their Smith stacks replaced with diamond stacks. As an experimental measure several passenger locomotives were equipped with diamond stacks. A test was conducted between these stacks on the Pittsburgh Division using locomotive #654, a new class C built at Altoona in August. The engine was assigned to a heavy express train running daily each way between Altoona and Pittsburgh. The test was in charge of two enginemen, who ran the train on alternate days. For the first two days the Smith stack was used. It was replaced for the next two days by a diamond stack of the Jewett type, which was in use on the PC&St.L. The test was continued for a month, and resulted in a sweeping success for the Smith stack.

On January 1, 1874, the Pennsylvania Railroad

*Figure 75. #950 (Baldwin, c/n 3339, August 1873, the first 2-8-0 on the PRR, was built by Baldwin in August 1873 at a cost of $17,000. Several similar 2-8-0's were built at the same time for the Philadelphia & Erie. The locomotive was not a PRR design but included a number of standard features. The four of this design were the only 2-8-0's on the PRR until the introduction of the Class I in 1875.* (Author's collection)

Company was operating 920 locomotives, 420 (45.7%) of which were classified as standard. Several of the PRR's earliest locomotives were still in operation, although in much-rebuilt form, for example #8, *Huntingdon*, built by Baldwin in 1849. Early locomotives of the Philadelphia & Columbia, Allegheny Portage, Camden & Amboy and New Jersey Railroad & Transportation Company were represented, although standard locomotives had already replaced many similar ones.

The roster of locomotive stock for January 1, 1874, represents the PRR at a point of transition. The character of the motive power was being stamped in standard configuration, and in a few short years the vast diversity of the older builders, with their independent ideas of valve gear and cutoff, would be a thing of the past. Laird had tried to bring some order to the roster in his rebuilding program, but it was Ricker's plan for standardization, implemented by Cassatt's administrative ability and Collin's designs, that would carry the day. Although the standard designs appropriated much of the progress in locomo-

tive development from the commercial builders, almost from the beginning Altoona pursued an independent course and in some measure led the way. It was only at the PRR's insistence that Baldwin built its first steel boiler. Locomotives of simple design were built in large numbers for system-wide operation. PRR locomotives soon developed an "Altoona" look that was immediately recognizable, comprising neat machines with a touch of style in the stack and domes to offset the utilitarian appearance. The photographs in this book represent the last of the early PRR.

The motive policy of the Pennsylvania Railroad was set in 1849 and basically never changed. Thomson wrote, ... *the general plan of the "Juniata" and "Huntingdon" having been arranged by myself of course is preferred* ..... Change the locomotives from the *Juniata* and *Huntingdon* to any Altoona-designed machine and substitute the names Theodore N. Ely, Alfred W. Gibbs, or James T. Wallis for Thomson, and with some interesting exceptions you have the story.

▲ *Figure 76.* #258, The Big Elephant, *(Baldwin, six 48" drivers, 18" x 22" cylinders). The city of Pittsburgh passed a resolution that locomotives operating on Liberty St. had to burn coke, steam must be prevented from blowing off, and the speed must not exceed 4 mph. Collin rebuilt #258, a Baldwin 4-6-0, for this service.* (C.H. Caruthers drawing; author's collection)

◄ *Figure 77.* #258, The Big Elephant *(Baldwin, c/n 1094, November 1862.) A 4-6-0 originally built with a tender for road service, it was later designated as a "383 type" (from the number of a typical engine). In 1874 it was changed to a tank engine for use on street track on Liberty Street, Pittsburgh. It was probably retired in 1880, because a Class B (D2) #258 was built that year. This picture was taken (probably not later than 1880) at old "GD" (then the east end of the Altoona Yard), which stood on the north side of the railroad, not far from the present (1938) "GD" (at milepost 129.5). The men in the picture are, left to right; Joseph H. Sands, Trainmaster, Altoona Yard (he later was General Manager, Norfolk & Western Ry.); members of 258's crew Albert R. McHugh, Engineman; William Zeigler, Brakeman; Alanzo Rollins, Conductor; James Ross, Fireman; James Fowler, Brakeman (standing on the pilot beam). Engine 258 was locally known in Altoona as the "big elephant," to distinguish her from the Class F (B1) and other smaller tank engines, which were called "little elephants."*
*(This information was written on the back of the photo by J.D. Lovell, of Hollidaysburg, Pa.)*

The branch that terminated at the Duquesne Freight Station at the "Point" in Pittsburgh originally ran down the middle of Liberty Street, one of the busiest thoroughfares in the city. In the 1870's, Liberty Street was a loathsome mixture of mud and the residue of the city's increasing horse-pulled traffic. The rails were of a type which enabled the vehicular traffic to traverse or leave them with ease, but were not well adapted to the performance of locomotives and were often covered with a black greasy muck, which rendered adhesion difficult. The locomotives in use were continually slipping, to the annoyance of the business community, whose second-story windows were at stack level.

The City of Pittsburgh passed an ordinance, which specified that locomotives operating on Liberty Street must use coke as fuel, steam must be prevented, as far as possible, from blowing off, and speed must not exceed 4 mph. In 1874, Collin, the PRR's Mechanical Engineer, took locomotive #258 and rebuilt her for service on Liberty Street. Its tender was removed, a coal bunker was installed on an extension of the frame at the rear end, and a large saddle tank was placed between the cab and the smokebox. A pipe was attached to the top of the Baldwin "exhaust pot" and was carried out though the left side of the saddle-tank. This device was so arranged that the exhaust could either be directed into the pipe and then into the saddle tank, or up the stack. This was controlled by a reach rod on the right side of the locomotive. Mufflers had not yet come into use on safety valves, so #258 was provided with a pipe extending from the backhead into the saddle tank, fitted with a globe valve which could be opened when the engine ap-

proached the blowing-off point, allowing the steam to escape into the tank.

#258 was a "condensing tank locomotive," which was typical of English practice when underground working was required. The first were developed by the Great Western Railway of England to service the Metropolitan Railway when it was opened on January 10, 1863. They were seven-foot gauge 2-4-0 tanks, designed by Daniel Gooch. Flap valves, worked by rods from the footplate, directed the exhaust steam either up the chimney (stack) or into a tank placed under the boiler, an awkward and ultimately unsuitable arrangement. When the Metropolitan itself took over working the line, they used Beyer-Peacock 4-4-0 tanks with condensing apparatus. The exhaust steam was directed into the top of the tank and was discharged upon the surface of the water, a much more satisfactory arrangement.

The problem with a condensing locomotive was that the exhaust tended to heat the water in the saddle tank and render the injectors ineffective. Fortunately #258 was equipped with both an injector and a crosshead pump. The exhaust also carried oil back into the tank, often causing trouble with the crosshead pump, as well as seriously polluting the tank water.

Collin supposed that the 94,300 lbs. weight of the locomotive would be sufficient for adhesion, and sandboxes could be omitted. In service this turned out to be incorrect, and sandboxes were added under the saddle tank. No means of escape for any surplus exhaust steam from the saddle-tank was provided, except through a safety valve on its top. This proved insufficient, and with the exhaust turned into the tank the locomotive was enveloped in a cloud of steam, which escaped through the riveting on the tank seams and around the manhole.

On November 27, 1876, a full report was made of the performance of engine #258 shifting at Pittsburgh by Sam Vauclain, together with suggestions made by himself and William Major. The conditions on Liberty Street, even with the added weight of the saddle tank and sanded rails, caused so much slipping that the coke fire languished and the steam pressure dropped, unless the steam was turned back up the stack. #258 was removed from this service, and until the track was elevated, standard shifters of the F and H classes were used.

The drawing of #258 by C.H. Carruthers (Fig. 76) shows the locomotive as originally rebuilt. The photograph (Fig. 77) shows it in service at Altoona in the late 1870's. Several changes are evident. The tank is larger than that on Carruthers' rendering. We cannot tell if the diversion pipe is still on the left side of the locomotive. The reach-rod controlling the exhaust is on the top of the tank, just to the left of the bell, but appears not to be connected. A standard PRR type has replaced the original Baldwin three-window cab. The sandbox is visible at the center of the bottom of the saddle tank. The pipe just in front of the sandbox may be an overflow pipe for the condensing arrangement. One can imagine the excitement that a shot of steam would cause, directed onto a passing team of horses.

# CHAPTER 4
## SHOPS AND ENGINEHOUSES IN 1874

When operations began on the PRR, the Company used the Dillerville, enginehouse and the Harrisburg enginehouse and shop of the Harrisburg, Portsmouth, Mountjoy & Lancaster. The PRR built its first shop at Mifflin in 1851 and began construction of a shop at Altoona. During the mid 1850's, as operations expanded, the Motive Power Department came to need more enginehouse room and shop capacity, especially at Mifflin, Altoona, Conemaugh and Pittsburgh. Harrisburg presented a special problem; the old HPM&L wooden buildings were small and a very present fire hazard. At Altoona, locomotive repair was being carried out at the enginehouse. This was inefficient and costly, and the space was needed for running repairs. The shop facilities at Altoona were continually expanded during these years.

With the purchase of the State Works in 1857, the PRR refitted the Parkesburg Shop of the Philadelphia & Columbia and closed the Allegheny Portage's Hollidaysburg and Johnstown Shops. The former P&C

***Figure 78.*** *Looking east from the 17th St. Bridge, the Altoona shops spread out along the south side of the railroad. This photo was probably taken in the early 1860's. The shifter is one of the Baldwin 0-6-0T flexible-beam truck engines. A Winans Camel is standing near the woodshed.*

*(Author's collection)*

83

West Philadelphia enginehouse proved to be insufficient, and improvements were made there. With the construction of a new shop at Harrisburg, the old P&C shops at Parkesburg were closed on April 1, 1861.

The traffic surge during the Civil War put a great deal of pressure on the locomotive facilities. As the number of locomotives increased, space to shelter them and perform running repairs was at a premium. During the late 1860's heavy repair and all new construction was centralized at Altoona. The PRR continued to expand its facilities to keep repair costs in hand and to ensure locomotives to handle the traffic. The lease of the United Railroads of New Jersey brought a whole new set of locomotive facilities. 1874 began another of the periodic depressions in the nation's economy, and the need to update and expand the Company's locomotive facilities was delayed for a few years.

The following is a summary of the men who were responsible for Motive Power on the PRR during the years shown. Titles varied with time.

| | Tenure | |
|---|---|---|
| J.P. Laird, Master of Machinery | 6/15/1862 to 2/1/1863 | |
| J. P. Laird, Superintendent of Motive Power & Machinery | 2/1/1863 | 7/15/1866 |
| R.E. Ricker, Superintendent of Motive Power & Machinery | 7/16/1866 | 10/15/1867 |
| A.J. Cassatt, Superintendent of Motive Power & Machinery | 11/16/1867 | 4/1/1870 |
| Isaac Dripps, Superintendent of Motive Power & Machinery | 4/1/1870 | 3/31/1872 |
| G.C. Gardner, Superintendent of Motive Power, PRR | 4/1/1872 | 2/28/1873 |
| Frank Thomson, Superintendent of Motive Power, PRR Grand Division | 3/1/1873 | 6/30/1874 |

**General Foreman, Altoona Shops**

| | | |
|---|---|---|
| J.B. Collin | 10/15/1864 | 4/1866 |

**Master Mechanic, Altoona Machine Shop**

| | | |
|---|---|---|
| T.W. Worsdell | 7/1/1866 | 10/1/1871 |
| G.W. Stratton | 10/1/1871 | 2/1/1906 |

**Assistant Master Mechanic, Altoona Machine Shop**

| | | |
|---|---|---|
| G.W. Stratton | 3/13/1867 | 10/1/1871 |

**General Foreman Altoona Car Shops**

| | | |
|---|---|---|
| John P. Levan | 8/1/1862 | 12/1/1904 |

**Mechanical Engineer, PRR**

| | | |
|---|---|---|
| J.B. Collin | 7/1/1866 | 3/20/1886 |

The following list contains the available information on each enginehouse. Where no information is shown, data were not available.

## PHILADELPHIA DIVISION

**West Philadelphia Enginehouse & Shop**
1858, enginehouse got sheet iron roof, new wood shed, extension to the machine shop

1863, temporary frame shed for locos, 220' x 40'
1866, new enginehouse, 44 stalls, 50' turntable, shop with 11 tracks

**Paoli Enginehouse**
1857, new enginehouse
1864, enlarge enginehouse to accommodate passenger loco for Paoli/Phila service
1865, two-stall brick enginehouse, to replace frame enginehouse destroyed by fire

**Parkesburg Enginehouse**
1857, old P&C Parkesburg Shop – 40' x 60' wooden boiler repair shop added
1861, closed and machinery transferred to Harrisburg
1868, brick enginehouse, 32' x 65'

**Lancaster Enginehouse**

**Dillerville Enginehouse**
1854, extension added
1856, new turntable

**Columbia Enginehouse**
1855, frame extension to enginehouse, new turntable
1858, new wood shed, extension to machine shop
1873, new 44-stall enginehouse and shops

**Waynesburg Enginehouse**
1861, one-stall enginehouse

**Middletown Branch Intersection Enginehouse**
1865, brick enginehouse, 66' x 32'

**York Enginehouse**

**Frederick Enginehouse**

## MIDDLE DIVISION

**Harrisburg Enginehouse & Shop**
1854, smithy extended
1858, three small enginehouses in use, two temporary
1860, new 42-stall enginehouse
1861, large machine shops completed
1865, frame enginehouse put up
1868, new 44-stall full circle enginehouse and shops

**Mifflin Enginehouse**
1851, shop complete; also called "Patterson Shops" for Pres. W.C. Patterson
1855, only 13 tracks available for locos
1869, closed 10/1/1869 – only small two-track repair shop remains

**Huntingdon Enginehouse**
1860, two-stall enginehouse for locos for Broad Top Coal trade
1862, 112' x 31' frame enginehouse and 50' iron turntable

**Spruce Creek Enginehouse**
1854, enginehouse & turntable put in for use of wood train engine

**Altoona Enginehouse** (eastern)
1851, construction started, originally eight stalls, with some used for car repair and paint shop.
? increased to 15 stalls
1862, 15 stalls added, now housing 30 locomotives

**Altoona Machine Shop**
1851, construction started
1853, machine shop brought into operation
1854, shops extended, new smithy - 18 forges, new foundry, extension to machine shop, new enginehouse with 26 stalls
1855, erecting shop and foundry opened
1858, extension of erecting and boiler shops, steam transfer table installed
1859, improvements
1863, formerly passenger car shop – added to the machine shop, new brass foundry
1864, addition to the machine shop
1865, new smith shop
1867, enlargement of the brass foundry
1870, car shops moved, facility used exclusively for locomotive building and repair
1872, new blacksmith shop, machine shop, foundry and engine and boiler house
1874, new erecting shop

## PITTSBURGH DIVISION

**Altoona Enginehouse** (western)
1867, new 44-stall enginehouse

**Newry Enginehouse**
1868, temporary enginehouse, 60' x 20' for two engines

**Gallitzin Enginehouse**
1863, enginehouse for M/W engine

**Cresson Enginehouse**

**Ebensburg Enginehouse**
1862, enginehouse and turntable

**Conemaugh Enginehouse**
1857, nine-stall addition to the enginehouse, making 15
1859, new machine shop and nine-stall extension
1862, 50' iron turntable
1866, enlarged engine shed

**New Florence Enginehouse**
1860, one stall

**Derry Enginehouse**
1868, frame enginehouse, 45' x 115', to hold six engines

**Latrobe ?**
had a one-stall enginehouse built in the 1850's

**Greensburg Enginehouse**
1862

**Irwin Enginehouse**
1862, frame enginehouse for two engines
1867, brick enginehouse, 32' x 64', to replace frame building destroyed by fire

**Penn Enginehouse**
1865, 21' x 60'

**Wall Enginehouse**
1859, brick two stalls - for locos for accommodation trains

**Brinton Enginehouse**
1866, enginehouse enlarged to accommodate local passenger loco

**Pittsburgh Enginehouse & Shops**
1852, construction started on 44-stall enginehouse, enough finished to accommodate 23 engines
1855, addition to enginehouse completed
1857, new turntable
1859, new machine shop and blacksmith shop
1866, temporary enginehouse, 32' x 200'
1867, new 38-stall enginehouse and shops
1868, new enginehouse, 55' x 262' for 15 engines, west of the passenger station for Panhandle

## LEWISTOWN DIVISION

**Lewistown Jct. Enginehouse**
? – enginehouse 61' x 61' with four tracks, two-track repair shop

## BEDFORD DIVISION

**Bedford Enginehouse**
**State Line Enginehouse**
? Four-stall round house with 50' turntable

## TYRONE DIVISION

**East Tyrone Enginehouse**
1862, 112' x 21' enginehouse
1863, brick enginehouse started
1864, brick enginehouse, 15 stalls

1865, 15-stalls added

1872, extension of enginehouse to full circle started

**Bellefonte Enginehouse (B&S)**

**Lock Haven Enginehouse (P&E)**

**Osceola Jct. Enginehouse**

**Philipsburg Enginehouse**

1864, frame, two stalls & iron turntable

1868, 31' x 68' extension added making room for four engines

**Clearfield Enginehouse**

1869, 57' x 31' enginehouse and turntable

## WESTERN PENNSYLVANIA DIVISION

**Blairsville Enginehouse**

1866, engine shed inadequate

1869, enginehouse burned on October 16, being rebuilt

repair shop 123' x 40'

**Indiana ?**

had a turntable in 1863

**Butler Jct. Enginehouse**

**Butler Enginehouse**

**Allegheny Enginehouse**

## NEW YORK DIVISION

**Jersey City Enginehouse**

(near the passenger station, not the later Waldo Avenue location)

Enginehouse 200' square, with 54' turntable, machine shop 125' x 23'

**Meadows Enginehouse & Shops**

Circular round house with 44 tracks and 50' turntable, semi-circular round house with

19 tracks, seven-stall erecting shop, boiler shop and machine shop

**New Brunswick Enginehouse**

**Frankford Jct. Enginehouse**

**West Philadelphia Enginehouse (Powelton Avenue)**

## BELVIDERE DIVISION

**Trenton Enginehouse (Coalport)**

**Phillipsburg Enginehouse**

**Lambertville Enginehouse (old Bel Del Shop)**

nine-stall enginehouse, repair, boiler and machine shop

**Manunka Chunk ?**

## AMBOY DIVISION

**South Amboy Enginehouse**

rectangular enginehouse 259' x 71' with five tracks, machine and repair shop

**Bordentown Enginehouse (old C&A Shop)**

**Camden Enginehouse**

Amboy Division enginehouse 201' x 47' with four tracks, small repair shop

PRR enginehouse 161' x 52' with four tracks

**Hightstown Enginehouse**

# CHAPTER 5
## LOCOMOTIVE PRACTICE

Throughout this book, some material has been repeated to complete discussions touching a subject from various directions. This section summarizes PRR early locomotive practice and includes both new and previously-discussed material. Interesting notes from original PRR sources have been interspersed where appropriate, to give the reader a sense of the development effort required.

See **Index to Figures** for illustrations.

### REPAIRS
#### 1/21/1874
Repairs from which to estimate time required.[155]

#1  New boiler and general repairs to machinery, 90 days.

#2  New firebox and general repairs to machinery, 75 days.

#3  Resetting tubes and general repairs to machinery, 40 days.

#4  Resetting tubes and light repairs to machinery, 25 days

#5  Turning of tires and light repairs to machinery, 20 days.

#6  Facing of valves and light repairs to machinery, 5 days.

#### 3/14/1874
#266 (4-6-0, BLW, February 1863) was started by William Kelly and it got away from him running through the roundhouse on the through track, up through the machine shop and jumped in the transfer pit & landed in the wheel shop door. Killed, Geo. Kaufman, broke James Bradley's right leg and broke 12 machines, more or less, one 15" new cylinder, two foot plates and bent main rod on a machine.[156]

### BOILER AND BOILER ACCESSORIES
#### Boilers
The first locomotives the PRR ordered had boilers equipped with Bury fireboxes. These were followed by boilers with a "stepped-up" raised section over the firebox. By 1854 the wagon-top type was in use. The early boilers were made of wrought iron. Baldwin built its first steel boiler for the PRR in July 1868 when they constructed the first of the class D 4-6-0's, #154 . The boilers on the standard designs were of soft crucible steel, either ⅜" or 5⁄16" thick.

#### 11/16/1870
Orders to wash boilers once a week on the Pittsburgh Division and once in four weeks on the Middle Division and to put in plugs opposite water grates to facilitate washing.[157]

#### 1/25/1872
Testing Boilers, Letter from ID [Isaac Dripps] ordering all boilers to be tested to 150# Hyd. press. Each new engine will be tested once a year for the first two years and every six months thereafter. A record must be kept in a book and signed by foreman of machine shop and boiler maker.[159]

#### 2/24/1872
Wagon Top Boilers. In noting your letter of the 13th inst. I would state that in construction of all wagon top boilers should have braces between each pair of crown bars and in boilers Class 90 or straight boilers the braces must be placed in alternate spaces between the pairs of crown bars. The crown sheets must also be changed in thickness from 2 wire gauge to 5⁄16".[158]

#### 4/17/1874
Make it a rule to put in crown braces when engs. come in for general repairs, except F, G, and H engines, which do not need them, provided they have cross braces or long staybolts between crown bars.[160]

#### Fireboxes
The earliest fireboxes on the PRR burned wood. They were constructed of wrought iron, but later copper ¾" thick was used extensively. With the advent of the use of bituminous coal, iron fireboxes were replaced by copper. A steel firebox of homogeneous cast-steel plates was installed and tried in 1861. The first new PRR locomotive equipped with a steel firebox was #231, a Baldwin 4-6-0 built in January 1862 (BLW #1029). The side sheets of the firebox were made of ¼" steel. Staybolts were ⅞" iron on 4½" centers. The PRR adopted water grates and the firebrick arch.

#### Smokestacks
The smokestacks of the first PRR locomotives were of the French & Baird balloon (bonnet) type.[161] While wood was the principal fuel the concern was the emission of sparks, and various forms of netting were included in the stacks. The only exception to the balloon stack was Ross Winans' peculiar stack on his coal burning Camel locomotives. A straight stack with a neat cast iron cap was introduced during the smoke consuming tests of 1859 and until 1862 was applied to most new locomotives and many old ones. The stack was entirely open, with no netting, and frequently large coals were emitted. In 1862, John Laird introduced his stack and all passenger locomotives and many freight locomotives

both new and rebuilt were equipped with it. From 1862-1866 a number of freight locomotives were equipped with the old balloon stack. In 1870, James Smith developed a spark arrestor for use with a straight stack. It was applied to both freight and passenger locomotives, but some coals were still thrown out. In 1873 the diamond stack replaced the straight stack with the Smith spark arrestor on some freight locomotives and express passenger locomo-tives. The fine dirt from the diamond stack proved to be very annoying to the passengers.

### 12/27/1870

Trial of 13 and 56, Engine 13 with Smith's stack and #56 with Laird stack.[162]

### 10/4/1872

Stacks - put straight stacks with perforated cones on all class A and E engines now building.[163]

### 7/9/1874

Having adopted the Smith Stack for passenger en-gine, we send tracing #2876.[164]

### 7/13/1874

Having made trial of diff. lengths of screens in Smith Stacks, 70" long is decided the best, & it must fit in the stack and around the nozzles.[165]

## THE DEVELOPMENT OF THE 4-6-0

*Figure 79.* #207 (Baldwin, c/n 640, March 1855). Built as Allegheny Portage T.H. Forsythe (48" drivers, 19" x 22" cylinders) and rebuilt at Altoona (August 1867?), #207 retains some of the features of PRR's earliest ten-wheelers, Black Oak , Aughwick and Blue Ridge. In its original form, #207 would have had hook motion valve gear and an auxiliary frame. Aside from the addition of a Laird stack, the original fittings are more or less intact. The forward connecting rod is of the "round" type used until the early 1850's. The rear connecting rod and main rod are a modified flat type. Note the pump operated off the rear driver.

(PRR photo ME1307A; author's collection)

**THE DEVELOPMENT OF THE 4-6-0**

*Figure 80.* *#1 (Baldwin, c/n 1009, September 1861). Built with Smith's patent boiler, this locomotive (48" drivers, 18½" x 22" cylinders) was the second to hold #1. Smith's patent boiler had a deep firebox, short tubes, and a long combustion chamber equipped with baffles. Note the long wagon top, and the slant to the cylinders.* (BLW photo 13154-18; Broadbelt collection; Author's collection)

## Feedwater Pumps

From 1849 to 1861, all PRR locomotives were equipped with either crosshead pumps or an eccentric pump driven off the rear driver to supply feedwater to the boiler. The major drawback of this type of pump was that the locomotive had to be in motion to get water into the boiler.

## Injectors

The Giffard injector was introduced into America by William Sellers & Company of Philadelphia. A jet of steam drawn from the boiler forced the feedwater through series of nozzles, increasing its velocity and achieving a pressure higher than that inside the boiler, so that the water was forced into the boiler though the check valves. In 1861 the PRR removed the pumps on many locomotives and installed Giffard-type injectors. The injector was located under the footboard alongside the firebox. The check valve was on the rear wall of the firebox casing, just above the mudring. This location was prone to leaks and the check valves were soon located well forward on the boiler barrel. At first one was used on each locomotive, but these early injectors frequently failed, making it necessary for the engine crew to dump the fire. Subsequently two injectors, or one injector and one

◄ *Figure 81.* *#5 (Baldwin, c/n 1446, January 1866). Note the wagon top with the long boiler barrel, crosshead pump between the frames, and balloon stack. The lettering style was in use from 1863-1867. 54" drivers, 18" x 22" cylinders.* (BLW photo 13154-38; Author's collection)

The preceeding three photographs show the development of the ten-wheeled freight locomotive on the PRR over an 11-year period, 1855-1866. #207 has a short firebox above the frames, while #'s 1 and 5 have a deep firebox between the axles of the second and third drivers. As development progressed the cylinders became more level and the distance between the wheels on the front truck spread.

squirt (a non-adjustable injector) were put on each locomotive. Trouble with the injectors persisted and in 1864 the Company equipped their locomotives with one injector on the left side and a pump on the right side.

### 9/9/1873

Injectors. Place them below footboard.[166]

### 7/20/1874

Have asked Mr. Collin to work up an injector of our own, suitable for our engines, to cost less than we have to pay.[167]

### Safety Valves

The earliest PRR locomotives were equipped with two spring-balance safety valves, usually located on the steam dome. On some locomotives there was an auxiliary column, which had one of the valves. "Pop" valves were first used in 1867. The typical practice was to have one pop valve and one spring-balance lever safety valve on each locomotive.

On October 20, 1872 the practice was put in place to have all safety valves blow off at 125 psig and have them in order when leaving the shop.[168]

### RUNNING GEAR
### Frames

The frame of the locomotive held the drivers in place, provided a bed for the cylinders, a support for

▶

*Figure 83.* #135 (Baldwin, c/n 736, December 1856). Leopard (four 66" drivers, 15" x 24" cylinders), was the second locomotive built by Baldwin for the PRR with Stephenson valve gear. Although rebuilt, #135 retains the two steam domes. The rear dome, over the firebox, has one pop valve and one spring loaded lever valve. The forward dome contained the throttle valve and carried the whistle. Note the crosshead pump and four bar crosshead. The locomotive is equipped with a "limelight." Note the gas tank on the pilot beam. The limelight was soon discontinued, as the beam thrown by the headlight was too intense. *(BLW photo ME1263A; author's collection)*

# THE DEVELOPMENT OF THE 4-4-0

*Figure 82.* #26 (Baldwin, c/n 460, December 1852). Butler *was the passenger version of the Baldwin eight-wheel C locomotive (four 60" drivers, 13½" x 22" cylinders). The photograph shows the minimal extent of rebuilding these 4-4-0's were subjected to during the 1860's. Originally equipped with 13½" x 22" cylinders, 60" drivers, and hook motion, the locomotive received new Stephenson valve gear, but the old Bury boiler is unaltered.* *(PRR photo ME1245A; author's collection)*

3/5/1869

**Chart 9**

**Frame Costs, Passenger and Freight** 169

| Passenger | Wt., lbs. | Cost | Freight | Wt., lbs. | Cost |
|---|---|---|---|---|---|
| 2 main frames | 2,058 | $186.20 | 2 main frames | 2,800 | $286.20 |
| 2 front ends | 1,524 | 91.00 | 2 front ends | 1,260 | 91.00 |
| 2 back braces | 186 | 13.00 | 2 back braces | 186 | 13.03 |
| 2 pedestal braces | 520 | 35.36 | 4 pedestal braces | 774 | 62.62 |
| 2 pedestal caps | 200 | 15.52 | 6 pedestal caps | 318 | 23.28 |
| Total | 4,518 | $341.08 | | 5,388 | $476.13 |

THE DEVELOPMENT OF THE 4-4-0

*Figure 84.* #387 (Baldwin, c/n 1636, June 1867). #387 (four 60" drivers, 17" x 24" cylinders) represents the "modern" 4-4-0 on the PRR. Note the flat rods.

(BLW photo; author's collection)

The preceeding three photographs show the development of the 4-4-0 into a modern locomotive. The Bury boiler, sloped cylinders and short wheelbase truck were replaced by the straight boiler and then the wagon top, the cylinders became level, and the wheelbase of the engine truck was spread.

the boiler, and handled the weight of the trailing load. The frame also had to withstand the thrusts of the reciprocating parts. Unlike their British counterparts with deep plate frames, American locomotives typically featured bar frames. The boiler provided the lateral strength for the locomotive, and the bar frame with its cross bracing provided a measure of flexibility on the rough American roadbed. The Winans Camels with their plate frames were atypical. The bar frames were made of wrought iron bars welded or riveted together. The journals were generally cast iron and the bearings made of brass.

Outside auxiliary frames were abandoned by the early 1860's.

2/25/1870: Letter by TWW (Thomas W. Worsdell), stating number of frames broken from April 1867 to August 1869.[170]

| | | |
|---|---|---|
| 22 | BLW | 8-whl, passenger |
| 16 | BLW | 10-wheel, freight |
| 2 | BLW | Shifters, 6-wheel |
| 10 | AMS | engine, six-wheel and pony |
| 11 | Laird | engine, like 201, 245 |
| 1 | S&P | ten-wheel |
| 1 | Norris-Lanc | ten-wheel |
| 1 | Jersey, old cl. | ten-wheel |
| 1 | Jersey, new cl. | ten-wheel |

66 engines total

### Engine Trucks

The engine trucks on the earliest PRR locomotives were short wheelbase, center-bearing. The Bissell truck was adopted in the late 1850's. Various improvements were carried out by the railroad. In 1865 the equalizing bars were placed between the frame and the knee braces, instead of above the frame. In 1868 the center plate was mounted on an independent frame hung from the main truck frame by four staggered eyebolts, arranged in such a way as to afford a slight lateral motion in rounding curves. When the patentee came forward and demanded what the PRR thought to be an excessive royalty for this device, the Company placed oak blocks between the auxiliary frame and the main frame to render the trucks practically rigid. The swing center truck suspended on links became standard and was first applied to #419, a Baldwin 4-4-0, in October 1867.

*Figure 85. #110 (Baldwin, c/n 1197, December 1863). The first locomotives purchased for shifting service were Baldwin flexible-beam-truck 0-6-0's with saddle tanks added. The cylinders, mounted high on the side of the smoke box, allowed for the lateral motion of the flexible-beam truck, which held the first two drivers. #110 has been shopped at Altoona and has been fitted with a Laird stack.* (BLW photo; author's collection)
▶

## THE DEVELOPMENT OF THE 0-6-0

Although the PRR operated locomotives with a single pair of lead wheels, these were rigidly mounted in the main frame. The first two-wheel "swing" truck came on the PRR in 1862. Laird rebuilt Winans Camel #131 as a 2-6-0 with his own two-wheel equalizer leading truck (**Fig. 39**). All of the Altoona rebuilds with a two-wheel engine truck used Laird's invention.

The use of chilled iron wheels was standard.

### Drivers

Drivers had cast iron centers, hollow spokes, and were counterbalanced with lead. The tires were originally of wrought iron, but later were replaced by steel. The exceptions were the F and H 0-6-0 shifters. The lead drivers on these locomotives had chilled iron tires.

### Valve Gears

The PRR used a variety of double-eccentric, hook-motion valve gears supplied by the various commercial builders. Some had independent half-stroke cutoff. The Winans and Smith & Perkins locomotives used a drop-hook valve gear with independent half-stroke cutoff. Until the adoption of the Stephenson link-motion, the PRR had tried about fifteen different types of valve gear.

▶

*Figure 86. #442 (Baldwin, c/n 1902, June 1869), one of the last non-standard locomotives purchased by the PRR. The cylinders are level and all drivers are held in the locomotive frame. #442 has an early style of Alligator crosshead.*
(BLW photo 13153-1; author's collection)

◀ *Figure 87.* #224 (Baldwin, c/n 1014, October 1861). #224 had a straight boiler and slightly slanted cylinders. #'s 231 and 232, built by Baldwin the next year, the same type as #224 but with 18" x 24" cylinders, were the first PRR locomotives to be built by Baldwin with steel fireboxes. #224 has a balloon stack and an injector. The PRR equipped locomotives exclusively with injectors for a short period, but because of problems moved to one injector and one pump. Note the iron pilot. *(BLW photo 8349; Broadbelt collection; author's collection)*

The first locomotive to be equipped with the link motion valve gear was *Wyalusing*, built by Richard Norris & Son in July of 1856. Baldwin was reluctant to abandon its own form of variable-cutoff valve gear. During December 1856, Baldwin built *Tiger*, #134, **(Fig. 125)** for the PRR with Stephenson link motion. This became standard on all new locomotives and many older locomotives were rebuilt with the new gear.

### Brakes

The PRR's locomotives were not equipped with engine brakes until the advent of air brakes. In order to stop the train, the engineman reversed the locomotive and whistled for brakes to be set on the cars. A tender brake was used to hold the locomotive when standing. With the advent of air brakes, cambrakes were applied between the drivers on four-wheeled locomotives and between the main and rear drivers on six-wheeled locomotives.

11/12/1873: Driver Brakes ordered to be put on 11 engines [Class H] with bracing.[171]

◀ *Figure 88.* #91 (Ross Winans, February 1854). In May 1867, Altoona substantially rebuilt #91, *Logan*, at a cost of $13,064. The loco received a new firebox, frame, cylinders, 48" drivers and valve gear. The only remaining Winans feature was the enormous steam dome, which was moved from near the front of the boiler on the Camels to the rear over the front of the firebox. #91 is equipped with Laird's design of crosshead, which became quite popular on American railroads after 1870. The stack is also of Laird's design. *(PRR photo; author's collection)*

## Cost of labor and material in attaching an Air Brake [172]

| | |
|---|---|
| Engine | 107.37 |
| Tender | 43.57 |
| Air pump complete with all pipes | 325.00 |
| Total | 475.94 |

## Lubrication

The PRR at first used a simple oil cup attached directly to the valve-box cover. In the autumn of 1861, Laird rebuilt a Norris 4-4-0, #59, built in 1853. This was the first PRR locomotive to have the oil cups placed in the cab. The connecting oil lines entered the top of the valve-box cover.

## OTHER COMPONENTS
### Cowcatchers

The PRR used iron pilots with transverse slats on its earliest locomotives. J. Edgar Thomson asked Baldwin for the drawings of the Philadelphia & Reading's pilot so that he could use it on the PRR's locomotives. Some Norris locomotives built in 1858, 1862 and 1863 were supplied with pilots having vertical wooden bars. In 1867 passenger locomotives were equipped with vertical wooden bar pilots and freight locomotives were equipped with iron "hencoop" pilots.

## Headlights

All PRR locomotives were equipped with square-case oil-burning headlights, generally fitted to brackets extending in front of the smokebox. The PRR experimented with a "limelight" in 1866, applying it to locomotive #135 **(Fig. 83)**. This burned gas from a tank carried on the pilot beam. It was removed after one year because of the difficulty in preventing too great a concentration of light in a single narrow beam. **Fig. 133** shows a limelight on #170.

11/11/1873: Tried the reflecting qualities of the various head lamps, viz. Williams burner our case, Hall burner (our own standard), Kelly burner. Hall burner in silvered mica reflector and Hall burner in silver plated reflector does best under all circumstances.[173]

## Bells

The earliest PRR locos did not have bells. They became standard about 1855.

## Sandboxes

Some early PRR locos did not have sandboxes. Soon the sandbox became standard equipment and a variety of shapes were used, generally installed on the front portion of the boiler. John Laird rebuilt a Norris 4-4-0 in 1861 with sandboxes under the running boards, but these were soon removed.

## Cabs

All PRR cabs were made of wood. Some passenger locomotives were equipped with black-walnut cabs finished with several coats of varnish.

## Tenders

Early tenders were equipped with six wheels fixed in pedestals, one fixed wheel with a four-wheel vibrating truck, or one rigid four-wheel truck and a four-wheel vibrating truck. They were soon superseded by the two-truck tender. With the adoption of the standard classes the tenders were standardized. Classes A, B, C, D, and E used the same tender.

| Class | Length | Water | Coal |
|---|---|---|---|
| A,B,C,D,E | 17'-6" | 2,400 gals. | 8,000 lbs. |
| F | Tank | 820 | 1,500 |
| G | 15'-8" | 1,600 | 6,500 |
| H | 16'½" | 2,000 | 5,000 |
| C anth | 19'-0" | 2,400 | 12,000 |

By the early 1870's, some passenger tenders on the Pittsburgh Division were equipped for scooping

water, and other Divisions followed.

11/10/1875: **Summary of Water Troughs on PRR** [174]

| Place | Division | Northward | Southward | Total |
|---|---|---|---|---|
| Monmouth Jct. | NY | 1,300 | 1,300 | 2,600 |
| Downingtown | Phila. | 840 | 840 | 1,680 |
| Dillerville | Phila. | | | 1,000 |
| Bixlers | Mid. | 1,200 | 1,210 | 2,410 |
| Jackstown | Mid. | 800 | | 800 |
| Sang Hollow | Pgh. | 800 | 1,200 | 2,000 |
| Millwood | Pgh. | 1,561 | 1,200 | 2,761 |
| Spring Hill | Pgh. | | | 800 |
| Remaining at Downingtown not put down | | | | 210 |
| Total | | | | 14,251 |

The 850 ft. which was laid at Leaman Place was taken up and taken to Downingtown where 680 ft. of it is included in the above and the balance 210 ft is now laying out of service at Downingtown as stated above.

02/10/1874: Safety Chains. On the 2nd inst. at #9 Bridge at 10:40 a.m. an accident occurred to Eng. 305 [4-6-0, BLW, September 1863], a Camel axle broke close to the wheel, but the safety chains held the truck off the bridge & the axle guard held the broken end of the axle. The opposite to the one, which broke off, fell inside the rail and ran alongside of the stringer. The Engineman felt the jar and stopped before he got off the bridge. The broken end of the axle and wheel did not lose out of its place. Axle was turned with a square shoulder when break occurred. Neither wheel was flat.[175]

## FUEL

The PRR began its operations by using wood for fuel. Wood sheds were established at frequent intervals, secured from local contractors. In 1854, the Company began to operate a wood train out of Spruce Creek, to harvest wood from its own holdings. Although the PRR passed through some of the richest coal lands in the state, these properties were not developed to any great extent until the mid-1850's; the PRR hauled only 523,223 tons of coal in 1860. As the coal lands were developed, interest in burning coal increased. This was due to not only to the cost but also to availability. Much of the best wood lands along the railroad were held in reserve by the charcoal iron industry, which flourished in the Upper Juniata Valley.

The first attempt to use coal was initiated by Enoch Lewis in a series of tests in 1851. The results were mixed at best. Using Allegheny coal (a generic term applied to Western Pennsylvania bituminous other than Pittsburgh coal) alone resulted in burned out grates and damaged fireboxes. Although Pittsburgh coal did not burn as hot the results from that type were deemed inconclusive. Lewis suggested that a mixture of coal and wood would permit a locomotive to run further without renewal of the fuel supply. That year the company used 20,463 cords of wood and 8,029 bushels of coal.

Extensive fuel tests were carried on in 1859. Interestingly, one of the major concerns was the offensive nature of coal smoke to the Company's gas passengers. These tests showed that coal could be used with little offense to the passengers from the smoke. The Company used a variety of strange and wonderful boiler and firebox arrangements in these tests; Dimpfel, Phleger, Smith, and Gill & Company fireboxes were tried. Grier, the Master of Machinery, was convinced of the practicality of substituting bituminous coal for wood and urged the Company to adopt the Gill & Company firebox arrangement at approximately $500 per engine.

In 1860 the PRR's fuel consumption was as follows:

| | Wood - cords | | Coal - tons | |
|---|---|---|---|---|
| | Consumed | On Hand | Consumed | On hand |
| Eastern | 11,183 | 10,674 | 23,774 | 4,479 |
| Middle | 24,352 | 6,754 | 31,032 | 1,553 |
| Western | 22,776 | 22,788 | 20,275 | 50 |

The cost of the coal consumed was $1,960.67

charged to passenger service and $69,673.66 charged to freight service. The cost for wood, which included the price of the wood and hauling, was $77,300.63 charged to passenger service and $67,463.32 charged to freight service. There was an additional cost for the wood: $12,499.63 in labor and $11,782.66 for preparation.

Laird, Grier's successor, converted all of the Company's locomotives to coal burning with the addition of a brick arch, for about $50 per engine. By 1862 all freight locomotives and ten passenger locomotives were burning coal and by 1864 all the Company's locomotives were changed to burn coal. The figures recorded for fuel consumption reported in the *Annual Reports* indicate that a mixture of coal and wood continued to be used.

### Fuel Costs in Dollars

| | Coal | | Wood | |
|---|---|---|---|---|
| | Freight | Passenger | Freight | Passenger |
| 1855 | $30,826 | | $57,237 | |
| 1860 | 89,673 | 1,960 | 7,463 | 77,300 |
| 1865 | 502,055 | 95,176 | 108,897 | 31,328 |
| 1870 | 465,617 | 89,992 | 18,648 | 72,789 |
| 1873* | 932,362 | 138,758 | 84,248 | 17,318 |

\* PRR Division

05/10/1873 - All engine coal is sent as "Run of Mine" - if there is any particular car load that is too bad for use, report it giving No. of car.[176]

11/6/1873: Trials of Anth. Coal - over Middle Div., 123m., Eng. 922, 17" x 25" cylinders, 60" drivers. Red Ash, White Ash, Buck Mtn., McNeely - Buck Mtn. is the cleanest.[177]

### Petroleum as Fuel -
### A Report by G. W. Stratton [178]

What are the facts and figures relating to the experiment by the PRR with petroleum as fuel for locomotives. During July and August 1870 a Mr. Whipple came to Altoona and with the assistance of Mr. T.W. Worsdell, the MM, a series of experiments

were made endeavoring to utilize petroleum as a fuel for locomotives. The arrangement for carrying out his intentions I will describe as nearly as possible from memory. I cannot learn that any reports were made of the experiments. Engine No. 141 was used. [4-6-0 BLW, c/n 1012, September 1861]

On the tender were placed tanks to hold a supply of petroleum, a generator to convert the oil into gas and a hand pump to transfer the oil from the fuel tank to the generator. From the generator on the tender was a pipe to conduct gas into [the] bottom of the firebox of the locomotive. The oil was converted to gas by heat, viz. - steam taken from the boiler, the generator having a great number of pipes in it to afford sufficient heating surface. The gas from the generator was very hot so that nothing but metal could stand it, and hence mechanical difficulties occurred of making a flexible connection between the tender and the engine. An expansion joint was made of a stuffing box and gland and ball and socket connections free enough to adjust themselves to the proper position on curves and the undulating movements of the engine and tender, or else the gas would escape and be wasted or take to fire. Asbestos packing was the only material that would stand the heat in the stuffing box of [the] expansion joint.

There seemed to be no trouble about making the gas in the generator and the gas when burned in the firebox would make steam, but the arrangements were not of a scale large enough to keep up a supply of gas to make steam in the quantity used by a locomotive. The engine starting at 125 psig pressure would in two miles run have but 30 to 40 lbs., then steam could be accumulated again for another two miles run, the grades on the mountain being the running ground.

At first a six ply gum hose was used to convey the gas from the generator to [the] firebox but this soon burned up under the intense heat of the gas, and once this hose burnt, it allowed the gas to escape which caught fire and enveloped cab, tender and people in flames, not seriously hurting anybody, Mr. Whipple only having sprained his ankle in jumping from the tender.

The steam to heat the generator was obtained from the boiler, and when steam was low the gas was made slowly. To start the apparatus steam was obtained from another boiler.

### Petroleum as Fuel, by Wm. T. Miller [179]

July 9, 1870, Whipple's Patent Fuel. Arrangements attached to Eng. #141 and tender. Machine was tested July 19 and 21; first trials made on July 23, 24 and 25. Your description of apparatus is good. The gas was superheated after steam was raised and of course caused great heat. The great-est difficulty experienced was that the generator would not make steam enough for use of engine and one or two cars. We never made at one heat, further than where Nick Heickey now lives, and often stopped four of five times between this and Kittanning Point.

On the August 11, we ran up to McDermitts starting with 125 lbs. steam and stopping with 35 lbs. steam and 25 lbs. gas. (The production of gas depended on the amount of steam and when steam went down so did gas.) We then blowed up to 95 lbs. steam and returned, combustion poor, and vapor wasted largely. Another set of burners were then put in firebox at door inclined toward flue sheet. A base plate had been put over water grates, covered with charcoal to assist in combustion and prevent draft.

After repairing, was ready on August 15 but Mr. Whipple was not present. These experiments were continued but with little success till abandoned. The apparatus would have done well, I think, on a stationary boiler, but not on a locomotive arranged as #141 was. The flame could not get further than the flue sheet, as there was no draft to induce it.

The complicity [complexity] and danger of the arrangement was another objection. One could hardly feel [safe] after it was fired up, as any defect was liable to cause an explosion - I do not know that anyone kept any figures on estimates of the experiments as the whole thing appeared to be done by Mr. Whipple as an experiment on his own. I do not remember how long the experiment lasted. Perhaps Jno. Carr has some facts, which bear on the case.

# CHAPTER 6
## LOCOMOTIVE LIVERIES

The following information is of a general nature and represents the practice that was typical for the period indicated. Locomotives were repainted as they were shopped and several different styles could exist at the same time. The Company moved toward a standardization of painting and lettering locomotives that was finally achieved with the introduction of the standard designs in 1868. The individual preferences of the various Company shops and patterns of the independent builders were superseded by standards set down in Altoona. Soon thereafter all locomotives carried a common livery.

### LOCOMOTIVE PAINTING
#### 1849 - 1854

The first locomotives of the PRR were rather plain and were painted a medium dark (Forest) green or occasionally a medium chocolate brown (the Norris engines), except for the boiler and smokebox, which were left unpainted. The boiler was decorated with brass bands, and some of the fittings were polished brass. The cabs were striped, depending on the style, with either a horizontal panel or several vertical panels beneath the windows. Horizontal panels were usually decorated with an arabesque of vine leaves or fruit. The side of the tender cistern was divided into panels by striping.

#### 1854 - 1862

At this time a highly elaborate style of painting prevailed, with the use of bright colors, polished brass work and detailed decoration. The famous lithograph of *Tiger* (BLW, c/n 731, 1857, **Fig. 125**) is representative of this trend. *Tiger* had vermilion wheel centers, a Russian Iron boiler jacket, green

domes with bright brass covers, highly decorated headlight and cab sides, and a pink tender with detailed striping and colorful arabesques and scrolls. During this period the side of the square headlight was frequently decorated with paintings of various scenes.

There was a similarity of paint schemes for both passenger and freight locomotives carried out by the Company's shops, with enough variation that it can-not be termed a standard pattern.

**Passenger locomotives**: *vermilion* - wheel centers, tender panels & dome bases; *burnt umber* - sandbox & tender cistern; *dark green* - frames; *chrome yellow* - tender collar or fender. The steam dome cover, boiler bands, and fittings were polished brass, the cab was varnished black walnut, the boiler was Russian Iron and the smokebox was unpainted.

**Freight locomotives**: *vermilion* - wheel centers;

*Figure 89.* #173 (Baldwin, c/n 590, May 1854). The former Philadelphia & Columbia Nebraska was rebuilt at Altoona in February 1867. #173 retains some of the livery of that period. Note the "painting" on the headlight, scroll work on the domes, and striping on the tender. A letter from T.W. Worsdell to his family in England contains a description of this style. The engines are ... painted most fantastically ... it makes them look very inferior to our finished engines, gilt is used lavishly, they don't seem to think that gold leaf costs anything. Chimneys were black, boiler barrels were slate blue, domes polished brass, sandboxes green and gold, cabs polished walnut with gilt lining, cylinders blue, framing dark green, wheel splashers emerald green and wheels vermilion and gilt.

*(PRR photo ME1265A; author's collection)*

*Figure 90. #332 (Baldwin, c/n 1346, March 1865) carries the livery applied from 1861-1867. The number is on the sandbox and "PENNA. R.R." is on the center panel of the tender. Note the arabesques at each end of the panel around the road name.*
(BLW photo; author's collection)

burnt umber - sandbox; *dark Tuscan red* - frame & cowcatcher; *Tuscan red* - border around the tender panels; *dark green* - tender cistern; *green* - cab panels & tender panels; *black* - dome bases and tender collar or fender. The steam dome cover, boiler bands and fittings were polished brass, the boiler of Russian Iron and the smokebox was unpainted.

The increased use of bituminous coal made this elaborate style difficult to maintain, since the loco was soon covered with sooty grime.

### 1862 - 1868

With the advent of John P. Laird as Master of Machinery, the Company began to standardize the painting of its locomotives as they passed through the shops. Dark colors were adopted, with each shop following their own designs. There was some reluctance to abandon the bright decorative colors. In 1864 the Company adopted black for the centers of locomotive drivers. In 1866 a uniformity of design in painting locomotives was adopted; black for the wheels and a warm shade of burnt umber (brown) for the other parts of the locomotive and tender. The boiler was Russian Iron and the smokebox was unpainted. This was not applied to locomotives supplied by outside builders, but was applied to locomotives rebuilt or shopped.

### 1868 Onward

When the standard designs were adopted in 1868, a uniform plan for finishing locomotives was achieved. They were painted a dark, black color. The jackets of the boilers were left unpainted until 1895. G.W. Stratton reported to Frank Thomson on November 26, 1873, that C anth. engine #'s 912 - 914, 921, and 922 were painted with McClaskys drop black and the balance with Reynolds. Two

◀ *Figure 91. #60 (Baldwin, c/n 1140, June 1863) shows the difficulty in making definitive statements about lettering styles. The locomotive has a painting on the headlight, decorative scrollwork, and "P.R.R." lettered on the tender.*
(BLW photo; author's collection)

schemes were being tried, the seven-coat plan and the 14-coat plan. In the seven-coat plan, the engines were painted with a coat of red lead, then a coat of lead color, two coats of drop black, two coats of engine rubbing varnish, and one coat of engine finishing varnish. The 14-coat plan had the addition of two coats of glazing and three of filling after the lead color, then another coat of lead color was applied and three coats of drop black. The engine was finished with two coats of engine rubbing varnish and one coat of engine finishing varnish.

#'s 944-949, class H, were noted on 12/02/1873 to have been painted according to the "seven-coat plan." [180]

By the mid 1870's, when James Dredge toured the Pennsylvania Railroad for the British magazine *Engineering*, the PRR was painting its locomotives a dark green color, because it was found to be more durable than black. *Engine 131 [Class E, April 1871] painted a dark green, put out February 15, 1875, and a letter from T.N. Ely dated 02-09-75 instructed us to paint all eng. green, both passenger and freight.*[181]

The materials specifications for painting a class C locomotive in 1876 were as follows:[182]

    7 lbs. of Swedish Green
    25 lbs. of Dark Brunswick Green
    4 lbs. of Roofing Brown
    20 lbs. Ironclad Paint
    2 gals Black Japan Varnish
    2 gals Rubbing Varnish
    1 gal Finish Varnish
    27 books of gold leaf

The locomotives and cars were painted in the Paint Shop, a 345 x 32-foot, one-story wooden building with two tracks. The equipment was run in the eastern doors, painted, and put out the western doors. The paint was mixed and stored in a separate building. The color consistency was maintained by having only one person mix the paint.

## LOCOMOTIVE LETTERING AND NUMERALS
### 1849 - 1854

A plate with the name of the locomotive was attached to the boiler near the smokebox. Occasionally the locomotive name appeared on the side of the tender. The road name did not appear.

### 1854 - 1862

Locomotive numbers were adopted in 1857 and appeared on a brass plate on the boiler near the smokebox or were painted on the sandbox. The name **PENNA. RR**, **PENNSYLVANIA RAIL ROAD**, or **PENNSYLVANIA RAILROAD COMPANY** appeared with various forms of scrollwork on the tender side.

### 1862 - 1868

In late 1863, Laird began to have the Company's locomotives lettered **PENNA. RR** on the center of the tender panel. This was discontinued in early 1867. The locomotive number was painted on the sandbox. Laird's rebuilds had the number on the side and front of the valve chamber. About this time the

***Figure 92.*** *#19 (Altoona, c/n 127, April 1872), Class E, illustrates the standard style of painting adopted in 1867. The locomotive was painted black; the boiler is Russian iron, and the tender is lettered "P.R.R." The striping has been simplified.*

*(PRR photo ME1009A; author's collection)*

number also appeared in a number plate on the center of the smokebox, and it was painted on the rear of the tender.

### 1868 Onward

The initials **P.R.R.** were centered on the center panel of the tender. The number was painted on the sandbox and on the rear of the tender. The number was cast on a round number plate with burnished brass letters and a black background, which was attached to the center of the smokebox.

## LOCOMOTIVE STRIPING
### 1849 - 1854

The earliest PRR locomotives carried a rather simple form of striping with what appears to be a double line of stripes forming a panel on the sandbox and two panels on the tender side. The cab was striped according to its design, either a single horizontal panel or four vertical panels.

### 1854 - 1862

During the period of extensive locomotive decoration the striping was supplemented by elaborate scrollwork and arabesques.

### 1862 - 1868

When Laird became Master of Machinery the striping was simplified but there appears to have been no standard. The matter of striping was left to the talents of the individual shops and their master painters. Arabesques and vine leaves still appear on the side of the tender.

Locomotives appearing in the burnt umber paint scheme were striped with yellow, set off by a smaller vermilion stripe.

### 1868 Onward

The standard designs introduced in 1868 adopted a common standard for all striping of new locomotives; older locomotives were repainted to conform. The locomotives were striped with a double band. The outside stripe was approximately ½" wide and was gold leaf for passenger and lemon yellow for freight. The inner stripe, ⅛" wide, was vermilion. The headlight was striped (double band) as well as the smoke stack. The sandbox and steam domes were striped, from top to bottom, just below the dome cover a large stripe and then a small stripe, then at the bottom of the dome above the dome saddle, a small stripe and then a large stripe. The cab panel was striped with a double band below the windows. There was a single stripe (gold/yellow) forming a panel on the tender collar. A single small stripe (gold/yellow) went around the cistern at the top.

The tender was divided into panels at the corners, ends and sides by a double band. At the bottom of the cistern there was a single stripe (gold/yellow), then a band of freight car color (red), and a final small stripe (gold/yellow). As noted in the double band striping the larger gold or yellow stripe was set off by a very narrow stripe of vermilion about 1" away. In 1881 this vermilion stripe was changed to white. The corners of the double-band stripes on the tender panels were ornate, with a 90-degree angle leading to a reversed 90-degree angle, tangent to an arc of about 4" radius, ending in another pair of 90-degree angles. These were replaced by a simple arc in 1881.

# CHAPTER 7
## LOCOMOTIVE NUMBERING ON THE PRR

Until 1857, the PRR used names for its locomotives. The locomotives built by Baldwin were usually named for the Counties of the Commonwealth. The first exception was the *True American*, built in August 1853. The locomotives built by Norris were named for natural features: mountains, valleys, rivers, and streams. The Smith & Perkins locomotives were named for cities, and the Winans Camels were named for mythical persons - *Thor* - or Indian tribes or chiefs. The three Seth Wilmarth locomotives were named *Antelope*, *Atlanta* (**Fig. 20**) and *Eagle*.

With the purchase of the Public Works in August 1857, named locomotives from the Philadelphia & Columbia and Allegheny Portage were added to the roster. Because some PRR locos carried the same names, numbers were assigned as follows:

| | |
|---|---|
| Pennsylvania Railroad | 1 - 140 |
| Philadelphia & Columbia | 141 - 195 |
| Allegheny Portage | 196 - 210 |
| Pennsylvania Railroad | 211 and up |

During the following years the PRR continued to add new equipment until the assigned numbers reached #574 in 1871. When a locomotive was retired or sold, a new locomotive would be assigned the number made vacant. When there were no more vacant numbers available the next highest unfilled number would be assigned. With the lease of the United Companies in June 1871 their locomotives were renumbered into the PRR series as follows:

| | | |
|---|---|---|
| Belvidere Delaware | #'s 575 - 600 | April 1872 |
| Camden & Amboy | #'s 601 - 700 | January 1872 |
| New Jersey RR & Transportation | #'s 701 - 751 | January 1872 |
| Camden & Amboy | #'s 752 - 770 | January 1872 |

By January 1, 1874, the numbers had reached #953. Within the numbers assigned, 33 were vacant, giving a total of 920 locomotives in the stock of equipment. #954 was used by a locomotive renumbered from the Alexandria & Fredericksburg Railway and #955 was not used until August 1882. Until that date, new equipment was numbered in the numbers below #954 made vacant by renumbering to controlled or affiliated lines, scrapping or sale.

### LOCOMOTIVE CLASSIFICATION ON THE PRR

The earliest classification system ranked locomotives by weight and type of service. *Mifflin* (**Figs. 95 and 96**), at 21 tons, was a First Class Passenger Engine, while *Juniata* (**Fig. 98**), at 19 tons, was considered a Second Class Passenger Engine. A particular locomotive's place in this system kept changing as newer and heavier locomotives were added to the roster.

For a while, the *Annual Reports* used a form of Baldwin's classification system of weight and number of drivers, but omitted the total number of wheels. This applied only to the engines purchased from Baldwin. In 1854 the PRR purchased 13 "24-ton C freight engines" from Baldwin — these were 4-4-0's with 54" drivers and 17" x 22" cylinders. Locomotives from the other builders, Norris for instance, were still reported by weight and service, First Class Passenger and so forth. The 0-8-0's from Winans and Baldwin were referred to as "heavy First Class assistant freight engines or pushers."

In 1866, the Company began to list locomotives by a more descriptive form of wheel arrangement and type of service: ten-wheel freight, eight-wheel passenger, and shifter.

The first real attempt to make some sense out of the variety of locomotives on the road is to be found in *A Collection of Photographs of Locomotives, Typical of Each Class on the Pennsylvania Railroad at This Date, Pennsylvania Railroad Company, Motive Power Department, May 1st 1868.* (See **Bibliography**.)

Each locomotive owned by the Company was listed in numerical order, originally from 1-440, in Index "A," found at the front of the book, with the locomotive that it was "like" listed beside it. A photograph of the "like" or "typical" locomotive was reproduced in the album section of the book. Locomotive #5 (**Fig. 81**), a Baldwin 4-6-0 with 18" x 22" cylinders and 54" drivers, was shown to be like engine #383 (**Fig. 55**), a locomotive with the same general dimensions that was pictured in the accompanying photographs. In this example, #5 was a "383 Class engine." In Index "B," the typical locomotives were listed — the locomotives illustrated by the photographs — with the numbers of the engines of the "same class" shown. Interestingly enough, beside #383 are listed the numbers of "like" locomotives with 48", 50½", 54" and 55" drivers. Locomotives like #14 (**Fig. 56**), a Millholland "Gunboat" built by Lancaster, have no "like" number shown beside it, because there was only one of that particular configuration on the road. The 26 Class, illustrated by engine 26, *Butler* (Fig. 82), a Baldwin 4-4-0 with a Bury boiler, has all the remaining Baldwin 4-4-0's with Bury boilers listed beside it, including #8, *Huntingdon*. It would appear that this classification system was for the benefit of operating personnel. Locomotives of like capacity and mechanical similarity were lumped together into a single class. This was a rather awkward and complicated system, and the register book itself was bulky and fragile.

The copy of the *Photographs of Locomotives Typical of each Class*, as we shall call it here, in the State Archives at Harrisburg, was used on the Pittsburgh Division. Since it was in regular use, the additions were either written in by hand or cut off the addition sheets and pasted beside the proper number. The last number added was #949 (Fig. 72), a class H, built in December 1873. An exact reproduction of the original condition of the book is not possible. The following can be reconstructed from Indexes A and B:

## CLASSES WITH MORE THAN ONE LOCOMOTIVE, AS OF MAY 1, 1868

Any important deviations from the typical locomotive are noted under remarks.

**Locomotives like #26** - Baldwin "C" 4-4-0 with Bury firebox and various size drivers and cylinders. Includes #'s 7, 8, 11, 12, 13, 16, 17, 18, 19, 20, 21, 22, 25, 28, 29, 31, 32, 33 (19 locomotives in the class). #16 has a different boiler and a 30" dome.

**Locomotives like #34** - Baldwin 0-6-0 tank engine. Includes #'s 35, 36, 37, 108, 112, 158, 171, 362, 363, 364, 365, 366, 367 (14 locomotives in the class)

**Locomotives like #42** - Baldwin "D" 4-6-0 of 1852-53. Includes #'s 49 and 62 (three locomotives in the class)

**Locomotives like #43** - Smith & Perkins six-wheeled freight locomotive with a wagon-top boiler and drop-hook valve gear. Includes #'s 41, 82, 99,101, 200 (six locomotives in the class). For #'s 41, 82, 101 the remarks show "pony wheels." Although the "typical" locomotive pictured is #43, a 4-6-0, most of the other locomotives remained as 2-6-0's. #99 was cut up and replaced by a class E in March 1869; it is unclear if it received a four-wheel engine truck.

**Locomotives like #45** - Baldwin flexible-beam-truck 0-8-0 rebuilt with a small wheel replacing the front driver. Includes #44 (two locomotives in the class)

**Locomotives like #46** - Baldwin "D" 4-6-0 and Norris 4-4-0 rebuilt as 2-6-0's. Includes #'s 38, 39, 47, 58, 81, 84 (eight locomotives in the class)

**Locomotives like #60** - Baldwin 4-4-0 (April 1866, 17" x 24"). Includes #'s 61 and 80 (three locomotives in the class)

**Locomotives like #77** - Smith & Perkins six-wheeled freight locomotives with a straight boiler and link motion rebuilt as a 4-6-0. Includes #s 76, 78, 89, 201 (five locomotives in the class).

**Locomotives like #91** - Winans Camel rebuilt as a 2-6-0 (June 1848, 19" x 24"), with level cylinders. Includes #'s 50, 51, 88, 121, 130 (six locomotives in the class)

**Locomotives like #94** - Baldwin flexible-beam-truck 0-8-0 rebuilt as a 2-6-0. Includes #95 (two locomotives in the class)

**Locomotives like #96** - Baldwin 0-4-0. Includes #'s 23, 24, and 92, all equipped with saddle tanks (four locomotives in the class)

**Locomotives like #98** - Baldwin flexible-beam-truck 0-8-0 rebuilt as a 2-8-0 tank engine. Includes #97 (two locomotives in the class)

**Locomotives like #106** - Baldwin freight 4-4-0 (April 1854, 17" x 22"). Includes #'s 66, 67, 69, 70, 72, 73, 75, 83, 100, 102, 103, 104, 105, 106, 113, 114, 122, 123, 125, 126 (21 locomotives in the class)

**Locomotives like #110** - Baldwin flexible-beam-truck 0-6-0 with a saddle tank, includes #'s 111, 140, 197, 215, 216, 247, 248, 252, 327, 328, 329, 330, 344, 345, 346 (16 locomotives in the class)

**Locomotives like #118** - Baldwin 4-6-0 (June 1848, 18" x 22" and 19" x 22"). Includes #117 (two locomotives in the class)

**Locomotives like #119** - Winans Camel rebuilt as a 2-6-0 (June 1848, 19" x 24") with slightly sloping cylinders. Includes #52 (two locomotives in the class)

**Locomotives like #129** - Baldwin flexible-beam-truck 0-8-0 rebuilt with an extended rigid frame. Includes #128 (two locomotives in the class)

**Locomotives like #135** - Baldwin 4-4-0 with 66" drivers and two steam domes. Includes #'s 132 and 134 (three locomotives in the class)

**Locomotives like #136** - Baldwin 4-4-0 (April 1855, 17" x 22"). Includes #139 (two locomotives in the class)

**Locomotives like #137** - Baldwin 4-6-0 (June 1854, 18" x 22") built 1864-65. Includes #'s 2, 6, 10, 63, 93, 107, 109, 115, 138, 280, 281, 282, 289, 290, 291, 292, 293, 294, 337 (20 locomotives in the class)

**Locomotives like #143** - Baldwin 0-4-0 tank engine. Includes #246 (two locomotives in the class)

**Locomotives like #145** - 4-4-0 with Brandt-style sloping cylinders (April 1860). Includes #'s 188, 189, 192, 193, 198 (six locomotives in the class)

**Locomotives like #148** – Altoona-built 4-4-0. Includes #'s 127 and 239 (three locomotives in the class)

**Locomotives like #166** - 4-4-0 with Brandt-style sloping cylinders (April 1866). Includes #'s 159, 160, 161, 162, 163, 164, 165, 172, 175 (ten locomotives in the class)

**Locomotives like #187** - 4-4-0 with Brandt-style sloping cylinders (April

1854). Includes #'s 176, 177, 178, 179, 183, 184, 185, 186 (nine locomotives in the class)

**Locomotives like #195** - 4-4-0 with Brandt-style sloping cylinders (April 1866). Includes #'s 181, 182, 194, 180 (five locomotives in the class)

**Locomotives like #205** - Norris 4-6-0 rebuilt as a 2-6-0. Includes #208 (two locomotives in the class)

**Locomotives like #207** - Baldwin 4-6-0 rebuilt as a 2-6-0 by Laird. Includes #206 (two locomotives in the class)

**Locomotives like #210** - Norris and Smith & Perkins engines rebuilt as 2-6-0's (June 1848, 18" x 24"). Includes #'s 74 and 204 (three locomotives in the class). Any important deviations from the typical locomotive are noted under remarks, and for #210, "has pony wheels and different dome."

**Locomotives like #212:** 2-4-0 and 4-4-0 passenger tank engines. Includes #251 (two locomotives in the class)

**Locomotives like #224:** Baldwin 4-6-0 (50" drivers, 16" x 22" cylinders). Includes #'s 1, 3, 4, 15, 141, 213, 214, 218, 219, 220, 221, 222, 225, 226, 227, 228, 229, 230, 231, 232 (21 locomotives in the class)

**Locomotives like #233:** Rogers 4-6-0. Includes #'s 234, 235, 236 (four locomotives in the class)

**Locomotives like #245:** 4-6-0 rebuilt to "Laird's plan" as 2-6-0. Includes #304 (two locomotives in the class)

**Locomotives like #283:** NJL&M 4-6-0 of 1865. Includes #'s 284, 285, 286, 287, 288 (six locomotives in the class)

**Locomotives like #297:** Norris 4-6-0 with 48" or 54" drivers and 18" x 22" cylinders. Includes #'s 238, 240, 272, 273, 274, 275, 275, 276, 277, 295, 296, 298, 299 (14 locomotives in the class)

**Locomotives like #325:** Baldwin 4-4-0 (66" drivers, 17" x 24" cylinders) built in 1864. Includes #'s 318, 319, 320, 321, 322, 323, 324, 326 (nine locomotives in the class)

**Locomotives like #339:** Baldwin 4-6-0 (48" drivers, 16" x 22" cylinders). Includes #'s 340, 341, 342, 343 (five locomotives in the class)

**Locomotives like #349:** Baldwin 4-4-0 (60" drivers, 16" x 24" cylinders) built in 1865. Includes #'s 331, 332, 333, 334, 335, 336, 350, 351, 352, 353 (11 locomotives in the class)

**Locomotives like #361:** Baldwin 4-4-0 (60" drivers, 16" x 24" cylinders) built in 1866. Includes #'s 356, 357, 358, 359, 360 (six locomotives in the class)

**Locomotives like #383:** a mixed class of Baldwin 4-6-0's with 48", 50½", 54" and 55" drivers and 18" x 22" cylinders. Includes #'s 5, 53, 64, 90, 116, 199, 241, 242, 243, 244, 249, 250, 253, 254, 255, 256, 257, 258, 259, 260, 262, 263, 264, 265, 266, 267, 268, 269, 270, 271, 300, 301, 302, 303, 305, 306, 307, 308, 309, 310, 311, 312, 313, 314, 315, 316, 317, 354, 355, 369, 370, 371, 372, 373, 374, 375, 376, 377, 378, 379, 380, 381, 382, 384 (65 locomotives in the class)

**Locomotives like #387:** Baldwin 4-4-0 (60" drivers, 17" x 24" cylinders) built in 1867. Includes #'s 385, 386, 388, 389, 390, 391, 392, 393, 394, 395, 396 (12 locomotives in the class)

**Locomotives like #407:** Norris-Lancaster 4-6-0. Includes #'s 397, 398, 399, 400, 401, 402, 403, 404, 405, 406, 408 (12 locomotives in the class)

**Locomotives like #417:** NJL&M 4-6-0, built in 1867. Includes #'s 409, 410, 411, 412, 423, 414, 415, 416, 418 (10 locomotives in the class)

**Locomotives like #421:** Baldwin 4-4-0 (66" drivers, 17" x 24" cylinders) built in 1867. Includes #'s 419, 420, 422 (four locomotives in the class)

## CLASSES WITH ONLY ONE LOCOMOTIVE IN THE CLASS, AS OF MAY 1, 1868

As previously noted, the original book was much amended and added to with pasted-in printed strips showing the replacement locomotives. Some of the information was difficult to decipher and there may be omissions in what follows. Most of these one-of-a-kind locomotives were quickly replaced. There were 19 pictured.

| | |
|---|---|
| #14 | a 4-6-0 Millholland "Gunboat," built by Norris-Lancaster. |
| #40 | a Seth Wilmarth 4-4-0. |
| #48 | a Winans Camel rebuilt as a 2-6-0. |
| #57 | a Norris 4-4-0 with 60" drivers. |
| #120 | a Baldwin 4-6-0, the former *Blue Ridge*. |
| #131 | a Winans Camel rebuilt as a 2-6-0. |
| #142 | a 4-4-0 built at Altoona (AMS c/n #1). |
| #169 | a Norris 4-4-0 with 60" drivers. |
| #173 | an ex-P&C Baldwin 4-4-0. |
| #174 | an ex-P&C Norris 4-6-0. |
| #203 | a Norris loco rebuilt as an 0-4-0T. |
| #209 | an ex-Norris 4-4-0. |
| #217 | a Baldwin 4-4-0T . |
| #237 | a Norris loco rebuilt as an 0-4-0T. |
| #261 | a Baldwin 4-4-0 rebuilt as a 2-6-0, with the note "See photo." |
| #278 | a Norris 4-4-0. |
| #279 | a Norris 4-4-0. |
| #347 | a Norris 4-4-0 rebuilt as a 2-6-0. |
| #348 | a Norris 4-4-0. |

## LOCOMOTIVES NOT PHOTOGRAPHED BUT INCLUDED, AS OF MAY 1, 1868

There were some locomotives that were classified as "Odd" that were not photographed and were noted as such. Some of these were already being replaced when the book was printed and the remarks are recorded below in italics. Others were replaced and hand-written notes indicated the replacement, while others had the original notations covered over by strips cut from the printed addition sheets.

#9   a Norris 4-4-0 of 1850.

#27   *Is being rebuilt in a New Passenger Engine like #421 - a Baldwin 4-4-0 of 1852.*

#30   *Vacant - a Baldwin 4-4-0 of 1867 sold to the StLV&TH in May 1868.*

#54   *Is being rebuilt into a First Class Passenger Engine like #421 - a Norris 4-4-0 of 1853.*

#55   *Not photographed, like 59 - a Norris 4-4-0 of 1853.*

#59   *Not photographed, like 55 - a Norris 4-4-0 of 1853.*

#65   a Norris 4-4-0 of 1853.

#68   a Norris 4-4-0 of 1853.

#79   *Rebuilding to Company Standard Ten-wheel Freight Engine - a Norris 4-4-0 of 1854.*

#85   *Not photographed, like 86 - a Norris 4-4-0 of 1854.*

#86   a Norris 4-4-0 of 1854.

#87   *Rebuilding to Company Standard Ten-wheel Freight Engine a Norris 4-4-0 of 1854.*

#124   *Odd - Rebuilt Camel - not photographed - a Winans camel rebuilt to a 2-6-0.*

#134   *Is being rebuilt into a First Class Passenger Engine like #421, a Baldwin 4-4-0 of 1856.*

#144   *Odd - not photographed - an ex-P&C Norris 4-4-0 of 1848.*

#146   a Norris 4-6-0 of 1860.

#147   an ex-P&C Norris 4-4-0 of 1849.

#149   an ex-P&C Norris 4-4-0 of 1849.

#150   an ex-P&C Norris 4-4-0 of 1849.

#151   *Not photographed - like 150 and 149 - an ex-P&C Norris 4-4-0 of 1849.*

#152   *Not photographed - like 153 - a Norris 4-6-0 of 1860.*

#153   a Norris 4-6-0 of 1860.

#154   *Odd - not photographed - an ex-P&C Norris 4-4-0 of 1851.*

#155   an ex P&C Norris 4-4-0 of 1851.

#156   *Odd - not photographed - a Baldwin 4-4-0 of 1859.*

#157   *Not photographed - like 149 - an ex-P&C Norris 4-4-0 of 1851.*

#170   an ex-P&C Norris 4-4-0 of 1854.

#190   an ex-P&C Baldwin 4-4-0 of 1856.

#191   an ex-P&C Norris 4-4-0 of 1856.

#196   *Odd - not photographed - ex-AP Norris 4-4-0 of 1851.*

#202   *Odd - not photographed - ex-AP Baldwin 4-6-0 of 1852.*

#211   *Odd - not photographed - a Baldwin flexible-beam truck 0-6-0 tender engine.*

#223   *Odd - not photographed - a Norris 4-6-0 of 1861.*

#368   *Odd - not photographed - a Lancaster 4-4-0 of 1867.*

The next system, in use until 1897, was initiated by the standard designs when a single letter was assigned to all locomotives built from the same drawings by the Company or by an outside contractor. A listing for January 1, 1873, shows the following:

## CLASSIFICATION FOR STANDARD ENGINES (ALTOONA, PA., JANUARY 1, 1873)

**Class A.**   Standard Passenger Engine – 17" x 24" cylinders, 66" drivers.

**Class B.**   Mountain Passenger Helper - a modification of class A, being in all respects like it, with the exception of cylinders, which are 18" x 24", 60" drivers.

**Class C.**   Used for Local and Fast Freight, and for Passenger Engine. Another modification of Class A - differing only in the diameter of, 60" drivers, and the boiler, which is larger.

**Class D.**   Standard Ten-wheel Freight Engine - 18" x 22" cylinders, and 54" drivers.

**Class E.**   Mountain Ten-wheel Freight Engine - a modification of class D, differing only in the drivers, which are 48" in diameter, and the boiler, which is larger.

**Class F.**   Standard Six-wheel Shifting Engine - 15" x 18" cylinders, with 44" drivers.

**Class G.**   Standard Light Passenger or Ballast Engine - 15" x 22" cylinders, with 55" drivers.

**Class H.**   Standard Six-wheel Shifting Engine with Tender – 15" x 22" cylinders, with 44" drivers.

By January 1, 1875, an additional two classes were added:

**Class C**   "Anthracite" Same as class C, with the exception of boiler and firebox, which are larger.

**Class Consolidation** – Ten-wheel Freight Engines – 20" x 24" cylinders, with eight driving wheels, 49" in diameter, built for anthracite coal, but now using soft coal.

**Note:** Many of the principal castings, such as driving boxes, eccentrics, eccentric straps, etc., are common to all the above classes.

The transition from one classification system to another took some time, even though the system in use was quite cumbersome. The classes in the *Photographs of Locomotives Typical of Each Class* continued for quite a while. The class A locomotives were first known as "First Class Passenger Engine like #421" The class A perpetuated the basic dimensions of the class #421, 17" x 24" cylinders, 66" drivers, and the photograph in the book was of #421. The class B had no representative photo in the book and was known as a "class B." The remaining classes were illustrated by photographs in the book and were so identified. The class C was identified as a class C, like #387. The photo of #387 is of a Baldwin built 4-4-0 with 60" drivers and 17" x 24" cylinders, built in June 1867 (c/n 1636). The others are shown by photos of engines of their respective class: the D like #168, the E like #218, the F like #440, and the class G like #247.

## COMPANIES BUILDING LOCOMOTIVES FOR THE PRR

In the cases of the Lambertville Shop, Bordentown Shop, Jersey City Shop, and West Philadelphia Shop, locomotives started before the PRR lease were completed under PRR ownership. New construction at these shops was terminated after the completion of the locomotives under construction.

**Chart 10**

### Locomotives Built New for the PRR, by Builder and Year

| Year | AMS | BLW | LLW | NJLM | NB | N-L | RN&S | RL&M | S&P | RW | SW |
|------|-----|-----|-----|------|----|-----|------|------|-----|----|----|
| 1848 |     | 2   |     |      |    |     |      |      |     |    |    |
| 1849 |     | 6   |     |      |    |     |      |      |     |    |    |
| 1850 |     | 11  |     |      | 1  |     |      |      |     |    |    |
| 1851 |     | 3   |     |      |    |     |      |      |     |    |    |
| 1852 |     | 16  |     |      |    |     |      |      | 1   |    | 2  |
| 1853 |     | 13  |     |      |    |     | 12   |      | 4   | 4  | 1  |
| 1854 |     | 17  |     |      |    |     | 10   |      | 7   | 2  |    |
| 1855 |     | 2   |     |      |    |     |      |      |     |    |    |
| 1856 |     | 7   |     |      |    |     | 2    |      | 3   | 5  |    |
| 1857 |     | 12  |     |      |    |     |      |      |     |    |    |
| 1858 |     |     |     |      |    |     | 1    |      |     |    |    |
| 1859 |     | 1   |     |      |    |     |      |      |     |    |    |
| 1860 |     |     | 1   |      |    |     | 3    |      |     |    |    |
| 1861 |     | 22  | 1   |      |    |     | 1    |      |     |    |    |
| 1862 |     | 27  |     |      |    |     | 9    | 4    |     |    |    |
| 1863 |     | 29  |     |      |    |     | 21   |      |     |    |    |
| 1864 |     | 36  |     |      |    |     | 2    |      |     |    |    |
| 1865 |     | 32  |     | 6    |    | 2   | 2    |      |     |    |    |
| 1866 |     | 32  |     |      |    |     |      |      |     |    |    |
| 1867 | 4   | 23  |     | 10   |    | 14  |      |      |     |    |    |
| 1868 | 7   | 21  |     |      |    |     |      |      |     |    |    |
| 1869 | 40  | *36 | #(6)|      |    |     |      |      |     |    |    |
| 1870 | 22  | 7   |     |      |    |     |      |      |     |    |    |
| 1871 | 38  |     |     |      |    |     |      |      |     |    |    |
| 1872 | 58  | 55  |     |      |    |     |      |      |     |    |    |
| 1873 | 68  | **82|     |      |    |     |      |      |     |    |    |
|      | 237 | 492 | 8   | 16   | 1  | 16  | 63   | 4    | 14  | 11 | 3  |

\*      "Last" non-standard locomotives were built by Baldwin.

\*\*    Four "experimental" non-standard 2-8-0's built by Baldwin.

\#      L.B. Tyng operated the Lancaster Locomotive Works during 1869-1870 and built six 4-6-0, (56", 18" x 22"), class D locomotives, which were immediately transferred to the Panhandle.

AMS   Altoona Machine Shop, Altoona, Pa.
BLW   Baldwin Locomotive Works, Philadelphia, Pa.
LLW   Lancaster Locomotive Works, Lancaster, Pa.
NJLM  New Jersey Locomotive & Machine Company, Paterson, N.J.
NB    Norris Brothers, Philadelphia, Pa.
N-L   Norris - Lancaster, Lancaster, Pa.
RN&S  Richard Norris & Son, Philadelphia, Pa.
RL&M  Rogers Locomotive & Machine Company, Paterson, N.J.
S&P   Smith & Perkins, Alexandria, Va.
RW   Ross Winans, Baltimore, Md.
SW   Seth Wilmarth (Union Iron Works), Boston, Ma.

# THE LOCOMOTIVE REGISTER
## CORRECTED TO JANUARY 1, 1874

The *Locomotive Register for January 1, 1874* represents only the locomotive stock of the Pennsylvania Railroad Company. The early locomotives acquired by the Company, with their wide variety of individual design and detail, were being replaced by the standard locomotives designed by the Mechanical Engineer's office at Altoona. Never again would the PRR roster contain such a mixture of builders and designs.

In the register contained herein, some locomotives listed are the third or fourth to hold a particular number. Quite a few new locomotives held PRR numbers for only a few months before being transferred (sold) to the P&E, PFt.W&C, or the PC&St.L, and were immediately replaced with new equipment.

## SOURCES

The locomotive register contained herein is not an official Company document. The date the Company published its first "official" register is uncertain. There were various locomotive lists held by motive power officials, or circulated among roundhouse foreman from time to time. There is evidence of the existence of a register for January 1, 1885, and the first register may have been published in 1880. The register books for Lines East were 3½" by 4⅝". Each page contained a block of 100 squares. Each square represented a number. There are ten locomotive numbers per row of squares and ten rows, for a total of 100 numbers per page. Pages had headings of 0 hundreds, 1 hundreds and so on. To find a locomotive #556 in the January 1, 1897 Register, for instance, you would turn to the 5 hundreds, go down 6 lines from 0 through 5 to the 50's line

and go over 7 squares from 0 through 6. There you would find #556 and read the following: Bald'n, DE, '72. Thus, #556 is held by a DE class 4-6-0 built by Baldwin in 1872. Where no builder is shown, the Altoona Machine Shop is understood. The Company continued to publish these registers for Lines East on a biannual basis until January 1, 1920, when they were discontinued. Lines West registers differed is size, and frequency of publication, and contained detailed specifications of each class.

The list of locomotives for January 1, 1874 contained in this book was compiled in February 1940 by the late Joseph D. Lovell of Hollidaysburg, Pa., from two small record books, bearing on the flyleaf the name G.W. Stratton, for many years the Master Mechanic at the Altoona Machine Shop. The first entries were apparently made about 1867. Replacement of locomotives during the following years was indicated in red ink. When Lovell copied the notebooks he added the builder's construction numbers. Some of the locomotives shown were known to have been Altoona rebuilds of locomotives built elsewhere. In such cases Lovell inserted the name of the original builder and "re-built Altoona" was noted. Lovell wrote that:

*... the following pages may contain errors and omissions. The purpose in compiling them, however was to record the information in the note books, rather than to make an authentic register.*

The Lovell material provided the basis for the register, which follows. Each number was checked with available Company records. The primary source was the *Record of Locomotives and Tenders*, large volumes measuring 16" x 21", with a page for each

number. (See **Bibliography**.) This record was kept in several hands over a period of years by clerks in the Motive Power Accountants Office. Each locomotive to hold a particular number is listed in vertical format, with specifications, rebuildings, renumberings, and final disposition. Further information was obtained from the *Pennsylvania Rail Road, Motive Power and Machinery Department, Register of Engines*. This hand-written record, entered on pre-printed pages, was corrected to February 1868. (See **Bibliography**.)

Since this register is a listing of the Company's equipment, the PRR records are treated as the primary source for dates and specifications. Where specifications differ from builder's lists this discrepancy may be due to a rebuilding by the PRR. The dates shown are the dates the PRR considered the locomotive to have originally come upon the road. Firebox renewals were usually shown in the PRR records. While these original Company records are not complete and there are omissions in specifications and dispositions, the list that follows is what the Company itself understood and listed its equipment to be.

## THE PHOTOGRAPHS

The images in this book are mainly official photographs taken by the PRR photographer at Altoona. They were originally contained in a book supplied to enginehouse foremen and various motive power officials, *A Collection of Photographs of Locomotives, Typical of Each Class on the Pennsylvania Railroad at This Date, Pennsylvania Railroad Company, Motive Power Department, May 1st, 1868*, which we have discussed at length previously. Original builders photographs and other PRR official photographs supplement them. Those in this book came for the most part from two albums assembled by the late Harvey Eldridge. Eldridge tried to locate at least one photo of each class of PRR locomotive. The early non-standard locos were grouped in numerical order in Volumes H and I. Eldridge acquired these photos over a period of years from the PRR.

## ARRANGEMENT OF THE REGISTER
### Number

A locomotive register is at best only a list of numbers assigned to equipment on a particular date. Since a locomotive roster is a dynamic and ever-changing thing, there are situations when there are disagreements between a register and other records which list equipment in use. In several instances the Stratton register shows a number vacant when other records show the number occupied. These situations are noted.

Numbers used: #'s 1-632, 634-795, 801-879, 906-953
Numbers vacant: #'s 633, 796 - 800, 879 - 905
920 numbers used, 33 numbers vacant
Total locomotives: 920

### Type

The "typing" of locomotives in the familiar Whyte classification, in the three number system showing engine truck, drivers and trailing truck was not formalized until 1900. In the Stratton register and other early PRR records locomotives were classified as Passenger, Freight, and Shifting. The standard classes, introduced in 1868, were identified by letters A through G with the later addition of H and C anth. The Whyte classification system is used in the following register to indicate the type of locomotive, as could best be determined from the information available.

As of January 1, 1874, the Following Types and Classes Were on the Road:

### NON-STANDARD CLASSES

| TYPE | QUANTITY |
|---|---|
| 0-4-0 | 5 |
| 0-4-0T | 6 |
| 0-6-0 | 0 |
| 0-6-0T | 30 |
| 2-2-2-0 | 1 |
| 2-4-0T | 1 |
| 2-6-0 | 48 |
| 2-8-0 | 4 |
| 4-2-0 | 2 |
| 4-4-0 | 242 |
| 4-4-0T | 1 |
| 4-6-0 | 160 |
| Total | 500 |

### STANDARD CLASSES

| CLASS | TYPE | QUANTITY |
|---|---|---|
| A | 4-4-0 | 13 |
| B | 4-4-0 | 4 |
| C | 4-4-0 | 36 |
| C anth | 4-4-0 | 12 |
| D | 4-6-0 | 221 |
| E | 4-6-0 | 68 |
| F | 0-6-0T | 24 |
| G | 4-4-0 | 18 |
| H | 0-6-0 | 24 |
| Total | | 420 |

### Builders Represented on the Road on January 1, 1874

The builder is the original builder of the particular locomotive, as indicated by the Stratton list and corrected by other records. The information on purchased or leased lines is not as complete as for locomotives purchased or built by the PRR itself. The builders are shown as follows:

| Abb. | Builder | Quantity on Road |
|---|---|---|
| AMS | PRR, Altoona Machine Shop | 234 |
| BLW | Baldwin Locomotive Works | 425 |
| B D | Belvidere Delaware, Lambertville Shop | 18 |
| BS | PRR, Bordentown Shop (ex-C&A) | 2 |
| C&A | Camden & Amboy, Bordentown Shop | 45 |
| DC&C | Danforth, Cooke & Company | 32 |
| JCS | PRR, Jersey City Shop (ex-NJRR&T) | 1 |
| JCLW | Jersey City Locomotive Works | 4 |
| LS | PRR, Lambertville Shop (ex-B D) | 1 |
| LLW | Lancaster Locomotive Works | 11 |
| NJL&M | New Jersey Locomotive & Machine Company | 25 |
| NJRT | NJRR&T, Jersey City Shop | 28 |
| NB | Norris Brothers | 6 |
| N-L | Norris, Lancaster | 13 |
| RN&S | Richard Norris & Son | 33 |
| RS | Robert Stephenson (England) | 1 |
| RL&M | Rogers Locomotive & Machine Company | 22 |
| RW | Ross Winans | 9 |
| S&P | Smith & Perkins | 5 |
| TL&M | Trenton Locomotive & Machine Mfg. Company | 4 |
| WPS | PRR, West Philadelphia Shop (ex-Phila. & Trenton) | 1 |
| | Total | 920 |

### Date

The date built is taken from various sources and corresponds to the original date given in the list of consecutive construction numbers of the locomotive's builder, or, where these dates are not available, the date when the locomotive came upon the railroad. Where these dates are in conflict with other lists and information it is usually for locomotives built at the end or the beginning of the month. The Put-On-Road date could differ from several days to several weeks from the builder's date. The builder's date itself might be the date finished, date first steamed, or the date sold.

## Construction Number

The Stratton list and other PRR sources do not contain construction numbers. These were added to the Stratton list by Lovell on his original copy and corrected by consulting various published and private materials.

## Class

The letter class is used to designate standard PRR-design locomotives drawn up beginning in 1867 and introduced into the locomotive stock in July 1868.

| | | |
|---|---|---|
| A | 4-4-0 | Passenger |
| B | 4-4-0 | Mountain Passenger Helper |
| C | 4-4-0 | Fast Freight and Passenger |
| D | 4-6-0 | Freight |
| E | 4-6-0 | Mountain Freight |
| F | 0-6-0T | Shifter |
| G | 4-4-0 | Light Passenger and Ballast Engine |

Added to the original classes before January 1, 1874 were:

| | | |
|---|---|---|
| H | 0-6-0 | Shifter (with tender) |
| C anth | 4-4-0 | Passenger (for burning anthracite) |

This system of classification was in effect until June 1897.

**Chart 11**

**Specifications for Standard Locomotives**

| Class | Type | Dr., in. | Cylinders, in. | BP, psig | BT | Grate, sq.ft. | Wt/WO. Lbs. | TE, lbs. |
|---|---|---|---|---|---|---|---|---|
| A | 4-4-0 | 68* | 17x24 | 125 | wt/cb | 16.10 | 77,770 | *10,200 |
| B | 4-4-0 | 62 | 18x24 | 125 | wt/cb | 17.60 | 80,500 | 12,540 |
| C | 4-4-0 | 62 | 17x24 | 125 | wt/cb | 17.60 | 79,100 | 11,190 |
| C anth | 4-4-0 | 62 | 17x24 | 125 | wt/cb | 29.13 | 81,800 | 11,190 |
| D | 4-6-0 | 56 | 18x22 | 125 | wt/cb | 14.50 | 84,300 | 12,730 |
| DE | 4-6-0 | 50 | 18x22 | 125 | wt/cb | 14.50 | 82,590 | 14,250 |
| E | 4-6-0 | 50 | 18x22 | 125 | wt/cb | 16.34 | 84,800 | 14,250 |
| F | 0-6-0T | 44 | 15x18 | 125 | st/cb | 10.70 | 71,300 | 9,200 |
| G | 4-4-0 | 56 | 15x22 | 125 | st/cb | 13.30 | 65,200 | 8,840 |
| H | 0-6-0 | 44 | 15x22 | 125 | st/cb | 13.20 | 64,700 | 11,250 |

BP = Boiler Pressure.
BT = Boiler type: wt/cb = wagon top with crown bars; st/cb = straight top with crown bars.
Grate = grate area of firebox.
Wt/WO = weight of the locomotive in working order.
TE = tractive effort.

* Some class A had 62" drivers; others were equipped with a straight boiler.

## Rebuilt

"Rebuilt" indicates a major change in the locomotive such as a change in wheel arrangement, driver size, cylinder size, etc. Information on rebuilding is far from complete. In some instances rebuilt locomotives are listed as new equipment in the PRR records.

The rebuilding is shown by listing the rebuilding date. The original dimensions of the locomotive are shown in the footnotes immediately following the roster.

## Drivers: Number and Diameter

PRR records show the number of drivers and diameter in inches for all non-standard locomotives. Where the information here disagrees with other listings, the discrepancy may be due to rebuilding. The PRR records show a variety of minor dimensional differences over a period of time. The dimensions shown here are the ones that appear in the *Record of Locomotives & Tenders* for the standard locomotives.

DE: indicates Class D locomotives rebuilt with 50" drivers and reclassified DE.

## Cylinders: Bore & Stroke

Discrepancies in cylinder bore and stroke may be due to rebuilding.

## Disposition

This information shows how a number was made vacant. Numbers were made vacant by scrapping, renumbering or sale. Equipment shown renumbered was transferred to leased or controlled lines (P&E, PFt.W&C, PC&St.L, and so forth) and was actually sold to those lines. The term "sold" is used for the sale of a locomotive to non-controlled and non-leased railroads or to used-equipment dealers and industrial concerns.

**c/u** Cut up, scrapped

**don** Donated

**ren** Renumbered to a leased or controlled railroad.

**so** Sold to a non-controlled, non-leased railroad, or to a used-equipment dealer or industrial concern for further operation.

**sg** Machinery scrapped and the locomotive boiler used as a steam generator or stationary boiler. The location where the boiler was installed is shown.

**TO**

The railroad, equipment dealer or industrial concern a particular locomotive was sold to:

A&RM — Alexander & Rich Mountain RR
AC&C — Altoona Coal & Coke, Altoona, Pa.
AHK — Albert H. King, Bordentown, N.J. (equipment dealer)
AWT — Auto Water Tank
B — Brackley
B&SRR — Bloomsburg & Sullivan RR
B&T — Brown & Thomas (equipment dealer)
BM&JHS — B.M.&J.H. Schanley (equipment dealer)
CB — Coxe Bros.: Delaware, Susquehanna & Schuylkill
C&H — Cooper & Hewitt
C&MR — Cumberland & Maurice River
CPa&W — Central Pennsylvania & Western
CPG — Charleroi Plate Glass
EH — E. Hardman
EHW — E.H. Wilson & Company (equipment dealer)
ERR — Edgewood RR
F&JAgRR — Freehold & Jamestown Agricultural RR (later PRR)
FHC — F.H. Clements

FMH — F.M. Hicks & Company (equipment dealer)
HB&Co — H. Bayard & Company
HCM — Hampton Coal Mines
JGB — J.G. Brill Coast Ry
JHB — J.H. Brakeley
JTD — J.T. Dyer Quarry Company
JTG — J.T. Gardner - equipment dealer
JW — J. Whitehead
KICo — Kemble Iron Company
L&RNG — Lancaster & Reading Narrow Gauge RR (not narrow gauge)
LEE&SW — Lake Erie, Evansville & Southwestern RR
LVRR — Ligonier Valley RR
NM — Nona Mills
NYE — New York Equipment Company (equipment dealer)
PCRR — Perry County RR
R — Ross
R&D — Richmond & Danville RR
S&A — Shenango & Allegheny RR
SC — Standard Coal Company
SCG — S.C. Glading (equipment dealer)
SI — Smithsonian Institution

SRR — Strasburg RR
US&S — Union Switch & Signal Company
UT — Union Transportation Company
WC — Wm. Collier

The leased or controlled lines that equipment was renumbered (sold) to:

B&P — Baltimore & Potomac Railroad
B D — Belvidere  Delaware Railroad
C&A — Camden & Atlantic Railroad
C&MV — Cincinnati & Muskingum Valley Railway
CC&IC — Columbus, Chicago & Indiana Central Railway
GR&I — Grand Rapids & Indiana Railroad
NCR — Northern Central Railway
NYP&N — New York, Philadelphia & Norfolk Railroad
P&BC — Philadelphia & Baltimore Central Railroad
P&E — Philadelphia & Erie Railroad
PC&St.L — Pittsburgh, Cincinnati & St. Louis Railway
PFt.W&C — Pittsburgh, Ft. Wayne & Chicago Railway
PW&B — Philadelphia, Wilmington & Baltimore Railroad
St.LV&TH — St. Louis, Vandalia & Terre Haute Railroad
TH&I — Terre Haute & Indianapolis Railroad
WJ — West Jersey Railroad

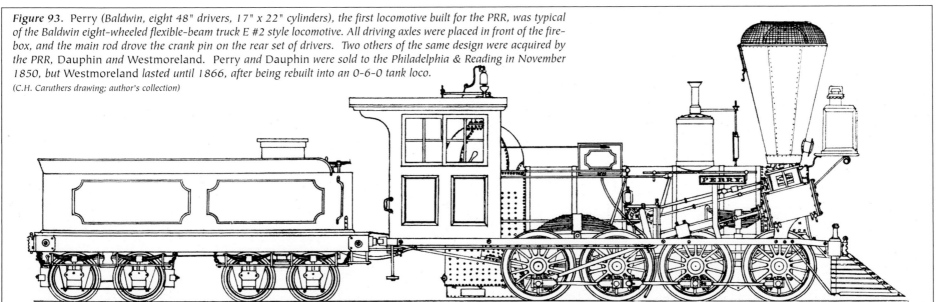

*Figure 93.* Perry *(Baldwin, eight 48" drivers, 17" x 22" cylinders), the first locomotive built for the PRR, was typical of the Baldwin eight-wheeled flexible-beam truck E #2 style locomotive. All driving axles were placed in front of the firebox, and the main rod drove the crank pin on the rear set of drivers. Two others of the same design were acquired by the PRR,* Dauphin *and* Westmoreland. Perry *and* Dauphin *were sold to the Philadelphia & Reading in November 1850, but* Westmoreland *lasted until 1866, after being rebuilt into an 0-6-0 tank loco.*
(C.H. Caruthers drawing; author's collection)

# LOCOMOTIVES OF THE PENNSYLVANIA RAILROAD as of January 1, 1874

**Attention:** A loco number with gray background indicates that there is additional information on this loco at the end of the chart.

| No. | Type | Builder | Date | C/N | Class | Rebuilt | Drivers, in. | Cylinder Bore & Stroke, in. | Disp. | Date | To | Notes |
|---|---|---|---|---|---|---|---|---|---|---|---|---|
| 1 | 4-6-0 | BLW | 9/1861 | 1009 | | | 48 | 18x22 | so | 4/1881 | WC | (Fig. 80) |
| 2 | 4-6-0 | BLW | 1/1865 | 1329 | | | 54 | 18x22 | c/u | 1/1880 | | Renumbered from 294, 1865. |
| 3 | 4-6-0 | BLW | 3/1861 | 94 | | | 50 | 18x22 | so | 4/1881 | WC | |
| 4 | 4-6-0 | AMS | 6/1869 | 25 | D | DE | | | ren | 11/1881 | CC&IC 456 | |
| 5 | 4-6-0 | BLW | 1/1866 | 1446 | | | 54 | 18x22 | c/u | 1875 | | (Fig. 81) |
| 6 | 4-6-0 | BLW | 12/1864 | 1312 | | | 54 | 18x22 | so | 8/1883 | SCB | |
| 7 | 4-6-0 | AMS | 4/1872 | 126 | E | | | | ren | 1/1891 | PRR 96 | |
| 8 | 4-4-0 | BLW | 11/1849 | 370 | | | 54 | 14x20 | c/u | 2/1876 | | *Huntingdon* |
| 9 | 4-6-0 | AMS | 7/1870 | 61 | E | | | | ren | 12/1881 | St.LV&TH 153 | |
| 10 | 4-6-0 | BLW | 11/1864 | 1313 | | | 54 | 18x22 | c/u | 1878 | | |
| 11 | 4-4-0 | AMS | 8/1869 | 34 | C | | | | ren | 10/1887 | C&A 503 | |
| 12 | 4-6-0 | AMS | 5/1870 | 56 | E | | | | ren | 3/1879 | PRR 1048 | |
| 13 | 4-4-0 | AMS | 4/1869 | 16 | A | | 68 | | ren | 12/1882 | NCR 111 | (Fig. 60) |
| 14 | 4-6-0 | N-L | 2/1867 | | | | 46 | 18x22 | c/u | 1879 | | (Fig. 56) |
| 15 | 4-6-0 | AMS | 12/1872 | 169 | E | | | | ren | 5/1886 | WJ 7 | |
| 16 | 4-4-0 | BLW | 9/1850 | 389 | | | 54 | 15x20 | c/u | 2/1874 | | *Columbia* |
| 17 | 4-4-0 | AMS | 11/1868 | 10 | A | | 68 | | ren | 12/1884 | WJ 29 | |
| 18 | 4-4-0 | BLW | 10/1850 | 390 | | | 54 | 15x20 | c/u | 3/1879 | | *Elk* |
| 19 | 4-6-0 | AMS | 4/1872 | 127 | E | | | | ren | 3/1879 | PRR 1065 | (Figs. 62 & 92) |
| 20 | 4-6-0 | AMS | 5/1872 | 128 | E | | | | ren | 11/1881 | St.LV&TH 117 | |
| 21 | 4-4-0 | AMS | 8/1869 | 35 | C | | | | so | 1/1889 | EHW | |
| 22 | 4-4-0 | AMS | 5/1872 | 129 | E | | | | ren | 3/1895 | C&MV 801 | |
| 23 | 0-4-0T | BLW | 5/1867 | 1629 | | | 48 | 14x22 | so | 10/1885 | EHW | |
| 24 | 0-4-0T | BLW | 5/1867 | 1631 | | | 48 | 14x22 | c/u | 12/1887 | | (Fig. 57) |
| 25 | 4-6-0 | AMS | 5/1872 | 130 | E | | | | ren | 4/1879 | NCR 36 | |
| 26 | 4-6-0 | AMS | 2/1873 | 170 | E | | | | so | 5/1890 | EHW | |
| 27 | 4-4-0 | AMS | 12/1868 | 11 | A | | 68 | | ren | 9/1885 | WJ 17 | |
| 28 | 4-4-0 | AMS | 11/1872 | 152 | A | | 68 | | ren | 4/1884 | WJ 28 | |
| 29 | 4-4-0 | AMS | 12/1870 | 72 | G | | | | so | 2/1890 | EHW | ex-PRR 367 |
| 30 | 4-4-0 | BLW | 6/1868 | 1751 | | | 60 | 14x24 | c/u | 2/1888 | | |
| 31 | 4-4-0 | AMS | 10/1868 | 9 | A | | 68 | | c/u | 11/1893 | | |
| 32 | 4-4-0 | BLW | 4/1852 | 471 | | | 60 | 15x20 | c/u | 9/1874 | | *Pike* |
| 33 | 4-4-0 | BLW | 5/1852 | 478 | | | 60 | 15x20 | c/u | 5/1875 | | *Union* |
| 34 | 0-6-0T | BLW | 7/1867 | 1646 | | | 44 | 15x18 | so | 9/1889 | EHW | (Fig. 101) |
| 35 | 0-6-0T | BLW | 7/1867 | 1647 | | | 44 | 15x18 | c/u | 5/1873 | | |

| No. | Type | Bldr. | Date | C/N | Class | Rebuilt | Driv., in. | Cyl., in. | Disp. | Date | To | Notes |
|---|---|---|---|---|---|---|---|---|---|---|---|---|
| 36 | 0-6-0T | BLW | 7/1867 | 1648 | | | 44 | 15x18 | c/u | 7/1887 | | |
| 37 | 0-6-0T | BLW | 7/1867 | 1649 | | | 44 | 15x18 | so | 1/1887 | AHK | |
| 38 | 4-6-0 | BLW | 10/1852 | 497 | | 10/1867 | 48 | 18x22 | c/u | 3/1877 | | Mercer |
| 39 | 4-6-0 | BLW | 10/1852 | 499 | | 9/1867 | 48 | 18x22 | so | 12/1882 | EHW | Berks |
| 40 | 4-6-0 | AMS | 5/1870 | 57 | E | | | | ren | 10/1890 | PRR 3009 | |
| 41 | 4-6-0 | S&P | 12/1852 | | | 1862 | 44 | 17x22 | c/u | 4/1873 | | Latrobe (Fig. 105) |
| 42 | 0-6-0T | AMS | 11/1869 | 46 | F | | | | c/u | 11/1896 | | (Fig. 107) |
| 43 | 4-6-0 | S&P | 12/1852 | | | ? | 44 | 17x22 | c/u | 3/1874 | | Altoona (Fig. 19) |
| 44 | 2-6-0 | BLW | 11/1857 | 787 | | 6/1867 | 44 | 18x20 | c/u | 1/1876 | | |
| 45 | 4-4-0 | AMS | 9/1869 | 36 | C | | | | ren | 7/1883 | PW&B 18 | |
| 46 | 2-6-0 | BLW | 1/1853 | 508 | | 5/1867 | 48 | 18x24 | so | 3/1887 | B&T | Lancaster (Fig. 109) |
| 47 | 2-6-0 | BLW | 1/1853 | 509 | | 12/1867 | 48 | 18x24 | c/u | 3/1877 | | Schuylkill |
| 48 | 0-6-0T | AMS | 12/1869 | 47 | F | | | | c/u | 9/1891 | | (Fig. 66) |
| 49 | 4-6-0 | AMS | 7/1870 | 65 | E | | | | ren | 1/1880 | GR&I 35 | |
| 50 | 2-6-0 | RW | 2/1853 | | | 12/1866 | 48 | 19x24 | c/u | 11/1881 | | Vulcan |
| 51 | 2-6-0 | RW | 2/1853 | | | 9/1866 | 48 | 19x24 | c/u | 4/1886 | | Cyclops |
| 52 | 2-6-0 | RW | 4/1853 | | | 8/1864 | 48 | 19x24 | c/u | 8/1879 | | Thor |
| 53 | 4-6-0 | BLW | 9/1865 | 1406 | | | 54 | 18x22 | so | 2/1887 | B&T | |
| 54 | 4-4-0 | AMS | 9/1868 | 7 | A | | 68 | | so | 2/1892 | EHW | |
| 55 | 4-4-0 | AMS | 11/1872 | 153 | A | | 68 | | ren | 6/1885 | WJ 14 | |
| 56 | 4-4-0 | AMS | 5/1869 | 17 | A | | 68 | | c/u | 6/1891 | | |
| 57 | 0-6-0T | AMS | 12/1869 | 48 | F | | | | so | 9/1889 | EHW | |
| 58 | 2-6-0 | RN&S | 6/1853 | 642 | | 12/1867 | 48 | 18x24 | so | 5/1883 | EHW | Youghiogheny |
| 59 | 4-4-0 | RN&S | 6/1853 | 643 | | | 60 | 16x24 | c/u | 2/1882 | | Monongahela (Fig. 112) |
| 60 | 4-4-0 | BLW | 6/1863 | 1140 | | | 66 | 17x24 | c/u | 1/1876 | | (Fig. 91) |
| 61 | 4-4-0 | BLW | 6/1863 | 1142 | | | 66 | 17x24 | so | 3/1887 | B&T | |
| 62 | 4-6-0 | AMS | 1/1869 | 12 | D | 11/1878 | DE | | ren | 1/1879 | PC&St.L 32 | |
| 63 | 4-6-0 | BLW | 9/1864 | 1284 | | | 54 | 18x22 | c/u | 5/1875 | | |
| 64 | 4-6-0 | BLW | 9/1865 | 1407 | | | 54 | 18x22 | c/u | 5/1875 | | |
| 65 | 4-6-0 | AMS | 3/1869 | 14 | D | ? | DE | | so | 5/1892 | EHW | |
| 66 | 4-6-0 | BLW | 8/1872 | 2864 | D | | | | ren | 4/1874 | PRR 1151 | |
| 67 | 4-4-0 | BLW | 9/1853 | 548 | | | 54 | 17x22 | c/u | 5/1875 | | Bucks |
| 68 | 0-6-0T | AMS | 12/1869 | 49 | F | | | | c/u | 8/1892 | | |
| 69 | 4-4-0 | BLW | 9/1853 | 550 | | | 55 | 17x22 | c/u | 5/1875 | | Carbon |
| 70 | 4-4-0 | BLW | 9/1853 | 551 | | | 54 | 17x22 | c/u | 3/1877 | | Chester |
| 71 | 2-6-0 | RN&S | 10/1853 | 649 | | 3/1868 | 48 | 18x24 | c/u | 4/1888 | | Loyalhanna |
| 72 | 4-4-0 | BLW | 10/1853 | 553 | | | 54 | 17x22 | c/u | 5/1875 | | Delaware |
| 73 | 4-4-0 | RN&S | 2/1854 | | | 5/1862 | 60 | 16x24 | c/u | 1/1885 | | Renumbered from 86. |
| 74 | 4-6-0 | S&P | 10/1853 | | | 2/1868 | 48 | 18x24 | c/u | 2/1874 | | Pittsburgh |
| 75 | 4-6-0 | AMS | 3/1869 | 15 | D | | | | so | 5/1892 | EHW | (Fig. 59) |
| 76 | 4-6-0 | BLW | 9/1872 | 2914 | D | 8/1880 | DE | | ren | 12/1880 | CC&IC 331 | |
| 77 | 4-6-0 | S&P | 12/1853 | | | 1865 | 44 | 17x22 | c/u | 12/1874 | | Johnstown (Fig. 115) |
| 78 | 4-6-0 | BLW | 10/1872 | 2957 | D | | | | c/u | 1/1893 | | |

| No. | Type | Bldr. | Date | C/N | Class | Rebuilt | Driv., in. | Cyl., in. | Disp. | Date | To | Notes |
|---|---|---|---|---|---|---|---|---|---|---|---|---|
| 79 | 4-6-0 | AMS | 8/1868 | 5 | D | | | | c/u | 2/1892 | | |
| 80 | 4-4-0 | BLW | 6/1863 | 1147 | | | 66 | 17x24 | c/u | 5/1878 | | |
| 81 | 2-6-0 | RN&S | 1/1854 | | | 6/1868 | 48 | 18x24 | so | 6/1882 | EHW | *Warrior Ridge* |
| 82 | 2-6-0 | S&P | 1/1854 | | | | 44 | 17x22 | c/u | 4/1874 | | *Bolivar* |
| 83 | 4-6-0 | AMS | 12/1871 | 110 | E | | | | c/u | 2/1894 | | |
| 84 | 2-6-0 | RN&S | 1/1854 | | | 7/1868 | 48 | 18x24 | so | 3/1887 | B&T | *Mahoney* |
| 85 | 4-4-0 | RN&S | 1/1854 | | | 12/1865 | 66 | 16x24 | c/u | 11/1875 | | *Nescopeck* (Fig. 49) |
| 86 | 0-6-0T | AMS | 11/1869 | 50 | F | | | | so | 4/1892 | K I Company | |
| 87 | 4-6-0 | AMS | 8/1868 | 6 | D | | | | so | 4/1891 | EHW | |
| 88 | 2-6-0 | RW | 2/1854 | | | 11/1867 | 48 | 19x24 | c/u | 7/1884 | | *Mountaineer* |
| 89 | 4-4-0 | AMS | 11/1870 | 68 | G | | | | c/u | 12/1892 | | *(Fig. 71)* |
| 90 | 4-6-0 | BLW | 5/1863 | 1131 | | 1/1869 | 54 | 18x22 | so | 7/1879 | WC | |
| 91 | 2-6-0 | RW | 2/1854 | | | 5/1867 | 48 | 19x24 | c/u | 2/1878 | | *Logan* (Fig. 88) |
| 92 | 0-4-0T | BLW | 3/1866 | 1474 | | | 48 | 14x22 | c/u | 4/1887 | | |
| 93 | 4-6-0 | BLW | 11/1864 | 1285 | | | 54 | 18x22 | c/u | 5/1875 | | |
| 94 | 2-6-0 | BLW | 2/1854 | 573 | | 12/1865 | 48 | 19x24 | c/u | 8/1879 | | *Quaker City* (Fig. 44) |
| 95 | 2-6-0 | BLW | 3/1854 | 574 | | 12/1865 | 48 | 19x24 | c/u | 1/1880 | | *Iron City* (Fig 117) |
| 96 | 0-4-0 | BLW | 7/1866 | 1495 | | | 48 | 14x22 | so | 11/1890 | BM&JHS | (Fig. 119) |
| 97 | 4-6-0 | AMS | 6/1869 | 26 | D | ? | DE | | ren | 9/1879 | CC&IC 304 | |
| 98 | 4-6-0 | AMS | 7/1870 | 66 | D | ? | DE | | ren | 12/1881 | CC&IC 457 | |
| 99 | 4-6-0 | AMS | 3/1869 | 27 | E | | | | ren | 4/1879 | PRR 1075 | |
| 100 | 4-6-0 | AMS | 2/1873 | 171 | E | | | | ren | 9/1889 | WJ 9 | |
| 101 | 4-4-0 | AMS | 11/1868 | 11-a | | | 62 | 17x24 | ren | 3/1895 | C&IE | (Fig. 120A & 120B) |
| 102 | 4-4-0 | BLW | 3/1854 | 582 | | | 54 | 17x22 | c/u | 5/1877 | | *Montour* |
| 103 | 4-4-0 | BLW | 4/1854 | 584 | | | 54 | 17x22 | c/u | 1/1880 | | *Monroe* |
| 104 | 4-4-0 | BLW | 4/1854 | 585 | | | 54 | 17x22 | c/u | 5/1878 | | *Northampton* |
| 105 | 4-4-0 | BLW | 4/1854 | 586 | | | 54 | 17x22 | c/u | 5/1878 | | *Perry* |
| 106 | 4-4-0 | AMS | 6/1869 | 28 | C | | | | ren | 7/1883 | PW&B 34 | |
| 107 | 4-6-0 | BLW | 9/1864 | 1286 | | | 54 | 18x22 | c/u | 7/1880 | | |
| 108 | 0-6-0T | BLW | 9/1865 | 1409 | | | 44 | 15x18 | c/u | 8/1879 | | (Fig. 53) |
| 109 | 4-6-0 | BLW | 11/1864 | 1315 | | | 54 | 18x22 | so | 8/1880 | EHW | |
| 110 | 0-6-0T | BLW | 12/1863 | 1197 | | | 44 | 15x18 | c/u | 1/1876 | | (Fig. 85) |
| 111 | 0-6-0T | BLW | 12/1863 | 1199 | | | 44 | 15x18 | so | 8/1890 | EHW | (Fig. 121) |
| 112 | 0-6-0T | BLW | 1/1865 | 1413 | | | 44 | 15x18 | c/u | 1/1885 | | |
| 113 | 4-4-0 | BLW | 10/1854 | 620 | | | 54 | 17x22 | so | 10/1874 | ERR | *Warren* |
| 114 | 4-4-0 | BLW | 10/1854 | 622 | | | 54 | 17x22 | c/u | 3/1877 | | *Wayne* |
| 115 | 4-6-0 | BLW | 12/1864 | 1317 | | | 54 | 18x22 | c/u | 1/1876 | | |
| 116 | 4-6-0 | BLW | 1/1866 | 1448 | | | 54 | 18x22 | c/u | 1/1880 | | |
| 117 | 4-6-0 | BLW | 5/1855 | 642 | | | 48 | 19x22 | c/u | 2/1878 | | *Black Oak* |
| 118 | 4-6-0 | AMS | 12/1872 | 166 | E | | | | c/u | 2/1894 | | |
| 119 | 2-6-0 | RW | 1/1856 | | | 1/1865 | 48 | 19x24 | c/u | 8/1879 | | *Corn Planter* (Fig. 122) |
| 120 | 4-6-0 | BLW | 1/1856 | 679 | | | 48 | 19x22 | c/u | 1/1876 | | *Blue Ridge* (Fig. 26) |
| 121 | 2-6-0 | RW | 1/1856 | | | 6/1866 | 48 | 19x24 | c/u | 5/1878 | | *Red Jacket* |

| No. | Type | Bldr. | Date | C/N | Class | Rebuilt | Driv., in. | Cyl., in. | Disp. | Date | To | Notes |
|---|---|---|---|---|---|---|---|---|---|---|---|---|
| 122 | 4-6-0 | AMS | 12/1871 | 111 | E | | | | c/u | 2/1900 | | |
| 123 | 4-6-0 | AMS | 5/1869 | 22 | | | | | c/u | 2/1894 | | |
| 124 | 2-6-0 | RW | 2/1856 | | | 2/1865 | 48 | 19x24 | c/u | 1/1880 | | Oneida |
| 125 | 0-6-0T | AMS | 12/1869 | 51 | F | | | | so | 7/1891 | EHW | |
| 126 | 4-4-0 | BLW | 8/1854 | 605 | | | 54 | 17x22 | c/u | 5/1875 | | Renumbered from 110, c.1863. |
| 127 | 4-4-0 | AMS | 9/1867 | 3 | | | 60 | 17x24 | so | 11/1886 | EHW | |
| 128 | 4-6-0 | AMS | 6/1870 | 62 | E | | | | c/u | 10/1893 | | |
| 129 | 0-6-0T | AMS | 12/1869 | 40 | F | | | | c/u | 12/1892 | | |
| 130 | 2-6-0 | RW | 4/1856 | | | 6/1867 | 48 | 19x24 | c/u | 11/1881 | | Mohawk |
| 131 | 4-6-0 | AMS | 4/1871 | 74 | E | | | | so | 12/1894 | NYE | |
| 132 | 4-6-0 | AMS | 5/1869 | 23 | E | | | | ren | 5/1886 | WJ 11 | |
| 133 | 4-4-0 | AMS | 10/1868 | 8 | A | | 68 | | ren | 6/1885 | WJ 13 | |
| 134 | 4-4-0 | BLW | 12/1856 | 731 | | | 66 | 15x24 | c/u | 5/1875 | | Tiger (Fig. 125) |
| 135 | 4-4-0 | BLW | 12/1856 | 736 | | | 66 | 16x24 | c/u | 5/1875 | | Leopard (Fig. 83) |
| 136 | 4-4-0 | AMS | 4/1869 | 18 | B | | | | so | 10/1895 | JGB | |
| 137 | 4-6-0 | BLW | 11/1864 | 1304 | | | 54 | 18x22 | c/u | 5/1873 | | (Fig. 126) |
| 138 | 4-6-0 | BLW | 11/1864 | 1305 | | | 54 | 18x22 | c/u | 3/1881 | | |
| 139 | 4-4-0 | BLW | 7/1857 | 770 | | | 54 | 17x22 | c/u | 5/1875 | | (Fig. 29) |
| 140 | 0-6-0T | BLW | 4/1863 | 1123 | | | 44 | 15x18 | c/u | 1/1880 | | Consolidation (Fig. 127) |
| 141 | 4-6-0 | BLW | 9/1861 | 1012 | | | 48 | 18x22 | c/u | 2/1878 | | |
| 142 | 4-4-0 | AMS | 1/1867 | 1 | | | 60 | 16x24 | ren | 6/1882 | PRR 3001 | (Fig. 51) |
| 143 | 0-4-0T | BLW | 7/1862 | 1068 | | | 36 | 11x16 | so | 6/1891 | EHW | (Fig. 128) |
| 144 | 4-6-0 | AMS | 4/1871 | 75 | E | | | | c/u | 2/1894 | | |
| 145 | 4-6-0 | AMS | 7/1870 | 63 | E | | | | ren | 8/1885 | NCR 50 | |
| 146 | 4-6-0 | AMS | 3/1872 | 122 | | | | | c/u | 11/1893 | | |
| 147 | 0-6-0T | AMS | 12/1869 | 41 | F | | | | out | 9/1892 | | |
| 148 | 4-4-0 | AMS | 6/1867 | 2 | | | 60 | 17x24 | so | 12/1882 | EHW | (Fig. 52) |
| 149 | 4-4-0 | AMS | 4/1869 | 19 | B | | | | c/u | 11/1893 | | |
| 150 | 4-4-0 | AMS | 2/1870 | 52 | A | | 62 | | c/u | 8/1891 | | |
| 151 | 4-4-0 | NB | 12/1849 | | | | 54 | 12x24 | c/u | 2/1874 | | Swatara |
| 152 | 4-4-0 | AMS | 10/1872 | 154 | C | | | | ren | 11/1881 | CC&IC 463 | |
| 153 | 4-4-0 | AMS | 10/1870 | 69 | G | | | | c/u | 4/1891 | | |
| 154 | 4-6-0 | BLW | 8/1868 | 1744 | D | | | | c/u | 4/1891 | | |
| 155 | 4-4-0 | AMS | 6/1869 | 29 | C | | | | so | 10/1891 | PCRR | |
| 156 | 4-4-0 | BLW | 4/1859 | 847 | | | 66 | 15x24 | c/u | 3/1877 | | (Fig. 30) |
| 157 | 4-4-0 | AMS | 12/1870 | 73 | G | | | | c/u | 9/1892 | | ex PRR 437 |
| 158 | 0-6-0T | BLW | 5/1866 | 1488 | | | 44 | 15x18 | c/u | 4/1887 | | |
| 159 | 4-4-0 | NJLM | 6/1853 | | | | 60 | 15x22 | c/u | 3/1877 | | Keystone |
| 160 | 4-4-0 | NJLM | 7/1853 | | | | 60 | 15x22 | c/u | 4/1887 | | Conowingo |
| 161 | 4-4-0 | AMS | 5/1869 | 21 | D | | | | so | 5/1892 | EHW | |
| 162 | 4-4-0 | NJLM | 5/1853 | | | | 60 | 15x22 | c/u | 7/1884 | | Minnesota |
| 163 | 4-4-0 | AMS | 10/1870 | 70 | G | | | | so | 10/1894 | EHW | |
| 164 | 4-4-0 | NJLM | 9/1853 | | | | 60 | 16x22 | c/u | 6/1875 | | Clinton |

| No. | Type | Bldr. | Date | C/N | Class | Rebuilt | Driv., in. | Cyl., in. | Disp. | Date | To | Notes |
|-----|------|-------|------|-----|-------|---------|-----------|-----------|-------|------|-----|-------|
| 165 | 4-4-0 | NJLM | 9/1853 | | | | 66 | 16x20 | c/u | 7/1884 | | *Atalanta* (Fig. 129) |
| 166 | 4-6-0 | BLW | 11/1872 | 3000 | D | 6/1879 | DE | | ren | 11/1882 | PW&B 102 | |
| 167 | 4-4-0 | BLW | 12/1853 | 566 | | | 55 | 17x22 | c/u | 2/1876 | | *Lehigh* |
| 168 | 4-6-0 | AMS | 12/1868 | 13 | D | 1880 | E | | ren | 11/1880 | PFt.W&C 80 | (Figs. 67 & 131) |
| 169 | 2-6-0 | RN&S | 4/1854 | | | 5/1866 | 60 | 16x24 | c/u | 4/1886 | | *President* (Fig. 132) |
| 170 | 4-6-0 | AMS | 5/1872 | 131 | E | | | | c/u | 1/1892 | | |
| 171 | 0-6-0T | BLW | 8/1866 | 1511 | | | 44 | 15x18 | c/u | 7/1888 | | |
| 172 | 4-4-0 | AMS | 9/1869 | 37 | C | | | | so | 11/1893 | LV | |
| 173 | 4-4-0 | BLW | 5/1854 | 590 | | 2/1867 | 60 | 16x24 | so | 5/1875 | R&D | *Nebraska* (Fig. 89) |
| 174 | 4-4-0 | AMS | 7/1869 | 30 | C | | | | c/u | 8/1894 | | |
| 175 | 4-4-0 | NJLM | 6/1854 | | | | 60 | 16x20 | c/u | 3/1877 | | *John Gilpin* |
| 176 | 4-4-0 | LLW | 12/1854 | | | | 60 | 16x20 | c/u | 3/1877 | | *Tam O'Shanter* |
| 177 | 4-4-0 | LLW | 1/1855 | | | | 54 | 16x20 | c/u | 1/1876 | | *Uncle Toby* |
| 178 | 4-4-0 | LLW | 3/1855 | | | | 60 | 16x22 | so | 5/1881 | JHB | *Bardolph* |
| 179 | 0-6-0T | AMS | 12/1869 | 42 | F | | | | c/u | 1/1895 | | |
| 180 | 4-4-0 | LLW | 11/1855 | | | | 60 | 16x22 | c/u | 7/1884 | | *Young America* |
| 181 | 4-4-0 | LLW | 12/1855 | | | | 60 | 17x20 | c/u | 3/1879 | | *Attila* |
| 182 | 4-4-0 | LLW | 2/1856 | | | | 54 | 17x20 | c/u | 3/1876 | | *Alaric* |
| 183 | 4-4-0 | AMS | 2/1870 | 53 | A | | 62 | | so | 2/1894 | NYE | |
| 184 | 4-4-0 | LLW | 3/1856 | | | | 60 | 16x22 | so | 4/1881 | WC | *My Son Samuel* |
| 185 | 4-4-0 | NJLM | 3/1856 | | | | 54 | 16x22 | c/u | 2/1874 | | *Yorick* |
| 186 | 4-4-0 | LLW | 4/1856 | | | | 60 | 16x22 | c/u | 1/1885 | | *Alert* |
| 187 | 4-4-0 | NJLM | 4/1856 | | | | 54 | 16x22 | c/u | 5/1875 | | *Corporal Trim* (Fig. 134) |
| 188 | 4-4-0 | LLW | 6/1856 | | | | 60 | 18x22 | c/u | 1/1876 | | *Fingal's Baby* |
| 189 | 4-4-0 | AMS | 2/1870 | 54 | A | | 68 | | ren | 1/1885 | WJ 30 | |
| 190 | 0-6-0T | AMS | 11/1869 | 43 | F | | | | c/u | 2/1894 | | |
| 191 | 4-6-0 | AMS | 5/1872 | 132 | E | | | | ren | 3/1895 | C&MV 809 | |
| 192 | 4-4-0 | RN&S | 7/1856 | | | | 54 | 18x22 | c/u | 1/1875 | | *G. Washington* |
| 193 | 4-4-0 | AMS | 2/1870 | 55 | A | | 68 | | c/u | 12/1892 | | |
| 194 | 4-4-0 | LLW | 2/1857 | | | | 60 | 16x22 | so | 2/1882 | EHW | *Hiawatha* |
| 195 | 4-4-0 | LLW | 2/1857 | | | | 60 | 16x22 | c/u | 1/1881 | | *Breckenridge* (Fig. 135) |
| 196 | 4-4-0 | BLW | 8/1868 | 1745 | D | 8/1879 | DE | | c/u | 12/1891 | | |
| 197 | 0-6-0T | BLW | 4/1863 | 1126 | | | 42 | 15x18 | c/u | 7/1873 | | |
| 198 | 4-6-0 | AMS | 5/1872 | 133 | E | | | | ren | 10/1886 | GR&I 60 | |
| 199 | 4-6-0 | BLW | 5/1863 | 1133 | | | 54 | 18x22 | so | 7/1879 | WC | |
| 200 | 4-6-0 | AMS | 12/1872 | 167 | E | | | | ren | 10/1890 | PRR 3011 | |
| 201 | 4-6-0 | AMS | 4/1871 | 76 | D | ? | DE | | ren | 10/1879 | CC&IC 328 | |
| 202 | 4-6-0 | BLW | 8/1868 | 1749 | D | | | | c/u | 3/1891 | | |
| 203 | 0-4-0T | NB | 6/1850 | | | 8/1865 | 43 | 11x24 | c/u | 1874 | | *Montgomery* (Fig. 136) |
| 204 | 2-6-0 | RN&S | 6/1854 | | | 12/1866 | 48 | 18x24 | c/u | 7/1884 | | *Jupiter* |
| 205 | 2-6-0 | RN&S | 4/1854 | | | 10/1866 | 60 | 19x24 | c/u | 1/1880 | | *Hercules* (Fig. 137) |
| 206 | 4-6-0 | AMS | 4/1872 | 125 | E | | | | so | 10/1895 | EHW | |
| 207 | 4-6-0 | AMS | 2/1873 | 173 | E | | | | so | 1/1896 | EHW | |

| No. | Type | Bldr. | Date | C/N | Class | Rebuilt | Driv., in. | Cyl., in. | Disp. | Date | To | Notes |
|---|---|---|---|---|---|---|---|---|---|---|---|---|
| 208 | 2-6-0 | RN&S | 4/1854 | | | 12/1865 | 60 | 19x24 | c/u | 5/1877 | | *Blair* (Fig. 138) |
| 209 | 4-6-0 | AMS | 5/1870 | 58 | D | | DE | | ren | 9/1897 | CC&IC 306 | |
| 210 | 2-6-0 | S&P | 9/1853 | | | 12/1866 | 48 | 18x24 | c/u | 4/1879 | | 63 via P&E (Fig. 139) |
| 211 | 4-6-0 | BLW | 8/1868 | 1747 | D | | | | ren | 4/1880 | St.LV&TH 174 | |
| 212 | 2-4-0T | BLW | 4/1861 | 1000 | | | 56 | 10x18 | so | 6/1882 | EHW | (Fig. 34) |
| 213 | 4-6-0 | BLW | 6/1861 | 1003 | | | 48 | 16x22 | c/u | 1/1875 | | |
| 214 | 4-6-0 | BLW | 7/1861 | 1004 | | | 50 | 16x22 | c/u | 5/1875 | | (Fig. 140) |
| 215 | 4-6-0 | AMS | 4/1869 | 20 | D | 7/1880 | DE | | ren | 12/1880 | PC&St.L 380 | |
| 216 | 4-6-0 | AMS | 4/1872 | 123 | E | | | | c/u | 11/1893 | | |
| 217 | 4-6-0 | AMS | 12/1872 | 168 | E | | | | ren | 5/1891 | C&A 509 | |
| 218 | 4-6-0 | AMS | 5/1869 | 24 | E | | | | ren | 5/1888 | WJ 32 | (Fig. 141) |
| 219 | 4-6-0 | AMS | 5/1870 | 59 | E | | | | c/u | 2/1894 | | |
| 220 | 4-6-0 | BLW | 11/1861 | 1017 | | | 48 | 18x22 | c/u | 3/1877 | | |
| 221 | 4-6-0 | BLW | 11/1861 | 1018 | | | 48 | 18x22 | c/u | 5/1875 | | |
| 222 | 4-6-0 | AMS | 8/1872 | 144 | E | | | | ren | 1/1880 | PC&St.L 16 | |
| 223 | 4-6-0 | RN&S | 10/1861 | | | | 48 | 15x24 | c/u | 2/1874 | | |
| 224 | 4-6-0 | BLW | 10/1861 | 1014 | | | 50 | 16x22 | c/u | 5/1875 | | (Fig. 87) |
| 225 | 4-6-0 | BLW | 11/1861 | 1021 | | | 48 | 18x22 | ren | 6/1882 | PRR 3021 | |
| 226 | 4-6-0 | BLW | 12/1861 | 1022 | | | 48 | 18x22 | c/u | 2/1878 | | |
| 227 | 4-6-0 | BLW | 12/1861 | 1023 | | | 48 | 18x22 | c/u | 1/1880 | | |
| 228 | 4-6-0 | BLW | 12/1861 | 1025 | | | 48 | 18x22 | c/u | 2/1878 | | |
| 229 | 4-6-0 | BLW | 1/1862 | 1027 | | | 48 | 18x22 | c/u | 5/1878 | | |
| 230 | 4-6-0 | BLW | 1/1862 | 1028 | | | 48 | 18x22 | so | 2/1887 | B&T | |
| 231 | 4-6-0 | BLW | 1/1862 | 1029 | | | 48 | 18x22 | c/u | 1/1876 | | |
| 232 | 4-6-0 | BLW | 1/1862 | 1030 | | | 48 | 18x22 | c/u | 3/1877 | | |
| 233 | 4-6-0 | RL&M | 2/1862 | 1009 | | | 48 | 18x22 | c/u | 2/1878 | | (Fig. 142) |
| 234 | 4-6-0 | RL&M | 3/1862 | 1011 | | | 48 | 18x22 | c/u | 2/1878 | | (Fig. 38) |
| 235 | 4-6-0 | RL&M | 4/1862 | 1012 | | | 48 | 18x22 | c/u | 5/1878 | | |
| 236 | 4-6-0 | AMS | 4/1872 | 124 | E | | | | so | 10/1894 | JTG | |
| 237 | 4-6-0 | AMS | 6/1870 | 60 | D | ? | DE | | ren | 9/1879 | CC&IC 319 | |
| 238 | 4-4-0 | AMS | 9/1869 | 38 | C | | | | so | 6/1894 | A&RM | (Fig. 63) |
| 239 | 4-4-0 | AMS | 10/1867 | 4 | | | 60 | 17x24 | c/u | 2/1881 | | |
| 240 | 4-6-0 | RN&S | 3/1862 | | | | 48 | 18x22 | c/u | 1/1875 | | |
| 241 | 4-6-0 | BLW | 1/1862 | 1032 | | | 48 | 18x22 | so | 10/1883 | EHW | |
| 242 | 4-6-0 | BLW | 1/1862 | 1034 | | | 48 | 18x22 | c/u | 3/1874 | | (Fig. 143) |
| 243 | 4-4-0 | AMS | 7/1869 | 31 | C | | | | so | 12/1893 | AWT | |
| 244 | 4-6-0 | BLW | 2/1862 | 1039 | | | 48 | 18x22 | c/u | 3/1885 | | |
| 245 | 2-6-0 | BLW | 10/1861 | 1013 | | 1866 | 54 | 18x24 | c/u | 5/1878 | | Ren. from 142 (Fig. 144) |
| 246 | 0-4-0T | BLW | 3/1862 | 1047 | | | 36 | 11x16 | so | 2/1891 | EHW | |
| 247 | 4-4-0 | AMS | 11/1870 | 71 | G | | | | so | 4/1891 | EHW | (Fig. 145) |
| 248 | 4-6-0 | AMS | 4/1871 | 77 | D | ? | DE | | ren | 9/1879 | CC&CI 308 | |
| 249 | 4-6-0 | BLW | 3/1862 | 1048 | | | 48 | 18x22 | c/u | 7/1884 | | |
| 250 | 4-6-0 | BLW | 4/1862 | 1049 | | | 48 | 18x22 | so | 2/1887 | B&T | |

| No. | Type | Bldr. | Date | C/N | Class | Rebuilt | Driv., in. | Cyl., in. | Disp. | Date | To | Notes |
|-----|------|-------|------|-----|-------|---------|-----------|-----------|-------|------|-----|-------|
| 251 | 4-4-0T | BLW | 4/1863 | 1129 | | | 56 | 10x20 | so | 3/1882 | EHW | (Fig. 146) |
| 252 | 4-6-0 | AMS | 7/1870 | 67 | E | | | | c/u | 1/1898 | | |
| 253 | 4-6-0 | BLW | 10/1862 | 1083 | | | 48 | 18x22 | c/u | 5/1875 | | |
| 254 | 4-6-0 | BLW | 10/1862 | 1085 | | | 48 | 18x22 | c/u | 9/1875 | | |
| 255 | 4-6-0 | BLW | 11/1862 | 1084 | | | 48 | 18x22 | c/u | 5/1875 | | |
| 256 | 4-6-0 | BLW | 11/1862 | 1086 | | | 48 | 18x22 | c/u | 2/1876 | | (Fig. 147) |
| 257 | 4-6-0 | BLW | 11/1862 | 1092 | | | 48 | 18x22 | c/u | 8/1879 | | |
| 258 | 4-6-0 | BLW | 11/1862 | 1094 | | | 48 | 18x22 | c/u | 1/1880 | | (Fig. 77) |
| 259 | 4-6-0 | BLW | 12/1862 | 1096 | | | 54 | 18x22 | c/u | 1/1880 | | |
| 260 | 4-6-0 | BLW | 12/1862 | 1098 | | | 54 | 18x22 | so | 4/1881 | WC | |
| 261 | 2-6-0 | BLW | 9/1862 | 1081 | | 7/1866 | 66 | 19x24 | c/u | 2/1883 | | (Fig 148) |
| 262 | 4-6-0 | BLW | 12/1862 | 1099 | | | 50 | 18x22 | c/u | 2/1880 | | |
| 263 | 4-6-0 | BLW | 1/1863 | 1100 | | | 54 | 18x22 | c/u | 5/1878 | | |
| 264 | 4-6-0 | BLW | 1/1863 | 1101 | | | 54 | 18x22 | c/u | 5/1878 | | |
| 265 | 4-6-0 | BLW | 1/1863 | 1102 | | | 54 | 18x22 | c/u | 2/1880 | | |
| 266 | 4-6-0 | BLW | 2/1863 | 1106 | | | 54 | 18x22 | c/u | 8/1879 | | |
| 267 | 4-6-0 | BLW | 2/1863 | 1107 | | | 54 | 18x22 | c/u | 1/1880 | | |
| 268 | 4-6-0 | BLW | 2/1863 | 1111 | | | 54 | 18x22 | c/u | 5/1878 | | |
| 269 | 4-6-0 | BLW | 2/1863 | 1113 | | | 54 | 18x22 | c/u | 1/1880 | | |
| 270 | 4-6-0 | BLW | 3/1863 | 1115 | | | 54 | 18x22 | so | 4/1881 | WC | |
| 271 | 4-6-0 | BLW | 4/1863 | 1119 | | | 54 | 18x22 | c/u | 5/1878 | | |
| 272 | 4-6-0 | RN&S | 11/1862 | | | | 54 | 18x22 | c/u | 5/1875 | | |
| 273 | 4-6-0 | RN&S | 12/1862 | | | | 54 | 18x22 | c/u | 5/1875 | | |
| 274 | 4-6-0 | RN&S | 12/1862 | | | | 54 | 18x22 | c/u | 5/1875 | | |
| 275 | 4-6-0 | RN&S | 12/1862 | | | | 54 | 18x22 | c/u | 5/1875 | | |
| 276 | 4-6-0 | RN&S | 12/1862 | | | | 54 | 18x22 | c/u | 6/1875 | | |
| 277 | 4-6-0 | RN&S | 1/1863 | | | | 54 | 18x22 | c/u | 5/1878 | | |
| 278 | 4-6-0 | BLW | 12/1872 | 3007 | D | 1881 | DE | | c/u | 8/1895 | | |
| 279 | 4-4-0 | RN&S | 4/1863 | 1068 | | | 66 | 17x24 | c/u | 5/1878 | | (Figs. 149 & 150) |
| 280 | 4-6-0 | BLW | 12/1864 | 1321 | | | 54 | 18x22 | c/u | 1/1876 | | |
| 281 | 4-6-0 | BLW | 10/1872 | 2956 | D | 1882 | DE | | c/u | 1/1895 | | |
| 282 | 4-6-0 | BLW | 12/1864 | 1325 | | | 54 | 18x22 | c/u | 5/1878 | | |
| 283 | 4-6-0 | NJLM | 1/1865 | 424 | | | 54 | 18x22 | c/u | 1/1880 | | (Fig. 151) |
| 284 | 4-6-0 | NJLM | 1/1865 | 435 | | | 54 | 18x22 | so | 8/1881 | EHW | |
| 285 | 4-6-0 | NJLM | 1/1865 | 426 | | | 54 | 18x22 | c/u | 1/1882 | | |
| 286 | 4-6-0 | NJLM | 1/1865 | 427 | | | 54 | 18x22 | c/u | 1/1885 | | |
| 287 | 4-4-0 | AMS | 8/1869 | 32 | C | | | | c/u | 11/1893 | | |
| 288 | 4-4-0 | AMS | 8/1869 | 33 | C | | | | c/u | 5/1894 | | |
| 289 | 4-6-0 | BLW | 12/1864 | 1326 | | | 54 | 18x22 | c/u | 3/1874 | | |
| 290 | 4-6-0 | BLW | 11/1864 | 1306 | | | 54 | 18x22 | c/u | 7/1884 | | |
| 291 | 4-6-0 | BLW | 11/1864 | 1307 | | | 54 | 18x22 | c/u | 5/1875 | | |
| 292 | 4-6-0 | BLW | 12/1872 | 3026 | D | 5/1880 | DE | | c/u | 7/1887 | | |
| 293 | 4-6-0 | BLW | 12/1864 | 1310 | | | 54 | 18x22 | so | 6/1882 | EHW | |

| No. | Type | Bldr. | Date | C/N | Class | Rebuilt | Driv., in. | Cyl., in. | Disp. | Date | To | Notes |
|---|---|---|---|---|---|---|---|---|---|---|---|---|
| 294 | 4-6-0 | BLW | 9/1864 | 1283 | | | 54 | 18x22 | c/u | 1/1880 | | Renumbered from 2, c.1865. |
| 295 | 4-6-0 | RN&S | 12/1863 | | | | 54 | 18x22 | c/u | 2/1874 | | |
| 296 | 4-6-0 | RN&S | 12/1863 | | | | 54 | 18x22 | c/u | 7/1873 | | |
| 297 | 4-6-0 | RN&S | 8/1863 | | | | 54 | 18x22 | c/u | 7/1874 | | Ren. from 289 (Figs. 152 & 153) |
| 298 | 4-6-0 | RN&S | 4/1864 | | | | 54 | 18x22 | c/u | 1/1876 | | |
| 299 | 4-6-0 | RN&S | 4/1864 | | | | 54 | 18x22 | c/u | 2/1874 | | |
| 300 | 4-6-0 | BLW | 5/1863 | 1136 | | | 54 | 18x22 | c/u | 1/1880 | | |
| 301 | 4-6-0 | BLW | 6/1863 | 1143 | | | 54 | 18x22 | c/u | 2/1888 | | |
| 302 | 4-6-0 | BLW | 7/1863 | 1144 | | | 54 | 18x22 | c/u | 9/1875 | | |
| 303 | 4-6-0 | BLW | 7/1863 | 1145 | | | 54 | 18x22 | c/u | 5/1878 | | |
| 304 | 4-6-0 | AMS | 7/1870 | 64 | E | | | | ren | 8/1886 | GR&I 61 | |
| 305 | 4-6-0 | BLW | 6/1863 | 1148 | | | 54 | 18x22 | c/u | 2/1876 | | |
| 306 | 4-6-0 | BLW | 7/1863 | 1153 | | | 54 | 18x22 | c/u | 2/1879 | | |
| 307 | 4-6-0 | BLW | 7/1863 | 1154 | | | 54 | 18x22 | c/u | 5/1878 | | |
| 308 | 4-6-0 | BLW | 7/1863 | 1155 | | | 54 | 18x22 | c/u | 5/1879 | | |
| 309 | 4-6-0 | BLW | 8/1863 | 1163 | | | 54 | 18x22 | so | 4/1880 | EHW | |
| 310 | 4-6-0 | BLW | 9/1863 | 1167 | | | 54 | 18x22 | c/u | 10/1887 | | |
| 311 | 4-6-0 | BLW | 9/1863 | 1169 | | | 54 | 18x22 | c/u | 5/1878 | | |
| 312 | 4-6-0 | BLW | 9/1863 | 1171 | | | 54 | 18x22 | c/u | 1/1880 | | |
| 313 | 4-6-0 | BLW | 2/1865 | 1207 | | | 54 | 18x22 | c/u | 5/1877 | | |
| 314 | 4-6-0 | BLW | 2/1864 | 1209 | | | 54 | 18x22 | c/u | 5/1877 | | |
| 315 | 4-6-0 | BLW | 3/1864 | 1219 | | | 54 | 18x22 | c/u | 1/1880 | | |
| 316 | 4-6-0 | BLW | 5/1864 | 1222 | | | 54 | 18x22 | c/u | 5/1878 | | |
| 317 | 4-6-0 | BLW | 8/1864 | 1261 | | | 54 | 18x22 | so | 7/1881 | EHW | |
| 318 | 4-4-0 | BLW | 5/1864 | 1242 | | | 66 | 17x24 | c/u | 4/1886 | | |
| 319 | 4-4-0 | BLW | 6/1864 | 1247 | | | 66 | 17x24 | c/u | 5/1878 | | |
| 320 | 4-4-0 | BLW | 6/1864 | 1249 | | | 66 | 17x24 | so | 9/1892 | EHW | |
| 321 | 4-4-0 | BLW | 7/1864 | 1259 | | | 66 | 17x24 | c/u | 5/1880 | | |
| 322 | 4-4-0 | BLW | 7/1864 | 1260 | | | 66 | 17x24 | c/u | 2/1878 | | |
| 323 | 4-4-0 | BLW | 8/1864 | 1262 | | | 66 | 17x24 | ren | 6/1882 | PRR 3002 | |
| 324 | 4-4-0 | BLW | 8/1864 | 1263 | | | 66 | 17x24 | c/u | 4/1886 | | |
| 325 | 4-4-0 | BLW | 8/1864 | 1266 | | | 66 | 17x24 | c/u | 3/1877 | | (Fig. 154) |
| 326 | 4-4-0 | BLW | 8/1864 | 1267 | | | 66 | 17x24 | c/u | 2/1876 | | |
| 327 | 0-6-0T | BLW | 4/1864 | 1229 | | | 44 | 15x18 | c/u | 1/1873 | | |
| 328 | 0-6-0T | BLW | 6/1864 | 1251 | | | 44 | 15x18 | c/u | 1/1882 | | |
| 329 | 0-6-0T | BLW | 6/1864 | 1254 | | | 44 | 15x18 | c/u | 3/1877 | | |
| 330 | 0-6-0T | BLW | 7/1864 | 1257 | | | 44 | 15x18 | c/u | 5/1877 | | |
| 331 | 4-4-0 | BLW | 3/1865 | 1344 | | | 66 | 17x24 | so | 5/1882 | EHW | (Fig. 155) |
| 332 | 4-4-0 | BLW | 3/1865 | 1346 | | | 66 | 17x24 | c/u | 1/1876 | | (Fig. 90) |
| 333 | 4-4-0 | BLW | 3/1865 | 1348 | | | 66 | 17x24 | so | 2/1887 | B&T | |
| 334 | 4-4-0 | BLW | 3/1865 | 1349 | | | 66 | 17x24 | so | 2/1887 | B&T | |
| 335 | 4-4-0 | BLW | 3/1865 | 1351 | | | 66 | 17x24 | c/u | 1/1880 | | |
| 336 | 4-4-0 | BLW | 3/1865 | 1352 | | | 66 | 17x24 | ren | 1/1882 | PRR 3003 | |

| No. | Type | Bldr. | Date | C/N | Class | Rebuilt | Driv., in. | Cyl., in. | Disp. | Date | To | Notes |
|-----|------|-------|------|-----|-------|---------|-----------|-----------|-------|------|-----|-------|
| 337 | 4-6-0 | BLW | 1/1865 | 1330 | | | 54 | 18x22 | c/u | 2/1875 | | |
| 338 | 4-6-0 | BLW | 8/1868 | 1750 | D | 1880 | DE | | c/u | 7/1893 | | |
| 339 | 4-6-0 | BLW | 1/1865 | 1335 | | | 54 | 16x22 | c/u | 1/1881 | | (Fig. 156) |
| 340 | 4-6-0 | BLW | 1/1865 | 1336 | | | 54 | 16x22 | so | 4/1881 | WC | |
| 341 | 4-6-0 | BLW | 2/1865 | 1338 | | | 54 | 16x22 | so | 4/1881 | WC | |
| 342 | 4-6-0 | BLW | 2/1865 | 1341 | | | 54 | 16x22 | c/u | 5/1878 | | |
| 343 | 4-6-0 | BLW | 3/1865 | 1342 | | | 54 | 16x22 | ren | 6/1882 | PRR 3004 | |
| 344 | 4-6-0 | BLW | 12/1872 | 3081 | D | | | | c/u | 1/1892 | | |
| 345 | 0-6-0T | BLW | 4/1865 | 1358 | | | 44 | 15x18 | c/u | 8/1891 | | |
| 346 | 0-6-0T | BLW | 4/1865 | 1365 | | | 44 | 15x18 | so | 2/1887 | B&T | |
| 347 | 2-6-0 | RN&S | 2/1865 | 1177 | | 12/1866 | 66 | 17x24 | so | 2/1884 | EHW | (Fig. 50) |
| 348 | 4-4-0 | AMS | 9/1869 | 39 | C | | | | c/u | 2/1894 | | |
| 349 | 4-4-0 | BLW | 12/1865 | 1436 | | | 66 | 17x24 | c/u | 2/1878 | | (Fig. 158) |
| 350 | 4-4-0 | BLW | 12/1865 | 1438 | | | 66 | 17x24 | so | 3/1887 | B&T | |
| 351 | 4-4-0 | BLW | 8/1865 | 1404 | | | 66 | 16x24 | c/u | 7/1876 | | |
| 352 | 4-4-0 | BLW | 10/1865 | 1412 | | | 66 | 16x24 | c/u | 1/1876 | | |
| 353 | 4-4-0 | BLW | 12/1865 | 1440 | | | 66 | 17x24 | c/u | 1/1880 | | |
| 354 | 4-6-0 | BLW | 1/1866 | 1450 | | | 54 | 18x22 | c/u | 1/1878 | | |
| 355 | 4-6-0 | BLW | 1/1866 | 1451 | | | 54 | 18x22 | c/u | 2/1880 | | |
| 356 | 4-4-0 | BLW | 1/1866 | 1452 | | | 60 | 16x24 | c/u | 2/1885 | | |
| 357 | 4-4-0 | BLW | 1/1866 | 1453 | | | 60 | 16x24 | so | 1/1882 | EHW | |
| 358 | 4-4-0 | BLW | 9/1866 | 1521 | | | 60 | 16x24 | so | 1/1887 | S&A | |
| 359 | 4-4-0 | BLW | 10/1866 | 1535 | | | 60 | 16x24 | so | 5/1875 | R&D | |
| 360 | 4-4-0 | BLW | 11/1866 | 1546 | | | 60 | 16x24 | so | 2/1887 | B&T | (Fig. 69) |
| 361 | 4-4-0 | BLW | 12/1866 | 1554 | | | 60 | 16x24 | so | 5/1875 | R&D | (Fig. 159) |
| 362 | 0-6-0T | BLW | 12/1865 | 1432 | | | 44 | 15x18 | so | 5/1887 | AHK | |
| 363 | 0-6-0T | BLW | 12/1865 | 1439 | | | 44 | 15x18 | c/u | 8/1892 | | |
| 364 | 0-6-0T | BLW | 12/1865 | 1441 | | | 44 | 15x18 | so | 2/1887 | B&T | |
| 365 | 0-6-0T | BLW | 12/1865 | 1442 | | | 44 | 15x18 | so | 12/1890 | EHW | |
| 366 | 0-6-0T | BLW | 2/1866 | 1462 | | | 44 | 15x18 | so | 9/1891 | EHW | |
| 367 | 0-6-0T | BLW | 12/1865 | 1430 | | | 44 | 15x18 | so | 2/1889 | EHW | Renumbered from 361. |
| 368 | 4-6-0 | BLW | 9/1868 | 1755 | D | ? | DE | | c/u | 1/1885 | | |
| 369 | 4-6-0 | BLW | 6/1866 | 1497 | | | 54 | 18x22 | c/u | 2/1875 | | |
| 370 | 4-6-0 | BLW | 7/1866 | 1499 | | | 54 | 18x22 | so | 3/1881 | EHW | |
| 371 | 4-6-0 | BLW | 3/1873 | 3152 | D | | E | | ren | 4/1882 | GR&I 51 | |
| 372 | 4-6-0 | BLW | 9/1866 | 1518 | | | 54 | 18x22 | c/u | 2/1878 | | |
| 373 | 4-6-0 | BLW | 10/1866 | 1534 | | | 54 | 18x22 | c/u | 2/1880 | | |
| 374 | 4-6-0 | BLW | 11/1866 | 1539 | | | 54 | 18x22 | c/u | 1/1880 | | |
| 375 | 4-6-0 | BLW | 11/1866 | 1542 | | | 54 | 18x22 | c/u | 6/1875 | | |
| 376 | 4-6-0 | BLW | 11/1866 | 1543 | | | 54 | 18x22 | c/u | 2/1880 | | |
| 377 | 4-6-0 | BLW | 11/1866 | 1544 | | | 54 | 18x22 | so | 8/1880 | EHW | |
| 378 | 4-6-0 | BLW | 11/1866 | 1545 | | | 54 | 18x22 | c/u | 1/1880 | | |
| 379 | 4-6-0 | BLW | 11/1866 | 1548 | | | 54 | 18x22 | so | 3/1887 | B&T | |

| No. | Type | Bldr. | Date | C/N | Class | Rebuilt | Driv., in. | Cyl., in. | Disp. | Date | To | Notes |
|---|---|---|---|---|---|---|---|---|---|---|---|---|
| 380 | 4-6-0 | BLW | 12/1866 | 1549 | | | 54 | 18x22 | c/u | 1/1885 | | |
| 381 | 4-6-0 | BLW | 12/1866 | 1550 | | | 54 | 18x22 | so | 7/1880 | EHW | |
| 382 | 4-6-0 | BLW | 12/1866 | 1552 | | | 54 | 18x22 | c/u | 2/1884 | | |
| 383 | 4-6-0 | BLW | 12/1866 | 1555 | | | 54 | 18x22 | c/u | 1/1880 | | (Fig. 55) |
| 384 | 4-6-0 | BLW | 12/1866 | 1558 | | | 54 | 18x22 | c/u | 1/1880 | | (Fig. 160) |
| 385 | 4-4-0 | BLW | 5/1867 | 1634 | | | 60 | 17x24 | so | 9/1886 | EHW | |
| 386 | 4-4-0 | BLW | 6/1867 | 1635 | | | 60 | 17x24 | so | 12/1886 | EHW | |
| 387 | 4-4-0 | BLW | 6/1867 | 1636 | | | 60 | 17x24 | c/u | 3/1885 | | (Fig. 84) |
| 388 | 4-4-0 | BLW | 6/1867 | 1637 | | | 60 | 17x24 | c/u | 6/1879 | | |
| 389 | 4-4-0 | BLW | 6/1867 | 1638 | | | 60 | 17x24 | so | 8/1886 | EHW | |
| 390 | 4-4-0 | BLW | 6/1867 | 1639 | | | 60 | 17x24 | c/u | 4/1885 | | |
| 391 | 4-4-0 | BLW | 6/1867 | 1640 | | | 60 | 17x24 | c/u | 10/1887 | | |
| 392 | 4-4-0 | BLW | 6/1867 | 1641 | | | 60 | 17x24 | c/u | 10/1883 | | |
| 393 | 4-4-0 | BLW | 7/1867 | 1645 | | | 60 | 17x24 | so | 1/1887 | S&A | |
| 394 | 4-4-0 | BLW | 9/1867 | 1659 | | | 60 | 17x24 | so | 4/1883 | EHW | |
| 395 | 4-4-0 | BLW | 9/1867 | 1663 | | | 60 | 17x24 | c/u | 8/1887 | | |
| 396 | 4-4-0 | BLW | 10/1867 | 1665 | | | 60 | 17x24 | c/u | 10/1895 | | |
| 397 | 4-6-0 | N-L | 4/1867 | | | | 54 | 17x24 | so | 2/1887 | B&T | |
| 398 | 4-6-0 | N-L | 4/1867 | | | | 54 | 17x24 | c/u | 12/1895 | | |
| 399 | 4-6-0 | N-L | 4/1867 | | | | 54 | 17x24 | c/u | 1/1881 | | |
| 400 | 4-6-0 | N-L | 4/1867 | | | | 54 | 17x24 | c/u | 10/1885 | | |
| 401 | 4-6-0 | N-L | 4/1867 | | | | 54 | 17x24 | c/u | 8/1887 | | |
| 402 | 4-6-0 | N-L | 4/1867 | | | | 54 | 17x24 | so | 3/1887 | B&T | |
| 403 | 4-6-0 | N-L | 5/1867 | | | | 54 | 17x24 | c/u | 1/1885 | | |
| 404 | 4-6-0 | N-L | 5/1867 | | | | 54 | 17x24 | c/u | 3/1887 | | |
| 405 | 4-6-0 | N-L | 5/1867 | | | | 54 | 17x24 | so | 3/1887 | B&T | |
| 406 | 4-6-0 | N-L | 5/1867 | | | | 54 | 17x24 | so | 2/1886 | SCB | |
| 407 | 4-6-0 | N-L | 5/1867 | | | | 54 | 17x24 | c/u | 3/1896 | | (Figs. 161 & 162) |
| 408 | 4-6-0 | N-L | 6/1867 | | | | 54 | 17x24 | sg | 6/1886 | | At Southwest Jct. |
| 409 | 4-6-0 | NJLM | 3/1867 | 483 | | | 54 | 18x22 | so | 2/1887 | B&T | |
| 410 | 4-6-0 | NJLM | 4/1867 | 484 | | | 54 | 18x22 | c/u | 8/1889 | | |
| 411 | 4-6-0 | NJLM | 4/1867 | 485 | | | 54 | 18x22 | c/u | 10/1880 | | |
| 412 | 4-6-0 | NJLM | 4/1867 | 486 | | | 54 | 18x22 | c/u | 8/1887 | | |
| 413 | 4-6-0 | NJLM | 4/1867 | 487 | | | 54 | 18x22 | c/u | 1/1887 | | |
| 414 | 4-6-0 | NJLM | 4/1867 | 488 | | | 54 | 18x22 | c/u | 9/1889 | | |
| 415 | 4-6-0 | NJLM | 4/1867 | 489 | | | 54 | 18x22 | c/u | 8/1889 | | |
| 416 | 4-6-0 | NJLM | 4/1867 | 409 | | | 54 | 18x22 | c/u | 9/1896 | | |
| 417 | 4-6-0 | NJLM | 4/1867 | 491 | | | 54 | 18x22 | c/u | 4/1887 | | (Fig. 163) |
| 418 | 4-6-0 | NJLM | 4/1867 | 492 | | | 54 | 18x22 | so | 7/1891 | EHW | |
| 419 | 4-4-0 | BLW | 8/1867 | 1651 | | | 66 | 17x24 | ren | 10/1881 | PRR 1095 | |
| 420 | 4-4-0 | BLW | 9/1867 | 1656 | | | 66 | 17x24 | c/u | 11/1894 | | |
| 421 | 4-4-0 | BLW | 9/1867 | 1657 | | | 66 | 17x24 | ren | 12/1881 | PRR 106 | (Fig. 54) |
| 422 | 4-4-0 | BLW | 9/1867 | 1658 | | | 66 | 17x24 | ren | 7/1885 | C&A 13 | (Fig. 164) |

| No. | Type | Bldr. | Date | C/N | Class | Rebuilt | Driv., in. | Cyl., in. | Disp. | Date | To | Notes |
|-----|------|-------|------|-----|-------|---------|-----------|-----------|-------|------|-----|-------|
| 423 | 4-6-0 | BLW | 10/1868 | 1766 | D | 6/1879 | DE | | c/u | 6/1893 | | |
| 424 | 4-6-0 | BLW | 10/1868 | 1767 | D | 4/1880 | DE | | c/u | 10/1887 | | |
| 425 | 4-6-0 | BLW | 10/1868 | 1769 | D | 4/1880 | DE | | c/u | 12/1891 | | |
| 426 | 4-6-0 | BLW | 11/1868 | 1771 | D | | | | c/u | 8/1874 | | |
| 427 | 4-6-0 | BLW | 11/1868 | 1775 | D | 3/1880 | DE | | c/u | 12/1891 | | |
| 428 | 4-6-0 | BLW | 11/1868 | 1778 | D | | | | so | 4/1891 | EHW | |
| 429 | 4-6-0 | BLW | 11/1868 | 1780 | D | | | | c/u | 6/1891 | | |
| 430 | 4-6-0 | BLW | 11/1868 | 1781 | D | 3/1879 | DE | | ren | 3/1879 | PRR 1081 | |
| 431 | 4-6-0 | BLW | 11/1868 | 1785 | D | 6/1880 | DE | | ren | 10/1880 | PC&St.L 316 | |
| 432 | 4-6-0 | BLW | 12/1868 | 1786 | D | | | | c/u | 4/1891 | | |
| 433 | 4-6-0 | BLW | 1/1869 | 1803 | D | | | | c/u | 2/1881 | | |
| 434 | 4-6-0 | BLW | 1/1869 | 1805 | D | | | | so | 2/1887 | B&T | (Fig. 68) |
| 435 | 0-6-0T | BLW | 11/1868 | 1795 | | | 44 | 15x18 | c/u | 1/1885 | | |
| 436 | 0-6-0T | BLW | 10/1868 | 1796 | | | 44 | 15x18 | c/u | 2/1886 | | |
| 437 | 0-6-0T | BLW | 12/1868 | 1807 | | | 44 | 15X18 | c/u | 6/1884 | | |
| 438 | 0-6-0T | BLW | 1/1869 | 1821 | | | 44 | 15x18 | c/u | 11/1887 | | |
| 439 | 0-6-0T | AMS | 12/1869 | 44 | F | | | | c/u | 2/1894 | | |
| 440 | 0-6-0T | AMS | 12/1869 | 45 | F | | | | so | 9/1889 | EHW | |
| 441 | 0-6-0T | BLW | 6/1869 | 1901 | | | 44 | 15x18 | c/u | 10/1886 | | |
| 442 | 0-6-0T | BLW | 6/1869 | 1902 | | | 44 | 15x18 | c/u | 7/1893 | | (Fig. 86) |
| 443 | 4-6-0 | BLW | 3/1869 | 1850 | D | 12/1884 | DE | | c/u | 1/1898 | | |
| 444 | 4-6-0 | BLW | 3/1869 | 1851 | D | | | | sg | 2/1892 | | At Philadelphia. |
| 445 | 4-6-0 | BLW | 3/1869 | 1853 | D | ? | DE | | ren | 11/1880 | GR&I 39 | |
| 446 | 4-6-0 | BLW | 3/1869 | 1855 | D | 12/1881 | DE | | ren | 8/1884 | PRR 3034 | |
| 447 | 4-6-0 | BLW | 7/1869 | 1913 | D | | | | c/u | 2/1892 | | |
| 448 | 4-6-0 | BLW | 7/1869 | 1917 | D | ? | DE | | ren | 10/1880 | GR&I 38 | |
| 449 | 4-6-0 | BLW | 7/1869 | 1918 | D | | | | c/u | 6/1895 | | |
| 450 | 4-6-0 | BLW | 7/1869 | 1919 | D | | | | c/u | 6/1896 | | |
| 451 | 4-6-0 | BLW | 7/1869 | 1922 | D | ? | DE | | ren | 8/1884 | PRR 3035 | |
| 452 | 4-6-0 | BLW | 10/1869 | 1973 | D | ? | DE | | ren | 2/1881 | PC&St.L 57 | |
| 453 | 4-6-0 | BLW | 10/1869 | 1974 | D | ? | DE | | ren | 12/1880 | CC&IC 329 | |
| 454 | 4-6-0 | BLW | 10/1869 | 1979 | D | ? | DE | | c/u | 2/1881 | | |
| 455 | 4-6-0 | BLW | 10/1869 | 1980 | D | | | | c/u | 9/1886 | | |
| 456 | 4-6-0 | BLW | 10/1869 | 1981 | D | | | | so | 6/1891 | EHW | |
| 457 | 4-6-0 | BLW | 10/1869 | 1982 | D | 1/1880 | DE | | ren | 1/1881 | PC&St.L 19 | |
| 458 | 4-6-0 | BLW | 11/1869 | 1985 | D | 3/1880 | DE | | ren | 12/1880 | PFt.W&C 79 | |
| 459 | 4-6-0 | BLW | 11/1869 | 1990 | D | | | | c/u | 3/1892 | | |
| 460 | 4-6-0 | BLW | 11/1869 | 1992 | D | | | | c/u | 4/1887 | | |
| 461 | 4-6-0 | BLW | 11/1870 | 2263 | D | 2/1880 | DE | | ren | 2/1880 | PFtW&C 69 | |
| 462 | 4-6-0 | BLW | 11/1870 | 2264 | D | 5/1879 | DE | | ren | 5/1879 | NCR 35 | |
| 463 | 4-6-0 | BLW | 12/1869 | 2014 | D | | | | c/u | 3/1891 | | |
| 464 | 4-6-0 | BLW | 12/1869 | 2015 | D | ? | DE | | ren | 5/1880 | GR&I 36 | |
| 465 | 4-6-0 | BLW | 12/1869 | 2016 | D | ? | DE | | ren | 11/1881 | StLV&TH 175 | |

| No. | Type | Bldr. | Date | C/N | Class | Rebuilt | Driv., in. | Cyl., in. | Disp. | Date | To | Notes |
|---|---|---|---|---|---|---|---|---|---|---|---|---|
| 466 | 4-6-0 | BLW | 12/1869 | 2018 | D | 12/1878 | DE | | ren | 1/1879 | PC&StL 37 | |
| 467 | 4-6-0 | BLW | 8/1869 | 1929 | D | 8/1880 | DE | | ren | 1/1880 | PC&StL 31 | |
| 468 | 4-6-0 | BLW | 8/1869 | 1930 | D | | | | so | 11/1898 | NYE | |
| 469 | 4-6-0 | BLW | 8/1869 | 1931 | D | 11/1878 | DE | | ren | 1/1879 | PC&StL 30 | |
| 470 | 4-6-0 | BLW | 8/1869 | 1932 | D | 5/1880 | DE | | ren | 12/1880 | PFW&C 87 | |
| 471 | 4-6-0 | BLW | 8/1869 | 1941 | D | 7/1879 | DE | | ren | 7/1879 | PFt.W&C 72 | |
| 472 | 4-6-0 | BLW | 8/1869 | 1928 | D | | | | c/u | 6/1892 | | |
| 473 | 4-6-0 | BLW | 9/1869 | 1961 | D | 2/1880 | DE | | ren | 2/1880 | PC&St.L 10 | |
| 474 | 4-6-0 | BLW | 9/1869 | 1960 | D | | | | c/u | 9/1891 | | |
| 475 | 4-6-0 | BLW | 10/1869 | 1964 | D | | | | ren | 11/1880 | CC&IC 320 | |
| 476 | 4-6-0 | BLW | 10/1869 | 1972 | D | 4/1880 | DE | | ren | 5/1880 | GR&I 37 | |
| 477 | 4-6-0 | BLW | 12/1869 | 2020 | D | 5/1879 | DE | | ren | 5/1879 | PFt.W&C 83 | |
| 478 | 4-6-0 | BLW | 1/1870 | 2050 | D | 12/1878 | DE | | ren | 1/1879 | PC&St.L 34 | |
| 479 | 4-6-0 | BLW | 1/1870 | 2051 | D | 2/1880 | DE | | ren | 3/1880 | PFW&C 84 | |
| 480 | 4-6-0 | BLW | 1/1870 | 2059 | D | ? | DE | | c/u | 5/1893 | | |
| 481 | 4-6-0 | BLW | 2/1870 | 2061 | D | | | | c/u | 9/1891 | | |
| 482 | 4-6-0 | BLW | 2/1870 | 2070 | D | | | | ren | 4/1891 | NYP&N 16 | |
| 483 | 4-6-0 | AMS | 10/1871 | 98 | D | 12/1878 | DE | | ren | 1/1879 | PC&St.L 14 | |
| 484 | 4-6-0 | AMS | 10/1871 | 99 | D | 8/1878 | DE | | ren | 12/1881 | PC&St.L 39 | |
| 485 | 4-6-0 | AMS | 10/1871 | 100 | D | ? | DE | | ren | 6/1884 | PRR 3036 | |
| 486 | 4-6-0 | AMS | 10/1871 | 101 | D | 4/1879 | DE | | ren | 8/1878 | PFt.W&C 77 | |
| 487 | 4-6-0 | AMS | 11/1871 | 102 | D | | | | c/u | 2/1892 | | |
| 488 | 4-6-0 | AMS | 11/1871 | 103 | D | | | | ren | 11/1881 | CC&IC 458 | |
| 489 | 4-6-0 | AMS | 11/1871 | 104 | D | | | | c/u | 12/1891 | | (Fig. 58) |
| 490 | 4-6-0 | AMS | 11/1871 | 105 | D | 1/1879 | DE | | ren | 6/1879 | PFt.W&C 71 | |
| 491 | 4-6-0 | AMS | 11/1871 | 106 | D | | | | c/u | 5/1894 | | |
| 492 | 4-6-0 | AMS | 11/1871 | 107 | D | | | | c/u | 3/1895 | | |
| 493 | 4-6-0 | AMS | 12/1871 | 108 | D | ? | DE | | c/u | 3/1893 | | |
| 494 | 4-6-0 | AMS | 12/1871 | 109 | D | | | | c/u | 8/1890 | | |
| 495 | 4-6-0 | AMS | 4/1871 | 78 | E | | | | ren | 3/1879 | PRR 1071 | |
| 496 | 4-6-0 | AMS | 5/1871 | 79 | E | | | | ren | 9/1885 | NCR 46 | |
| 497 | 4-6-0 | AMS | 5/1871 | 80 | E | | | | c/u | 5/1892 | | |
| 498 | 4-6-0 | AMS | 5/1871 | 81 | E | | | | c/u | 11/1892 | | |
| 499 | 4-6-0 | AMS | 5/1871 | 82 | E | | | | c/u | 5/1894 | | |
| 500 | 4-6-0 | AMS | 5/1871 | 83 | E | | | | c/u | 11/1893 | | |
| 501 | 4-6-0 | AMS | 5/1871 | 84 | E | | | | so | 4/1893 | EHW | |
| 502 | 4-6-0 | AMS | 5/1871 | 85 | E | | | | c/u | 5/1894 | | |
| 503 | 4-4-0 | AMS | 8/1871 | 92 | C | | | | ren | 8/1882 | PW&B 97 | |
| 504 | 4-4-0 | AMS | 8/1871 | 93 | C | | | | ren | 8/1882 | PW&B 98 | |
| 505 | 4-4-0 | AMS | 8/1871 | 94 | C | | | | c/u | 3/1894 | | |
| 506 | 4-4-0 | AMS | 8/1871 | 95 | C | | | | c/u | 3/1894 | | |
| 507 | 4-4-0 | AMS | 9/1871 | 96 | C | | | | ren | 12/1882 | P&E 2093 | |
| 508 | 4-4-0 | AMS | 9/1871 | 97 | C | | | | ren | 9/1882 | PW&B 99 | |

| No. | Type | Bldr. | Date | C/N | Class | Rebuilt | Driv., in. | Cyl., in. | Disp. | Date | To | Notes |
|-----|------|-------|------|-----|-------|---------|-----------|-----------|-------|------|------|-------|
| 509 | 0-6-0T | AMS | 6/1871 | 86 | F | | | | so | 9/1889 | EHW | |
| 510 | 0-6-0T | AMS | 6/1871 | 87 | F | | | | so | 4/1898 | FHC | |
| 511 | 0-6-0T | AMS | 6/1871 | 88 | F | | | | c/u | 10/1895 | | |
| 512 | 0-6-0T | AMS | 6/1871 | 89 | F | | | | c/u | 2/1899 | | |
| 513 | 0-6-0T | AMS | 6/1871 | 90 | F | | | | so | 12/1896 | HC | |
| 514 | 0-6-0T | AMS | 6/1871 | 91 | F | | | | so | 9/1896 | HB&Co | |
| 515 | 4-6-0 | AMS | 1/1872 | 112 | E | | | | c/u | 12/1898 | | |
| 516 | 4-6-0 | AMS | 2/1872 | 113 | E | | | | ren | 12/1881 | St.LV&TH 178 | |
| 517 | 4-6-0 | AMS | 2/1872 | 114 | E | | | | so | 11/1900 | NM | |
| 518 | 4-6-0 | AMS | 2/1872 | 115 | E | | | | so | 4/1895 | EHW | |
| 519 | 4-6-0 | AMS | 2/1872 | 116 | E | | | | ren | 4/1879 | NCR 45 | |
| 520 | 4-6-0 | AMS | 2/1872 | 117 | E | | | | c/u | 2/1894 | | |
| 521 | 4-6-0 | AMS | 3/1872 | 118 | E | | | | c/u | 3/1900 | | |
| 522 | 4-6-0 | AMS | 3/1872 | 119 | E | | | | c/u | 9/1894 | | |
| 523 | 4-6-0 | AMS | 3/1872 | 120 | D | ? | DE | | ren | 11/1881 | CC&IC 455 | |
| 524 | 4-6-0 | AMS | 3/1872 | 121 | E | | | | c/u | 9/1894 | | |
| 525 | 4-6-0 | BLW | 3/1872 | 2702 | D | | | | c/u | 3/1892 | | |
| 526 | 4-6-0 | BLW | 3/1872 | 2703 | D | | | | sg | 4/1892 | | At Mifflin. |
| 527 | 4-6-0 | BLW | 3/1872 | 2712 | D | 1/1880 | DE | | c/u | 8/1901 | | |
| 528 | 4-6-0 | BLW | 3/1872 | 2715 | D | | | | c/u | 1/1893 | | |
| 529 | 4-6-0 | BLW | 3/1872 | 2717 | D | 12/1878 | DE | | ren | 12/1879 | PC&St.L 13 | |
| 530 | 4-6-0 | BLW | 3/1872 | 2733 | D | 6/1879 | DE | | ren | 9/1879 | PFt.W&C 82 | |
| 531 | 4-6-0 | BLW | 3/1872 | 2729 | D | ? | DE | | c/u | 10/1891 | | |
| 532 | 4-6-0 | BLW | 4/1872 | 2735 | D | 6/1879 | DE | | ren | 11/1881 | St.LV&TH 176 | |
| 533 | 4-6-0 | BLW | 4/1872 | 2738 | D | | | | c/u | 3/1887 | | |
| 534 | 4-6-0 | BLW | 4/1872 | 2739 | D | 9/1880 | DE | | so | 3/1894 | NYE | |
| 535 | 4-6-0 | BLW | 4/1872 | 2745 | D | | | | c/u | 2/1892 | | |
| 536 | 4-6-0 | BLW | 4/1872 | 2749 | D | 3/1879 | DE | | ren | 10/1879 | PFt.W&C 62 | |
| 537 | 4-6-0 | BLW | 4/1872 | 2751 | D | 7/1880 | DE | | so | 5/1897 | NYE | |
| 538 | 4-6-0 | BLW | 4/1872 | 2753 | D | ? | DE | | c/u | 12/1895 | | |
| 539 | 4-6-0 | BLW | 5/1872 | 2770 | D | 2/1880 | DE | | ren | 2/1880 | PC&St.L 38 | |
| 540 | 4-6-0 | BLW | 5/1872 | 2771 | D | 4/1879 | DE | | c/u | 7/1888 | | |
| 541 | 4-6-0 | BLW | 5/1872 | 2785 | D | | | | c/u | 2/1894 | | |
| 542 | 4-6-0 | BLW | 5/1872 | 2786 | D | | | | c/u | 2/1894 | | |
| 543 | 4-6-0 | BLW | 5/1872 | 2798 | D | 8/1879 | DE | | c/u | 8/1891 | | |
| 544 | 4-6-0 | BLW | 5/1872 | 2801 | D | 4/1880 | DE | | c/u | 9/1894 | | |
| 545 | 4-6-0 | BLW | 7/1872 | 2854 | D | 5/1880 | DE | | c/u | 8/1891 | | |
| 546 | 4-6-0 | BLW | 7/1872 | 2860 | D | | | | c/u | 5/1895 | | |
| 547 | 4-6-0 | BLW | 8/1872 | 2884 | D | 1/1879 | DE | | ren | 12/1881 | CC&IC 454 | |
| 548 | 4-6-0 | BLW | 8/1872 | 2889 | D | | | | c/u | 4/1890 | | |
| 549 | 4-6-0 | BLW | 8/1872 | 2885 | D | 1/1879 | DE | | ren | 3/1879 | PRR 1076 | |
| 550 | 4-6-0 | BLW | 8/1872 | 2896 | D | 1/1879 | DE | | ren | 1/1879 | PC&St.L 12 | |
| 551 | 4-6-0 | BLW | 9/1872 | 2912 | D | 1/1879 | DE | | ren | 11/1881 | PC&St.L 28 | |

| No. | Type | Bldr. | Date | C/N | Class | Rebuilt | Driv., in. | Cyl., in. | Disp. | Date | To | Notes |
|-----|------|-------|------|-----|-------|---------|-----------|-----------|-------|------|-----|-------|
| 552 | 4-6-0 | BLW | 9/1872 | 2913 | D | 12/1878 | DE | | so | 8/1890 | EHW | |
| 553 | 4-6-0 | BLW | 9/1872 | 2919 | D | | | | c/u | 2/1892 | | |
| 554 | 4-6-0 | BLW | 9/1872 | 2921 | D | | | | c/u | 2/1892 | | |
| 555 | 4-6-0 | BLW | 12/1872 | 3036 | D | 4/1879 | DE | | ren | 4/1879 | PFt.W&C 38 | |
| 556 | 4-6-0 | BLW | 12/1872 | 3033 | D | ? | DE | | ren | 12/1890 | PRR 3023 | |
| 557 | 4-6-0 | BLW | 12/1872 | 3039 | D | 1881 | DE | | c/u | 3/1893 | | |
| 558 | 4-6-0 | BLW | 12/1872 | 3043 | D | | | | ren | 4/1891 | NYP&N 17 | |
| 559 | 4-6-0 | BLW | 12/1872 | 3045 | D | 1881 | DE | | c/u | 7/1892 | | |
| 560 | 4-6-0 | BLW | 12/1872 | 3046 | D | | | | so | 12/1890 | EHW | |
| 561 | 4-6-0 | BLW | 12/1872 | 3049 | D | | | | c/u | 11/1895 | | |
| 562 | 4-6-0 | BLW | 12/1872 | 3051 | D | ? | DE | | ren | 12/1880 | PFt.W&C 78 | |
| 563 | 4-6-0 | BLW | 12/1872 | 3056 | D | | | | so | 9/1889 | EHW | |
| 564 | 4-6-0 | BLW | 12/1872 | 3062 | D | | | | so | 1/1893 | CB | |
| 565 | 4-6-0 | BLW | 12/1872 | 3064 | D | 5-1880 | DE | | c/u | 5/1893 | | |
| 566 | 4-6-0 | BLW | 12/1872 | 3067 | D | | | | c/u | 4/1896 | | |
| 567 | 4-6-0 | BLW | 12/1872 | 3070 | D | | | | ren | 5/1883 | PW&B 103 | |
| 568 | 4-6-0 | BLW | 12/1872 | 3071 | D | | | | ren | 3/1891 | NYP&N 15 | |
| 569 | 4-6-0 | BLW | 12/1872 | 3074 | D | ? | DE | | c/u | 3/1893 | | |
| 570 | 4-4-0 | AMS | 12/1872 | 165 | C | | | | ren | 8/1883 | PW&B 37 | |
| 571 | 4-4-0 | AMS | 12/1872 | 161 | C | | | | ren | 1/1883 | CC&IC 332 | |
| 572 | 4-4-0 | AMS | 12/1872 | 162 | C | | | | ren | 5/1882 | PW&B 88 | |
| 573 | 4-4-0 | AMS | 12/1872 | 163 | C | | | | ren | 6/1883 | GR&I 56 | (Fig. 165) |
| 574 | 4-4-0 | AMS | 12/1872 | 164 | C | | | | ren | 12/1881 | CC&IC 461 | |
| 575 | 4-2-0 | BLW | 12/1852 | 502 | | | 66 | 12x18 | so | 4/1881 | WC | Ex-B D 2. |
| 576 | 4-2-0 | BLW | 12/1852 | 503 | | | 66 | 12x18 | so | 7/1879 | C&H | Ex-B D 3. |
| 577 | 4-4-0 | AMS | 8/1873 | 206 | C | | | | ren | 3/1881 | NCR 100 | |
| 578 | 4-4-0 | AMS | 8/1873 | 207 | C | | | | ren | 10/1881 | B&P 21 | |
| 579 | 4-4-0 | BLW | 8/1856 | 710 | | | 54 | 15x22 | so | 4/1881 | WC | Ex-B D 10. |
| 580 | 4-4-0 | BLW | 8/1853 | 543 | | | 66 | 15x22 | so | 4/1881 | WC | Ex-B D 6. |
| 581 | 4-4-0 | BLW | 9/1853 | 545 | | | 66 | 15x22 | so | 4/1881 | WC | Ex-B D 7. |
| 582 | 4-4-0 | B D | 6/1867 | | | | 66 | 15x22 | c/u | 5/1880 | | Ex-B D 19. |
| 583 | 4-4-0 | B D | 10/1870 | | | | 66 | 15x22 | ren | 6/1882 | PRR 3005 | Ex-B D 25. |
| 584 | 4-4-0 | DC&C | 9/1860 | | | | 48 | 16x22 | so | 4/1881 | EH | Ex-B D 13. |
| 585 | 4-4-0 | B D | 12/1868 | | | | 54 | 16x22 | ren | 6/1882 | PRR 3006 | Ex-B D 9. |
| 586 | 4-4-0 | B D | 6/1864 | | | | 54 | 16x22 | ren | 6/1882 | PRR 3007 | Ex-B D 14. |
| 587 | 4-4-0 | B D | 1/1865 | | | | 54 | 16x22 | ren | 6/1882 | PRR 3008 | Ex-B D 15. |
| 588 | 4-4-0 | B D | 1/1867 | | | | 54 | 16x22 | ren | 6/1882 | PRR 3009 | Ex-B D 18. (Fig. 166) |
| 589 | 4-4-0 | B D | 1/1868 | | | | 54 | 16x22 | ren | 6/1882 | PRR 3010 | Ex-B D 20. |
| 590 | 4-4-0 | B D | 7/1868 | | | | 54 | 16x22 | ren | 6/1882 | PRR 3011 | Ex-B D 21. |
| 591 | 4-4-0 | B D | 6/1869 | | | | 54 | 16x22 | ren | 6/1882 | PRR 3012 | Ex-B D 22. |
| 592 | 4-4-0 | B D | 5/1870 | | | | 54 | 16x22 | ren | 6/1882 | PRR 3013 | Ex-B D 24. |
| 593 | 4-4-0 | B D | 6/1871 | | | | 66 | 16x22 | ren | 6/1882 | PRR 3014 | Ex-B D 27. |
| 594 | 4-4-0 | TL&M | 12/1854 | | | | 48 | 16x24 | so | 4/1881 | WC | Ex-B D 8. |

| No. | Type | Bldr. | Date | C/N | Class | Rebuilt | Driv., in. | Cyl., in. | Disp. | Date | To | Notes |
|-----|------|-------|------|-----|-------|---------|------------|-----------|-------|------|-----|-------|
| 595 | 4-6-0 | AMS | 3/1873 | 174 | E | | | | ren | 4/1879 | PRR 1010 | |
| 596 | 4-4-0 | TL&M | 3/1857 | | | | 54 | 16x24 | so | 4/1881 | WC | Ex-B D 12. |
| 597 | 2-6-0 | B D | 12/1869 | | | | 48 | 16x22 | ren | 6/1882 | PRR 3015 | Ex-B D 23. |
| 598 | 2-6-0 | B D | 2/1871 | | | | 48 | 16x22 | ren | 6/1882 | PRR 3016 | Ex-B D 25. |
| 599 | 2-6-0 | B D | 3/1872 | | | | 48 | 16x22 | ren | 6/1882 | PRR 3017 | Ex-B D 30. |
| 600 | 2-6-0 | LS | 12/1872 | | | | 48 | 16x22 | ren | 6/1882 | PRR 3018 | Ex-B D 31. |
| 601 | 2-2-2-0 | RS | 8/1831 | 25 | | | 54 | 9x20 | don | 2/1885 | SI | Ex-C&A 1. |
| 602 | 4-4-0 | DC&C | 1859 | | | | 66 | 14-1/2x24 | c/u | 4/1876 | | Ex-C&A 2. |
| 603 | 4-4-0 | DC&C | 1859 | | | | 66 | 14-1/2x24 | c/u | 4/1876 | | Ex-C&A 3. |
| 604 | 4-4-0 | DC&C | 1859 | | | | 66 | 14-1/2x24 | c/u | 4/1876 | | Ex-C&A 4. (Fig. 167) |
| 605 | 4-4-0 | DC&C | 1859 | | | | 66 | 14-1/2x24 | so | 3/1881 | JHB | Ex-C&A 5. |
| 606 | 4-4-0 | C&A | 1864 | | | | 66 | 14x26 | c/u | 1/1875 | | Ex-C&A 6. |
| 607 | 4-4-0 | C&A | 1864 | | | | 66 | 14x26 | c/u | 1/1876 | | Ex-C&A 7. |
| 608 | 4-4-0 | C&A | 1865 | | | | 66 | 14x26 | c/u | 1/1876 | | Ex-C&A 8. |
| 609 | 4-4-0 | C&A | 1865 | | | | 66 | 15x26 | so | 11/1881 | EHW | Ex-C&A 9. |
| 610 | 4-4-0 | C&A | 1865 | | | | 66 | 15x26 | so | 7/1879 | C&MR | Ex-C&A 10. |
| 611 | 4-4-0 | C&A | 1865 | | | | 66 | 15x26 | so | 4/1881 | WC | Ex-C&A 11. |
| 612 | 4-4-0 | C&A | 1864 | | | | 60 | 16x24 | so | 4/1880 | JHB | Ex-C&A 12. |
| 613 | 4-4-0 | DC&C | 1864 | | | | 60 | 16x24 | so | 5/1875 | R&D | Ex-C&A 13. |
| 614 | 4-4-0 | DC&C | 1865 | | | | 54 | 16x24 | so | 1/1889 | EHW | Ex-C&A 14. |
| 615 | 4-4-0 | DC&C | 1865 | | | | 54 | 16x22 | so | 1/1889 | EHW | Ex-C&A 15. |
| 616 | 4-4-0 | DC&C | 1865 | | | | 54 | 16x22 | so | 11/1890 | EHW | Ex-C&A 16. |
| 617 | 4-4-0 | DC&C | 1865 | | | | 54 | 16x22 | so | 1/1876 | F&JAgRR | Ex-C&A 17. |
| 618 | 4-4-0 | C&A | 1866 | | | | 66 | 15x26 | so | 4/1880 | WC | Ex-C&A 18. |
| 619 | 4-4-0 | C&A | 1866 | | | | 66 | 15x26 | so | 9/1878 | WC | Ex-C&A 19. |
| 620 | 4-4-0 | C&A | 1845 | | | | 60 | 15x24 | c/u | 4/1877 | | Ex-C&A 20. |
| 621 | 4-4-0 | DC&C | 1858 | | | | 60 | 13x22 | c/u | 11/1881 | | Ex-C&A 21. |
| 622 | 4-4-0 | B D | 6/1866 | | | | 66 | 14x22 | ren | 6/1882 | PRR 3030 | Ex-B D 17 (Fig. 168) |
| 623 | 4-4-0 | DC&C | 1858 | | | | 66 | 14x24 | c/u | 4/1879 | | Ex-C&A 23. |
| 624 | 4-4-0 | DC&C | 1858 | | | | 66 | 14x24 | so | 9/1872 | SCG | Ex-C&A 24. |
| 625 | 4-4-0 | B D | 8/1865 | | | | 66 | 14x22 | ren | 6/1882 | PRR 3021 | Ex-B D 16 |
| 626 | 4-4-0 | AMS | 11/1872 | 155 | C | | | | ren | 8/1881 | NCR 106 | |
| 627 | 4-4-0 | AMS | 11/1872 | 156 | C | | | | ren | 8/1882 | PW&B 95 | |
| 628 | 4-4-0 | C&A | 1868 | | | | 60 | 16x22 | c/u | 5/1878 | | Ex-C&A 28. |
| 629 | 4-4-0 | NB | 1/1850 | | | 1855 | 72 | 13x38 | c/u | 4/1874 | | Ex-C&A 29. |
| 630 | 4-4-0 | NB | 2/1850 | 445 | | 1856 | 72 | 13-1/2x38 | c/u | 4/1874 | | Ex-C&A 30. |
| 631 | 4-4-0 | NB | 1850 | | | 1857 | 72 | 13-1/2x38 | c/u | 4/1874 | | Ex-C&A 31. |
| 632 | 4-4-0 | NB | 1850 | | | 1862 | 72 | 13-1/2x38 | c/u | 4/1874 | | Ex-C&A 32. |
| 633 | | | | | | | | | | | | |
| 634 | 4-6-0 | TL&M | 1852 | | | 4/1869 | 48 | 18x30 | so | 10/1879 | EHW | Ex-C&A 34. |
| 635 | 4-6-0 | C&A | 1852 | | | ? | 48 | 18x30 | c/u | 2/1874 | | Ex-C&A 35. (Fig. 170) |
| 636 | 4-4-0 | RN&S | 1853 | | | | 54 | 14x24 | so | 11/1874 | SCG | Ex-C&A 36. |
| 637 | 4-4-0 | RN&S | 1853 | | | 1856 | 72 | 13-1/2x38 | so | 7/1874 | SCG | Ex-C&A 37. |

| No. | Type | Bldr. | Date | C/N | Class | Rebuilt | Driv., in. | Cyl., in. | Disp. | Date | To | Notes |
|---|---|---|---|---|---|---|---|---|---|---|---|---|
| 638 | 4-6-0 | AMS | 9/1872 | 145 | E | | | | so | 3/1895 | L&RNG | |
| 639 | 4-6-0 | AMS | 2/1873 | 172 | E | | | | ren | 05/79 | NCR 34 | |
| 640 | 4-4-0 | DC&C | 4/1853 | | | | 66 | 15x20 | so | 3/1874 | F&JAgRR | Ex-C&A 40. |
| 641 | 4-4-0 | RL&M | 6/1853 | 399 | | | 66 | 15x20 | c/u | 1/1880 | | Ex-C&A 41. |
| 642 | 4-6-0 | TL&M | 1854 | | | ? | 48 | 18x30 | so | 7/1874 | SCG | Ex-C&A 42. |
| 643 | 4-6-0 | B D | 9/1871 | | | | 48 | 17x22 | ren | 6/1882 | PRR 3032 | Ex-B D 28. |
| 644 | 4-6-0 | B D | 12/1871 | | | | 48 | 17x22 | ren | 6/1882 | PRR 3033 | Ex-B D 29. |
| 645 | 4-4-0 | BLW | 1/1854 | 570 | | | 60 | 15x22 | c/u | 1/1878 | | Ex-C&A 45. |
| 646 | 4-4-0 | RN&S | 1853 | | | | 60 | 15x22 | so | 10/1874 | SCG | Ex-C&A 46. |
| 647 | 4-4-0 | NJL&M | 1852 | | | | 60 | 16x20 | so | 7/1879 | EHW | Ex-C&A 47. (Figs. 171A & B) |
| 648 | 4-4-0 | RL&M | 10/1854 | 541 | | | 66 | 15-1/2x20 | c/u | 5/1878 | | Ex-C&A 48. |
| 649 | 4-4-0 | RL&M | 11/1854 | 544 | | | 66 | 15-1/2x20 | c/u | 2/1875 | | Ex-C&A 49. |
| 650 | 4-4-0 | RL&M | 11/1854 | 548 | | | 66 | 15-1/2x20 | c/u | 4/1877 | | Ex-C&A 50. |
| 651 | 4-4-0 | AMS | 12/1872 | 157 | C | | | | ren | 6/1881 | NCR 104 | |
| 652 | 4-4-0 | AMS | 8/1873 | 208 | C | | | | ren | 11/1882 | PRR 2020 | |
| 653 | 4-4-0 | AMS | 12/1872 | 158 | C | | | | so | 3/1894 | NYE | (Fig. 64) |
| 654 | 4-4-0 | AMS | 8/1873 | 209 | C | | | | ren | 5/1881 | PRR 1035 | |
| 655 | 4-4-0 | AMS | 9/1873 | 210 | C | | | | ren | 2/1883 | PRR 2106 | |
| 656 | 4-4-0 | RN&S | 1853 | | | 1870 | 60 | 15x22 | c/u | 5/1878 | | Ex-C&A 56. |
| 657 | 4-4-0 | RN&S | 1853 | | | 1871 | 60 | 15x22 | c/u | 4/1874 | | Ex-C&A 57. |
| 658 | 4-4-0 | C&A | 1860 | | | | 68 | 14x26 | c/u | 2/1875 | | Ex-C&A 58. |
| 659 | 4-4-0 | NJLM | 1861 | | | | 60 | 16x24 | so | 5/1879 | WC | Ex-C&A 59. |
| 660 | 4-4-0 | DC&C | 1861 | | | | 54 | 16x24 | so | 5/1878 | WC | Ex-C&A 60. |
| 661 | 4-4-0 | DC&C | 1861 | | | 1871 | 58 | 16x24 | ren | 6/1882 | PRR 3019 | Ex-C&A 61. |
| 662 | 4-4-0 | AMS | 12/1872 | 159 | C | | | | ren | 8/1882 | PB&W 96 | |
| 663 | 4-4-0 | C&A | 1862 | | | | 66 | 14-1/2x26 | so | 7/1885 | EHW | Ex-C&A 63. |
| 664 | 4-4-0 | AMS | 9/1873 | 211 | C | | | | ren | 11/1881 | CC&IC 459 | |
| 665 | 4-4-0 | DC&C | 1862 | | | | 60 | 16x24 | so | 4/1882 | EHW | Ex-C&A 65. |
| 666 | 4-4-0 | DC&C | 1862 | | | | 60 | 16x24 | so | 3/1886 | EHW | Ex-C&A 66. |
| 667 | 4-4-0 | DC&C | 1862 | | | | 60 | 16x24 | so | 3/1881 | EHW | Ex-C&A 67. |
| 668 | 4-4-0 | AMS | 12/1872 | 160 | C | | | | ren | 12/1881 | CC&IC 462 | |
| 669 | 4-4-0 | DC&C | 1862 | | | | 60 | 16x24 | c/u | 3/1874 | | Ex-C&A 69. |
| 679 | 2-6-0 | C&A | 1867 | | | | 54 | 17x24 | ren | 6/1882 | PRR 3020 | Ex-C&A 79. |
| 680 | 4-6-0 | C&A | 1867 | | | | 54 | 17x24 | c/u | 5/1878 | | Ex-C&A 80. |
| 681 | 4-4-0 | C&A | 1868 | | | | 66 | 16x24 | so | 12/1891 | EHW | Ex-C&A 81. |
| 682 | 4-4-0 | C&A | 6/1868 | | | | 66 | 16x24 | so | 12/1891 | EHW | Ex-C&A 82. |
| 683 | 4-4-0 | C&A | 12/1868 | | | | 66 | 16x24 | so | 8/1889 | UT 1 | Ex-C&A 83. |
| 684 | 4-4-0 | C&A | 1869 | | | | 66 | 16x24 | so | 8/1888 | UT | Ex-C&A 84. |
| 685 | 2-6-0 | C&A | 4/1869 | | | | 54 | 17x24 | so | 4/1878 | EHW | Ex-C&A 85. |
| 686 | 4-4-0 | C&A | 1869 | | | | 60 | 17x24 | so | 12/1885 | SC | Ex-C&A 86. |
| 687 | 4-4-0 | C&A | 8/1869 | | | | 60 | 17x24 | c/u | 3/1880 | | Ex-C&A 87. |
| 688 | 4-4-0 | C&A | 1869 | | | | 60 | 17x24 | c/u | 4/1880 | | Ex-C&A 88. |
| 689 | 4-4-0 | C&A | 1869 | | | | 66 | 16x24 | so | 6/1886 | EHW | Ex-C&A 89. |

| No. | Type | Bldr. | Date | C/N | Class | Rebuilt | Driv., in. | Cyl., in. | Disp. | Date | To | Notes |
|---|---|---|---|---|---|---|---|---|---|---|---|---|
| 690 | 4-4-0 | C&A | 3/1870 | | | | 66 | 16x24 | c/u | 12/1894 | | Ex-C&A 90. |
| 691 | 4-4-0 | C&A | 4/1870 | | | | 66 | 16x24 | so | 8/1887 | EHW | Ex-C&A 91. |
| 692 | 4-4-0 | C&A | 6/1870 | | | | 66 | 16x24 | so | 7/1891 | UT | Ex-C&A 92. |
| 693 | 4-4-0 | C&A | 1870 | | | | 60 | 17x24 | so | 12/1893 | EHW | Ex-C&A 93. |
| 694 | 4-4-0 | C&A | 10/1870 | | | | 60 | 17x24 | so | 12/1893 | EHW | Ex-C&A 94. |
| 695 | 4-4-0 | C&A | 12/1870 | | | | 60 | 17x24 | so | 10/1880 | EHW | Ex-C&A 95. |
| 696 | 4-4-0 | C&A | 2/1871 | | | | 60 | 17x24 | so | 8/1888 | UT | Ex-C&A 96. |
| 697 | 4-4-0 | C&A | 4/1871 | | | | 60 | 17x24 | so | 8/1886 | EHW | Ex-C&A 97. |
| 698 | 4-4-0 | C&A | 6/1871 | | | | 60 | 17x24 | so | 12/1893 | EHW | Ex-C&A 98. |
| 699 | 4-4-0 | BS | 1/1872 | | | | 66 | 17x24 | c/u | 12/1894 | | |
| 700 | 4-4-0 | BS | 4/1872 | | | | 66 | 17x24 | c/u | 12/1894 | | |
| 701 | 0-4-0 | NJRT | 9/1869 | | | | 48 | 14x22 | so | 2/1884 | EHW | Ex-NJRR&T 1. |
| 702 | 4-4-0 | NJRT | 5/1869 | | | | 60 | 16x22 | so | 7/1882 | EHW | Ex-NJRR&T 2. |
| 703 | 4-4-0 | NJRT | 4/1868 | | | | 60 | 16x22 | so | 4/1881 | WC | Ex-NJRR&T 3. |
| 704 | 4-4-0 | NJRT | 3/1866 | | | | 66 | 16x24 | so | 4/1881 | EH | Ex-NJRR&T 4. |
| 705 | 0-4-0 | RL&M | 3/1865 | 1247 | | | 48 | 14x22 | so | 2/1884 | EHW | Ex-NJRR&T 5. |
| 706 | 0-4-0 | RL&M | 3/1865 | 1249 | | | 48 | 14x22 | so | 3/1885 | EHW | Ex-NJRR&T 6. |
| 707 | 4-4-0 | NJRT | 4/1865 | | | | 66 | 15x20 | c/u | 12/1880 | | Ex-NJRR&T 7. |
| 708 | 4-4-0 | RL&M | 5/1865 | 1261 | | | 66 | 16x22 | so | 3/1886 | EHW | Ex-NJRR&T 8. |
| 709 | 4-4-0 | NJRT | 1/1868 | | | | 60 | 16x22 | ren | 11/1879 | WJ 1 | Ex-NJRR&T 9. |
| 710 | 4-4-0 | NJRT | 12/1868 | | | | 66 | 16x22 | c/u | 3/1882 | | Ex-NJRR&T 10. |
| 711 | 4-4-0 | NJRT | 7/1868 | | | | 66 | 16x24 | c/u | 1/1876 | | Ex-NJRR&T 11. |
| 712 | 4-4-0 | NJRT | 2/1866 | | | | 66 | 15x20 | so | 4/1881 | WC | Ex-NJRR&T 12. |
| 713 | 4-4-0 | NJRT | 1865 | | | 5/1872 | 60 | 13x20 | so | 6/1877 | WC | Ex-NJRR&T 13. |
| 714 | 4-4-0 | NJRT | 1867 | | | | 60 | 14x20 | c/u | 1/1876 | | Ex-NJRR&T 14. |
| 715 | 4-4-0 | NJRT | 9/1867 | | | | 66 | 15x20 | ren | 1/1876 | C&MV 808 | Ex-NJRR&T 15. |
| 716 | 4-4-0 | RL&M | 1851 | 259 | | 1867 | 72 | 15x20 | c/u | 4/1874 | | Ex-NJRR&T 16. |
| 717 | 4-4-0 | NJRT | 6/1869 | | | | 66 | 16x20 | so | 2/1884 | EHW | Ex-NJRR&T 17. |
| 718 | 4-4-0 | NJRT | 1865 | | | | 66 | 15x20 | so | 7/1882 | EHW | Ex-NJRR&T 18. |
| 719 | 4-4-0 | NJRT | 5/1859 | | | | 66 | 15x22 | so | 3/1874 | SCG | Ex-NJRR&T 19. |
| 720 | 4-4-0 | NJRT | 6/1866 | | | | 60 | 15x20 | so | 6/1888 | AHK | Ex-NJRR&T 20. |
| 721 | 4-4-0 | NJRT | 7/1865 | | | | 60 | 15x20 | c/u | 5/1875 | | Ex-NJRR&T 21. |
| 722 | 4-4-0 | NJRT | 1865 | | | | 66 | 15x22 | c/u | 11/1881 | | Ex-NJRR&T 22. |
| 723 | 4-4-0 | JCLW | 1865 | | | | 66 | 16x22 | c/u | 3/1874 | | Ex-NJRR&T 23. |
| 724 | 4-4-0 | NJRT | 1857 | | | | 66 | 16x22 | c/u | 7/1874 | | Ex-NJRR&T 24. |
| 725 | 4-4-0 | NJRT | 11/1869 | | | | 60 | 16x22 | so | 6/1881 | EHW | Ex-NJRR&T 25. |
| 726 | 4-4-0 | NJLM | 1857 | | | | 66 | 15x22 | ren | 2/1876 | C&MV 806 | Ex-NJRR&T 26. |
| 727 | 4-4-0 | RL&M | 1859 | 880 | | | 66 | 16x22 | so | 6/1877 | WC | Ex-NJRR&T 27. |
| 728 | 4-6-0 | JCLW | 1859 | | | | 50 | 16x22 | so | 3/1886 | EHW | Ex-NJRR&T 28. |
| 729 | 4-4-0 | RL&M | 1859 | 923 | | | 66 | 16x22 | c/u | 7/1874 | | Ex-NJRR&T 29. |
| 730 | 4-4-0 | JCLW | 1864 | | | | 66 | 16x24 | c/u | 3/1874 | | Ex-NJRR&T 30. |
| 731 | 4-4-0 | JCLW | 1865 | | | | 60 | 16x24 | so | 3/1874 | SCG | Ex-NJRR&T 31. |
| 732 | 4-4-0 | RL&M | 8/1863 | 1090 | | | 60 | 16x22 | so | 3/1886 | EHW | Ex-NJRR&T 32. |

| No. | Type | Bldr. | Date | C/N | Class | Rebuilt | Driv., in. | Cyl., in. | Disp. | Date | To | Notes |
|---|---|---|---|---|---|---|---|---|---|---|---|---|
| 733 | 4-4-0 | RL&M | 10/1863 | 1103 | | | 60 | 16x22 | so | 4/1881 | WC | Ex-NJRR&T 33. |
| 734 | 4-4-0 | RL&M | 10/1863 | 1104 | | | 60 | 16x22 | so | 4/1881 | WC | Ex-NJRR&T 34. |
| 735 | 2-6-0 | RL&M | 10/1863 | 1106 | | | 54 | 17x22 | so | 10/1879 | EHW | Ex-NJRR&T 35. |
| 736 | 2-6-0 | RL&M | 11/1863 | 1107 | | | 54 | 17x22 | c/u | 8/1880 | | Ex-NJRR&T 36. (Fig. 172) |
| 737 | 4-4-0 | RL&M | 9/1864 | 1198 | | | 60 | 16x22 | so | 3/1881 | EHW | Ex-NJRR&T 37. |
| 738 | 4-4-0 | RL&M | 10/1864 | 1202 | | | 60 | 16x22 | so | 3/1881 | EHW | Ex-NJRR&T 38. |
| 739 | 2-6-0 | RL&M | 1/1865 | 1227 | | | 54 | 17x22 | so | 10/1879 | EHW | Ex-NJRR&T 39. |
| 740 | 4-4-0 | RL&M | 2/1865 | 1239 | | | 60 | 16x22 | so | 4/1881 | WC | Ex-NJRR&T 40. |
| 741 | 4-4-0 | NJRT | 11/1869 | | | | 60 | 16x22 | so | 6/1889 | EHW | Ex-NJRR&T 41. |
| 742 | 4-4-0 | NJRT | 1870 | | | | 60 | 16x22 | so | 6/1889 | EHW | Ex-NJRR&T 42. |
| 743 | 4-4-0 | NJRT | 1870 | | | | 60 | 16x22 | so | 10/1880 | EHW | Ex-NJRR&T 43. |
| 744 | 4-4-0 | NJRT | 10/1870 | | | | 66 | 16x22 | so | 1/1879 | LEE&SW | Ex-NJRR&T 44. |
| 745 | 4-4-0 | NJRT | 7/1871 | | | | 60 | 17x22 | so | 2/1884 | EHW | Ex-NJRR&T 45. |
| 746 | 4-4-0 | JCS | 12/1872 | | | | 60 | 17x22 | c/u | 4/1892 | | |
| 747 | 4-4-0 | NJRT | 12/1870 | | | | 56 | 17x22 | so | 3/1886 | EHW | Ex-NJRR&T 47. |
| 748 | 4-4-0 | NJRT | 4/1871 | | | | 56 | 17x22 | so | 3/1886 | EHW | Ex-NJRR&T 48. |
| 749 | 4-4-0 | NJRT | 10/1871 | | | | 66 | 17x22 | so | 7/1888 | EHW | Ex-NJRR&T 49. (Fig. 173) |
| 750 | 4-4-0 | WPS | 12/1872 | | | | 66 | 17x22 | c/u | 12/1892 | | |
| 751 | 4-6-0 | BLW | 12/1872 | 3028 | D | 2/1879 | DE | | ren | 4/1879 | NCR 42 | |
| 752 | 2-6-0 | BLW | 8/1871 | 2544 | | | 54 | 17x24 | ren | 6/1882 | PRR 3002 | Ex-C&A 152. |
| 753 | 2-6-0 | BLW | 8/1871 | 2540 | | | 54 | 17x24 | ren | 6/1882 | PRR 3023 | Ex-C&A 153. |
| 754 | 2-6-0 | BLW | 9/1871 | 2554 | | | 54 | 17x24 | ren | 6/1882 | PRR 3024 | Ex-C&A 154. |
| 755 | 2-6-0 | BLW | 9/1871 | 2560 | | | 54 | 17x24 | ren | 6/1882 | PRR 3025 | Ex-C&A 155. |
| 756 | 2-6-0 | BLW | 9/1871 | 2562 | | | 54 | 17x24 | ren | 6/1882 | PRR 3026 | Ex-C&A 156. |
| 757 | 2-6-0 | DC&C | 12/1871 | | | | 54 | 17x24 | ren | 6/1882 | PRR 3027 | Ex-C&A 157. |
| 758 | 2-6-0 | DC&C | 12/1871 | | | | 54 | 17x24 | ren | 6/1882 | PRR 3028 | Ex-C&A 158. |
| 759 | 2-6-0 | DC&C | 12/1871 | | | | 54 | 17x24 | so | 4/1887 | EHW | Ex-C&A 159. |
| 760 | 2-6-0 | DC&C | 10/1871 | | | | 54 | 17x24 | so | 1/1890 | EHW | Ex-C&A 160. |
| 761 | 2-6-0 | DC&C | 10/1871 | | | | 54 | 17x24 | ren | 6/1882 | PRR 3029 | Ex-C&A 161. |
| 762 | 4-4-0 | C&A | 8/1871 | | | | 66 | 17x24 | so | 12/1888 | EHW | Ex-C&A 162. |
| 763 | 4-4-0 | C&A | 10/1871 | | | | 66 | 17x24 | so | 12/1893 | EHW | Ex-C&A 163. |
| 764 | 4-4-0 | C&A | 1866 | | | | 54 | 13x20 | so | 3/1886 | EHW | Ex-C&A "A". (Fig. 174) |
| 765 | 4-4-0 | C&A | 1866 | | | | 54 | 13x20 | so | 4/1881 | WC | Ex-C&A "B". |
| 766 | 4-4-0 | C&A | 1866 | | | | 54 | 13x20 | so | 10/1874 | PSR | Ex-C&A "C". |
| 767 | 4-4-0 | C&A | 1866 | | | | 54 | 13x20 | so | 6/1888 | HCM | Ex-C&A "D". |
| 768 | 4-4-0 | DC&C | 4/1857 | | | | 60 | 13x20 | c/u | 7/1878 | | Ex-C&A "E". |
| 769 | 4-4-0 | DC&C | 1856 | | | | 66 | 13x22 | so | 4/1879 | WC | Ex-C&A "F". |
| 770 | 0-4-0 | DC&C | 8/1856 | | | | 40 | 11x20 | so | 3/1886 | EHW | Ex-C&A "G". |
| 771 | 4-6-0 | AMS | 6/1872 | 134 | E | | | | ren | 3/1879 | PRR 1008 | |
| 772 | 4-6-0 | AMS | 7/1872 | 135 | D | ? | DE | | ren | 9/1879 | CC&IC 312 | |
| 773 | 4-6-0 | AMS | 7/1872 | 136 | E | | | | ren | 3/1879 | PRR 1054 | |
| 774 | 4-6-0 | AMS | 7/1872 | 137 | E | | | | c/u | 2/1894 | | |
| 775 | 4-6-0 | AMS | 7/1872 | 138 | E | | | | so | 1/1895 | JTG | |

| No. | Type | Bldr. | Date | C/N | Class | Rebuilt | Driv., in. | Cyl., in. | Disp. | Date | To | Notes |
|-----|------|-------|------|-----|-------|---------|-----------|-----------|-------|------|-----|-------|
| 776 | 4-6-0 | AMS | 7/1872 | 139 | E | | | | ren | 4/1879 | NCR 54 | |
| 777 | 4-6-0 | AMS | 8/1872 | 140 | D | ? | DE | | ren | 9/1879 | CC&IC 313 | |
| 778 | 4-6-0 | AMS | 8/1872 | 141 | E | | | | ren | 10/1881 | PC&StL 3 | |
| 779 | 4-6-0 | AMS | 8/1872 | 142 | E | | | | c/u | 8/1892 | | |
| 780 | 4-6-0 | AMS | 8/1872 | 143 | E | | | | ren | 6/1883 | NCR 82 | |
| 781 | 0-6-0 | AMS | 10/1872 | 146 | H | | | | c/u | 11/1893 | | |
| 782 | 0-6-0 | AMS | 10/1872 | 147 | H | | | | so | 8/1894 | JTG | |
| 783 | 0-6-0 | AMS | 10/1872 | 148 | H | | | | c/u | 5/1896 | | |
| 784 | 0-6-0 | AMS | 10/1872 | 149 | H | | | | so | 8/1894 | JTG | |
| 785 | 0-6-0 | AMS | 10/1872 | 150 | H | | | | so | 12/1894 | JTG | |
| 786 | 0-6-0 | AMS | 11/1872 | 151 | H | | | | c/u | 9/1894 | | |
| 787 | 0-6-0 | AMS | 3/1873 | 178 | H | | | | so | 10/1894 | JTG | |
| 788 | 0-6-0 | AMS | 3/1873 | 179 | H | | | | c/u | 5/1894 | | |
| 789 | 0-6-0 | AMS | 4/1873 | 180 | H | | | | ren | 7/1883 | PRR 2053 | |
| 790 | 0-6-0 | AMS | 4/1873 | 181 | H | | | | c/u | 2/1894 | | |
| 791 | 0-6-0 | AMS | 4/1873 | 182 | H | | | | so | 11/1894 | JTG | |
| 792 | 0-6-0 | AMS | 4/1873 | 183 | H | | | | c/u | 5/1894 | | |
| 793 | 4-6-0 | AMS | 3/1873 | 175 | E | | | | c/u | 3/1897 | | |
| 794 | 4-6-0 | AMS | 3/1873 | 176 | E | | | | ren | 5/1879 | NCR 53 | |
| 795 | 4-6-0 | AMS | 3/1873 | 177 | E | | | | ren | 5/1879 | NCR 76 | |
| 801 | 4-6-0 | BLW | 3/1873 | 3140 | D | ? | DE | | c/u | 7/1898 | | |
| 802 | 4-6-0 | BLW | 3/1873 | 3145 | D | | | | c/u | 8/1895 | | |
| 803 | 4-6-0 | BLW | 3/1873 | 3144 | D | ? | DE | | c/u | 11/1900 | | |
| 804 | 4-6-0 | BLW | 3/1873 | 3146 | D | | | | c/u | 10/1894 | | |
| 805 | 4-6-0 | BLW | 3/1873 | 3158 | D | ? | DE | | ren | 12/1890 | PRR 3026 | |
| 806 | 4-6-0 | BLW | 3/1873 | 3157 | D | ? | DE | | c/u | 12/1900 | | |
| 807 | 4-6-0 | BLW | 3/1873 | 3159 | D | | | | c/u | 9/1892 | | |
| 808 | 4-6-0 | BLW | 3/1873 | 3173 | D | | | | ren | 6/1890 | NYP&N 13 | |
| 809 | 4-6-0 | BLW | 3/1873 | 3176 | D | ? | DE | | c/u | 7/1895 | | |
| 810 | 4-6-0 | BLW | 4/1873 | 3181 | D | ? | DE | | c/u | 1/1898 | | |
| 811 | 4-6-0 | BLW | 4/1873 | 3183 | D | ? | DE | | ren | 4/1874 | PRR 1152 | |
| 812 | 4-6-0 | BLW | 4/1873 | 3188 | D | ? | DE | | ren | 12/1878 | NCR 47 | |
| 813 | 4-6-0 | BLW | 4/1873 | 3191 | D | ? | DE | | c/u | 7/1890 | | |
| 814 | 4-6-0 | BLW | 4/1873 | 3201 | D | | | | so | 1/1893 | CB | |
| 815 | 4-6-0 | BLW | 4/1873 | 3202 | D | ? | DE | | ren | 12/1881 | St.LV&TH 149 | |
| 816 | 4-6-0 | BLW | 4/1873 | 3204 | D | ? | DE | | c/u | 3/1893 | | |
| 817 | 4-6-0 | BLW | 4/1873 | 3206 | D | | | | ren | 7/1879 | PFt.W&C 73 | |
| 818 | 4-6-0 | BLW | 4/1873 | 3211 | D | | | | c/u | 9/1894 | | |
| 819 | 4-6-0 | BLW | 4/1873 | 3213 | D | | | | c/u | 2/1894 | | |
| 820 | 4-6-0 | BLW | 5/1873 | 3223 | D | | | | c/u | 7/1893 | | |
| 821 | 4-6-0 | BLW | 5/1873 | 3224 | D | ? | DE | | so | 4/1891 | EHW | |
| 822 | 4-6-0 | BLW | 5/1873 | 3228 | D | | | | ren | 6/1882 | P&BC 201 | |
| 823 | 4-6-0 | BLW | 5/1873 | 3231 | D | ? | DE | | c/u | 11/1893 | | |

| No. | Type | Bldr. | Date | C/N | Class | Rebuilt | Driv., in. | Cyl., in. | Disp. | Date | To | Notes |
|---|---|---|---|---|---|---|---|---|---|---|---|---|
| 824 | 4-6-0 | BLW | 5/1873 | 3232 | D | ? | DE | | ren | 5/1874 | PRR 1153 | |
| 825 | 4-6-0 | BLW | 5/1873 | 3236 | D | | | | ren | 1/1881 | PC&St.L 58 | |
| 826 | 4-6-0 | BLW | 5/1873 | 3244 | D | ? | DE | | so | 1/1893 | EHW | |
| 827 | 4-6-0 | BLW | 5/1873 | 3246 | D | ? | DE | | so | 1/1893 | CB | |
| 828 | 4-6-0 | BLW | 5/1873 | 3250 | D | | | | ren | 4/1892 | WJ 13 | |
| 829 | 4-6-0 | BLW | 5/1873 | 3254 | D | | | | so | 9/1889 | EHW | |
| 830 | 4-6-0 | BLW | 5/1873 | 3255 | D | ? | DE | | c/u | 5/1898 | | |
| 831 | 4-6-0 | BLW | 5/1873 | 3257 | D | ? | DE | | ren | 12/1880 | PC&St.L 33 | |
| 832 | 4-6-0 | BLW | 6/1873 | 3275 | D | ? | DE | | ren | 1/1879 | PC&St.L 36 | |
| 833 | 4-6-0 | BLW | 6/1873 | 3278 | D | ? | DE | | c/u | 3/1892 | | |
| 834 | 4-6-0 | BLW | 6/1873 | 3285 | D | | | | ren | 4/1880 | St.LV&TH 173 | |
| 835 | 4-6-0 | BLW | 6/1873 | 3287 | D | | | | ren | 11/1882 | PW&B 101 | |
| 836 | 4-6-0 | BLW | 6/1873 | 3289 | D | ? | DE | | so | 2/1893 | EHW | |
| 837 | 4-6-0 | BLW | 6/1873 | 3291 | D | ? | DE | | c/u | 5/1902 | | |
| 838 | 4-6-0 | BLW | 6/1873 | 3290 | D | | | | ren | 5/1891 | WJ 25 | |
| 839 | 4-6-0 | BLW | 6/1873 | 3292 | D | | | | c/u | 2/1901 | | |
| 840 | 4-6-0 | BLW | 6/1873 | 3299 | D | ? | DE | | so | 3/1896 | NYE | |
| 841 | 4-6-0 | BLW | 6/1873 | 3300 | D | ? | DE | | c/u | 9/1891 | | |
| 842 | 4-6-0 | BLW | 7/1873 | 3301 | D | ? | DE | | ren | 5/1882 | GR&I 52 | |
| 843 | 4-6-0 | BLW | 7/1873 | 3302 | D | ? | E | | ren | 11/1880 | PFt.W&C 41 | |
| 844 | 4-6-0 | BLW | 7/1873 | 3303 | D | | | | c/u | 5/1893 | | |
| 845 | 4-6-0 | BLW | 7/1873 | 3304 | D | ? | E | | ren | 10/1879 | PFt.W&C 6 | |
| 846 | 4-6-0 | BLW | 7/1873 | 3311 | D | ? | DE | | ren | 12/1878 | NCR 51 | |
| 847 | 4-6-0 | BLW | 7/1873 | 3315 | D | ? | E | | ren | 1/1881 | PFt.W&C 60 | |
| 848 | 4-6-0 | BLW | 6/1873 | 3316 | D | ? | DE | | ren | 4/1874 | PRR 1154 | |
| 849 | 4-6-0 | BLW | 7/1873 | 3317 | D | | | | c/u | 9/1891 | | |
| 850 | 4-6-0 | BLW | 7/1873 | 3323 | D | | | | c/u | 6/1895 | | |
| 851 | 4-6-0 | BLW | 7/1873 | 3326 | D | | | | ren | 6/1890 | NYP&N 14 | |
| 852 | 4-6-0 | BLW | 8/1873 | 3333 | D | | | | ren | 9/1892 | PRR 833 | |
| 853 | 4-6-0 | BLW | 8/1873 | 3335 | D | | | | ren | 9/1892 | PRR 852 | |
| 854 | 4-6-0 | BLW | 8/1873 | 3340 | D | ? | DE | | c/u | 3/1893 | | |
| 855 | 4-6-0 | BLW | 8/1873 | 3342 | D | | | | c/u | 1/1893 | | |
| 856 | 4-6-0 | BLW | 8/1873 | 3343 | D | ? | DE | | c/u | 6/1892 | | |
| 857 | 4-6-0 | BLW | 8/1873 | 3345 | D | | | | c/u | 6/1893 | | |
| 858 | 4-6-0 | BLW | 8/1873 | 3346 | D | | | | c/u | 6/1893 | | |
| 859 | 4-6-0 | BLW | 8/1873 | 3347 | D | | | | c/u | 12/1895 | | |
| 860 | 4-6-0 | BLW | 8/1873 | 3354 | D | | | | so | 4/1897 | NYE | |
| 861 | 4-6-0 | BLW | 8/1873 | 3352 | D | 9/1880 | DE | | ren | 11/1882 | PW&B 100 | |
| 862 | 4-6-0 | BLW | 8/1873 | 3356 | D | 7/1879 | DE | | ren | 10/1879 | PFt.W&C 86 | |
| 863 | 4-6-0 | BLW | 8/1873 | 3361 | D | 11/1878 | DE | | ren | 1/1879 | PC&St.L 26 | |
| 864 | 4-6-0 | BLW | 8/1873 | 3370 | D | 1/1880 | DE | | c/u | 6/1892 | | |
| 865 | 4-6-0 | BLW | 8/1873 | 3372 | D | 5/1880 | DE | | c/u | 5/1893 | | |
| 866 | 4-6-0 | BLW | 9/1873 | 3380 | D | | | | ren | 7/1883 | P&BC 215 | |

| No. | Type | Bldr. | Date | C/N | Class | Rebuilt | Driv., in. | Cyl., in. | Disp. | Date | To | Notes |
|-----|------|-------|------|-----|-------|---------|-----------|-----------|-------|------|-----|-------|
| 867 | 4-6-0 | BLW | 9/1873 | 3376 | D | | | | c/u | 3/1891 | | |
| 868 | 4-6-0 | BLW | 9/1873 | 3382 | D | ? | DE | | so | 3/1896 | NYE | |
| 869 | 4-6-0 | BLW | 9/1873 | 3387 | D | 4/1880 | DE | | so | 4/1895 | NYE | |
| 870 | 4-6-0 | BLW | 9/1873 | 3390 | D | | | | c/u | 12/1894 | | |
| 871 | 4-6-0 | BLW | 9/1873 | 3396 | D | 5/1880 | DE | | c/u | 5/1893 | | |
| 872 | 4-6-0 | BLW | 9/1873 | 3395 | D | | | | c/u | 2/1898 | | |
| 873 | 4-6-0 | BLW | 9/1873 | 3402 | D | | | | c/u | 5/1893 | | |
| 874 | 4-6-0 | BLW | 9/1873 | 3406 | D | | | | so | 5/1888 | AC&C | |
| 875 | 4-6-0 | BLW | 9/1873 | 3407 | D | 10/1879 | DE | | ren | 1/1879 | PC&St.L 35 | |
| 876 | 4-6-0 | BLW | 9/1873 | 3409 | D | | | | so | 3/1894 | NYE | |
| 877 | 4-6-0 | BLW | 9/1873 | 3414 | D | | | | c/u | 2/1894 | | |
| 878 | 4-6-0 | BLW | 9/1873 | 3412 | D | | | | c/u | 5/1895 | | |
| 906 | 0-6-0T | AMS | 4/1873 | 184 | F | | | | c/u | 9/1896 | | |
| 907 | 0-6-0T | AMS | 4/1873 | 185 | F | | | | so | 9/1892 | US&S | |
| 908 | 0-6-0T | AMS | 5/1873 | 186 | F | | | | so | 7/1897 | NYE | |
| 909 | 0-6-0T | AMS | 5/1873 | 187 | F | | | | so | 9/1892 | CPG | |
| 910 | 0-6-0T | AMS | 5/1873 | 188 | F | | | | so | 9/1889 | JW | |
| 911 | 0-6-0T | AMS | 5/1873 | 189 | F | | | | c/u | 8/1895 | | |
| 912 | 4-4-0 | AMS | 5/1873 | 190 | C anth | | | | c/u | 4/1896 | | (Fig. 73) |
| 913 | 4-4-0 | AMS | 6/1873 | 191 | C anth | | | | so | 10/1895 | CPa&W | |
| 914 | 4-4-0 | AMS | 6/1873 | 192 | C anth | | | | c/u | 2/1895 | | |
| 915 | 4-4-0 | AMS | 6/1873 | 193 | C anth | | | | c/u | 7/1896 | | |
| 916 | 4-4-0 | AMS | 6/1873 | 194 | C anth | | | | c/u | 4/1896 | | |
| 917 | 4-4-0 | AMS | 6/1873 | 195 | C anth | | | | ren | 7/1884 | PRR 3007 | |
| 918 | 4-4-0 | AMS | 6/1873 | 196 | C anth | | | | ren | 7/1890 | PRR 3002 | |
| 919 | 4-4-0 | AMS | 7/1873 | 197 | C anth | | | | ren | 9/1890 | PRR 3014 | |
| 920 | 4-4-0 | AMS | 7/1873 | 198 | C anth | | | | c/u | 7/1902 | | |
| 921 | 4-4-0 | AMS | 7/1873 | 199 | C anth | | | | c/u | 12/1898 | | |
| 922 | 4-4-0 | AMS | 7/1873 | 200 | C anth | | | | ren | 7/1884 | PRR 3008 | |
| 923 | 4-4-0 | AMS | 7/1873 | 201 | C anth | | | | so | 4/1893 | B&SRR | (Fig. 74) |
| 924 | 4-4-0 | AMS | 9/1873 | 212 | B | | | | c/u | 6/1896 | | |
| 925 | 4-4-0 | AMS | 9/1873 | 213 | B | | | | ren | 8/1899 | WJ 6 | (Fig. 61) |
| 926 | 4-4-0 | AMS | 9/1873 | 214 | G | | | | c/u | 9/1892 | | |
| 927 | 4-4-0 | AMS | 10/1873 | 215 | G | | | | so | 2/1890 | EHW | |
| 928 | 4-4-0 | AMS | 10/1873 | 216 | G | | | | c/u | 7/1891 | | |
| 929 | 4-4-0 | AMS | 10/1873 | 217 | G | | | | ren | 9/1896 | PRR 46 | |
| 930 | 4-4-0 | AMS | 10/1873 | 218 | G | | | | ren | 10/1899 | PRR 558 | (Fig. 70) |
| 931 | 4-4-0 | AMS | 10/1873 | 219 | G | | | | c/u | 2/1894 | | |
| 932 | 4-4-0 | AMS | 10/1873 | 220 | G | | | | c/u | 1/1891 | Machinery only. | Boiler transferred to 930. |
| 933 | 4-4-0 | AMS | 10/1873 | 221 | G | | | | c/u | 5/1889 | | |
| 934 | 4-4-0 | AMS | 11/1873 | 222 | G | | | | c/u | 2/1892 | | |
| 935 | 4-4-0 | AMS | 11/1873 | 223 | G | | | | so | 11/1892 | SRR | |
| 936 | 4-4-0 | AMS | 11/1873 | 224 | G | | | | c/u | 4/1891 | | |

| No. | Type | Bldr. | Date | C/N | Class | Rebuilt | Driv., in. | Cyl., in. | Disp. | Date | To | Notes |
|-----|------|-------|------|-----|-------|---------|-----------|-----------|-------|------|------|-------|
| 937 | 4-4-0 | AMS | 11/1873 | 225 | G | | | | ren | 6/1891 | PRR 44 | |
| 938 | 0-6-0 | AMS | 12/1873 | 226 | H | | | | c/u | 4/1898 | | |
| 939 | 0-6-0 | AMS | 12/1873 | 227 | H | | | | so | 6/1897 | NYE | |
| 940 | 0-6-0 | AMS | 12/1873 | 228 | H | | | | c/u | 7/1892 | | |
| 941 | 0-6-0 | AMS | 12/1873 | 229 | H | | | | c/u | 5/1893 | | |
| 942 | 0-6-0 | AMS | 12/1873 | 230 | H | | | | so | 7/1902 | EHW | |
| 943 | 0-6-0 | AMS | 12/1873 | 231 | H | | | | ren | 5/1890 | C&A 506 | |
| 944 | 0-6-0 | AMS | 12/1873 | 232 | H | | | | c/u | 7/1893 | | |
| 945 | 0-6-0 | AMS | 12/1873 | 233 | H | | | | c/u | 2/1895 | | |
| 946 | 0-6-0 | AMS | 12/1873 | 234 | H | | | | so | 10/1894 | JTG | |
| 947 | 0-6-0 | AMS | 12/1873 | 235 | H | | | | ren | 7/1890 | WJ 15 | |
| 948 | 0-6-0 | AMS | 12/1873 | 236 | H | | | | so | 1/1895 | EHW | |
| 949 | 0-6-0 | AMS | 12/1873 | 237 | H | | | | so | 3/1895 | EHW | (Fig. 72) |
| 950 | 2-8-0 | BLW | 8/1873 | 3339 | | | 48 | 20x24 | c/u | 7/1894 | | (Fig. 75) |
| 951 | 2-8-0 | BLW | 8/1873 | 3337 | | | 48 | 20x24 | c/u | 1/1895 | | |
| 952 | 2-8-0 | BLW | 8/1873 | 3348 | | | 48 | 20x24 | c/u | 7/1894 | | |
| 953 | 2-8-0 | BLW | 8/1873 | 3351 | | | 48 | 20x24 | c/u | 5/1882 | | |

## Notes on rebuildings:

38   Rebuilt from 4-6-0 (44, 18x22) AMS 10/1867.

39   Rebuilt from 4-6-0 (44, 18x22) AMS 9/1867.

41   Rebuilt from 2-6-0 (44, 17x22) AMS 1862.

43   Rebuilt from 2-6-0 (44, 17x22) AMS ?

44   Rebuilt from 0-8-0 (44, 18x20) AMS ?

46   Rebuilt from 2-6-0 (44, 18x22) AMS 5/1867.

47   Rebuilt from 2-6-0 (44, 18x24) AMS 12/1867.

50   Rebuilt from 0-8-0 Camel (44, 19x22) AMS 12/1866.

51   Rebuilt from 0-8-0 Camel (44, 19x22), AMS 9/1866.

52   Rebuilt from 0-8-0 Camel (44, 19x22), AMS 8/1864.

58   Rebuilt from 4-4-0 (60, 16x24), AMS 12/1867.

71   Rebuilt from 4-4-0 (60, 16x24), AMS 3/1868.

73   Rebuilt from 4-4-0 (54, 16x24), AMS 5/1862, originally named *Nanticoke*.

74   Rebuilt from 2-6-0 (44, 17x22), AMS 2/1868.

77   Rebuilt from 2-6-0, AMS, 1865.

81   Rebuilt from 4-4-0 (54, 16x24), AMS 6/1868.

84   Rebuilt from 4-4-0 (54, 16x24), AMS 7/1868.

85   Rebuilt from 4-4-0 (54, 16x24), AMS 12/1865.

88   Rebuilt from 0-8-0 Camel (44, 19x22), AMS 11/1867.

91   Rebuilt from 0-8-0 Camel (44, 19x22), AMS 5/1867.

94   Rebuilt from 0-8-0 (44, 19x22), AMS 12/1865.

95   Rebuilt from 0-8-0 (44, 19x22), AMS 12/1865.

119   Rebuilt from 0-8-0 Camel (44, 19x22), AMS 1/1865.

121   Rebuilt from 0-8-0 Camel (44, 19x22), AMS 6/1866.

| | |
|---|---|
| 124 | Rebuilt from 0-8-0 Camel (44, 19x22), AMS 2/1865. |
| 126 | Originally named *Sullivan*. |
| 130 | Rebuilt from 0-8-0 Camel (44, 19x22), AMS 6/1867. |
| 134 | Rebuilt from 4-4-0 (66, 15x24) ? |
| 135 | Rebuilt from 4-4-0 (66, 15x24) ? |
| 141- | The original locos holding PRR #s 141-210 (those with names) were purchased from the State Works and came into possession of PRR 8/1857. |
| 195 | #'s 141- 195 were from the Philadelphia & Columbia and #s 196-210 were from the Allegheny Portage. |
| 147 | Given to J.T. Dyer to replace an engine destroyed by the PRR. |
| 169 | Rebuilt from 4-4-0 (60, 16x22), AMS 05/1866. |
| 173 | Rebuilt from 4-4-0 (60, 16x22), AMS 02/1867. |
| 175 | Rebuilt from 4-4-0 (60, 16x22) ? |
| 177 | Rebuilt from 4-4-0 (60, 16x22) ? |
| 182 | Rebuilt from 4-4-0 (60, 17x22) ? |
| 187 | Rebuilt from 4-4-0 (54, 16x22) ? |
| 192 | Rebuilt from 4-4-0 (60, 18x22) ? |
| 203 | Rebuilt from 4-4-0 (54, 12x24), AMS 8/1865. |
| 204 | Rebuilt from 4-6-0 (48, 17x24), AMS 12/1866. |
| 205 | Rebuilt from 4-6-0 (48, 17x24), AMS 10/1866. |
| 208 | Rebuilt from 4-6-0 (48, 17x24), AMS 12/1865. |
| 210 | Rebuilt from 4-6-0 (44, 17x22), AMS 12/1866.  Former PRR 63, transferred to P&E and returned. |
| 245 | Rebuilt from 4-6-0 (48, 18x22), AMS 1866. |
| 261 | Rebuilt from 4-4-0 (66, 16x24), AMS 7/1866. |
| 347 | Rebuilt from 4-4-0 (66, 17x24), AMS 12/1866.  Blew up at Duncannon, Pa., 9/5/1865. |
| 480 | Shown as vacant on the Stratton register. |
| 481 | Shown as vacant on the Stratton register. |
| 482 | Shown as vacant on the Stratton register. |
| 601 | The *John Bull* was built as a 0-4-0, but the C&A did not connect the drivers, and added a truck to support the cow-catcher.  It ran as a 2-2-2-0. |
| 620 | PRR records show #620 filled by URR&CCo #20 79" drivers, 4/1860. 14x24 may be the dimensions for URR&C Company #20. |
| 620 | Rebuilt from 4-4-0 (54, 13x20). |
| 629 | Rebuilt by the C&A from a Crampton style 6-2-0 (96, 13x38). |
| 630 | Rebuilt by the C&A from a Crampton style 6-2-0 (96, 13-1/2x38). |
| 631 | Rebuilt by the C&A from a Crampton style 6-2-0 (96, 13-1/2x38). |
| 632 | Rebuilt by the C&A from a Crampton style 6-2-0 (96, 13-1/2x38). |
| 634 | Rebuilt by the C&A from a "Monster" 0-8-0 (48, 18x30). |
| 635 | Rebuilt by the C&A from a "Monster" 0-8-0 (48, 18x30). |
| 637 | Rebuilt by the C&A from a Crampton style 6-2-0 (84, 13-1/2x38). |
| 642 | Rebuilt by the C&A from a "Monster" 0-8-0 (48, 18x30). |
| 674 | Traded for West Jersey #5; #5 cut up in 1874. |
| 699 | Completed after lease of C&A by PRR. |
| 700 | Completed after lease of C&A by PRR.  #700 shown as vacant in the Stratton register. |
| 719 | Rebuild of RL&M #381 1853. |
| 722 | Rebuild of RL&M #475 1854. |
| 724 | The Stratton list corrected by Lovell and the NJRR&T January 1, 1867 *Register* show #724 as Mason #44 1856. |
| 725 | Rebuild of RL&M #648 1856. |

| 726 | The Stratton list corrected by Lovell and the NJRR&T January 1, 1867 *Register* show Mason #77, 1857. |
| 746 | Completed after the PRR lease. |
| 750 | Completed after the PRR lease. |
| 796-800 | Vacant. |
| 879-905 | Vacant. |

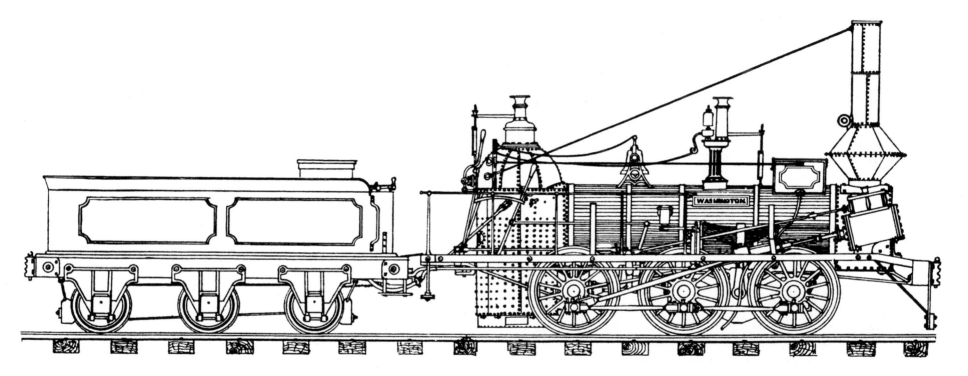

## Six-coupled Locomotive "Washington," built by The Baldwin Locomotive Works, 1847

*Figure 94.* #4, Washington (*Baldwin, six 46" drivers, 13" x 16" cylinders*), *a Baldwin flexible-beam-truck six-wheeler, was built for the HPM&L in 1847. The loco was not built with a cab, and the components of the Bury firebox are quite evident in the drawing. After the PRR acquired the H&L locos, a cab was added. The stack is an inverted diamond.*
(*C.H. Caruthers drawing; author's collection*)

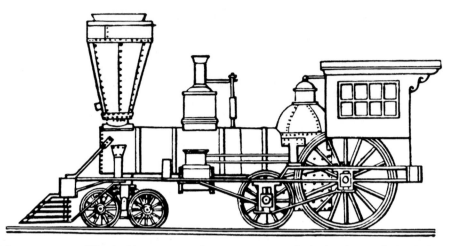

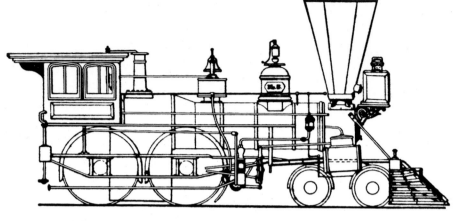

The " Mifflin," P. R. R.

*Figure 95*. #5, Mifflin (Baldwin, two 72" drivers, 14" x 20" cylinders). *This rough sketch shows the first locomotive to pull a train in revenue service on the PRR. A Baldwin Special A Class, Mifflin and her two sisters,* Blair *and* Indiana, *had a carrying wheel in front of the 72" driver, controlled by a lever which shifted the weight from the carrying wheel when the locomotive was starting. Note the cylinder placement.* (Author's collection)

*Figure 96*. #5, Mifflin, *as rebuilt in 1855 as a 4-4-0. The cylinders were moved to the smoke box, a new boiler was built with a wagon top firebox, the old Bury firebox was eliminated, and a new frame was constructed with four 66" drivers.* (Author's collection)

◄

*Figure 97*. #6, Blair, *as rebuilt in 1854 as a 4-4-0. The cylinders were moved to the smoke box, the carrying wheel was removed, and a new frame with four 72" drivers was fabricated.* Blair *retained the old Bury firebox.* (Author's collection)

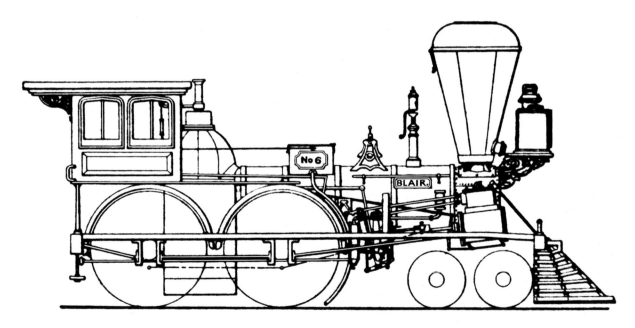

The " Blair," P. R. R.

**Figure 98.** #7, Juniata (Baldwin, four 54" drivers, 15" x 30" cylinders), a Baldwin class C locomotive, was the first 4-4-0 built for the PRR. The whistle and one safety valve were on the column on the first boiler course and a second safety valve was on the Bury dome. The loco was equipped with Baldwin's half-stroke-cutoff valve gear. Typical of the PRR's early locos, no road name appears on the tender. Twenty-three of this general type were built between November 1849 and January 1852. *(C.H. Caruthers drawing; author's collection)*

**Figure 99.** #10, Indiana (Baldwin, two 72" drivers, 14" x 20" cylinders), remained in service virtually unchanged until 1863, except for the removal of the carrying wheel. Mifflin, Blair and Indiana were the only inside connected locomotives purchased by the PRR. The cylinders drove a crank axle on the single main driver. *(Author's collection)*

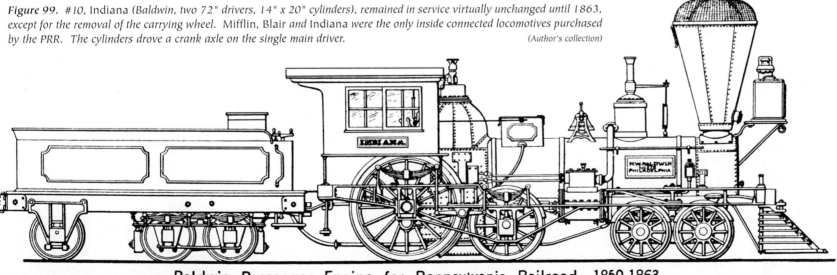

## Baldwin Passenger Engine for Pennsylvania Railroad, 1850-1863.

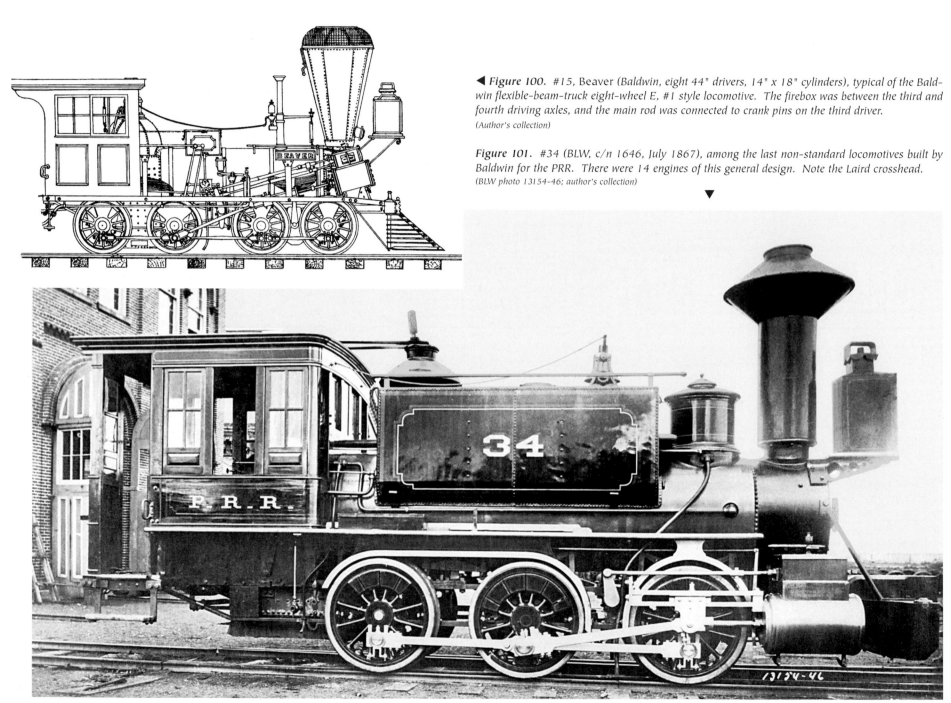

◀ *Figure 100.* #15, Beaver (*Baldwin, eight 44" drivers, 14" x 18" cylinders), typical of the Baldwin flexible-beam-truck eight-wheel E, #1 style locomotive. The firebox was between the third and fourth driving axles, and the main rod was connected to crank pins on the third driver.* (Author's collection)

*Figure 101.* #34 (*BLW, c/n 1646, July 1867), among the last non-standard locomotives built by Baldwin for the PRR. There were 14 engines of this general design. Note the Laird crosshead.* (BLW photo 13154-46; author's collection)

▼

303

*Figure 102.* #39, Berks *(Baldwin, six 44" drivers, 18" x 22" cylinders), was one of six coal-burning Baldwin D locomotives built with a raised firebox, four-wheel vibrating truck, and whistle on a column on the boiler waist.*
(Author's collection)

▶

*Figure 103.* #40, Atalanta *(Wilmarth, four 78" drivers, 16" x 22" cylinders), was one of three fast passenger locomotives constructed by Seth Wilmarth of Boston. Wilmarth began to build locos in 1848 and was ruined in 1854 when the Erie could not pay for a large order.* Atalanta *had a troubled existence; she struck a tree on Christmas Day 1854 and was overturned. After being rebuilt and placed back on the road in March 1855 she struck a rock and was "wrecked worse than before."*
(Author's collection)

▶

*Figure 104.* Atalanta *(#40), as rebuilt.* Atalanta *was again rebuilt at Altoona in 1865. The locomotive received a new boiler, cylinders and spread engine truck. The drivers were reduced to 60".*   (Author's collection)

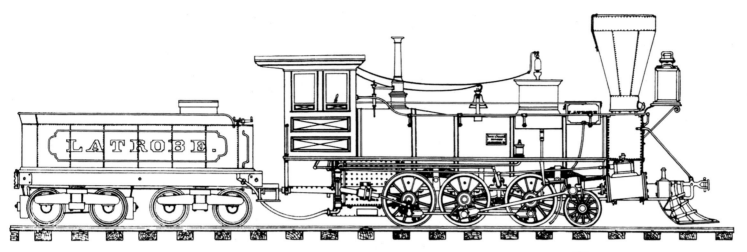

◀ *Figure 105*. #41, Latrobe (*Smith & Perkins, six 44" drivers, 17" x 22" cylinders*), *the first locomotive built by Smith & Perkins of Alexandria, Virginia for the PRR. Latrobe and Altoona had wagon-top boilers and mixed frames. Bar frames extended from the pilot beam to the front of the firebox, where slab frames were used. The engine truck was held in pedestals and had only a slight lateral movement.* (Author's collection)

▶ *Figure 106*. #42, Cumberland (*Baldwin, six 44" drivers, 18" x 22" cylinders*), *one of six Baldwin D coal-burning locomotives, having a single leading wheel with boxes set in rigid pedestal jaws. In 1855 the single wheels were removed and a four-wheel vibrating truck was substituted.* (Author's collection)

◀ *Figure 107*. #42 (*AMS, c/n 46, November 1869*), *Class F. #42 was photographed sometime after 1880 when capped stacks were applied to freight and shifting locomotives. The loco is equipped with air brakes, but aside from the stack is unchanged from when built. Note the early form of Alligator crosshead.* (Author's collection)

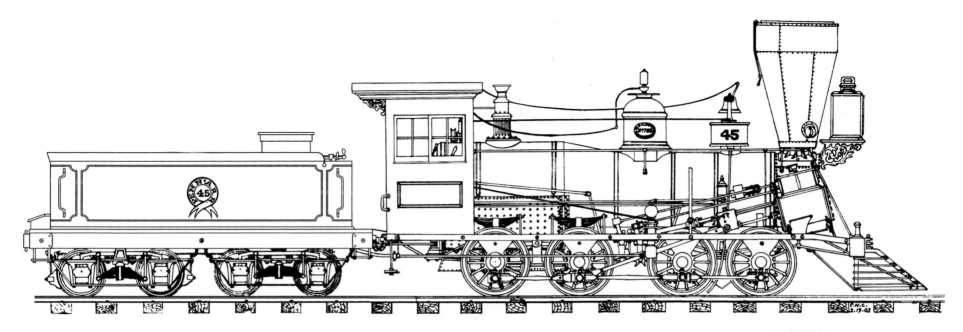

▲

*Figure 108.* #45 (Baldwin, six 44" drivers, 18" x 20" cylinders), built in November 1857 to replace Northumberland, a Baldwin D-Class 4-6-0, which was sold to the Steubenville & Indiana. The engine is a flexible-beam-truck E #3 with the firebox above the axles of the rear driver. In comparing the drawing of #45 with the drawings of Beaver and Perry, the advance in the design of the flexible-beam truck loco is evident. Gone is the Bury firebox. Baldwin continued to build flexible-beam-truck locos until 1866.
(Author's collection)

▶

*Figure 109.* #46 (Baldwin, c/n 508, January 1853). Built as Lancaster, a Baldwin "D" 2-6-0 with a rigid engine truck, #46 was rebuilt at Altoona in May 1867 for $14,202. Not much of the old Lancaster is left; the loco received a new boiler, link motion, cylinders and new wheel arrangement as well as Laird's crosshead and two bar guide and stack. (Author's collection)

139

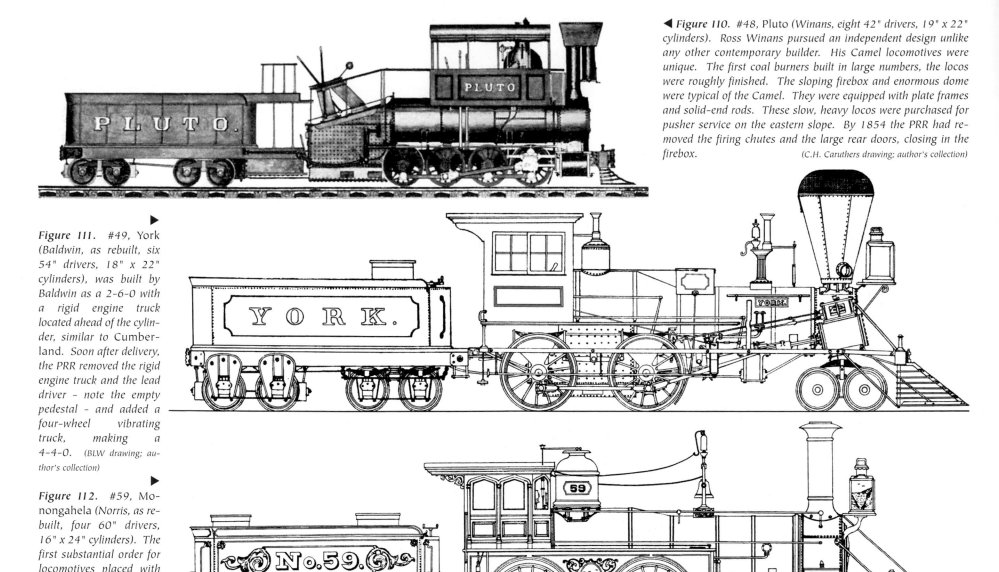

▲ *Figure 110.* #48, Pluto (Winans, eight 42" drivers, 19" x 22" cylinders). *Ross Winans pursued an independent design unlike any other contemporary builder. His Camel locomotives were unique. The first coal burners built in large numbers, the locos were roughly finished. The sloping firebox and enormous dome were typical of the Camel. They were equipped with plate frames and solid-end rods. These slow, heavy locos were purchased for pusher service on the eastern slope. By 1854 the PRR had removed the firing chutes and the large rear doors, closing in the firebox.* (C.H. Caruthers drawing; author's collection)

*Figure 111.* #49, York ▶ (Baldwin, as rebuilt, six 54" drivers, 18" x 22" cylinders), *was built by Baldwin as a 2-6-0 with a rigid engine truck located ahead of the cylinder, similar to Cumberland. Soon after delivery, the PRR removed the rigid engine truck and the lead driver - note the empty pedestal - and added a four-wheel vibrating truck, making a 4-4-0.* (BLW drawing; author's collection)

*Figure 112.* #59, Mo- ▶ nongahela (Norris, as rebuilt, four 60" drivers, 16" x 24" cylinders). *The first substantial order for locomotives placed with Richard Norris & Son was in 1853 for two classes of 4-4-0's with 16" x 24" cylinders, one with 72" drivers and the other with 60" drivers. Mononga- hela was rebuilt in 1861 and only the cylinders, "D"-shaped smokebox and first three rings of the boiler barrel were retained. The firebox was fitted with a Gill & Co. smoke consuming device. The sandboxes were placed under the running boards in the wheel covers. This was the first PRR locomotive to have the oil cups placed in the cab, with the connecting pipes following the steam supply pipes instead of having the cups at the top of the valve chest.* (C.H. Caruthers drawing; author's collection)

End View of "Buckhorns"

M.W. BALDWIN - PENNSYLVANIA R.R. - 24 OF THIS TYPE BUILT **C** FROM SEPT'R 1850 TO MARCH 1859 FOR

ADAMS.

**Figure 113.** #63, Philadelphia (Smith & Perkins, six 44" drivers, 17" x 24" cylinders). The second group of Smith & Perkins pseudo-Moguls, ten built between 1853 and 1854, had straight top boilers with copper fireboxes. Many were rebuilt with four-wheel trucks. (Author's collection)

**Figure 114.** #66, Adams (Baldwin, four 54" drivers, 17" x 22" cylinders), a development of the Baldwin C-Class 4-4-0 for freight service (**Fig. 98**). The improved design discarded the Bury firebox and replaced it with a small wagon-top. A standpipe with a safety valve was located about mid-point on the firebox and another safety valve and whistle were located on the steam dome. About 24 of these were built for freight service between Harrisburg and Altoona. (C.H. Caruthers drawing; author's collection)

**Figure 115.** #77 (Smith & Perkins, December 1853). Johnstown, built by Smith & Perkins as a 2-6-0 with a rigid engine truck, was rebuilt at Altoona in 1863 with a new engine truck, cylinders, and link motion. Note the original "buckhorn" with the whistle and spring-balanced lever safety valve that protrudes through the sand-box. Originally equipped with copper fireboxes, these locomotives gave good service as coal burners. Note the cinder chute used for cleaning the cinders trapped by the screens in the balloon stack. (Author's collection)

Total Weight 54,900 lbs. On Drivers 34,300 lbs.
Fuel, Wood. Worn out in 1869.

Cylinders 16" x 24"
Drivers 54"
Boiler 44"

**Figure 116.** *#79, Nittany (Norris, four 54" drivers, 16" x 24" cylinders). Built by Richard Norris & Son,* Nittany *was the first of eight similar 4-4-0's for freight service. Note the spring arrangement between the two drivers, above the running board.*

*(C.H. Caruthers drawing; author's collection)*

M.W. BALDWIN & CO, LOCOMOTIVE BUILDERS,
PHILADELPHIA.

Lith & Printed in Colors by L.N. Rosenthal, Philadelphia.

**Figure 117.** *#95, Iron City (Baldwin, eight 43" drivers, 19" x 22" cylinders). Another Baldwin flexible-beam-truck E #3 0-8-0,* Iron City *and her sisters* Quaker City, Pennsylvania *and* Bedford *were purchased for helper service on the eastern slope. The locomotive had a wagon-top boiler, two steam domes (one over the firebox and another on the boiler waist, which had the whistle), Baldwin's variable cutoff and auxiliary frames.*

*(BLW drawing photocopy; author's collection)*

**Figure 118.** *#96, Allegrippus (Norris, six 44" drivers, 17" x 22" cylinders). Norris built two of these for the PRR,* Allegrippus *and* Kittatinny, *similar in design to the Smith & Perkins pseudo-Moguls. The driving wheels were set close together, with the leading wheels held in rigid jaws just behind the cylinders. This made for a rather short wheelbase. Note the half-elliptic springs between the rear and main driver, and between the front driver and leading wheel. In his article (Railroad Gazette, May 4, 1900, p.290) on these locos, Caruthers suggests that they had fireboxes with sloping tops. The valve gear was the Norris V-hook with independent half-stroke cutoff. Both were transferred to the Steubenville & Indiana.*

*(C.H. Caruthers drawing; author's collection)*

*Figures 120A, 120B.* #101 (Altoona, c/n 11a, November 1868). #101 is somewhat of a mystery. Not shown in the list used to construct the "official" consecutive list of locomotives built by the Altoona Machine Shop, the badge plate has the date November 1868. The traditional list of locomotives built at Altoona has inserted #101 between AMS c/n 11, November 1868 (PRR #27, Class A) and AMS c/n 12 (PRR #62, Class D). The locomotives is not a standard design, although it has standard features and was later classified Odd Class A. It has a straight boiler, 62" drivers and 17" x 24" cylinders.

(Engineman's side view is PRR photo ME3139A; both are from the author's collection) ▼

▲

*Figure 119.* #96 (Baldwin, c/n 1495, July 1866), lasted on the roster until November 1890, when it was sold for further operation. Note the arabesques on the cab and tender.
(PRR photo ME1292A; author's collection)

143

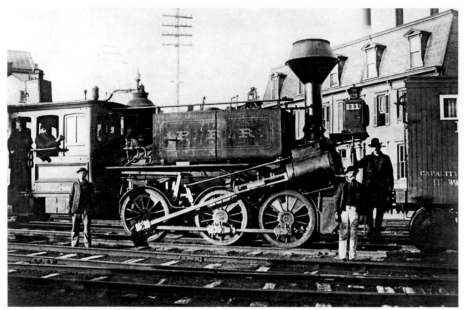

*Figure 121.* #111 *(Baldwin, c/n 1199, December 1863). An "in service" photograph shows the injector just in front of the cab.*
(Author's collection)

*Figure 122.* #119 *(Ross Winans, January 1856). Corn Planter, a Winans Camel, was rebuilt at Altoona at a cost of $8,825 in January 1865 with slant cylinders. Later conversions had level cylinders. Note the injector under the cab. Locomotives rebuilt later in 1865 had a pump on the engineman's side.*
(PRR photo ME1317A; author's collection)

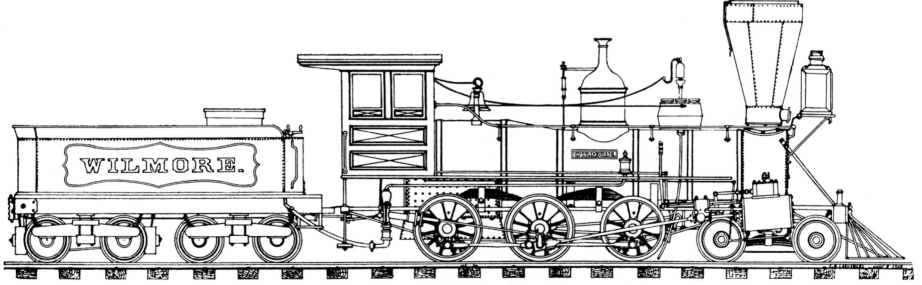

*Figure 123.* #127, Wilmore *(Smith & Perkins, six 44" drivers, 17" x 22" cylinders), and her sisters* Cresson *and* Gallitzin, *were the last locos that the PRR ordered from Smith & Perkins. They were an improvement over the earlier pseudo-Mogul type and represented conventional mechanical practice for the mid-1850's. The boilers were of the wagon-top type with the steam dome in the middle boiler course. In typical Smith & Perkins practice, the whistle stand passed up through the sand box. The valve gear was of the "suspended-link," or Gooch, type.*
(C.H. Caruthers drawing; author's collection)

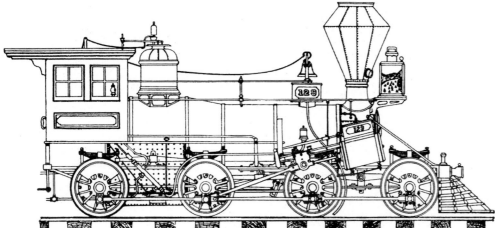

Number 129—After Remodeling at Altoona in 1864.

◀ *Figure 124.* #129 (Baldwin (as rebuilt) eight 43" drivers, 18" x 20" cylinders), was built to replace a Smith & Perkins 4-6-0 of the same number which was transferred to the Steubenville & Indiana. The loco began life as a typical Baldwin flexible-beam-truck 0-8-0. During Laird's tenure it was rebuilt; the flexible-beam truck was removed, the frame lengthened and the front driver placed in front of the cylinders. The original intent of the flexible-beam loco - adaptability to the uneven track structure of American railroads - was entirely compromised by this monster. *(C.H. Caruthers drawing; author's collection)*

*Figure 125.* #134, Tiger (Baldwin, four 66" drivers, 18" x 24" cylinders), the first Baldwin engine on the PRR with link motion. The engine sported a Russian iron boiler jacket, brass domes, red wheels and a pink tender. ▶ *(Reed Kinnert drawing; author's collection)*

◀ *Figure 126.* #137 (Baldwin, c/n 1304, November 1864). Equipped with a steel firebox and a 3½" combustion chamber, 20 were built to this design with 54" drivers and 18" x 24" cylinders. The locomotives were equipped with two primitive injectors, or "squirts." *(PRR photo ME1324A; author's collection)*

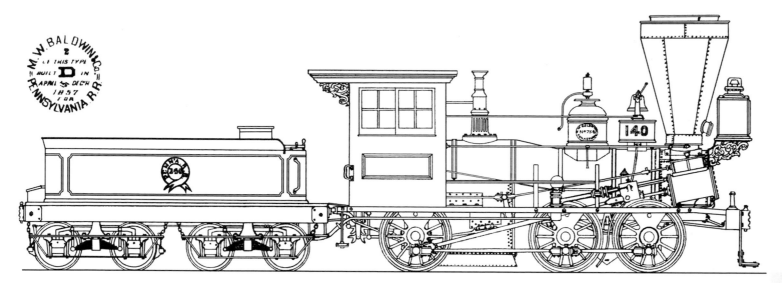

*Figure 127.* #140, Consolidation (Baldwin, six 44" drivers, 14½" x 18" cylinders), was the last named loco purchased by the PRR; the name might refer to the impending addition of the State roads to the Company. It is a Baldwin flexible-beam-truck 0-6-0, a forerunner of the "distributing" loco or shifter. The "first" locos used specifically as shifters by the PRR were Baldwin's with flexible-beam-trucks and side tanks.
(C.H. Caruthers drawing; author's collection)

*Figure 128.* #143 (Baldwin, c/n 1068, July 1862), was tiny, weighing only 34,935 lbs. and built with 11" x 16" cylinders and 36" drivers. Note the sandbox for the front drivers under the slanted cylinders. The builder's information is on the valve chest. #143 was sold in 1891 for further operation.
(BLW photo 13154-23; author's collection)

*Figure 129.* #165 (New Jersey, *four 60" drivers, 16" x 22" cylinders), the former Philadelphia & Columbia* Atalanta. *Although this Caruthers drawing shows it to be built by the Lancaster Locomotive Works,* Atalanta *was built by the New Jersey Locomotive & Machine Company in September 1853. #165 is a typical Brandt locomotive without modification. The valve chambers sloped outward and down, and the throttle was located in the steam dome on the boiler waist.*
(C.H. Caruthers drawing; author's collection) ▶

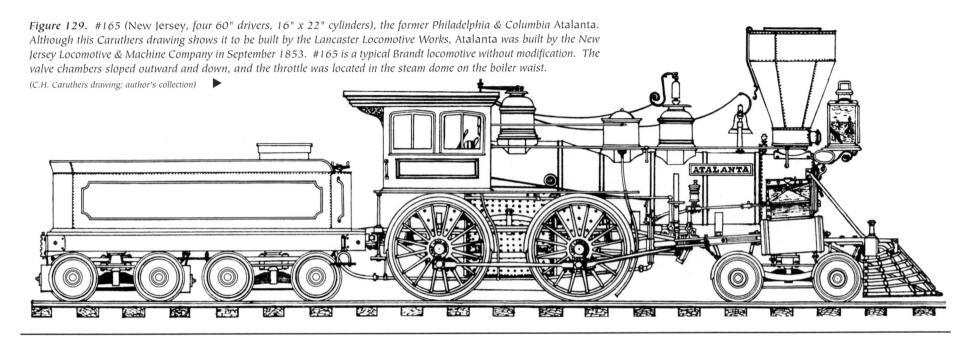

## Pennsylvania Railroad Locomotive Which Hauled the Train of the Prince of Wales in 1860.

*Figure 130.* #166 (New Jersey, *four 60" drivers, 16" x 22" cylinders), the former Philadelphia & Columbia* Wheatland, *is another example of a Brandt locomotive. A column for the safety valve has replaced the rear steam dome, and a straight stack has been fitted.*

(C.H. Caruthers drawing; author's collection)

*Figure 131.* #168 (Altoona, c/n 13, December 1868), D Class. The first standard freight locomotives built at Altoona had Laird stacks; later they were built with diamond stacks. The loco has one crosshead pump and one injector. Some D locomotives were rebuilt with 50" drivers and reclassified DE. This was the third PRR locomotive to carry #168. Note the number on the snowplow pilot.
(PRR photo; author's collection)

*Figure 132.* #169 (Richard Norris & Son, April 1854). Built as President for the Philadelphia & Columbia and taken into PRR stock in August 1857, #169 was rebuilt into a 2-6-0 at Altoona for $14,506 in May 1866 during the end of Laird's term as Master of Machinery. The loco has a Laird stack and crosshead. Note the water pump running off the rear driver. The crosshead pump was hard on the crosshead and occasionally forced the crosshead guide out of line.
(PRR photo ME1266A; author's collection)

◄ **Figure 133.** *#170 (Richard Norris & Son, May 1854). The former P&C Governor, photographed at Harrisburg, has been considerably rebuilt. Note the tank for the "lime-light" on the pilot. The locomotive in the background is a Philadelphia & Reading machine.* (Railroad Museum of Pennsylvania)

**Figure 134.** *#187 (New Jersey Loco. & Mach., April 1856). The Corporal Trim was typical of the 4-4-0's used in freight service on the P&C. Although built after John Brandt left Paterson for Lancaster, the loco was turned out in "Brandt" style with twin steam domes and sloping valve chests. This style of cylinder arrangement was so popular with the P&C that they had Norris of Philadelphia build several that were similar.* (PRR photo ME1312A; author's collection) ▼

M.E.1312A

◄ *Figure 135.* #195 *(Lancaster Loco. Works, February 1857). Ex-P&C John C. Breckenridge is another Brandt locomotive. When Brandt was Superintendent at Lancaster he had the builder, date built and his name put on the brass hub plates on each driver axle.* #195 *was rebuilt at Altoona, the front steam dome was removed and higher drivers (60" to 66") put on. In the PRR's Register of Engines, both the NJL&M and Lancaster locomotives are shown as built by Brandt.*
(PRR photo ME1321A; author's collection)

*Figure 136.* #203 *(Norris Bros., June 1850), began life as a 4-4-0, Montgomery, on the Allegheny Portage. Altoona rebuilt it in August 1865 as an 0-4-0T shifter for $4,027. The engine retained its Bury firebox, but Stephenson valve gear replaced the old hook motion. Note the sandbox beside the Laird stack. The photograph gives an excellent view of Laird's crosshead.*
(PRR photo; author's collection) ►

*Figure 137.* #205 (Richard Norris & Son, April 1854). The former Allegheny Portage Hercules was rebuilt at Altoona from a 4-6-0 with 48" drivers and 17" x 24" cylinders to a 2-6-0 with 19" x 24" cylinders and 60" drivers in December 1866. These high-wheeled Moguls were used as passenger helpers on the eastern slope from Altoona to Gallitzin. Equipped with a new boiler, frame, Laird stack and crossheads, the rebuilding information is on the side of the valve chest – "Rebuilt at Altoona Shops 1866." *(PRR photo; author's collection)*

*Figure 138.* #208 (Richard Norris & Son, April 1854). The former Allegheny Portage Blair is shown in the February 1868 Register of Engines as "rebuilt Laird & Collin design." *(Railroad Museum of Pennsylvania)*

◄

*Figure 139.* #210 (Smith & Perkins, September 1853?). Philadelphia (#63) and Wilkinsburg (#93), Smith & Perkins 2-6-0's with rigid engine trucks, were sent to the Philadelphia & Erie in 1864. They were later returned to the PRR and one of them was numbered #210 - likely #63, and rebuilt at Altoona. The first #210 was a 4-6-0 with a Phleger boiler used in the smoke consuming tests of 1859. The locomotive pictured here retains the old Smith & Perkins boiler and domes. It has a "buckhorn," with the safety valves and whistle extended up through the sandbox. The locomotive has a new frame, cylinders and drivers and a Laird stack and crossheads. #210 was destroyed in the Pittsburgh riots of 1877.

*(PRR photo ME1277A; author's collection)*

M. W. BALDWIN & CO., Locomotive Builders, PHILADELPHIA.

▲ *Figure 140.* #214 (Baldwin, c/n 1004, July 1861). Equipped with a Smith boiler, #214 appears to have the sandboxes under the skirting below the running boards; note the sand pipes between the first and second drivers. #1 **(Fig. 80)** is quite similar, but with a sandbox where the bell is on #214. There are two badge plates or builder's plates on the skirting. Both read "M.W. Baldwin & Co."; the one nearest the front has the date while the rear plate has the builder's number. (BLW photo 13154-13; author's collection)

▶

*Figure 142.* #233 (Rogers Loco. & Mach., c/n 1009, February 1862). One of the few Rogers locomotives on the PRR, there were only four in this class. #233 has a roomy cab and an injector between the drivers. The position of the injector, next to the firebox, must have caused problems with the early application of the squirt. (PRR photo ME1275A; author's collection)

**Figure 141.** #218 (Altoona, c/n 24, May 1869) E. Designed for "mountain freight service," the E class locomotives had 50" drivers and a slightly different boiler than the D. #218 is equipped with a pump and an injector. The PRR used iron pilots on its freight locomotives. (PRR photo 1327A; author's collection)

**Figure 143.** #242 (Baldwin, c/n 1034, January 1862), has a Smith boiler, which had a large deep firebox and a 4"-long combustion chamber. A considerable amount of air was admitted through 24 hollow staybolts in the back leg of the firebox and about 100 perforations in the door. The combustion chamber was divided in half by a midfeather. (PRR photo; author's collection)

**Figure 144.** #245 (Baldwin, c/n 1013, October 1861), looked like #242 when built. The long boiler section in front of the cab, typical of the Smith boiler, is quite visible. Originally a 4-6-0 with 49" drivers and 18½" x 22" cylinders, #245 was rebuilt with 54" drivers and 18" x 22" cylinders. The PRR crudely retouched the right-hand portion of the skyline. (PRR photo ME1273A; author's collection)

153

*Figure 145.* #247 (Altoona, c/n 71, November 1870), class G. The G was the lightest of the standard classes and designated as "light passenger or ballast engines." They were used for special passenger assignments and in branch line passenger service. Several were rebuilt and used as "official" locomotives for Company service.
(PRR photo; author's collection)

*Figure 146.* #251 (Baldwin, c/n 1129, April 1863). Originally built for branch line passenger service, #251 was frequently used on the official photographer's train. The locomotive was sold to E.H. Wilson & Co., a used-equipment dealer, in March 1882.
(Author's collection)

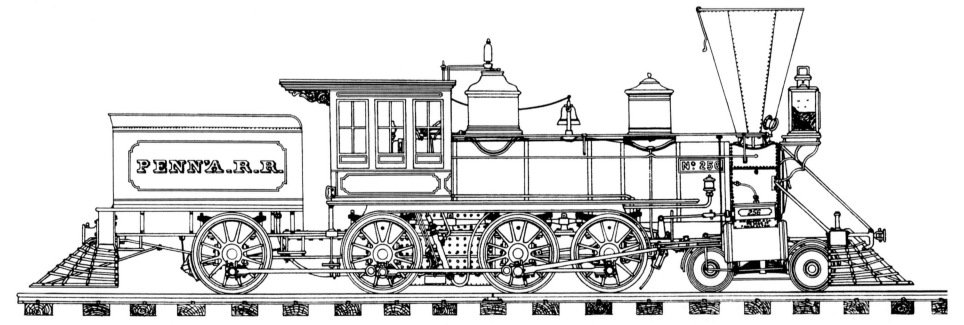

## Number 256—Tender on Extension of Engine Frame with Drivers Underneath, 1865.

*Figure 147.* #256 (Baldwin, as rebuilt, eight 48" drivers, 18" x 22" cylinders), was built by Baldwin as a 4-6-0. Laird removed the tender, extended the frame, and added an additional driver, making a 4-8-0T. The length of the wheelbase created problems, and the loco was converted back to a 4-6-0.
(C.H. Caruthers drawing; author's collection)

◄

**Figure 148.** *#261 (Baldwin, c/n 1081, September 1862). Rebuilt from a 4-4-0 by Altoona in July 1866 as a high driver (66") 2-6-0 for $14,884, #261 was used in passenger service on the Pittsburgh Division.* (Author's collection)

**Figure 149.** *#279 (Norris, four 66" drivers, 17" x 24" cylinders). Richard Norris & Son of Philadelphia was reaching the end of its production when #279 was built. The PRR was never an enthusiastic Norris customer. The placement of the injector alongside the firebox created problems.* (C.H. Caruthers drawing; author's collection)

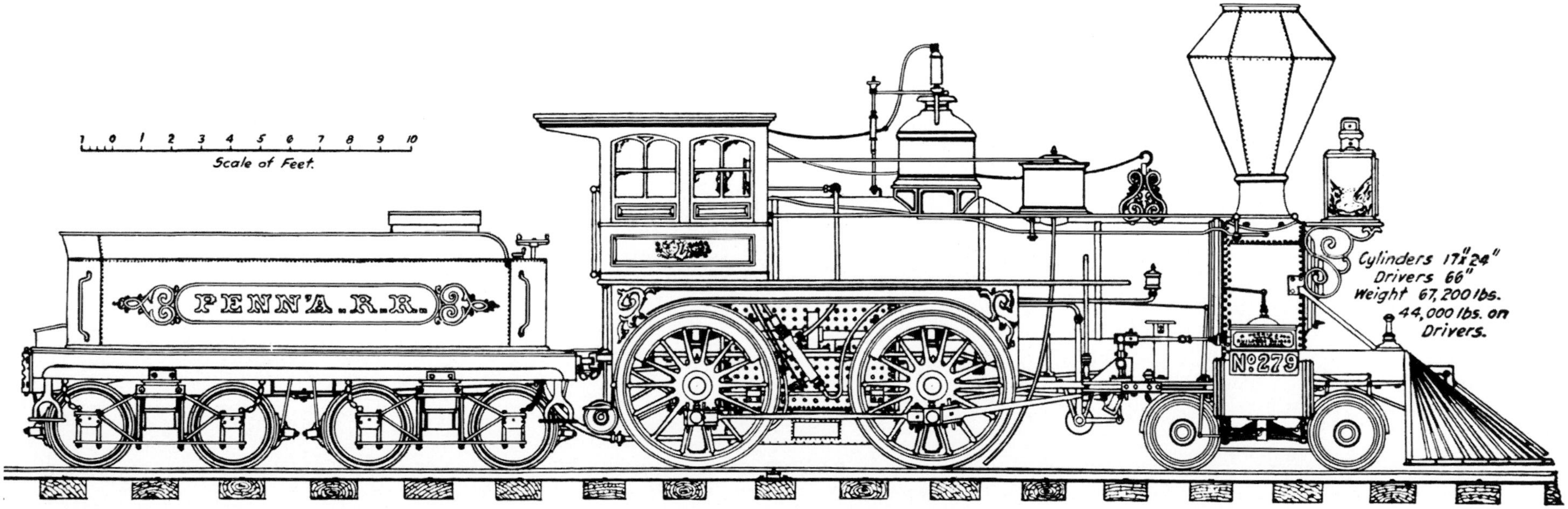

▼

Scale of Feet.

PENN'A. R. R.

Cylinders 17"x 24"
Drivers 66"
Weight 67,200 lbs.
44,000 lbs. on
Drivers.

N° 279

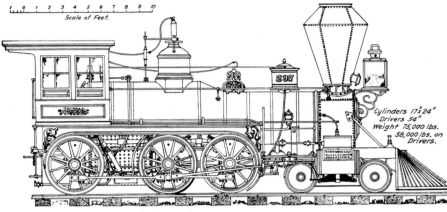

*Figure 152.* #297 (Norris, six 54" drivers, 17" x 24" cylinders), represents a "modern" freight locomotive: spread engine truck, level cylinders, link valve gear and wagon-top boiler. Norris' insistence on using the "D"-shaped smokebox is atypical of the most advanced practice.
(C.H. Caruthers drawing; author's collection)

▲ *Figure 150.* #279 (Richard Norris & Son, c/n 1068, April 1863). Rebuilt at Altoona, #279 was photographed before the finishing touches were applied.
(PRR photo ME1271A; author's collection)

▶

*Figure 151.* #283 (New Jersey Loco. & Mach., January 1865). Built at the height of the inflation caused by the Civil War, the PRR paid the NJL&M $30,900 (which included war tax) for #283. Note the rods to the water pump and cylinder cocks.
(PRR photo; author's collection)

*Figure 153.* #297 *(Richard Norris & Son, August 1863). By the mid-1860's the 4-6-0 had become the standard freight locomotive on the PRR; the products of the various builders had more or less the same specifications. Norris and Rogers used the D-shaped smokebox later than the other builders.*
(PRR photo 13154-29; author's collection)

*Figure 154.* #325 *(Baldwin, c/n 1266, August 1864), a modern 4-4-0 with a wagon top boiler, level cylinders and link motion. There were 21 of this general design put into service between 1863 and 1865.*
(BLW photo ME1269A; author's collection)

*Figure 156.* #339 (Baldwin, c/n 1335, January 1865). *After introducing the injector in 1861, problems developed. By late 1864, the PRR reverted to one pump on the right side of the engine and one injector on the left.* (PRR photo; author's collection)

*Figure 155.* #331 (Baldwin, c/n 1344, March 1865). *The PRR had just paid $31,227 for #331 when it had the sad task of pulling Mr. Lincoln's funeral train in April 1865.* (Author's collection)

◄

*Figure 157.* #348 (Richard Norris & Son, c/n 1178, March 1865). *Norris built locomotives in 1865, but by 1866 production had stopped. The plant was offered for sale in 1867. A comparison of #348 with Baldwin-built #349 (**Fig. 158**, December 1865) shows that Norris did not keep up with developments in locomotive building. The Baldwin has a round smokebox, while the Norris has the old D-shaped smokebox. The locomotive is equipped with the Loughridge brake; note the wheel behind the rear driver.* (PRR photo ME1305A; author's collection)

▶ *Figure 158.* #349 (Baldwin, c/n 1436, December 1865), has a Laird stack, but no road name on the tender. Note the side sheet on the pilot.
(PRR photo ME1303A; author's collection)

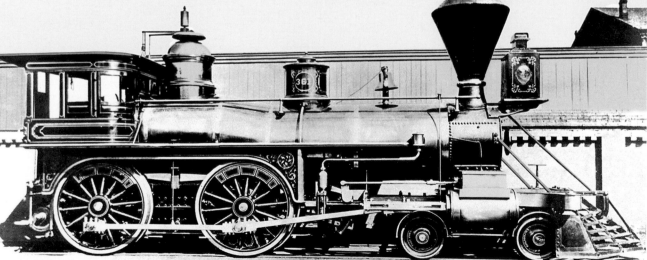

◀ *Figure 159.* #361 (Baldwin, c/n 1554, December 1866). In a year the price of a 4-4-0 had dropped about $15,000. #361 cost $16,275. Note the interesting cab with the curved front corner windows.
(Author's collection)

*Figure 160.* #384 (Baldwin, c/n 1558, December 1866). Note that the lever that operates the cylinder cocks is connected to a rod that runs through the handrail. There were 12 locomotives of this design. (BLW photo 13154-41; author's collection)

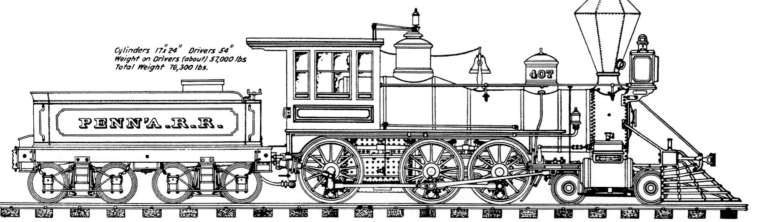

Cylinders 17"x 24"  Drivers 54"
Weight on Drivers (about) 57,000 lbs.
Total Weight 76,300 lbs.

PENN'A.R.R.

*Figure 161.* #407 (Norris-Lancaster, six 54" drivers, 17" x 24" cylinders). Two of the Norris brothers, James and Edward, began to build locomotives at the old Lancaster Works in competition with Richard Norris & Son of Philadelphia. The PRR purchased 12 of these locos from Norris-Lancaster. (C.H. Caruthers drawing; author's collection)

*Figure 162.* #407 (Norris-Lancaster, May 1867). The Lancaster Works failed in 1857, but in 1863 James Norris, a brother of the Philadelphia builder, leased the plant. James died in 1864 and his brother, Edward, operated the works. Lancaster built a few locomotives for the PRR, but closed in 1868. These Lancaster ten-wheelers were long-lived locomotives; the last one was cut up in March 1893. #407 ended up as a stationary boiler at South West Junction, Greensburg Pa., in June 1886. *(PRR photo ME1291A; author's collection)*

▶

*Figure 163.* #417 (New Jersey Loco. & Mach., c/n 491, April 1867), displays a number of features that were to characterize the PRR standard designs. Equipped with a Laird stack and iron pilot, there were ten of this design. Sister #416 remained in service until it was cut up in August 1896. *(Author's collection)*

*Figure 164.* #422 (Baldwin, c/n 1658, September 1867), one of the last non-standard 4-4-0's built for the PRR by Baldwin. On May 14, 1871, #422 came in for repairs at Altoona, estimated to cost $1,262.73, having run 153,280 miles on the Middle Division. *(Railroad Museum of Pennsylvania)*

**Figure 165.** *#573 (Altoona, Class C), one of Collin's standard locomotives. The C, intended for both passenger and freight, proved to be very useful engines and more were built than any of the other standard 4-4-0 designs.*

(C.H. Caruthers drawing; author's collection) ▶

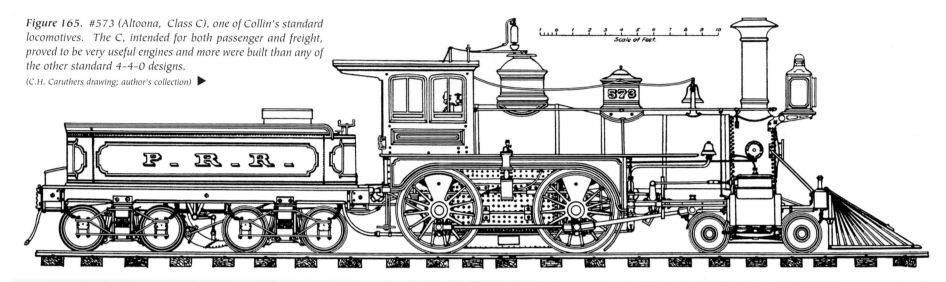

**Figure 166.** *#588 (B D, Lambertville Shops, January 1867). Ex-Belvidere Delaware Rancocas was photographed in June 1882, when the loco was renumbered to 3009. The only PRR influence is the diamond stack and sandbox.*

(Author's collection)

◀ *Figure 167.* #604 (*Danforth, Cooke & Co., 1859*). *Ex-Camden & Amboy #4, the locomotive is equipped with the C&A's unusual box tender. Note the "aliens" riding the tailgate; they're the result of earlier photoretouching.* (Author's collection)

*Figure 168.* #622 (*B D, Lambertville Shops, June 1866*), ex-Belvidere Delaware Warren. *Note the filler pipe extending through the tender roof, and the oval cab windows.* (Author's collection)

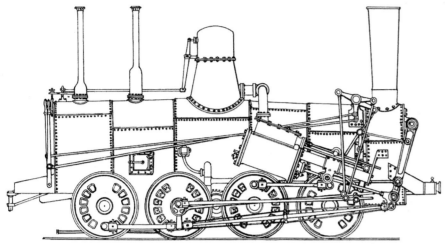

*From a Drawing by C. H. Caruthers*
**The "Monster," Camden & Amboy R. R., as originally built**

**Figure 169.** *Camden & Amboy "Monster", eight 44" drivers, 18" x 30" cylinders. In 1836, Isaac Dripps designed a heavy partially gear-driven 0-8-0 anthracite-burning freight locomotive for the Camden & Amboy. Six Monsters were built; two at Bordentown and four by the Trenton Locomotive Works.* (C.H. Caruthers drawing; author's collection)

**POP SAFETY VALVES ARE ON TOP OF DOME COVER. WHISTLE CONCEALS THEM**

**Fig. 3—Rebuilt Monster, 1869.**

**Figure 170.** *#635, rebuilt "Monster." The Monster 0-8-0's were rebuilt into semi-conventional 4-6-0's in the 1860's, and in this form passed into the PRR roster.*
(C.H. Caruthers drawing; author's collection)

**Figures 171A, 171B.** *#647 (New Jersey Loco. & Mach., 1852), ex-Camden & Amboy #47. Note the Brandt cylinders.* (Railroad Museum of Pennsylvania)
*A retouched version (at right) appeared at the bottom of the PRR double-page ad (and poster), "Working Partners," that appeared in mid-1946.* (Chuck Blardone collection)

*Figure 172.* NJRR&T #36 (Rogers Loco. & Mach., c/n 1107, November 1863), one of the first true Mogul locomotives, with a swing truck. It was renumbered to #736 when it was absorbed into the PRR roster.  (Author's collection)

*Figure 173.* #749 (New Jersey RR & Transp., October 1871), was ex-NJRR&T #49, built in the Jersey City Shops.  (Railroad Museum of Pennsylvania)

▶

*Figure 174.* *#764 (Camden & Amboy, 1866), ex-Camden & Amboy "A," built at the Bordentown Shops.*
(Railroad Museum of Pennsylvania)

*Figure 175.* *C&A #28 (Norris Brothers, c/n 420, May 1849), one of seven Crampton type locomotives built for the C&A by Norris Bros. of Philadelphia. It had 13" x 34" cylinders and 84" drivers.*
(Author's collection)

▼

*Figure 176.* C&A #30 (Norris Brothers, c/n 445, January 1850). *This photo gives a good view of the valve gear of these remarkable engines.*
(Author's collection)

▶

▲ *Figure 177.* This locomotive may represent one of the Cramptons rebuilt to a 4-4-0.
(PRR photo 3119; author's collection)

◄

*Figure 178.* This unidentified C&A locomotive was a product of the Bordentown Shops.
(PRR photo ME3230A; author's collection)

BUILT AT THE C. & A. R. R. CO.'S SHOPS,

Photographed by Sexton & Tantum.

BORDENTOWN, N. J.

# APPENDICES
## APPENDIX A
### THE PRR'S FIRST LOCOMOTIVE

The question of priority is always interesting—what came first? The first of anything may not be all that significant other than its claim to priority in time. This is especially true of things mechanical. The first locomotive built for a railroad may represent an anomaly, a mistake those hired to run and repair the engine may soon regret, yet, there is something compelling about identifying it, if only to set the record straight. A good bit of ambiguity surrounds the identity of the PRR's first locomotive. This has thickened rather than dispelled over the years.

### BEYOND THE *JOHN BULL*

The identity of the PRR's first locomotive was not seriously considered as long as the railroad had a real, live antique in its stable. The PRR inherited the *John Bull* when it leased the Camden & Amboy in 1871. *John Bull*, built by Robert Stephenson in June 1831, was a unique artifact. Assembled in the first decade of railroading as a commercial venture, *John Bull* was one of the few English locomotives imported to America during the railroad's initial development on this continent. It was displayed by the PRR during the United States Centennial in 1876 and at the National Railway Appliance Exposition at Chicago in 1883. In 1884, the locomotive was donated to the Smithsonian Institution and exhibited in the East Hall of Arts. In 1893, *John Bull* was withdrawn from the museum by the PRR, operated under its own power to the World's Columbian Exposition at Chicago, and then returned to the Smithsonian and put on permanent display.

The commitment to *John Bull* as the symbol of the road's early motive power can be fully appreciated when one realizes that the PRR's upper management had a full-size operating model built in 1940 at the Company's Juniata Shop, for exhibition at public events. This *John Bull* is now on display at the Railroad Museum of Pennsylvania, at Strasburg, Pa. Almost nothing of the design of *John Bull* was perpetuated on the PRR except for the most basic elements, the contained smokebox, tubular boiler and rear firebox.

### THE FIRST OF THESE NEW ENGINES

Very likely the first attempt to deal with the question of priority is to be found in J. Elfreth Watkins' unpublished history of the PRR.[183] Watkins (1852–1903), a civil engineer employed by the PRR, had a passion for engineering history. After he lost a leg in an accident, he was assigned by the PRR to work at the Smithsonian's Arts and Industry Building and was involved in the transfer of the *John Bull* to the Smithsonian.[184]

Watkins was given the task of writing a history of the PRR, but the work did not meet with the approval of the management and was never published. In that history, Watkins noted that the first mention of locomotives is to be found in the *Minutes of the Board of Directors* for September 27, 1848.[185] J. Edgar Thomson recommended the purchase of two or three locomotives for construction purposes. Watkins reports the financial arrangements for the purchase of three locomotives from Baldwin amounting to $27,900, and then writes *the first of these new engines delivered to the Pennsylvania Railroad Company was the "Mifflin".*[186]

Paul T. Warner, in his series of articles, "Motive Power Development on the Pennsylvania Railroad System: 1831–1924,"[187] written on behalf of the Baldwin Locomotive Company, began his discussion by introducing the first locomotive Baldwin appears to have built for the PRR. *Records show that the first Baldwin locomotives completed for the Pennsylvania were the "Dauphin" and "Perry," which were finished by the builders in November 1848, previous to the opening of the road. They bore construction numbers 333 and 334, and were finally placed in service on the new line in November 1849, and January 1850, respectively.*[188]

Warner follows Watkins' lead in affirming in the next paragraph that: *Records indicate that the first Baldwin engine built for the Pennsylvania to be actually placed in service on the road was the "Mifflin," a fast passenger locomotive completed in July 1848.*[189] Warner's work has been widely available and thus most subsequent histories have repeated his assumptions.[190] The priority of *Mifflin* is perpetuated in the *Centennial History of the Pennsylvania Railroad Company*: *Also in 1848, the company placed its first order for the new equipment it expected to use on its line. Three locomotives were ordered for delivery in 1849, which were to be named the "Mifflin", the "Indiana", and the "Blair" ... The "Mifflin" hauled the first train from Harrisburg to Lewistown on the historic*

*September 1.*[191] The priority of *Mifflin* is again affirmed in the section on "Locomotives." *The first locomotive built for the Company and placed in passenger service was the "Mifflin" built by Baldwin in September, 1849 ... Baldwin also built the "Dauphin" and "Perry" for the Company in 1849 and 1850, but after a short service on the Pennsylvania they were sold to the Philadelphia & Reading.*[192]

## SHOW OR INDICATE

When Warner uses the terms "records show" or "records indicate," it is important that the records themselves are clearly identified. An unintended confusion exists because Warner may be alluding to two completely different sets of records when he refers to *Dauphin* and when he refers to *Mifflin*.

The history of the early Pennsylvania Railroad locomotives can be traced in the extant documents of the Baldwin Locomotive Works, especially the *Register of Engines Made By M.W. Baldwin.*[193] This record, compiled by Baldwin, is a handwritten list of locomotives built by the Baldwin works and arranged numerically, with a number assigned to each locomotive, along with a date, record of the purchasing railroad, and the major mechanical specifications. I assume that when Warner states that the "record shows," this is the document he is referring to. The first locomotive that Baldwin sold to the PRR is *Dauphin*, construction number 333, with a date of November 17, 1848.

In the case of *Mifflin*, the record Warner refers to may be one of several "official" records. The early *Annual Reports* of the Pennsylvania Railroad, beginning in 1850, list the locomotives which were owned by the company, arranged alphabetically by name. The builder is shown as well as the mileage and expenses charged to each particular locomotive for fuel, repair, and so forth. There is a column that shows the date "Placed On Road." This date is repeated in the PRR *Record of Locomotives and Tenders*, which was prepared in the 1890's from earlier records. The Chief Clerk of Motive Power, who since 1854 was Benjamin F. Custer, kept this information.[194] When the "records indicate" that *Mifflin* was the first engine actually placed in service on the Pennsylvania, the records are the "Placed On Road" dates found in the *Annual Reports* and later the PRR *Historical Record of Locomotives*.

A list of the first 20 locomotives of the Pennsylvania Railroad according to the "Placed On Road" date is shown in **Chart 12** (to the right).

The date shown in the Baldwin records is the date of sale or the date of shipping rather than the date of completion or the date on which the locomotive was first steamed. This would explain the variety of dates that pertain to the early Baldwin records. The earliest builder's date, discounting the Harrisburg & Lancaster locomotives which were added to the PRR stock on October 16, 1849, are for the *Dauphin* and *Perry*, November 17, 1848. The earliest "Placed-On-Road" date is for *Mifflin*, September 1, 1849.

## THOMSON AND BALDWIN

After his appointment as Chief Engineer of the Pennsylvania Railroad in April 1847, J. Edgar Thomson continued in his previous position as Chief Engineer of the Georgia Railroad until 1852.[195] During this time, Thomson, who was then in Harrisburg, continued to order locomotives from Baldwin for the Georgia Railroad.[196] In March 1848, Baldwin sent Thomson drawings for a freight locomotive for his *Pennsylvania road.*[197] The locomotive was similar to those built by Baldwin under contract for the Baltimore & Ohio, and he noted they would probably weigh about 22 tons. Baldwin was interested in an order from Thomson as it would *much facilitate my position to make a number together.*[198] Baldwin further suggested that if Thomson ordered these machines it would *perhaps put pressure on the Harrisburg Company to order also.*[199] Baldwin was interested in spreading the development costs of the B&O locomotives over a number of orders for similar machines;[200] *then I can do something profitable in this affair, which cannot be well asked, by taking them singly as you know.*[201]

**Chart 12**

**First 20 PRR Locomotives Placed on Road**

| Name | Bldr. | c/n | Builder's Date | Date Placed on Road | | |
| --- | --- | --- | --- | --- | --- | --- |
| | | | | 12/31/1851 Annual Report | Watkins | Record of Locomotives and Tenders |
| Mifflin | BLW | 356 | 7/12/1849 | 9/1/1849 | 9/1/1849 | 9/1849 |
| Blair | BLW | 371 | 12/14/1849 | 9/23/1849 | 9/23/1849 | 9/1849 |
| Clay * | WmN | | 1838 | 10/16/1849 | 10/16/1849 | 10/1849 |
| Franklin * | BLW | 306 | 8/24/1847 | 10/16/1849 | 10/16/1849 | 10/1849 |
| Harrisburg * | BLW | 64 | 2/18/1837 | 10/16/1849 | 10/16/1849 | 10/1849 |
| D.R. Porter * | WmN | | 1839 | 10/16/1849 | 10/16/1849 | 10/1849 |
| Penrose * | BLW | 84 | 6/29/1837 | 10/16/1849 | 10/16/1849 | 10/1849 |
| Washington * | BLW | 293 | 2/15/1847 | 10/16/1849 | 10/16/1849 | 10/1849 |
| Juniata | BLW | 369 | 10/29/1849 | 11/2/1849 | 11/2/1849 | 11/1849 |
| Dauphin | BLW | 333 | 11/17/1848 | 11/5/1849 | 11/5/1849 | 11/1849 |
| Huntingdon | BLW | 370 | 11/19/1849 | 11/16/1849 | 11/16/1849 | 11/1849 |
| Perry | BLW | 334 | 11/17/1848 | 1/10/1850 | 1/10/1850 | 1/1850 |
| Cambria | NB | | 1/1850 | 1/22/1850 | 1/22/1850 | 1/1850 |
| Indiana | BLW | 372 | 12/31/1849 | 1/22/1850 | 1/22/1850 | 1/1850 |
| Allegheny | BLW | 385 | 6/27/1850 | 7/9/1850 | 7/9/1850 | 7/1850 |
| Clarion | BLW | 386 | 6/28/1850 | 7/22/1850 | 7/22/1850 | 7/1850 |
| Clinton | BLW | 387 | 8/14/1850 | 9/5/1850 | 9/5/1850 | 9/1850 |
| Westmoreland | BLW | 357 | 4/3/1849 | 9/7/1850 | 9/7/1850 | 9/1850 |
| Beaver | BLW | 388 | 8/21/1850 | 9/10/1850 | 8/21/1850 | 9/1850 |
| Columbia | BLW | 389 | 8/27/1850 | 9/18/1850 | 9/18/1850 | 9/1850 |

* These locomotives were purchased by the PRR from the Harrisburg, Portsmouth, Mountjoy & Lancaster Rail-Road Company when the line was leased by the PRR.

BLW   Baldwin Locomotive Works
WmN   William Norris
NB      Norris Brothers

Thomson was not impressed with the weight of 22 tons for a freight locomotive. In June he wrote to Baldwin for specifications for an eight-wheel locomotive not to exceed 20 tons. "I think we may be in the market for it during the fall..." [202] Initially Baldwin suggested several types of eight-wheelers; an 0-8-0, a 4-4-0, or the locomotive he was making for the Central Vermont (a 4-2-2-0).[203] Thomson asked for an eight-wheel freight machine with all wheels connected. "We would secure it for transportation of materials previous to the opening of the road and to be a model locomotive." [204] Baldwin then suggested either an 18-ton machine that could be made off the same drawings as the locomotives he was now building for the Georgia road or a 22-ton machine "like these we are making for the B&O."[205] Thomson responded that the new road had grades of only 16 feet to the mile to Lewistown and 21 feet to the mile to the mountain. "I should therefore hardly think it policy to exceed 20 tons in the weight of a locomotive." [206]

Sometime between June and September, 1848, Thomson visited Philadelphia, met with Baldwin, and discussed the engines that Baldwin had built for the B&O.[207] Locomotive orders were down from the previous year and Baldwin was now stuck with the three refused by the B&O because they did not meet contract specifications. Thomson had still not made up his mind on the "proper description of the freight engines we should first get on the road." [208]

In late September, Baldwin called on Samuel Merrick, the PRR's president, and made a bargain based on the proposition he had submitted to Thomson.[209] The whole agreement was subject to Thomson's approval. Due to a *continuation of adverse circumstances,* Baldwin found himself in need of a large sum of ready cash in short order.[210] He returned to the PRR offices with the intention of getting an advance in City bonds from the Company by placing two of the locomotives in the PRR's possession. Unfortunately, Merrick was out of town and no one was willing to do anything until he returned. When Merrick returned, the PRR Board wanted to bind Baldwin not to put the City bonds on the market if Thomson should approve the contract. Baldwin, who needed an immediate infusion of cash to meet his obligations, wrote to Thomson on September 29, complaining bitterly about his treatment and added *I cannot by any means keep that amount of capital locked up and continue any business.*[211]

On October 4, 1848, the Board acted to authorize Merrick and Thomson to inspect the locomotives, and if found suitable, purchase them from Baldwin.[212] Thomson wrote on October 8, informing Baldwin that the Board had referred the purchase of the locomotives to himself and Merrick, and that he would be absent until November 10, "In the meantime talk over the financial part of the question with him." Thomson mentioned that "the one you proposed to have on hand next spring will not be called for and you can turn it over to the B&O." [213]

A suitable agreement was finally worked out, because on October 18, 1848, Merrick recommended that the Board approve the purchase of the "three" locomotives built by Baldwin for the B&O for $27,900, to be paid for by the transfer of $19,400 in Philadelphia bonds, 100 shares of new PRR stock valued at $5,000, and the balance due of $3,500 on 100 shares of PRR stock that Baldwin had purchased but not finished paying for.[214]

Thomson finally answered Baldwin's letter of September 29 on November 3. He admitted that he mistook Baldwin's figures and had responded to the Board that Baldwin had only two engines for sale, a matter which Thomson thought of no consequence. He stated that he would be in Philadelphia the next week and would "confirm the trade if it will pass muster." [215] Thomson informed Baldwin that the committee (finance committee of the PRR Board) was afraid that if Baldwin sold his Philadelphia bonds below par it would adversely affect the remaining City bonds the PRR held.

The Board met on November 22, 1848, and Merrick read the contract and receipts of Baldwin in reference to the settlement for locomotives and tenders.[216] The Board authorized that an order (Order #449) be drawn in favor of Baldwin for $19,200. Unfortunately, the Board action does not tell us what the $19,200 represents. It is $600 more than the price of two locomotives at $9,300 each.

The PRR had received only two locomotives from Baldwin by early December 1848. They were flexible-beam-truck freight engines (21-ton, eight-wheel E, #2) which had all of their drivers placed in front of the firebox, with the main rod connected to the rear, rather than to the third driver.[217] Baldwin wrote to Thomson on December 8 that "the two engines are now in the Depot – one at Dillerville, and the other at Harrisburg." [218] Thomson responded that managers of the H&L were scared at the weight of his new machines, and he had assured them that with eight wheels the new locomotives were not much heavier on the rails than their own six-wheel machine.[219]

A month after the arrival of the first two locomotives, Thomson wrote to Baldwin that *I would be glad if you could dispose of that third engine to the B&O. We shall have more freight engines than we want for twelve months to come with the three but shall be deficient in passenger machines.*[220] What were the three freight engines that Thomson alludes to? Certainly two were *Dauphin* and *Perry.* The third was *Washington,* a flexible-beam-truck 0-6-0, which the PRR got with the lease of the Harrisburg & Lancaster.

The "third engine" Thomson suggested that Baldwin dispose of to the B&O was *Westmoreland.*[221] Thomson then changed his mind and agreed to take the machine. *After consideration, I have concluded in as much as we have two of those large freight engines it would be best to take the third and not stock our road with so great a variety of machines. We should be able to get through with this winter's busi-*

*ness without her.*[222] He was in no hurry for delivery, *You can take your time on the large freight machine, as we shall not require her until we have more road.*[223] The *Westmoreland*, which came on the PRR in the spring of 1850, continued in service until 1863, when it was rebuilt at the Altoona Shop by Laird. The third pair of drivers was removed and a saddle tank was added. It ran in the Altoona yards in this condition until 1866 or 1867, when it was scrapped.[224]

The further history of *Dauphin* and *Perry* in PRR service was of rather short duration. They appeared in the 1850 *Annual Report* (the first report to contain a roster of locomotives) but were absent in the 1851 report. Both were sold to the Philadelphia & Reading and arrived on that road October 1850. The P&R in turn sold them to the Huntingdon & Broad Top Mountain Railroad. The H&BTM records indicate that the P&R sold *Perry* in November 1861 and *Dauphin* in March 1863.[225] Both were scrapped in December 1867.

## BEGINNING IN DAUPHIN COUNTY

We can safely say that *Dauphin*, not *Mifflin*, was the PRR's first locomotive. It is not coincidental that the locomotive was named *Dauphin*. The PRR initially named its locomotives for the counties of the Commonwealth that the railroad passed through, beginning at Harrisburg in Dauphin County. Progressing west, the line passed through Perry, Juniata, Mifflin, Huntingdon, and Blair Counties. The Western Division began in Blair County and passed through Cambria, Indiana, Westmoreland, and Allegheny Counties.

How did the PRR lay rail on the first 61 miles of track between Harrisburg and Lewistown? J. Elfreth Watkins suggested that Thomson recommended the purchase of two or three locomotives from Baldwin for construction purposes;[226] Thomson's letter to Baldwin confirms this ... *The engine we may want first will be a freight machine ... for transportation of materials previous to the opening of the road.*[227] From the materials available it is clear that *Dauphin* and *Perry* were acquired for this work.

Why has *Mifflin* been credited as the first Pennsylvania Railroad locomotive? It is true that it pulled the first passenger train on the PRR from Harrisburg to Lewistown on September 1, 1849. The critical issue is again dates and what they mean. The earliest "Placed On Road" date is September 1, 1849 for *Mifflin*. September 1, 1849 is the day that the PRR began revenue operation, when it became a railroad. There was no operating entity running trains in revenue service known as the Pennsylvania Railroad before that date. *Mifflin* was the first locomotive to operate in revenue service, but not the first locomotive acquired by the PRR, or the first locomotive to operate over the PRR track in Company service.[228]

## THE FIRST LOCOMOTIVE TO ARRIVE

*Mifflin* may not have been be the first locomotive to arrive in Lewistown. The *Lewistown Gazette* recorded that *the first locomotive arrived at Lewistown on Thursday afternoon* [August 23, 1849] *with a train of lumber cars. The road will be opened for travel on Friday or Saturday next.*[229] Unfortunately the newspaper did not record the name of the locomotive involved, but the type of service might suggest a locomotive other than the high-drivered *Mifflin*.

A week later the same paper reported that *a large party of ladies and gentlemen from Harrisburg ... arrived here on Thursday last* [August 30, 1849], *and after a stay of three hours returned homewards ... it was altogether a private affair.*[230] The *Pennsylvania Telegraph* of Harrisburg reported *that part of the Eastern Division of the Central Railroad extending from Harrisburg to Lewistown, a distance of 60 miles, was opened for travel on Thursday last* [August 30, 1849] *... a few minutes past 8 o'clock a train consisting of a large class of locomotive and four large and splendid passenger cars ... left the Depot and arrived at Lewistown at 11:00 a.m.*[231] One might assume that this trip was handled by *Mifflin*.

*Mifflin* was clearly identified in an article approximately a month later. *We left Lewistown on Thursday of last week* [November 8, 1849] *for the purpose of meeting our friends of the press in Harrisburg, but a "screw" becoming loose and a rod bent in the Prince of Engines, the Mifflin, we were unable to reach that place until late in the evening. Our detention, however, at Millerstown, although of four or five hours duration ... The perseverance of the engineers having at last effected the necessary repairs, we moved on and soon reached Harrisburg.*[232]

## PLACED ON THE ROAD

After the first few locomotives were acquired, the date on the Baldwin lists, the sale or shipping date, and the "Placed On Road" date are reasonable, and for the most part allow time for a locomotive to get from Philadelphia to Harrisburg, be set up, and then be placed on the road. How does one explain the difference between the dates Baldwin shipped the locomotives and the "Placed On Road" dates for *Dauphin* (November 5, 1849), *Perry* (January 10, 1850) and *Westmoreland* (September 7, 1850)? Until further evidence is found, these may be the dates that the Chief Engineer turned them over to the Superintendent of Transportation for use in revenue service. *Dauphin* was "placed on road" after the railroad was opened to Lewistown on September 1, 1849. *Perry* was "placed on road" after the railroad was opened to McVeytown on December 14, 1849. *Westmoreland* was held until just before the connection was opened with the Portage Railroad at Portage Intersection on September 15, 1850.

# APPENDIX B
## WHAT WAS THE FIRST LOCOMOTIVE BUILT AT THE ALTOONA MACHINE SHOP?

### THE ALTOONA MACHINE SHOP CONSTRUCTION LIST

The commonly-accepted list of locomotives built by the Altoona Machine Shop was most recently published by the National Railway Historical Society in 1984, *Pennsylvania Railroad Altoona Machine Shops Construction Number List: 1866-1904*. The list was complied by Joseph D. Lovell of Hollidaysburg, Pa., and had wide circulation among those interested in the PRR; Charles B. Chaney, Alan O. Geertz, Charles E. Fisher, H.R. Johannessen, and Harold Goldsmith, among others.

The most interesting thing about the list is the preface that has traditionally accompanied it. Apparently the work of J.D. Lovell, a portion of it follows:

*The list was compiled from an official list of Consecutive Construction numbers from 1-1770 evidently not kept concurrently, but probably made about 1892; and from official lists for the rest of the numbers. The information obtained from the foregoing was checked with the official builder records and official locomotive registers and some differences found. Where they occurred the data entered herein is that which appeared to be correct ... No construction numbers were placed on badge plates of Altoona Machine Shop engines prior to July, 1892; 1770 being the first number appearing. Before that time construction numbers were not used to and did not serve as an official means of record or identification. The construction numbers from 1-1769 therefore represent only a sequence of construction, which in some instances may be incorrectly stated. Comparison of the year built of the above numbers as shown herein with official registers show a difference in some instances. The engines affected are those built near or at the close of the year ... The information under remarks was obtained from various sources, both official and unofficial. Construction #1 is shown on the official list as engine #347, 12/1866. Notes by C.H. Caruthers on his drawing of this engine state that it was built by R. Norris & Son in 1856, construction #1177, rebuilt as a 2-6-0 at Altoona 1866, rebuilt to a 4-4-0 about 1870 and cut up in 1876. The list completely omitted engine #142 which is conceded to be the first engine built completely new at Altoona. In this list, the #142 has been substituted for the #347. The official list also omits Odd Class A #101 (straight boiler and 62" drivers). Official photographs of it are extant on which with a magnifying glass — "Altoona Shop November 1868" — is easily discernible on the badge plate. Official records show this as placed on the road December 1868.*

I am indebted to Roger Keyser for raising questions about the "traditional" Altoona Machine Shop list, and agree with him that the list is questionable at best and probably ultimately worthless as an historical document, in its present form.

On July 27, 1891, the first locomotive was turned out at the new Juniata Shops, just east of Altoona in the borough of Juniata.[233] It had an oval badge plate with the date "7-1891," the class "R," and the construction number "1" in the center, "Juniata Shops" along the top curve of the plate, and "Altoona" along the curve at the bottom of the plate. The locomotives built at the Altoona Machine Shop beginning in 1868, with the first standard locomotive, were equipped with a round badge plate which read "Altoona Shops" around the top of the plate, and "August 1868" around the bottom, with the date changing where necessary for each subsequent locomotive. No construction numbers were issued to any locomotive built at any of the PRR shops prior to 1891. The "new oval badge plate" with a construction number was first used on Altoona Machine Shop #1771 on July 22, 1892.[234]

In order to have a construction number (#1771) for the oval plate on Northern Central #146, a Class P 4-4-0, someone in the Motive Power Department, probably the Motive Power Clerk, Benjamin F. Custer, who had held that post since the early 1850's, had to come up with the number. Lovell's introduction, quoted above, mentions that his list is from a list of consecutive construction numbers "not kept concurrently but probably made about 1892." So far this "official" consecutive construction list has not surfaced. One wonders who made the list Lovell consulted, and what the compiler of that list used for sources. Lovell admits that other "official" boiler lists, registers, and so forth were used to corroborate and correct the list. The "traditional" ("Lovell") list does not have any notes that point out these disagreements. Lovell mentions that where disagreements occurred, the date used was that which appeared to be correct. I assume that he used his own judgment in this matter. It appears that as the list circulated it was further amended and corrected as various persons saw fit.

In the preface to the "Lovell list," reference is made to the "official list" compiled in 1892, which shows the first locomotive built at Altoona as #347. Lovell is correct in stating that #347 was built by Richard Norris & Son of Philadelphia. A 4-4-0, it came on the road in February 1865 (RN&S #1177, April 1864, 17" x 24") and exploded at Duncannon, Pa., on September 5, 1865. It was rebuilt at Altoona in December 1866 as a 2-6-0 with 66" drivers and 17" x 24" cylinders. The February 1869 *Register of Locomotives* notes the locomotive as Company-built, with a new steel firebox furnished in January 1867.

Lovell notes that the list omitted #142, which was conceded to be the first engine built completely new at Altoona (conceded by whom?). The "Lovell list" shows four American Standard 4-4-0's, #'s 142, 148, 127 and 239, as Altoona Machine Shops #1-4, built during 1867.

## THE ALTOONA MACHINE SHOP

One wonders why it took the PRR so long to begin to build locomotives in their own shops, when many smaller roads with less-well-equipped facilities were doing so. Between 1864 and 1866 the little Belvidere Delaware had already built six in its small shop at Lambertville, New Jersey, and the Lancaster Locomotive Works, a modest commercial establishment in an H-shaped building, functioned with an erecting shop of 50 ft. x 158 ft., with six bays, turning out a new locomotive approximately every 2½ weeks in 1856.

The possibility of building a locomotive depends on several factors: physical facilities - space and machinery - and personnel - experienced men. In his book *American Locomotive Builders*, John H. White suggests that:

*... there was no mystery in locomotive construction to an experienced stationary engine builder. He could copy the work of another man as well as anyone. If he had only a moderate size machine shop equipt with a large lathe, a drill press, and the capacity to assemble boilers, he could build a locomotive ... before 1880 most American locomotives were fairly small machines. Eight wheelers were common. Weights rarely exceeded thirty tons. The individual parts were fairly manageable. Big overhead cranes were not really needed. Hand powered swing cranes, blocks, jacks and enough strong backs could jockey most parts around the shop.[235]*

The development of the physical facilities of the Altoona Machine Shop can be gleaned from the Company's *Annual Reports*. Construction of what was to be the Company's chief shops was started in 1851, and completed and brought into operation in 1853. It consisted of a long one-story building, which housed a machine shop, paint shop, wood working shop, blacksmith shop, foundry, and space for locomotive repair. There was an eight-stall enginehouse, which served as a passenger and freight car repair shop and paint shop. During the next several years the shops were expanded with the addition a new smithy of 18 forges, a new foundry, and an extension to the machine shop. In 1855 an erecting shop and foundry were opened. In 1858 the erecting shop and boiler shop were enlarged.

In 1854 a new 26-stall enginehouse was built at Altoona. The reports of the Master of Machinery over several years in the *Annual Reports* reveal the need for more space. In the 1857 *Annual Report*, Alexander McCausland alluded to the extent of the problem:

*An early completion of the extension to the erecting and boiler shop already commenced, is urgently required to relieve the Round House; which building is not at all calculated for other than its legitimate business, owing to constant exposure, deficient light,*

*and annoyance from smoke and steam rendering it almost impossible for the person in charge to have a proper supervision of his men. Only repairs of a trifling nature ought, under any circumstances, to be made, there being no facilities with regard to tools and power. The fact of a large portion of the general repairs on Freight engines being made in the Round House, has largely added to the expense of repairs.*

*Our present demands for Engine accommodation require thirty tracks, whereas in the present building there are only twenty-six, a portion of which are constantly occupied by extra Engines, and those undergoing general repairs, causing on the average of six Engines to be nightly exposed to the severe weather on the Mountain Division. A temporary building, with accommodations to house six Engines, is strongly recommended.[236]*

The shops at Altoona developed in a helter-skelter fashion, with additions made as the need arose. In 1862, the old semicircular enginehouse was enlarged to accommodate 30 engines. In February 1867 another new circular enginehouse was completed to handle the Pittsburgh Division engines.

From the above, and the constant references to the need for expanded enginehouse and shop facilities in the *Annual Reports*, one might glean that the major problem at Altoona was space. Toward the end of 1867 this was beginning to be alleviated. The West Philadelphia enginehouse and shop had come on line, servicing the Philadelphia Division engines. Completed in 1866, it had 44 stalls; the shop facilities included a machine shop and erecting shop, with 11 tracks. At Harrisburg, there were two enginehouses, one with 42 stalls and the other, when finished in 1868, with 44. There was also a machine shop and an erecting shop with nine tracks, which handled the general and running repairs for the Middle Division. At Pittsburgh a new 44 stall enginehouse and shops for running repairs were completed in 1867. With the completion of the new 44 stall Pittsburgh Division enginehouse, at Altoona in February 1867, there was now enough room to house the locomotives and provide for the necessary running repairs. With no more extensive additions to the shops at Altoona, it appears that, with the expansion of shop facilities at the major terminals, Altoona could now handle general repairs and begin new construction.

The facilities for locomotive repair and construction were composed of two sets of buildings with a steam transfer table, added in 1858, between them. The northernmost structure formed a "T," with the leg of the "T" a two-floor brick building, comprising the machine shop on the first floor and the vise shop on the second. At the top of the "T" was the erecting shop, 326' long and 62'- 6" wide, with the long side facing the transfer table. Across the transfer table to the south was a brick building in the shape of an "E," with the back of the "E" facing the transfer table. The leg of the "E" on the west side of the building housed the blacksmith shop. The middle leg accommodated the wheel shop and another blacksmith shop. The leg on the south side housed the boiler shop, flanging shop, and tank shop. The foundry, in a separate building, supplied castings to all the other PRR shops. As noted, there were three enginehouses. Between the shop buildings and the main line was a 26-track enginehouse used for testing engines, light repairs, and setting up tenders. The paint shop was a long two-track wooden building to the east of the facilities.

Although James Dredge referred to the facility as "old and not over commodious," through the end of 1873 the PRR turned out 237 new locomotives from these shops. It wasn't until 1874 that a new three-track erecting shop, 350' long by 66'- 6" wide, with two overhead traveling cranes, was completed.

Altoona had the machinery to engage in new construction as early as 1856, when the shops began firebox renewal. In 1857, 18 new copper fireboxes were put in, *York* (#49) had an iron firebox put in designed for difficult use, and *Blue Ridge* (#120) was altered with a combustion chamber added. The next year 22 new copper fireboxes were put in. By 1866, 21 locos were rebuilt with new boilers, 31 were equipped with new fireboxes, and 23 half-fireboxes were installed.

The problem was one of shop space and the rapid increase in the number of locomotives. In 1856, there were 133 and, with the addition in 1857 of the locomotives from the Public Works, the number jumped to 211. There were 434 on the road ten years later. That year, Altoona built 14 new locomotives, made general repairs to 234, ordinary repairs to 358, and put in 31 new steel fireboxes.

To build a locomotive "new" required the ability to form a boiler; boilers were not large, but were made of several iron tubes fit into one another. Building a new locomotive also require the ability to forge a throat sheet. This was perhaps the most difficult piece of work. Also required was the capacity to produce the necessary forgings, and a lathe large enough to bore out cylinders. The PRR had all of this. Many components were purchased from outside suppliers, such as springs, axles, locomotive tires, and wheels.

PRR had the physical capacity to build a new locomotive before they actually did. The rebuilding program, started by John Laird in 1862, included new boilers and fireboxes on many of the rebuilds. #52, a Winans Camel built in April 1853, was rebuilt by Laird at Altoona in August 1864 as a 2-6-0 with a new frame, drivers, lead truck, link-motion valve gear, boiler and firebox. The only remnant of the old Camel was the enormous steam dome. Between 1863 and 1868, Altoona rebuilt approximately 62 locomotives as "new" machines.

As to the question of personnel, the answer is difficult without more biographical documentation. Both Laird and Collin had experience at several commercial locomotive builders, and Thomas W. Worsdell, the Master Mechanic at Altoona Machine Shop, had locomotive construction experience at one of the most advanced locomotive building establishments in England, the London & Northwestern's shops at Crewe.

## WOULD THE PRR BUILD NEW NON-STANDARD LOCOMOTIVES IN 1867?

Why would the PRR build new non-standard locomotives at Altoona on the eve of a broad revision of the Company's locomotive policy? In the *Twenty Second Annual Report* for the year 1868 (dated February 2, 1869), on page 40, A.J. Cassatt, Superintendent of Motive Power & Machinery, writes:

*During the past year the importance of arriving as soon as possible at a system of perfect uniformity in plans and patterns, the first decided effort in which direction was made by my predecessor, was kept steadily in view. The importance of this subject, both as a measure of efficiency, cannot be too highly estimated, for with such a system only can the cost of repairs of locomotives, and the proportion of engines out of service be reduced to a minimum. During the past year complete detailed drawings were prepared for all the standard locomotives, and in all those purchased or built at the Company's shops, these plans have been closely adhered to.*[237]

The above quote reveals the "official concern" as being repair costs and the proportion of locomotives out of service for repair. The issue of standardization was primarily a matter of cost reduction. By 1865, the Company had achieved a certain level of standardization under the direction of Laird. First, the locomotives purchased from commercial builders had a *wheel base that will secure the easiest and best riding machine, and at the same time diminish wear and tear of the engine and of the road.*[238] The Company had settled on 4-4-0's with 60" drivers for both passenger and freight and 66" drivers for passenger, and 4-6-0's with 50" to 54" drivers for freight. Second, Laird recommended the *proper counterbalancing of the reciprocating parts and a valve motion which, while it is simple and durable in its parts, is the most economical and effective in operation.*[238] The PRR locomotive of this era followed a standard design with a spread engine truck, level cylinders, a wagon-top boiler, and Stephenson valve gear. Laird proceeded to rebuild a number of early PRR locomotives with these standard features.

The problem facing the PRR was not standard design — that had been achieved — but interchangeability of parts. The components of the locomotives purchased from the commercial builders and those of Laird's own rebuilds were not interchangeable from one to another. Cassatt was proposing that the Company design locomotives in which the various components were interchangeable as far as possible, not only among the same class, but among different classes.

Progress in engineering matters is fairly rational; it builds slowly upon previous stages. It seems possible within the context of engineering development to see the Company building new locomotives while this program of standardization was being developed.

The first four locomotives traditionally designated as AMS c/n's 1-4 were built while Ricker, Cassatt's predecessor, held the office of Superintendent of Motive Power & Machinery. Cassatt refers specifically to Ricker as initiating the first effort at standardization. Given the mechanical specifications of the first four locomotives: #142 (61" drivers, 16" x 24" cylinders), and #'s 148, 127, 239, (60" drivers, 17" x 24" cylinders), it is possible that #142 was the first attempt at the Company's own design for a 4-4-0, and #'s 148, 127, and 239 were modifications as they worked out a suitable design. The minor differences in firebox size and heating surface could be ascribed to initial attempts to develop uniformity of details. With the information from these four in hand, Collin may have proceeded to develop the plans and patterns for the Company's standard locomotives.

Ultimately the decision to buy or build goes to cost. Interestingly, the Company did both. This may have been related to the question of capacity and ability to deliver.

### WHEN DID THE PRR BUILD ITS FIRST NEW LOCOMOTIVE?

Again we need to refer to Cassatt's statement, quoted above. He uses the phrase "during the past year" twice; once in reference to the managerial decision and direction, *the importance in arriving as soon as possible at a system of perfect uniformity,* and once in reference to the preparation of drawings and the construction of the first locomotives to these plans. What did Cassatt mean by the phrase "during the past year"? The report was for 1868. It is clear that Cassatt is referring to 1868 when he writes "during the past year." This would indicate that the design and drafting of the plans for the standard classes took place during 1868, and likely were not completed until later.

A brief review of the chronology of additions to the roster may be helpful.

| | |
|---|---|
| 7/15/1866 | (J.P. Laird resigned, R.E. Ricker appointed) |
| 1/1867 | #142 built |
| 6/1867 | #148 built |
| 9/1867 | #127 built |
| 10/15/1867 | (R.E. Ricker resigned) |
| 10/1867 | #238 built (rebuilt ?) |
| 11/16/1867 | (A.J. Cassatt appointed) |

On July, 27, 1868, the first standard loco (class D) was turned out by Baldwin. On August 10, 1868, the first standard loco (class D) was turned out by Altoona. The usual dates for AMS c/n's 1-4 are:

| | |
|---|---|
| January 1867 | #142 [239] |
| June 1867 | #148 |
| September 1867 | #127 |
| October 1867 | #239 |

This might indicate that #142 was constructed, the plans modified, and #148 built, followed by #'s 127 and 239.

Note the PUT-ON-ROAD date for the first of each of the standard locomotives.

| | |
|---|---|
| August 1868 | Class D 4-6-0 |
| September 1868 | Class A 4-4-0 |
| April 1869 | Class B 4-4-0 |
| June 1869 | Class E 4-6-0 |
| June 1869 | Class C 4-4-0 |
| November 1869 | Class F 0-6-0T |
| November 1870 | Class G 4-4-0 |

The D and A were built first, with two different driver sizes on the A. Then, eight months later, the first B was built. The E closely followed, with a different driver and firebox size than the D. The C was first built the same month as the E, and was quite similar to the B. The F, which was dissimilar from the other classes, was not built until a year and three months after the first standard loco was turned out. The G, again quite dissimilar, followed a year later. In total, the standard classes were introduced over a period of two years and three months. It is conceivable that the drawings and patterns for the seven classes were not completed during 1868, but took a longer period.

Cassatt's report suggests that the basic managerial decision to proceed with a program of standard plans and patterns for locomotives was made during Ricker's tenure, but their specific development, which actually resulted in their first standard locomotive, was not undertaken until 1868, so there may well have been design development before the standard plans were implemented. Does Cassatt's comment on the "first decided effort" refer to #'s 142, 148, 127, and 239, built under Ricker's direction?

### NEW CONSTRUCTION OR REBUILDS?

The rebuilding program initiated by Laird and continued by his successors until 1868 complicates the question. During this period, many older locomotives were rebuilt with new valve gear, fireboxes, boilers and wheel arrangements, but usually retained their former numbers. Were there previous locomotives holding #'s 142, 148, 127 and 239 that could have been rebuilt?

A further complication is introduced by the PRR's method of record keeping. The *Record of Locomotives and Tenders* often shows a locomotive as cut up, and a new locomotive built by the Company and assigned the same number. Photographs and other official records show that this was not new construction at all, but a complete rebuilding of the earlier locomotive. Examples are the Winans Camels. The rebuilt locomotive was recapitalized as a new piece of equipment in the records.

## ALTOONA MACHINE SHOP #1
### 1st #142 - A Baldwin Six-Wheeler.

The original locomotive to hold #142 was *Atlas* (15-ton, six-wheel Baldwin class D, 42" drivers, 14" x 18" cylinders), a flexible-beam-truck 0-6-0 with a Bury firebox, built by Baldwin in April 1845 (#232) for the Philadelphia & Columbia, and relettered and renumbered as PRR #142 in 1857. The *Fourteenth Annual Report* for 1860 lists #142 (48" drivers, 13⅝" x 22" cylinders) as a shifting engine in good order. In the *Fifteenth Annual Report* for 1861, #142 has the notation, *in Altoona Shop for general repairs*. Apparently the engine was not worth repairing and it was cut up during 1862.

There was little of 1st #142 that would have been used in a "modern" locomotive of 1862. The frame and flexible-beam truck would have been obsolete, and the Bury-style boiler with the large dome over the firebox had been replaced in practice by the wagon-top boiler.

### 2nd #142 - Was It or Wasn't It?

The Baldwin consecutive construction list shows PRR #142, c/n 1013, as a 4-6-0 built in October 1861 with 48" drivers and 18½" x 22" cylinders. It appears that BLW #1013 was put on the road as #142 and was renumbered immediately upon delivery to #245. The *Valuation Record* has a note for #245 - "came as #142." Some locomotive rosters, especially the roster prepared by Allen O. Geertz, shows Baldwin #1013 as #142.

### 3rd #142 - The Mystery Engine

The *Sixteenth Annual Report* for 1862 lists the following after #142: Baldwin, April 1862 (60" drivers, 16" x 22" cylinders). The date is the date "put on road," and not necessarily the date built. A search of the *Baldwin Construction List* shows no unidentified 4-4-0 built for the PRR in April 1862, nor does it show a 4-4-0 with these dimensions built during that period that might have been refused and then sold to the PRR.

The *PRR Locomotive Valuation Register* shows a cost of $8,000 listed for #142, charged to repairs. The builder is noted as the Baldwin Locomotive Works; the date is April 1862. "Repair" in the *PRR Locomotive Valuation Register* does not necessarily mean that the locomotive was repaired. The PRR typically charged new construction to repair. Second #140 shows $7,750 charged to repair. This was a new locomotive, Baldwin c/n 1123, of April 1863. Other new construction was charged to "C&E," Capital & Expense. It is also significant that the *PRR Locomotive Valuation Register* does not show any reduction in the cost of the locomotive due to credit from old material.

The *Sixteenth Annual Report* shows repair costs to #142 of $7,953.67. There is a note at the end of that report which states *Purchased to replace old engines #s 142*

*and 143 condemned*. Unfortunately the printer did not add the asterisk to indicate which were the new locomotives in the roster. One can only assume that new #142 replaced old #142.

If this locomotive was 3rd, not 2nd #142, where did it come from? There is no notation in the *Annual Report* of any transfer of a locomotive from a subsidiary road to the PRR.

### 4th #142 - Altoona Machine Shop #1?

Is it possible that 3rd #142 was rebuilt at Altoona in late 1866 and early 1867 and identified as AMS #1? Could 3rd #142 have been scrapped after a short life of four years, due to an accident, or perhaps was it transferred (leased) to a subsidiary line?

In the *Twentieth Annual Report* for 1866 (dated February 19, 1867) the General Superintendent notes that Laird resigned July 15, 1866 and the position was filled by Ricker, Superintendent of the TH&I. Ricker reports as follows on page 45:

**Engines acquired to fill vacant numbers:**

| | |
|---|---|
| 10-Wheel Freight | 2 |
| 8-Wheel Passenger | 7 |
| Shifting | 8 |
| **Engines rebuilding to fill a vacant number:** | 1 |

**Engines acquired to fill condemned numbers:**

| | |
|---|---|
| Shifting | 5 |
| From P&E (Perkins Freight Engines) | 3 |

**Additional numbers:**

| | |
|---|---|
| New 10-Wheel Freight | 16 |

**Ricker noted the following under repairs:**

| | |
|---|---|
| 21 rebuilt, including new boilers | 21 |
| New fireboxes | 31 |
| New half-fireboxes | 23 |

The significant element in this report is that one locomotive is shown as "rebuilding" to fill a vacant number and that 21 locomotives are shown as having been rebuilt with new boilers. Was the locomotive "rebuilding" #142? The term "rebuilding," as the PRR uses it in its official records, is not employed in a consistent fashion. In some instances it means that the number is being rebuilt and not the machinery, i.e., #142 is "rebuilding" by the construction of a new piece of machinery to fill #142. If 3rd #142 was being rebuilt — used in conjunction with the actual machinery here - why was one loco shown as "rebuilding" to fill a vacant number rather than being listed with the 21 locomotives that received new boilers? To put it in PRR terminology was #142, filled by "rebuilding," namely, the construction of a new locomotive?

The issue is further complicated by the cylinders on #142. They are unlike the cylinders on #148 and also unlike the cylinders on the standard locomotives. There is a strip where the valve chest is connected to the cylinder with three bolts in it. The valve chest extends out beyond the cylinder. This type of cylinder can be seen on the following Altoona rebuilds: #'s 94, 169, 205 278, and 347, originally built by Norris, #s 36 and 173 originally built by Baldwin, and #210, built by Smith & Perkins.

The cost for #142 is shown as $11,576, while the cost for #148 is $13,870.35. The costs attributed to #142 appear to be about $1,000 below the cost of a new locomotive in 1867. Does this indicate that #142 was extensively rebuilt, or that a "new" locomotive was built and assigned #142 and that approximately $1,000 of the parts of former #142 were used? This might be the tender and certain fittings, but the PRR Locomotive Valuation Register does not does not show any reduction in the cost of the locomotive due to credit from old material. The price would seem to include a new boiler and firebox, and perhaps cylinders. #142 had an iron firebox, according to the Register of Engines, February 1868, and this might account in part for the cost differential between #142 and #148.

There remains a real question if in fact #142 is the first locomotive to be built new at Altoona. Since there was a locomotive that can be identified as holding #142 (BLW, April 1862), was that earlier #142 rebuilt as 4th #142? Since the price must have included a new boiler and firebox, are we to consider this new construction? It would have been assigned a new boiler number, if they had been in use then.

I opt (with reservations) for 4th #142 as Altoona Machine Shop c/n #1, because the cost suggests a new boiler and the Register of Engines, February 1868 shows a new iron firebox installed with the date of December 1866.

In the copy of A Collection of Photographs, Typical of each class on the Pennsylvania Railroad at this date; May 1st 1868 on file at the State Archives in Harrisburg, written by hand below the photograph of #142 are the words "Altoona #1 - the 1st engine built new by Altoona Shops - November 1866." Unfortunately, this note appears to be a later addition.

## ALTOONA MACHINE SHOP #2
### 1st #148 - A Norris 4-4-0
PRR #148 (April 1860, 11" x 26") was first assigned in August 1857 to Wissahicken, built by Norris Brothers in May 1849 for the Philadelphia & Columbia. The typical Norris 4-4-0 of this period had a Bury boiler, short-wheelbase engine truck, and sloping cylinders. A note in the Geertz roster shows 1st #148 cut up in 1866.

### 2nd #148 - Altoona Machine Shop #2
The photo of #148 shows a modern 4-4-0 with none of the old Norris features.

Was first #148 scrapped in 1866, and a new 4-4-0, AMS c/n #2, built to fill the number?

The Register of Engines, February 1868 shows #148 (4-4-0, 17" x 24" cylinders), built by the Company with a steel firebox (the firebox date is December 1866). The Record of Locomotives and Tenders shows #148 built by the Company in December 1866 at a cost of $13,870.35.

The old Wissahicken was probably scrapped, and a new 4-4-0 built to replace it. As noted, the difference in price between #148 and #142 might include the cost differential between an iron and a steel firebox.

I opt for the opinion that #148 was "constructed entirely new" at Altoona.

### The Philadelphia & Erie Connection
There is a note in a roster by Alan Geertz which states that 2nd #148 was ex-Philadelphia & Erie #1022. The loco was supposedly sent to the PRR and rebuilt.

There are four locomotives in the P&E roster that disappear before February 1866: #'s 1014, 1022, 1034, and 1035. The PRR Annual Reports generally show the transfer of locomotives. There is no record of the transfer of these four locomotives from the P&E to the PRR. The Twentieth Annual Report for 1866, noted above, shows the transfer of three locomotives from the P&E to the PRR in 1864, with the note that they are old Perkins freight engines. To confuse matters, only two Perkins engines appear to have been transferred to the P&E; they did not receive their former numbers when transferred back to the PRR, and only one new number seems to have been assigned, #210. That leaves one locomotive that was transferred back to the PRR unidentified as to type and builder.

## ALTOONA MACHINE SHOP #3
### 1st #127 - A Smith & Perkins Ten-wheeled Freight Engine.
The first locomotive to hold #127 was Wilmore, a Smith & Perkins 4-6-0 built in April 1856 (44" drivers, 17" x 22" cylinders). In 1858 it was transferred to the Steubenville & Indiana and named Mingo Chief. Accompanying C.H. Caruthers' article on the PRR's Smith & Perkins locomotives in the Railroad Gazette, April 19, 1907, Vol. XLII, #16, p.554, is a drawing of Wilmore. Caruthers writes that I am credibly informed that one of them which had been renamed "Mingo Chief" at the time of transfer, continued in service until 1881. Since the first locomotive to hold #127 was operating until 1881 on the Panhandle, there is no apparent candidate for rebuilding.

### 2nd #127 - Altoona Machine Shop, c/n #3
The second locomotive to hold #127 could have been built new at Altoona. The Register of Engines, February 1868 shows #127 (60" drivers, 17" x 24" cylinders) built by the Company with a steel firebox (firebox date December 1866). The PRR Record of Locomotives and Tenders reports a price of $13,766.43.

## ALTOONA MACHINE SHOP #4
### 1st #239 - A Norris Ten-Wheeled Freight Engine

The first locomotive to hold #239 was a 4-6-0 built by Richard Norris & Son in March 1862 (49" drivers, 18" x 22" cylinders). A minute in the *Minute Book of the Board of Directors* for January 9, 1867, in reference to the payment of a death benefit, states that engine #239 exploded at East Liberty, Pa., on December 21, 1865.[240]

### 2nd #239 - A Rebuild, and not Altoona Machine Shop, c/n #4?

The *Register of Engines* for February 1868 has a note following #239: "rebuilt." Of all the locomotives under discussion, #239 is the only one to have this note. It is possible that the Norris Ten-wheeler, #239, which exploded, was rebuilt to a 4-4-0 (60" drivers, 17" x 24" cylinders) and that #239 was not built new as AMS c/n 4.

The *PRR Record of Locomotives and Tenders* shows the cost of 2nd #239 as $13,766.43. This is similar to the price listed for #'s 148 and 127, and would indicate the cost of a new locomotive and not a rebuilding. How much of #239 was left after the explosion?

## TO SUM UP THE INFORMATION WE HAVE DISCUSSED SO FAR:
### The different dates and the costs are as follows:

|  | #142 | #148 | #127 | #239 |
|---|---|---|---|---|
| J. D. Lovell's Roster | 12/1866 | 6/1867 | 9/1867 | 10/1867 |
| Charles Fisher's Roster | 11/1866 | 6/1867 | 9/1867 | 10/1867 |
| 02/68 Register | 1/1867 | 6/1867 | 9/1867 | 10/1867 |
| Placed on Road* | 1/1867 | 12/1866 | 12/1866 | 10/1867 |
| Valuation Register | 1/1867 | 12/1866 | 12/1866 | 9/1867 |
| Firebox Date ** | 12/1866 | 12/1866 | 12/1866 | 10/1867 |
| Cost * | $11,756.00 | $13,870.35 | $13,766.43 | $13,765.75 |

* *Record of Locomotives & Tenders*
** *Register of Engines, February 1868*

| Dimensions | #142 | #148 | #127 | #239 |
|---|---|---|---|---|
| Drivers, dia., in. | 61 | 62 | 62 | 62 |
| Cylinders, in. | 16 x 24 | 17 x 24 | 17 x 24 | 17 x 24 |
| Grate Surface, sq.ft. | ? | 14.0 | 14.2 | 14.0 |
| Heating Surface, sq.ft. | ? | 1123.7 | 1286.7 | 1156.8 |
| Wt., on Drivers, lbs. | 42,100 | 42,600 | 42,600 | 42,600 |
| Wt., Working Order, lbs. | 67,500 | 66,000 | 66,000 | 66,000 |

In "Index A" of *A Collection of Photographs, Typical of each class on the Pennsylvania Railroad at this date; May 1st 1868*, #142 is shown as a single locomotive in the class #142 and #'s 127, 148 and 239 are shown as the three locomotives of the class #148.

## WILL THE REAL ALTOONA MACHINE SHOP #1 PLEASE STAND UP?

If all this were not enough, a recent study of the PRR's facilities at Altoona reports that:

*The first locomotive built at Altoona was passenger engine #86 completed in May of 1862. This engine had four 66" drivers and weighed 69,400 pounds. The engine number was changed to #73 in 1869 and it was cut up for scrap in 1885. Another early engine, often mistakenly referred to as the first Altoona engine, was passenger engine #142 built in January of 1867. This engine was slightly smaller in that it weighed 66,000 pounds, but otherwise of similar design as #86.*[241]

The source for the information is given as a letter from J.A. Lockard to H.T. Cover in 1949.[242]

Locomotive #86 was built as *Nanticoke*, a 4-4-0 (54" drivers, 16" x 24" cylinders) by Richard Norris & Son in February 1854. The *Annual Report* for 1861 shows the engine in the Altoona Shop being rebuilt, retaining its 4-4-0 wheel arrangement and cylinder dimensions, but with 66" drivers. The increased weight from 58,500 to 69,400 pounds very likely includes a new boiler. The *Register of Engines, February 1868*, lists #86 as built by Norris with 67" drivers and 16" x 24" cylinders. The locomotive is recorded as having received a new copper firebox in October 1860. It was renumbered to #73 in July 1870. The *Locomotive Register for January 1, 1885* shows locomotive #73 as an Odd 4-4-0 built by Richard Norris & Son. In the *Register of Engines, February 1868*, the builder for #142 is shown as "Company."

The jarring impact of this bit of information is not that #73 (*nee #86*) was the first locomotive built at Altoona, but that the Company did not know which actually was the first locomotive built at Altoona.

## SEVERAL OPTIONS

Let me suggest several options to clear up the mystery of Altoona Machine Shop c/n 1.

### #101

#101 is a mystery engine, built with standard features by Altoona Machine Shop in November 1868, and later classified "Odd A." A note in *A Collection of Photographs, Typical of each class on the Pennsylvania Railroad at this date; May 1st 1868* reads that "1st 101 was cut up and replaced by a standard 5 ft. whl. passenger engine the same throughout as engine (#)421 with the addition of a straight boiler on 5 ft. wheels." The locomotive has been included in the Lovell list as construction #11a.

## Possibility #1

The Lovell list incorrectly identifies AMS c/n 1 as #142. The mystery engine, 3rd #142, Baldwin April 1862, was rebuilt. AMS c/n 1 is actually #148. PRR #79, usually assigned AMS c/n 5, is actually AMS c/n 4. AMS c/n's 5-11 are actually AMS c/n's 4-10 and PRR #101 is AMS c/n 11, not c/n 11a. The list would look as follows:

| AMS c/n | PRR # | Class |
|---|---|---|
| 1 | 148 | 148 |
| 2 | 127 | 148 |
| 3 | 239 | 148 |
| 4 | 79 | D |
| 5 | 87 | D |
| 6 | 54 | A |
| 7 | 133 | A |
| 8 | 31 | A |
| 9 | 17 | A |
| 10 | 27 | A |
| 11 | 101 | A Odd |

## Possibility #2

The Lovell list correctly identifies AMS c/n's 1-3 as #'s 142, 148 and 127, but AMS c/n 4 is #79, the first standard class D built by Altoona. This locomotive has been misidentified as AMS c/n 5. #239, long identified as AMS c/n 4, is a rebuild, as the *Register of Engines, Corrected to February 1868* reports. Thus AMS c/n's 5-11 are actually AMS c/n's 4-10, and c/n 11a is really AMS c/n 11. The rest of the AMS list is substantially correct.

| AMS c/n | PRR # | Class |
|---|---|---|
| 1 | 142 | 142 |
| 2 | 148 | 148 |
| 3 | 127 | 148 |
| 4 | 79 | D |
| 5 | 87 | D |
| 6 | 54 | A |
| 7 | 133 | A |
| 8 | 31 | A |
| 9 | 17 | A |
| 10 | 27 | A |
| 11 | 101 | A Odd |

## Possibility #3

The Lovell list is actually correct and #101 was overlooked in the formulation of the original consecutive construction list. Locomotives #'s 142, 148, 127 and 239 were actually the first four locomotives built new at Altoona.

# APPENDIX C
## TOTAL OF LOCOMOTIVES ON THE PRR BY YEAR
### FROM THE ANNUAL REPORTS OF THE COMPANY 1851 ONWARD

| Year | Total |
|---|---|
| 1849 | 12 |
| 1850 | 24 |
| 1851 | 26 |
| 1852 | 44 |
| 1853 | 79 |
| 1854 | 115 |
| 1855 | 118 |
| 1856 | 133 |
| 1857 | 216 |
| 1858 | 209 |
| 1859 | 205 |
| 1860 | 211 |
| 1861 | 229 |
| 1862 | 255 |
| 1863 | 290 |
| 1864 | 321 |
| 1865 | 352 |
| 1866 | 384 |
| 1867 | 428 |
| 1868 | 477 |
| 1869 | 482 |
| 1870 | 514 |
| 1871 | 554 |
| 1872 | 776 (does not include P&E) |
| 1873 | 921 (does not include P&E) |

The figures are for December 31 of the year listed.

The total shown in the *Annual Reports* may disagree with other reports because of the way in which locomotives are listed. The *Annual Report* for 1857 shows the total of the Company locomotives and the additions from the Philadelphia & Columbia and Allegheny Portage. Included in this total are five condemned locomotives from the State Works, which never received PRR numbers.

The list of locomotives on the road in the 1857 *Annual Report* shows only 211. Other totals include leased locomotives, which do not show on the list of locomotives on the road.

The first two totals (1849 and 1850) are reconstructed from the list of locomotives on the road for 1851, tables in J. Elfreth Watkins, *History of the Pennsylvania Railroad Company 1846-1896*, and the Baldwin Construction list.

1872 and 1873 show the following totals: 1872 - PRR 554, URRofNJ 222, P&E 130 for a total of 906; 1873 - PRR 662, URRofNJ 259, P&E 150, for a total of 1,071.

# APPENDIX D

### Chart 13

| Classes | A | B | C | D | E | F | G | H | Ca | Odd |
|---|---|---|---|---|---|---|---|---|---|---|
| Robert E. Ricker, 7/16/1866 - 10/15/1867 | | | | | | | | | | 4 |
| A. J. Cassatt, 11/16/1867 - 4/1/1870 | 11 | 2 | 12 | 8 | 6 | 12 | | | | 1 |
| Isaac L Dripps, 4/1/1870 - 3/31/1872 | | | 6 | 12 | 38 | 6 | 6 | | | |
| G. Clinton Gardner, 4/1/1872 - 2/28/1873 | 2 | | 12 | | 30 | | | 6 | | |
| Frank Thomson, 3/1/1873 - 1/1/1874** | | 2 | *10 | | 4 | 6 | 12 | 18 | 12 | |
| Total | 13 | 4 | 40 | 20 | 78 | 24 | 18 | 24 | 12 | 5 |

236 locomotives built at Altoona between 12/1866 and 12/1873

* 4 went to the P&E.

** Thomson served as Superintendent of Motive Power, PRR Grand Division until June 30, 1874; the numbers of engines shown are those built prior to January 1, 1874.

# APPENDIX E
# LOCOMOTIVES BUILT BY BALDWIN FOR THE PRR
## THE BALDWIN CLASSIFICATION SYSTEM

In the 1840's through the 1860's, Baldwin classified its locomotives by weight, the total number of wheels, and the number of driving wheels. The capital letter indicated the number of drivers, with one exception, the Class A. A = special locomotives, B = two drivers, C = four drivers, D = six drivers, and E = eight drivers. In this system the PRR's *Juniata*, a 4-4-0, was a 19-ton, eight-wheel C.

## THE LOCOMOTIVES BALDWIN BUILT

**Chart 14** shows the locomotives that Baldwin built for the Pennsylvania Railroad from November 1848 through January 1868. They are listed by their Baldwin classification, the wheel arrangement according to the Whyte System, the diameter of the drivers, the bore and stroke of the cylinders, the date assigned by Baldwin to the first locomotive of its "class" built, the construction number in the consecutive Baldwin construction list, the PRR's name or number of the first locomotive of the class, and the total number of locomotives built to those specifications.

### Chart 14

### PRR Locos Built by Baldwin, November 1848 to January 1868

| Baldwin Type | Type | Drivers, in. | Cylinders, in. | Date Built | c/n | Name or # | Quantity Built |
|---|---|---|---|---|---|---|---|
| 21-ton, 8-wheel E | 0-8-0 | 42 | 17x22 | 11/7/1848 | 333 | *Dauphin* | 3 |
| 18-ton, 8-wheel A | 4-2-2-0 | 72 | 14x20 | 7/12/1849 | 356 | *Mifflin* | 3 |
| 19-ton, 8-wheel C | 4-4-0 | 54 | 14x20 | 10/20/1849 | 369 | *Juniata* | 2 |
| 19-ton, 8-wheel C | 4-4-0 | 54 | 14-1/2x20 | 6/27/1850 | 385 | *Allegheny* | 2 |
| 19-ton, 8-wheel C | 4-4-0 | 54 | 15x20 | 8/15/1850 | 387 | *Clinton* | 14 |
| 18-ton, 8-wheel E | 0-8-0 | 42 | 14-1/2x18 | 8/21/1850 | 388 | *Beaver* | 1 |
| 18-ton, 8-wheel C | 4-4-0 | 60 | 13-1/2x22 | 11/7/1850 | 404 | *Wyoming* | 4 |
| 19-ton, 8-wheel C | 4-4-0 | 60 | 15x20 | 4/6/1852 | 471 | *Pike* | 1 |
| 25-ton, 10-wheel D | 4-6-0 | 44 | 18x22 | 8/7/1852 | 487 | *Bedford* | 6 |
| 25-ton, 10-wheel D | 2-6-0 | 44 | 18x22 | 12/13/1852 | 505 | *Cumberland* | 6 |
| 23-ton, 8-wheel C | 4-4-0 | 66 | 16x22 | 8/29/1853 | 546 | *True American* | 5 |
| 24-ton, 8-wheel C | 4-4-0 | 54 | 17x22 | 9/12/1853 | 547 | *Adams* | 24 |
| 20-ton, 8-wheel E | 0-8-0 | 43 | 19x22 | 2/16/1854 | 573 | *Quaker City* | 4 |
| 23-ton, 8-wheel C | 4-4-0 | 72 | 16x22 | 12/6/1854 | 626 | *Belle* | 2 |
| 27-ton, 10-wheel D | 4-6-0 | 48 | 19x22 | 5/3/1855 | 642 | *Black Oak* | 3 |
| 25-ton, 8-wheel C | 4-4-0 | 66 | 15x24 | 12/4/1866 | 731 | *Tiger* | 2 |
| 17-ton, 6-wheel C | 0-6-0 | 44 | 14-1/2x18 | 4/21/1857 | 754 | *Consolidation* | 2 |
| 25-ton, 8-wheel C | 4-4-0 | 66 | 15-1/2x24 | 5/30/1857 | 761 | *Hornet* | 3 |
| 24-ton, 8-wheel C | 4-4-0 | 56 | 17x22 | 6/23/1857 | 766 | 136 | 4 |
| 25-ton, 8-wheel E | 0-8-0 | 43 | 18x20 | 10/15/1857 | 787 | 44 | 4 |
| 27-ton, 10-wheel D | 4-6-0 | 50 | 18-1/2x22 | 3/18/1861 | 994 | 3 | 1 |
| 15-ton, 6-wheel C | 2-4-0T | 56 | 10x18 | 2/28/1861 | 1000 | 212 | 1 |
| 26-ton, 10-wheel D | 4-6-0 | 50 | 16-1/2x22 | 6/8/1861 | 1003 | 213 | 3 |
| 15-ton, 8-wheel C | 4-4-0T | 56 | 10x18 | 7/6/1861 | 1005 | 217 | 1 |
| 20-ton, 6-wheel D | 0-6-0T | 44 | 15x18 | 8/8/1861 | 1006 | 215 | 15 |
| 27-ton, 10-wheel D | 4-6-0 | 48 | 18-1/2x22 | 9/4/1861 | 1009 | 1 | 2 |
| 27-ton, 10-wheel D | 4-6-0 | 48 | 18x22 | 9/21/1861 | 1011 | 15 | 22 |
| 10-ton, 4-wheel C | 0-4-0 | 36 | 11x16 | 3/29/1862 | 1047 | 246 | 2 |
| 28-ton, 10-wheel D | 4-6-0 | 48 | 18-1/2x22 | 8/19/1862 | 1075 | 251 | 1 |
| 28-ton, 8-wheel C | 4-4-0 | 66 | 16-1/2x24 | 9/3/1862 | 1081 | 261 | 1 |
| 28-ton, 10-wheel D | 4-6-0 | 48 | 18x22 | 10/16/1862 | 1083 | 253 | 7 |
| 28-ton, 10-wheel D | 4-6-0 | 50-1/2 | 18x22 | 12/19/1862 | 1098 | 260 | 5 |
| 28-ton, 10-wheel D | 4-6-0 | 54 | 18x22 | 1/24/1863 | 1106 | 266 | 64 |
| 15-ton, 8-wheel C | 4-4-0T | 56 | 10x20 | 4/29/1863 | 1129 | 251 | 1 |
| 28-ton, 8-wheel C | 4-4-0 | 66 | 17x24 | 5/30/1863 | 1140 | 60 | 15 |
| 25-ton, 10-wheel D | 4-6-0 | 54 | 16x22 | 2/11/1865 | 1334 | 338 | 6 |
| 27-ton, 8-wheel C | 4-4-0 | 66 | 17x24 | 3/13/1865 | 1344 | 331 | 6 |
| 27-ton, 8-wheel C | 4-4-0 | 66 | 16x24 | 8/30/1865 | 1404 | 351 | 4 |
| 21-ton, 6-wheel D | 0-6-0T | 44 | 15x18 | 9/27/1865 | 1409 | 108 | 18 |
| 27-ton, 8-wheel C | 4-4-0 | 60 | 16x24 | 1/26/1866 | 1425 | 358 | 6 |
| 14-ton, 4-wheel C | 0-4-0 | 50 | 14x22 | 3/31/1866 | 1474 | 92 | 2 |
| 28-ton, 10-wheel D | 4-6-0 | 55 | 18x22 | 10/1/1866 | 1534 | 373 | 13 |
| 14-ton, 4-wheel C | 0-4-0T | 48 | 14x22 | 5/24/1867 | 1631 | 24 | 1 |
| 28-1/2-ton, 8-wheel C | 4-4-0 | 60 | 17x24 | 5/31/1867 | 1634 | 385 | 9 |
| 28-1/2-ton, 8-wheel C | 4-4-0 | 66 | 17x24 | 8/5/1867 | 1651 | 419 | 4 |
| 28-1/2-ton, 8-wheel C | 4-4-0 | 60-3/4 | 17x24 | 9/25/1867 | 1659 | 394 | 4 |

This listing gives an idea of the size of the lots in which Baldwin built locomotives for the PRR. The 64 built as 28-ton ten-wheel D's with 18" x 22" cylinders and 54" drivers were turned out from January 24, 1863 through January 22, 1868 in small lots. Several photos of these locos are included and the slight differences between those built in various lots are evident.

# APPENDIX F
# REVENUE, PASSENGERS, AND TONS CARRIED

### Chart 15

### Revenue ($)

| Year | Passengers | Emigrants | Troops | Mail | Express | Freight | Misc. |
|---|---|---|---|---|---|---|---|
| 1855 | 680,463 | | | | | 1,183,556 | |
| 1860 | 1,453,992 | | | 74,503 | 75,120 | 4,191,783 | 137,300 |
| 1865 | 4,053,872 | 188,320 | 1,278,844 | 80,130 | 113,313 | 11,193,565 | 248,712 |
| 1870 | 3,595,371 | 162,671 | | 146,743 | 310,785 | 12,793,160 | 522,974 |
| 1873 | 4,169,141 | 230,529 | | 158,287 | 450,241 | 19,608,555 | 269,253 |

In 1863, $370,313 was shown for Extra Express Freight.

### Chart 16

### Passengers and Tons Carried

| Year | Passengers Carried | Tonnage | Coal (included in tonnage) |
|---|---|---|---|
| 1855 | | 365,006 | |
| 1860 | | 1,346,525 | 523,233 |
| 1865 | 2,861,836 | 2,798,810 | 1,074,757 |
| 1870 | 4,352,769 | 5,804,051 | 2,550,389 |
| 1873 | 5,879,684  PRR | 9,998,794  PRR | 4,527,501  PRR |
| 1873 | 8,003,043  URRofNJ | 3,051,577  URRofNJ | 415,940  URRofNJ |
| 1873 | 397,153  B D | 1,444,573  B D | 1,224,528  B D |

# APPENDIX G
# SPECIFICATIONS OF THE STANDARD CLASSES

### Chart 17

### Dimensions for Standard Engines

| Class | Cylinders, in. | Service | Drivers No. | Drivers Dia., in. | Weight (lbs.) on: Drivers | Weight (lbs.) on: Truck | Weight (lbs.) on: Total |
|---|---|---|---|---|---|---|---|
| A | 17x24 | Pass'r | 4 | 66 | 46,500 | 25,400 | 71,900 |
| B | 18x24 | Pass'r | 4 | 60 | 49,300 | 25,700 | 75,000 |
| C | 17x24 | Pass'r | 4 | 60 | 45,200 | 26,300 | 71,500 |
| C | 17x24 | Frt | 4 | 60 | 44,600 | 25,700 | 70,300 |
| D | 18x22 | Frt | 6 | 54 | 55,400 | 22,000 | 77,500 |
| E | 18x22 | Frt | 6 | 48 | 57,500 | 19,000 | 77,100 |
| F | 15x28 | Shift'r | 6 | 44 | Tank | | 63,500 |
| G | 15x22 | Pass'r. & Frt. | 4 | 54 | 39,200 | 20,800 | 60,000 |

### Chart 18

### Cylinders and Pistons for Standard Engines

| Class | Cylinders Diam. | Cylinders Stroke | Cylinders Center to Center | Weights Rough | Weights Finish | Weights Linking Head Alone | Piston Thickness, in. | Piston 2 Rings, ea., in. | Piston Rod Diam., in. | Piston Rod Center of piston to end of rod. in. |
|---|---|---|---|---|---|---|---|---|---|---|
| A | 17 | 24 | 81 | 2,200 | 1,834 | 150 | 4-3/4 | 1-1/2x3/4 | 2-1/2 | 42-3/8 |
| B | 18 | 24 | 81 | 2,200 | 1,834 | 150 | 4-3/4 | 1-1/2x3/4 | 2 7/8 | 42-3/8 |
| C | 17 | 24 | 81 | 2,200 | 1,834 | 150 | 4-3/4 | 1-1/2x3/4 | 2-1/2 | 42-3/8 |
| D | 18 | 22 | 81 | 2,300 | 1,820 | 165 | 4-3/4 | 1-1/2x3/4 | 2 7/8 | 40-3/8 |
| E | 18 | 22 | 81 | 2,300 | 1,820 | 165 | 4-3/4 | 1-1/2x3/4 | 2 7/8 | 40-3/8 |
| F | 15 | 18 | 81 | 1,770 | 1,390 | 140 | 4-3/4 | 1-1/2x3/4 | 2-1/4 | 36-1/2 |
| G | 15 | 22 | 81 | 1,775 | 1,500 | 145 | 4-3/4 | 1-1/2x3/4 | 2-1/2 | 40-3/8 |

For 2-1/2-inch piston rods, 4-inch diameter stuffing box
For 2-7/8-inch piston rods, 4-1/4-inch diameter stuffing box
For 2-1/4-inch piston rods, 3-3/4-inch diameter stuffing box
All valve rods are 1-1/2-inch diameter with 2-3/4-inch stuffing box

### Chart 19

### Driving wheels for Standard Engines
*All dimensions are in inches.*

| Class | Driver Diameter* | Width of Face | Dish Inside | Through Hub | Between Hubs | Between Rims | Lead of Cranks | Weight, lbs. | Weight of Lead for Center Balance, pounds per wheel |
|---|---|---|---|---|---|---|---|---|---|
| A | 62 | 5-1/4 | 1/2 | 7 | 54-5/8 | 53-1/2 | Left hand | **1,610 | 283 main, 192 back |
| B | 56 | 5-3/8 | 1/2 | 7 | 54-5/8 | 53-1/2 | Left hand | 1,530 | 337 |
| C | 56 | 5-3/8 | 1/2 | 7 | 54-5/8 | 53-1/2 | Left hand | 1,530 | 337 |
| D | 50 | 5-3/8 | 1/2 | 7 | 54-5/8 | 53-1/2 | Left hand | 1,210 | 310 |
| E | 44 | 5-3/8 | 1/2 | 7 | 54-5/8 | 53-1/2 | Left hand | 1,050 | 300 |
| F | | | | | | | | 750 | 110 |
| G | 50 | 5-1/4 | 1/2 | 7 | 54-5/8 | 53-1/2 | Left hand | 1,210 | 310 |

* Diameter is for driver center, not including tire
** New = 1,673 lbs.

181

## Chart 20

### Driving Axles for Standard Engines

*All dimensions are in inches.*

| Class | Finished Sizes | | Centers Of Journal | Length of Journal | Rough | | |
|---|---|---|---|---|---|---|---|
| | Dia. | Length | | | Length | Dia. | Wt., Lbs. |
| A | 6-1/2 | 68-3/8 | 47 | 7-1/2 | 69 | 6-7/8 | 750 |
| B | 6-1/2 | 68-3/8 | 47 | 7-1/2 | 69 | 6-7/8 | 750 |
| C | 6-1/2 | 68-3/8 | 47 | 7-1/2 | 69 | 6-7/8 | 750 |
| D | 6-1/4 | 68-3/8 | 47 | 7-1/2 | 69 | 6-5/8 | 720 |
| E | 6-1/4 | 68-3/8 | 47 | 7-1/2 | 69 | 6-5/8 | 720 |
| F | 6-1/4 | 68-3/8 | 47 | 7-1/2 | 69 | 6-5/8 | 720 |
| G | 6-1/4 | | | | | | |

Finished weight of axles, main and back, A, B and C: 637 lbs.
Finished weight of axles, main and others, D, E, F and G: ?

## Chart 21

### Engine Trucks for Standard Engines

*All dimensions are in inches.*

| Class | Wheels | | Frame | | | | | Axles | | |
|---|---|---|---|---|---|---|---|---|---|---|
| | Dia. | Ctrs. | Long | Wide | Section | Dia. | Length | Journal | Wheel Fit | |
| A | 30 | 68 | 92 | 48 | 3-1/2 x 1-1/2 | 4-1/2 | 66 | 7-1/2 x 4-1/4 | 6-3/4 x 1-1/4 | |
| B | 28 | 68 | 92 | 48 | 3-1/2 x 1-1/2 | 4-1/2 | 66 | 7-1/2 x 4-1/4 | 6-3/4 x 1-1/4 | |
| C | 28 | 68 | 92 | 48 | 3-1/2 x 1-1/2 | 4-1/2 | 66 | 7-1/2 x 4-1/4 | 6-3/4 x 1-1/4 | |
| D | 28 | 68 | 92 | 48 | 3-1/2 x 1-1/2 | 4-1/2 | 66 | 7-1/2 x 4-1/4 | 6-3/4 x 1-1/4 | |
| E | 26 | 68 | 92 | 48 | 3-1/2 x 1-1/2 | 4-1/2 | 66 | 7-1/2 x 4-1/4 | 6-3/4 x 1-1/4 | |
| F | 26 | 68 | 92 | 48 | 3-1/2 x 1-1/2 | 4-1/2 | 66 | 7-1/2 x 4-1/4 | 6-3/4 x 1-1/4 | |
| G | 28 | 68 | 92 | 48 | 3-1/2 x 1-1/2 | 4-1/2 | 66 | 7-1/2 x 4-1/4 | 6-3/4 x 1-1/4 | |

Between hub 52", length of hub 6-3/4", axle projects 1/4", springs 13 plates, 36" centers of bearings, plates 3-1/2" x 3/8".
Equalizers, section 4" x 1" on each side of frame.
Upper centers of cradle 28", lower centers 31".
Length of cradle links 6" centers.
Diameter of cast center pin, 12". Diameter of wrought center, 3-3/4".

## Chart 22

### Size and Weights of Boiler Flues for Standard Engines

| Class | No. of Tubes | Length, ft. & in. | Diameter, in. | Thickness, gauge | Wt. of One Tube, lbs. | Wt. of Set, lbs. |
|---|---|---|---|---|---|---|
| A | 142 | 11-1-1/2 | 2-1/4 | #11 | 25 | 3,550 |
| B | 155 | 10-8-3/4 | 2-1/4 | #11 | 24 | 3,720 |
| C Frt | 138 | 10-9 | 2-1/4 | #11 | 24 | 3,312 |
| C Pass | 151 | 11-1-3/4 | 2-1/4 | #11 | 25 | 3,775 |
| D | 119 | 12-10-1/2 | 2-1/2 | #11 | 38 | 4,522 |
| E | 123 | 12-4-3/4 | 2-1/2 | #11 | 37 | 4,551 |
| F | 95 | 12-11 | 2-1/4 | #11 | 29 | 2,755 |
| G | 130 | 9-9 | 2 | #11 | 20 | 2,600 |
| #46 | 105 | 14-8-1/2 | 2-1/2 | #11 | 40 | 4,200 |

## Chart 23

### Boilers, Fireboxes and Boiler Shells for Standard Engines

*All dimensions are in inches unless otherwise stated.*

| Class | Boiler Shell | | Wagon Top | Dome Length | Firebox Shell | | Flues | | Heating Surface, sq.ft. |
|---|---|---|---|---|---|---|---|---|---|
| | Diam., in. | Length, ft. & in. | | | Width | Diam. | Diam. | Length* | |
| A | 49-3/8 | 21-5-1/2 | 8 | 30 | 76 | 42-1/8 | 2-1/4 | 11-0-7/16 | 914.0 |
| B | 50 | 20-3-1/8 | 8 | 30 | 82 | 42-1/4 | 2-1/4 | 10-8 | 964.4 |
| C Frt. | 50-5/8 | 20-8-1/8 | Straight | 30 | 82 | 42-1/8 | 2-1/4 | 10-8 | 858.6 |
| C Pass. | 51-3/8 | 20-3-1/8 | Straight | 30 | 82 | 42-1/4 | 2-1/4 | 11-0-11/16 | 974.0 |
| D | 49-3/8 | 21-5-1/2 | 8 | 30 | 69-1/2 | 42-1/8 | 2-1/2 | 12-9-1/2 | 996.1 |
| E | 50 | 21-5-1/2 | 8 | 30 | 76-1/2 | 42-1/8 | 2-1/2 | 13-3-3/4 | 991.0 |
| F | 43-7/8 | 19-5-1/4 | Straight | 30 | 53-1/2 | 42-1/8 | 2-1/4 | 12-10-1/2 | 711.7 |
| G | 46 | 17-5-5/8 | Straight | 30 | 64 | 42-1/8 | 2 | 9-8 | 663.0 |

* Effective length between tubesheets. Used in the calculation of the heating surface of flues.

## Chart 24

### Heating Surface of Standard Engines

| Class | Firebox | | | | | | Heating Surface, sq.ft. | Max. Grate Dia. x Thickness, in. | Combustion Chamber Length, in. |
|---|---|---|---|---|---|---|---|---|---|
| | Length, in. | Width, in. | Depth, in. | Above Center, in. | Heating Surface, sq.ft. | Grate Area, sq.ft. | | | |
| A | 67 | 35 | 67-1/4 | 9-1/4 | 109.3 | 16.2 | 1,023.3 | 1-7/8 x 1/4 | 6 |
| B | 72 | 35 | 67-1/4 | 10-1/4 | 116.0 | 17.6 | 1,080.4 | 1-7/8 x 1/4 | 4-1/2 |
| C Frt. | 72-1/2 | 35 | 64-1/4 | 7-1/4 | 111.2 | 17.6 | 969.8 | 1-7/8 x 1/4 | 4-1/2 |
| C Pass. | 72-1/2 | 35 | 64-1/4 | 8 | 108.3 | 17.6 | 1,082.8 | 1-7/8 x 1/4 | |
| D | 61 | 35 | 64-1/2 | 9 | 100.0 | 14.8 | 1,096.1 | 1-7/8 x 1/4 | 6 |
| E | 67-3/8 | 35 | 64-3/4 | 9-1/4 | 103.0 | 16.3 | 1,094.0 | 1-7/8 x 1/4 | 4 |
| F | 44-1/4 | 35 | 51-1/2 | 5-1/2 | 63.8 | 10.7 | 775.5 | 1-7/8 x 1/4 | |
| G | 54-3/4 | 35 | 59 | 5-1/2 | 85.4 | 13.3 | 748.4 | 1-7/8 x 1/4 | 4 |

## Smoke Boxes of Standard Engines

| Class | Smokebox Size, in. |
|---|---|
| A&B | 50 x 33¼ |
| C Pass | 51 x 33¼ |
| C Ft | 50⅛ x 33¼ |
| D & E | 50⅛ x 33¼ |
| F & G | 46 x 30¼ |

## Boiler Class C - Steel Sheets for Boiler
*All dimensions are in inches.*

### Class C Freight

| | | | |
|---|---|---|---|
| 1 Barrel | A | 163¾ x 34¼ x 5/16 | |
| | A1 | 163¾ x 34¼ x 5/16 | |
| | A2 | 159¾ x 34¼ x 5/16 | |
| | A3 | 157¾ x 34¼ x 5/16 | |
| 1 Smokebox | B | 156¼ x 31⅜ x ⅜ | |
| 1 Roof | D1 | 110¾ x 62 x ⅜ | |
| | D2 | 109¾ x 28¼ x 5/16 | |
| 2 Sides | E | 87¼ x 60½ x ⅜ | |
| 1 Front Flue Sheet | H | 52¾ dia., ½ thick | |
| 1 Throat | G | 55 x 38 x ⅜ | |
| 1 Dome | K | 97¼ x 38 x 5/16 | |
| Cost | | $11,721.31 | |

### Class C Passenger

| | | | |
|---|---|---|---|
| 1 Barrel | A | 167½ x 34¼ x ⅜ | |
| | A1 | 165 x 34¼ x ⅜ | |
| | A2 | 162¾ x 34¼ x ⅜ | |
| | A3 | 100¼ x 38¼ x ⅜ | |
| 1 Smokebox | B | 159½ x 31⅜ x ⅜ | |
| 1 Roof | D1 | 91½ x 62¼ x ⅜ | |
| | D2 | 90½ x 28¼ x ⅜ | |
| 2 Sides | E | 78¾ x 57¼ x ⅜ | |
| Backhead | F | 87 x 60¾ x ⅜ | |
| 1 Throat | G | 61 x 61 x ⅜ | |
| 1 Front Flue Sheet | H | 53¾ dia x ½ | |
| 1 Dome | K | 97½ x 38 x 5/16 | |
| Cost | | $11,789.71 | |
| Engines built in 1869: | | #'s 11, 21, 45, 172, 238 | |
| Engines built in 1871: | | #'s 503-508 | |
| Cost | | Plain, $11,749.01; scoop, $12,098.18 | |

## Steel Firebox for One Engine
*All dimensions are in inches.*

### Freight

| | | |
|---|---|---|
| 2 Sides | M | 77½ x 67 x ¼ |
| 1 Crown | N | 77½ x 47½ x ¼ |
| 1 Door | O | 66½ x 44 x ¼ |
| 1 Flue | P | 36 x 47½ x ⅜ |
| 1 Throat | Q | 47 x 47½ x ¼ |

### Passenger

| | | |
|---|---|---|
| 2 Sides | M | 66¼ x 72½ x ¼ |
| 1 Crown | N | 72 x 48¾ x 5/16 |
| 1 Door | O | 66¾ x 44 x ¼ |
| 1 Flue | P | 100¼ x 38¼ x ⅜ |

## Class C Boiler - Revised 3/28/1873
*All dimensions are in inches.*

| | | |
|---|---|---|
| 1 Barrel | A | 161¾ x 38½ x 5/16 |
| | A1 | 159¾ x 36½ x 5/16 |
| | A2 | 159¾ x 34¼ x 5/16 |
| 1 Smokebox | B | 156¼ x 31⅛ x ⅜ |
| 1 Slope | C | 87 x 45 x ⅜ |
| 1 Roof | D | 100¾ x 54¼ x ⅜ |
| | D1 | 99¾ x 28¼ x ⅜ |
| 2 Sides | E | 78¾ x 59¾ x ⅜ |
| Backhead | F | 94¼ x 60 x ⅜ |
| 1 Throat | G | 55 x 46½ x ⅜ |
| 1 Frn't Flue Sheet | H | 52¾ dia., ½ thick |
| 1 Waist | I | 101¼ x 39 x ⅜ |
| 1 Dome | K | 97½ x 32 x 5/16 |

### Class C Firebox

| | | |
|---|---|---|
| 2 Sides | M | 77½ x 68¾ x 5/16 |
| 1 Crown | N | 77 x 47½ x 5/16 |
| 1 Door | O | 69½ x 43¾ x 5/16 |
| 1 Flue | P | 47½ x 40 x ½ |
| 1 Flue | P | 100¼ x 38¼ x ⅜ |
| 1 Throat | Q | 45½ x 41½ x 5/16 |

November - December 1872: Engine #'s 152, 626, 627, 651, 653, 662, 668, 570-574.

## NOTES ON SOURCES

The material on the growth of PRR from 1849 to 1873 revolves around the person of J. Edgar Thomson. I have used James A. Ward's *J. Edgar Thomson: Master of the Pennsylvania* and the histories of the PRR by Sipes, and by Burgess & Kennedy.

The material on the development of the PRR's motive power has been organized around the persons who served as Master of Machinery and later Superintendent of Motive Power & Machinery or Superintendent of Motive Power. This approach is novel; most American railroad mechanical history focuses on the machine rather than on the persons who developed and administered the motive power policy and designed the locomotives. The biographical information came from *The Biographical Directory of the Railway Officials of America, Railroad Gazette, Railway Age Gazette*, and *Railway Age*. This material has been supplemented by the *Pennsylvania Railroad Motive Power Personnel Records*.

The most available general history on the PRR's motive power development is found in the three articles by Paul T. Warner, published in the April, July and October 1924 issues of *Baldwin Locomotives*. The April issue contains the PRR's early motive power history. These articles were republished in book form by the Pennsylvania Railroad in 1924 and later reprinted by Owen Davies. Charles Fishers' article in *R&LHS Bulletin #86* simply repeats much of Warner's work.

Warner notes in his acknowledgments the contribution made by the articles of the late C.H. Caruthers appearing in various railroad journals. I have made extensive use of Caruthers' articles and drawings, which come from a first-hand observation of the PRR's early motive power. C.H. Caruthers spent his early years in and around Altoona, Pa., and was on hand to see many of the locomotives he writes about. He appears to have had some mechanical training and later served as foreman in the shops of a car builder, was the master mechanic of a substantial coke operation in the Connellsville area, and then operated a machinery business in Pittsburgh. I have been able to look over a portion of Caruthers' personal correspondence thanks to the generosity of the late Harry Albrecht. Caruthers' interest in locomotives is rather amazing. He carried on an extensive correspondence with Snowden Bell, Mathias Forney, and others. While he was researching the Winans Camels he paid a photographer to climb under one of the remaining Camels to take a picture of the eccentrics. The volume and extent of his correspondence shows that he did not rely on his memory but was continually checking on information, asking for drawings and seeking confirmation of his recollections from a variety of railway officials and operating personnel.

This material was woven into the story told by the detailed reports of the Master of Machinery and later Superintendent of Motive Power & Machinery or Superintendent of Motive Power, appearing in the Pennsylvania Railroad's *Annual Reports*. The development of PRR motive power can be traced by the facts, figures and commentary provided there. This is especially true of the development of coal burning on the PRR. These were supplemented by the notations in the *Master Mechanic's Notebooks*. These 19 books contain a variety of entries by George W. Stratton relating to PRR motive power practice.

The *Minute Books* of the Board of Directors and the Road Committee, while not revealing the reasons for decisions, show clearly the actions of those bodies in regard to the purchase of locomotives. The most revealing material to be found was in the *Letterbooks* of Matthias W. Baldwin at the Historical Society of Pennsylvania. These books contain both the letters received and the letters sent by Baldwin. The early exchanges between Baldwin and Thomson cleared up a number of questionable points and revealed some of the reasons for the decisions that were made.

The listing of motive power facilities was gleaned from the *Annual Reports* and listings provided in Coverdale & Colpitts. The mechanical practices were compiled from Caruthers' articles, especially his "Successive Experiments and Improvements on Locomotives of the Pennsylvania Railroad" in the *Railroad Gazette*, and the unpublished work of Charles Chaney, *Pennsylvania Railroad Locomotive Practice: 1867-1897*, and the *Annual Reports*. The painting and lettering of PRR locomotives was gathered from Caruthers' observations and material in Dredge.

The source for the roster is G.W. Stratton's register books, copied by Joseph D. Lovell.

## BIBLIOGRAPHY
### Original Sources

Baldwin Locomotive Works, *Letterbooks*, Baldwin Locomotive Works Papers, Historical Society of Pennsylvania, Philadelphia, Pa.

_____, *Register of Engines Made By M.W. Baldwin*, State Archives, Harrisburg, Pa.

Knight, Jonathan and Latrobe, Benjamin H., *Report Upon The Policy and Management of Several of the Principal Rail Roads in the Northern and Middle States*, 1838, reprint, Boston, Railway & Locomotive Historical Society, 1927.

Pennsylvania Railroad Company, *A Collection of Photographs, Typical of each class on the Pennsylvania Railroad at this date; May 1st 1868*, PRR Office of the Secretary, Library Reference Materials (1834-1968), Penn Central Railroad Collection, MG-286, Pennsylvania State Archives, Harrisburg, Pa.

_____, *Annual Report to the Stockholders*, #1, October 30, 1847, through #27, February 10, 1874, Altoona Public Library, Altoona, Pa.

_____, *Description of Locomotives and Tenders*, location unknown.

_____, *Historical Record of Locomotives*, location unknown.

_____, *Letterbook of J. Edgar Thomson, Chief Engineer, 1847-1851*, PRR Office of the Secretary, Library Reference Materials (1834-1968), Penn Central Railroad Collection, MG-286, Pennsylvania State Archives, Harrisburg, Pa.

_____, J.A.Lockard to H.T. Cover, January 31, 1949, Box 486, Chief of Motive Power File, Pennsylvania Railroad Collection, Acc. #1810, Hagley Museum and Library, Wilmington, Del.

_____, *Master Mechanic's Notebooks A-N*, Folders 13-1 to 13-17, Slot Location 9/3324, Box 13, PRR Office of the Secretary, Library Reference Materials (1834-1968), Penn Central Railroad Collection, MG-286, Pennsylvania State Archives, Harrisburg, Pa.

_____, *Minute Books of the Board of Directors of the Pennsylvania Rail Road Company,1847-1957*, Vol. 1, PRR Office of the Secretary, Library Reference Materials (1834-1968), Penn Central Railroad Collection, MG-286, Pennsylvania State Archives, Harrisburg, Pa.

_____, *Motive Power Personnel Records*, PRR Office of the Secretary, Library Reference Materials (1834-1968), Penn Central Railroad Collection, MG-286, Pennsylvania State Archives, Harrisburg, Pa.

_____, *Pennsylvania Locomotives Before 1868*, PRR Office of the Secretary, Library Reference Materials (1834-1968), Penn Central Railroad Collection, MG-286, Pennsylvania State Archives, Harrisburg, Pa.

_____, *Record of Locomotives and Tenders*, Roger L. Keyser Collection, PRRT&HS Archives, Lewistown, Pa.

_____, *Register of Engines, Corrected to February 1868, Motive Power and Machinery Department*, Roger L. Keyser Collection, PRRT&HS Archives, Lewistown, Pa.

_____, *Road Committee Minutes*, PRR Office of the Secretary, Library Reference Materials (1834-1968), Penn Central Railroad Collection, MG-286, Harrisburg, Pa.

Roberts, Solomon W, *Reminiscences of the First Railroad Over the Allegheny Mountain*, Read Before the Historical Society of Pennsylvania, April 8th, 1878.

_____, *P.R.R Locomotive Valuation Register* (photocopy), Roger L. Keyser Collection, PRRT&HS Archives, Lewistown, Pa.

Tibby, Matthew, *Personal Reminiscences of the Early Days of the Pennsylvania Railroad at Pittsburgh*, PRR, Office of the Secretary, Library Reference Materials (1834-1968), Penn Central Railroad Collection, MG-286, Pennsylvania State Archives, Harrisburg, Pa.

Welch, Sylvester, *Sylvester Welch's Report on the Allegheny Portage Railroad*, 1833, reprint, York, Pa.: American Canal & Transportation Center, 1975.

Wilson, William Hasell, *The Columbia-Philadelphia Railroad and its Successor*, 1896: reprint, York, Pa.: American Canal & Transportation Center, 2nd printing, 1992.

## Secondary Sources

Binder, Frederick M., *Coal Age Empire*, Harrisburg: Pennsylvania Historical & Museum Commission, 1974.

Brown, John K., *The Baldwin Locomotive Works: 1831-1915*, Baltimore: Johns Hopkins University Press, 1995.

Burgess, George H. and Kennedy, Miles C., *Centennial History of the Pennsylvania Railroad Company 1846-1946*, Philadelphia: Pennsylvania Railroad Company, 1949.

Chaney, Charles, *Pennsylvania Railroad Locomotive Practice: 1867-1897*, unpublished.

Coverdale and Colpitts, Consulting Engineers, *The Pennsylvania Railroad Company: Corporate, Financial and Construction History Lines Owned, Operated and Controlled to December 31, 1945*, Volumes I-IV, Allen, Lane and Scott, 1946.

Dredge, James, *The Pennsylvania Railroad: Its Origin, Construction and Management*. London & New York: John Wiley & Sons, 1879.

Gardner, G. Clinton, "The Rolling Stock of the Pennsylvania Railroad," *Van Nostrand's Eclectic Engineering Magazine*, Vol. 6, No. 39, March 1872, pp.302-307.

Jacobs, Harry A., *The Juniata Canal and Old Portage Railroad*, Altoona, Pa., Blair County Historical Society, 1941, reprinted 1969.

Kline, Benjamin F. G., *The Odyssey of Five Locomotives: 1835-1965*, reprint, Lancaster, Pa., Lancaster County Historical Society.

Lovell, Joseph D., *Pennsylvania Railroad Altoona Machine Shop: Construction Number List, 1866-1904*, National Railway Historical Society, 1984.

Page, John C., *A Special Study, Pennsylvania Railroad Shops and Works, Altoona, Pennsylvania*, United States Department of the Interior, National Parks Service, May 1989.

Patton, J. Howard, *Scrapbook of Pennsylvania Railroad Locomotives, 1909-1912*, PRR Office of the Secretary, Library Reference Materials (1834-1968), Penn Central Railroad Collection, MG-286, Pennsylvania State Archives, Harrisburg, Pa.

Sinclair, Angus, *Development of the Locomotive Engine*, Cambridge, Ma.: MIT Press 1970, Annotated Edition.

Sipes, William B., *The Pennsylvania Railroad: Its Origin, Construction, Condition and Connections*, Philadelphia: PRR Passenger Department, 1875.

Talbott, Elisha H., and Hobart, Horace Reynolds, *The Biographical Directory of the Railway Officials of America: An alphabetical list of general and division officers of railways on the American continent, with a record of their railway service*, various years.

Ward, James A. *J. Edgar Thomson: Master of The Pennsylvania*, Westport, Ct.: Greenwood Press, 1980.

Warner, Paul T., *Motive Power Development on the Pennsylvania Railroad 1831-1924*, Philadelphia: Pennsylvania Railroad, 1924.

Watkins, J. Elfreth, *History of the Pennsylvania Railroad Company 1846-1896*, Philadelphia, Pa.: n.p.1896.

White, John H., *A Short History of American Locomotive Builders In The Steam Era*, Washington D.C.: Bass Inc., 1982.

_____, *American Locomotives: An Engineering History, 1830-1880*, Baltimore: Johns Hopkins Press, 1968.

_____, *The John Bull: 150 Years a Locomotive*, Washington D.C.: Smithsonian Institution, 1981.

## Articles

Caruthers, C. H., "A Baldwin Freight Engine of 1850," *Locomotive Engineering*, June 1899, pp.292-293.

_____, "A Baldwin Saddle-Tank Locomotive of 1861," *Railway & Locomotive Engineering*, May 1902, pp.228-229.

_____, "Baldwin Locomotives for the Pennsylvania Railroad," *The Railroad Gazette*, Vol. XXX, No.18, May 6, 1898, pp.321-322.

_____, "Early Baldwin Locomotives on the Pennsylvania Railroad," *Locomotive Engineering*, February 1898, pp.110-111.

_____, "Early Valve Gears on the Pennsylvania Railroad," *The Railroad Gazette*, Vol. XLI, No. 7, August 27, 1906, pp.141-143.

_____, "Fast Passenger Locomotives on the Pennsylvania Railroad in 1850," *The Railroad Gazette*, Vol. XXXI, No. 30, July 28, 1899.

_____, "Locomotive Development on the Pennsylvania Railroad 1849-1905," *The Railroad Gazette*, Vol. XXXVIII, No. 17, April 23, 1905, pp.396-398.

_____, "Old Norris Freight Engines on the Pennsylvania Railroad," *The Railroad Gazette*, Vol. XXXII, No.18, p.290.

_____, "Painting of Pennsylvania Locomotives," *Pennsylvania Railroad: Locomotive and Cars, Stations, Bridges and Structures, Information and Data Book*, Yardley, Pa., E.P. Alexander, n.d.

_____, "Seth Wilmarth's Locomotives," *The Railroad Gazette*, Vol. XLIII, No. 13 September 27, 1907, pp.357-360.

_____, "Smith & Perkins, and Their Locomotives," *The Railroad Gazette*, Vol. XLII, No.16, April 19, 1907, pp.552-556.

_____, "Smith & Perkins Last Type of Locomotives," *Locomotive Engineering*, December 1900, p.519.

_____, "The Dimpfel Boiler," *Railway & Locomotive Engineering*, January 1903, p.43.

_____, "The Norris Locomotive Works, Part III," *Railroad Age Gazette*, Vol. XLVII, August 20, 1909, pp.313-315.

_____, "The Phleger Locomotive," *Locomotive Engineering*, October 1900, pp.438-439.

_____, "The Smith & Perkins Locomotive," *Locomotive Engineering*, Vol. 9, 1896, pp.905-906.

_____, "The Smoke Consuming Question Forty-Eight Years Ago," *The Railroad Gazette*, Vol. XLIII, No. 24, December 13, 1907, pp.719-724.

_____, "Successive Experiments and Improvements on Locomotives of the Pennsylvania Railroad," *The Railroad Gazette*, Vol. XLII, February 22, 1907, pp.235-241.

Fisher, Charles E., "Steam Locomotives of the Pennsylvania System," *Railway & Locomotive Historical Society, Bulletin No. 89*, November 1953; *Bulletin No. 90*, May 1954; *Bulletin No. 91*, October, 1954.

Ward, James A., "J. Edgar Thomson and the Georgia Railroad, 1834-1847," *Railway Locomotive & Historical Society, Railroad History #134*, Spring 1976.

## Index to Figures

*Engine Names are in Italics.*

## Index to Figures (continued)

*Engine Names are in Italics.*

## Newspapers

*Lewistown Gazette*, Lewistown, Pa., Saturday, August 25, 1849.

──────────, Saturday, September 1, 1849.

──────────, Saturday, November 17, 1849.

*Pennsylvania Telegraph*, Harrisburg, Pa., Wednesday, September 5, 1849.

## Other

Caruthers, C.H., "A drawing of the 'Perry'," *The Railroad Gazette*, July 26, 1907, p.99.

Letter from George M. Hart to Charles E. Fisher, March 20, 1943. The source of the correspondence contained in the letter is *Philadelphia & Columbia Railroad, Reports and Miscellaneous Documents*, Volume 2, #15.

## FOOTNOTES

The purpose of the two Latin abbreviations sprinkled through the footnotes is to avoid repeatedly setting out each reference in full. "Ibid." means "in the same place." This is used when the reference is the same as the one immediately preceding. "Op. cit." means "in the work cited." This is used when the reference is the same as set forth in a previous footnote for the same work.

Regarding *Master Mechanics Notebooks* references, multi-volume sets of the same work are considered as one reference after the first one, not a new one for each volume. That is the way the *MMN* footnotes after #149 (which cites the best archival reference we have.) are treated. They all came from the same place, so it would have been burdensome and unnecessary to separately set out each volume in full.

1. James A. Ward, *J. Edgar Thomson: Master of the Pennsylvania*, Westport, Ct., Greenwood Press, 1980, p.141.

2. The PRR had only an indirect half interest in the Indianapolis & St. Louis, which eventually became part of the NYC.

3. William Hassel Wilson, *The Columbia-Philadelphia Railroad and its Successor*, 1896, reprint, York, Pa., American Canal & Transportation Center, 2nd printing, 1992.

4. Ibid., pp.16 et. seq.

5. J. Knight & Benj. H. Latrobe, *Report Upon The Policy and Management of Several of the Principal Rail Roads in the Northern and Middle States*, 1838, reprint, Boston, Mass., Railway & Locomotive Historical Society, 1927, p.32.

6. Copies of these letters were contained in a letter from George M. Hart to Charles E. Fisher on March 20, 1943. The source of the letters is *Philadelphia & Columbia Railroad, Reports and Miscellaneous Documents*, Volume 2, #15.

7. William B. Sipes, *Pennsylvania Railroad, Historical & Descriptive*, Philadelphia, Pa., The Passenger Department (PRR), 1875, p.8. This is probably a later, romanticized version, like the story about the *Tom Thumb* and the horse. Presumably, it refers to the opening excursion of April 15-16, 1834. Contemporary newspaper accounts merely refer to the locomotive as too small; that is, not powerful enough.

8. Knight & Latrobe, op. cit., p.31.

9. A complete account of coal burning may be found in Frederick Moore Binder, *Coal Age Empire: Pennsylvania Coal and its Utilization to 1860*, Harrisburg, Pa., Pennsylvania Historical & Museum Commission, 1974, pp.117, et. seq.

10. *Pennsylvania State Journal*, 1835-36, Vol. I, p.57.

11. *Pennsylvania State Journal*, 1840, Appendix to Vol. II, p.71.

12. *Lewistown Gazette*, Lewistown, Pa., Saturday, February ?, 1850.

13. Benjamin F.G. Kline, *The Odyssey of Five Locomotives: 1835-1965*, reprint, Lancaster, Pa., Lancaster County Historical Society.

14. Solomon W. Roberts, *Reminiscences of the First Railroad Over the Allegheny Mountain*, read before the Historical Society of Pennsylvania, April 8, 1878.

15. *Sylvester Welch's Report on the Allegheny Portage Railroad*, 1833, reprint, York, Pa.: American Canal & Transportation Center, 1975.

16. Harry A. Jacobs, *The Juniata Canal and Old Portage Railroad*, Altoona, Pa.: Blair County Historical Society, 1941, reprinted 1969, p.8.

17. Roberts, op. cit.

18. Pennsylvania Railroad Company, *Minute Books of the Board of Directors of the Pennsylvania Rail Road Company, 1847-1957*, Vol. I, minutes for April 9, 1847, PRR Office of the Secretary, Library Reference Materials (1834-1868), Penn Central Railroad Collection, MG-286, Pennsylvania State Archives, Harrisburg, Pa.

19. Pennsylvania Railroad Company, *First Annual Report of the Chief Engineer, June 12, 1848*, Philadelphia, Pa., John C. Clark, 1848, Pennsylvania Railroad Technical & Historical Society, reprint edition, 1997, p.3.

20. *History of that Part of The Susquehanna & Juniata Valleys Embraced by the Counties of Mifflin, Juniata, Perry, Union And Snyder in the Commonwealth of Pennsylvania*, Vol. II, Philadelphia: Everets, Peck & Richards, 1886, p.440.

21. Ward, op. cit., p.76.

22. Pennsylvania Railroad Company, *Road Committee Minutes*, minutes for October 27, 1848, PRR Office of the Secretary, Library Reference Materials (1834-1868), Penn Central Railroad Collection, MG-286, Pennsylvania State Archives, Harrisburg, Pa.,

23. Pennsylvania Railroad Company, *Fourth Annual Report of the Directors of the Pennsylvania Railroad Company to the Stockholders, December 31, 1850*, p.40.

24. For a discussion of the PRR's first locomotive, see Appendix A.

25. Pennsylvania Railroad Company, *Road Committee Minutes*, op. cit., minutes for October 3, 1848.

26. J. Edgar Thomson, *Letterbook of J. Edgar Thomson, Chief Engineer, 1847-1851*, JET to S.V. Merrick, October 2, 1848, PRR Office of the Secretary, Library Reference Materials (1834-1868), Penn Central Railroad Collection, MG-286, Pennsylvania State Archives, Harrisburg, Pa.,

27. The Baldwin classification system is discussed in Appendix E.

28. Baldwin Locomotive Works Papers, *Letterbooks*, Historical Society of Pennsylvania, Philadelphia, Pa., Matthias W. Baldwin to J. Edgar Thomson, September 21, 1848.

29. Pennsylvania Railroad Company, *Board of Directors Minute Books*, op. cit., Volume I, minutes for October 18, 1848.

30. Ibid., minutes for November 22, 1848.

31. C.H. Caruthers, "A Baldwin Freight Engine of 1850," *Locomotive Engineering*, June 1899, pp.292-293.

32. Pennsylvania Railroad Company, *Board of Directors Minute Books*, op. cit., Vol. I, minutes for January 3, 1849.

33. Ibid., minutes for June 17, 1849.

34. Ibid., minutes for April 18, 1849.

35. Ibid., minutes for November 28, 1849.

36. Baldwin, *Letterbooks*, op. cit., MWB to H.R. Campbell, May 9, 1848. This letter was addressed to Gov. Paine, but was sent to H.R. Campbell and not given to Gov. Paine.

37. Ibid., MWB to Gov. Paine, May 9, 1848.

38. Ibid.

39. The fifth Class A was the *Susquehanna*, (#381, May 16, 1850), sold to the Hudson River Railroad.

40. Baldwin, *Letterbooks*, op. cit., JET to MWB, June 16, 1848.

41. Ibid., MWB to JET, June 17, 1848. "Your" passenger engine probably refers to the *Arrow*, a 12-ton, eight-wheel C (4-4-0, c/n #319) that Baldwin sent to the Georgia Railroad on November 22, 1847.

42. Ibid.

43. Ibid., JET to MWB, July 17, 1849.

44. William Pettit was a draftsman at Baldwin and worked with Matthias Baldwin on design. John K. Brown, *The Baldwin Locomotive Works: 1831-1915*, Baltimore, Md., Johns Hopkins University Press, 1995, p.101.

45. Baldwin, *Letterbooks*, op. cit., JET to MWB, July 21, 1849.

46. For a description of these locomotives see, C. H. Caruthers, "Fast Passenger Locomotives on the Pennsylvania Railroad," *Railroad Gazette*, Vol. XXXI, No. 30, July 28, 1899.

47. Baldwin, *Letterbooks*, op. cit., JET to MWB, June 5, 1849.

48. The "Placed on Road" dates show that the *Mifflin* was put on the road September 1, 1849, the *Blair* on September 23, 1849, and the *Indiana* on January 22, 1850. Note the discrepancy in Baldwin's date and the "Placed on Road" date for the *Blair*.

49. Herman Haupt, *Reminiscences Of The Early History Of The Pennsylvania Railroad Company*, undated, p.8, in Pennsylvania Railroad Company, Miscellaneous, Vol. I, Hill Railway Library Collection, University of Wisconsin, Madison, Wis.

50. *History of that Part of The Susquehanna and Juniata Valleys*, op. cit., Vol. II, p.441.

51. Pennsylvania Railroad Company, *Board of Directors Minute Books*, op. cit., Volume I, minutes for April 5, 1848.

52. Baldwin, *Letterbooks*, op. cit., JET to MWB, September 24, 1848.

53. Ibid., MWB to JET, September 25, 1848. The dates in this exchange show that the mail between Harrisburg and Philadelphia was faster in 1848 than it is today.

54. Pennsylvania Railroad Company, *Board of Directors Minute Books*, op. cit., Volume I, November 7, 1849, letter from H. Haupt reporting that the *D.R. Porter* had run off the track and has been considerably damaged, no persons were injured.

55. Ibid., minutes for January 12, 1848.

56. *History of that Part of The Susquehanna and Juniata Valleys*, op. cit., Vol. II, p.441.

57. Baldwin, *Letterbooks*, op. cit., MWB to JET, November 30, 1848, December 4, 1848, December 12, 1848.

58. Ibid., JET to MWB, April 25, 1849.

59. Ibid., JET to MWB, April 30, 1849.

60. Ibid., JET to MWB, November 25, 1849.

61. Pennsylvania Railroad Company, *Board of Directors Minute Books*, Vol. I, minutes for January 9, 1850.

62. Ibid., minutes for January 19, 1850

63. Pennsylvania Railroad Company, *Board of Directors Minute Books*, Volume I, minutes for January 23, 1850.

64. Ibid., minutes for October 17, 1849.

65. Thomson, *Letterbooks*, op. cit., Norris Brothers to JET, February 9, 1850 and February 14, 1850.

66. Ibid., M.W. Baldwin to JET, February 14, 1850.

67. Pennsylvania Railroad Company, *Board of Directors Minute Books*, op cit., Volume I, minute for February 20, 1850.

68. Thomson, *Letterbooks*, op. cit., JET to Board, February 16, 1850.

69. Ibid.

70. Ibid.

71. Baldwin, *Letterbooks*, op. cit., JET to MWB, January 22, 1850.

72. Ibid., JET to MWB, January 26, 1850.

73. Ibid.

74. Ibid., JET to MWB, February 20, 1850.

75. For a further discussion of the influence of master mechanics on the locomotive builder, see Brown's *Baldwin Locomotive Works*, op. cit., pp.63-66.

76. C.H. Caruthers, "Early Baldwin Locomotives on the Pennsylvania Railroad," *Locomotive Engineering*, February 1898, pp.100-111.

77. Pennsylvania Railroad Company, *Fourth Annual Report*, op. cit., p.62.

78. Baldwin, *Letterbooks*, op. cit., MWB to JET, December 8, 1848.

79. Pennsylvania Railroad Company, *Board of Directors Minute Books*, op. cit., Volume I, minute for July 10, 1850

80. Ibid, minutes for April 30, 1851.

81. Pennsylvania Railroad Company, *Fifth Annual Report of the Directors of the Pennsylvania Railroad Company to the Stockholders*, February 2, 1852, pp.65-66.

82. Matthew Tibby, "Personal Reminiscences of the Early Days of the Pennsylvania Railroad at Pittsburgh, April 27, 1893," manuscript in PRR Office of the Secretary, Library Reference Materials (1834-1868), Penn Central Railroad Collection, MG-286, Pennsylvania State Archives, Harrisburg, Pa.

83. The *Heisley* was the former Harrisburg & Lancaster *David R. Porter*, a Norris 4-2-0 (48" drivers, 10" x 20" cylinders), which was wrecked in November 1849, killing a civil engineer by the name of Heisley. The loco was rebuilt to a 4-4-0 at Harrisburg in August 1851 and renamed *Heisley*.

84. Brinton's Station was between Braddock and East Pittsburgh.

85. Beatty's Station was just west of Latrobe.

86. The *Henry Clay*, a 4-2-0, was a Norris product from the HPM&L, acquired by the PRR on October 16, 1849.

87. Tibby, op. cit.

88. Tibby refers to Radebaugh's as Rhodebaugh's (this pronunciation is common among local residents today).

89. Ibid.

90. George W. Grier was later Master of Machinery from 1858 to1862.

91. C.H. Caruthers, "Early Baldwin Locomotives on the Pennsylvania Railroad," op. cit., pp.100-111. Angus Sinclair in his *Development of the Locomotive Engine*, Cambridge, Mass., MIT Press, 1970, Annotated Edition, pp.337-338, describing the first ten-wheel locomotive (4-6-0) built by Norris in 1847 for the P&R, states that it was so successful the PRR ordered 20 of them. The first 4-6-0's on the PRR were the six noted above from Baldwin; Norris didn't supply a 4-6-0 until

92. C.H. Caruthers, "Smith & Perkins and Their Locomotives," *Railroad Gazette*, Vol. XLII, #16, April 19, 1907, pp.552-556.

93. Pennsylvania Railroad Company, *Fifth Annual Report*, op. cit., p.62.

94. A. Howry Espenshade, *Pennsylvania Place Names*, Baltimore, Md.: Genealogical Publishing Company, 1925, reprint, 1995, pp.176-177.

95. Pennsylvania Railroad Company, *Fifth Annual Report*, op. cit., p.65.

96. Ibid., p.64.

97. C. H. Caruthers, "Baldwin Locomotives for the Pennsylvania Railroad," *Railroad Gazette*, Vol. XXX, #18, May 6, 1898, p.332.

98. Pennsylvania Railroad Company, *Board of Directors Minute Books*, op. cit., Vol. I, minutes for December 12, 1849.

99. C.H. Caruthers, "Seth Wilmarth's Locomotives," *Railroad Gazette*, Vol. XLII, September 27, 1907, pp.357-360.

100. Ibid., p.360.

101. C.H. Caruthers, "The Norris Locomotive Works, Part III," *Railroad Age Gazette*, August 20, 1904, p.313.

102. C.H. Caruthers, ""Smith & Perkins and Their Locomotives," op. cit., pp.553-555 and "The Smith & Perkins Locomotive," *Locomotive Engineering*, Vol. 9, 1896, pp.905-6.

103. Baldwin, *Letterbooks*, op. cit., JET to MWB, January 1,1849.

104. For a description of Winans' Camels see John H. White, *American Locomotives: An Engineering History, 1830-1880*, Baltimore, Md., Johns Hopkins Press, 1968, pp.347-357.

105. C.H. Caruthers, "The Norris Locomotive Works, Part III," op. cit., p.315.

106. C.H. Caruthers, "Old Norris Freight Engine on the PRR," *Railroad Gazette*, XXXII, Vol. 18, p.290.

107. The *Allegrippus* was named for *Alleguippas* (or *Allaguipas*), an Iroquois chief, whose son, *Cashiowaya*, rendered service to the English during the French and Indian War. See George P. Donehoo, *A History of Indian Villages and Place Names in Pennsylvania*, Harrisburg, Pa., 1928, reprinted Baltimore, Md., Gateway Press, 1977, p.6.

108. Pennsylvania Railroad Company, *Eighth Annual Report of the Directors of the Pennsylvania Railroad Company to the Stockholders*, February 5, 1855, p.52.

109. C.H. Caruthers, "Early Valve Gear on the PRR," *Railroad Gazette*, Vol. XLI, #7, August 27, 1906, pp.141-143.

110. C.H. Caruthers, "The Norris Locomotive Works, Part III," op. cit., p.313.

111. Pennsylvania Railroad Company, *Fourth Annual Report*, op. cit., p.43.

112. Pennsylvania Railroad Company, *Eighth Annual Report*, op. cit., p.30.

113. Pennsylvania Railroad Company, *Ninth Annual Report of the Directors of the Pennsylvania Railroad Company to the Stockholders*, February 4, 1856, p.46.

114. Pennsylvania Railroad Company, *Tenth Annual Report of the Directors of the Pennsylvania Railroad Company to the Stockholders*, February 2, 1857, p.39

115. C.H. Caruthers, "Smith & Perkins Last Type of Locomotive," *Locomotive Engineering*, December 1900, p.519.

116. Pennsylvania Railroad Company, *Eighth Annual Report*, op. cit., p.50.

117. Pennsylvania Railroad Company, *Ninth Annual Report*, op. cit., p.49.

118. Pennsylvania Railroad Company, *Eleventh Annual Report of the Directors of the Pennsylvania Railroad Company to the Stockholders*, February 1, 1858, p.34.

119. Ibid., p.14

120. Ibid., p.33.

121. C.H. Caruthers, "Locomotive Development on the Pennsylvania Railroad 1849-1905," *Railroad Gazette*, Vol. XXXVIII, #17, April 23, 1905.

122. C.H. Caruthers, "The Phleger Locomotive," *Locomotive Engineering*, October 1900, pp.438-439.

123. Pennsylvania Railroad Company, *Twelfth Annual Report of the Board of Directors of the Pennsylvania Railroad Company to the Stockholders*, February 7, 1859, pp.84-91.

124. C.H. Caruthers, "The Dimpfel Boiler," *Railway & Locomotive Engineering*, January 1903, p.43.

125. Pennsylvania Railroad Company, *Thirteenth Annual Report of the Board of Directors of the Pennsylvania Railroad Company to the Stockholders*, February 6, 1860, p.27.

126. Also see Frederick M. Binder, *Coal Age Empire*, Harrisburg, Pa., Pennsylvania Historical & Museum Commission, 1974, pp.126-129.

127. C.H. Caruthers, "The Smoke Consuming Question Forty-Eight Years Ago," *Railroad Gazette*, Vol. XLIII, December 13, 1907, pp.719-723.

128. Pennsylvania Railroad Company, *Thirteenth Annual Report*, op. cit., p.27.

129. *American Railroad Journal*, May 25, 1860, June 16, 1860 and July 14, 1860.

130. C.H. Caruthers reported seeing #215 in the late summer of 1861 in Pittsburgh. "A Baldwin Saddle Tank of 1862," *Railway & Locomotive Engineering*, May 1902.

131. C.H. Caruthers, "Successive Experiments and Improvements on Locomotives of the Pennsylvania Railroad," *Railroad Gazette*, Vol. XLII, #86, February 22, 1907, p.237.

132. Pennsylvania Railroad Company, *Fifteenth Annual Report of the Board of Directors of the Pennsylvania Railroad Company to the Stockholders*, February 3, 1862, p.13

133. Pennsylvania Railroad Company, *Fourteenth Annual Report of the Board of Directors of the Pennsylvania Railroad Company to the Stockholders*, February 4, 1861, p.46.

134. The Winans Camels leased from the P&R were *Colorado*, *Mississippi*, *New Jersey* and *Connecticut*. The *Pawnee* class ("pseudo-Moguls") were *Comanche*, *Tecumseh*, *Wabash* and *Wissahicken*.

135. The Second Class freight locomotive was #142, a 4-4-0 with 60" drivers and 16" x 22" cylinders, built by Baldwin in April 1862. The Baldwin construction record shows no locomotive sold to the PRR in April 1862.

136. Pennsylvania Railroad Company, *Sixteenth Annual Report of the Board of Directors of the Pennsylvania Railroad Company to the Stockholders*, February 2, 1863, pp.30-31.

137. Ibid., p.30.

138. Pennsylvania Railroad Company, *Seventeenth Annual Report of the Board of Directors of the Pennsylvania Railroad Company to the Stockholders*, February 16, 1864, p.37.

139. Ibid., p.33.

140. This note, in the Pennsylvania Railroad Company, *Twentieth Annual Report of the Board of Directors of the Pennsylvania Railroad Company to the Stockholders*, February 19, 1867, is problematic; there were only two Perkins engines sent to the P&E according to C.H. Caruthers, "Smith and Perkins and Their Locomotives," op. cit., p.554. Two Smith & Perkins locos, #'s 63 and 93, were sent to the P&E in 1864. Two Baldwin 4-6-0's were built in 1864 and filled these numbers. The *Register of Engines, February 1868*, shows #210 as "Company"-built, with a new copper firebox, dated March 1867. Caruthers claims that this is one of the Smith & Perkins locos, rebuilt. A photo shows the typical S&P "buckhorn" on the boiler waist. Second #210, a Norris 4-6-0 with a Phleger boiler, passed out of service between 1869 and 1872. (Caruthers, "The Phleger Locomotive," op. cit., p.439). The disposition of the second S&P loco is unknown, as is the identity of the third.

141. #142 may not have been the first locomotive built new at Altoona. See Appendix B for a further discussion.

142. Pennsylvania Railroad Company, *Twenty First Annual Report of the Board of Directors of the Pennsylvania Railroad Company to the Stockholders*, February 18, 1868, p.50.

143. *Railroad Gazette*, May 25, 1894, Vol. 26, p.379.

144. Pennsylvania Railroad Company, *Twenty First Annual Report*, op. cit., p.39.

145. Pennsylvania Railroad Company, *Twenty Second Annual Report of the Board of Directors of the Pennsylvania Railroad Company to the Stockholders*, February 16, 1869, p.35.

146. Ibid., p.40.

147. Between May 1867 and January 1868, Baldwin built three 4-4-0's and nine 4-6-0's, which temporarily held PRR #'s 429-440 before being transferred to the PC&C.

148. The Baldwin record of construction has a date of July 27, 1868 for #154. The August date is the "Put On Road" date, when the locomotive was officially added to the equipment. This information is in the *Register of Engines Made by M.W. Baldwin*, a copy of which is at the Pennsylvania State Archives, Harrisburg, Pa

149. See Appendix G for the original specifications for the first seven classes, from the *Master Mechanic's Notebooks A-F*, PRR Office of the Secretary, Library Reference Materials (1834-1868), Penn Central Railroad Collection, MG-286, Pennsylvania State Archives, Harrisburg, Pa.

150. The *Master Mechanic's Notebook B*, ibid, has a date of March 28, 1873 for the revised Class C boiler, pp.76-77.

151. The identity of these two locomotives is unknown.

152. Pennsylvania Railroad Company, *Twenty Fifth Annual Report of the Board of Directors of the Pennsylvania Railroad Company to the Stockholders*, February 20, 1872, p.38.

153. Sipes, op. cit., p.27.

154. *Master Mechanic's Notebook D*, op. cit., p.199.

155. *Master Mechanic's Notebook A*, op. cit., p.168.

156. Ibid., p.84.

157. Ibid., p.2.

158. Ibid., p.9.

159. Ibid., p.6.

160. Ibid., p.16.

161. Pennsylvania Railroad Company, *Board of Directors Minute Books*, op. cit., Volume I, minutes for April 18, 1849. The Board approved a contract with French & Baird for the use of their patent spark arrester.

162. *Master Mechanic's Notebook A*, op. cit., p.73.

163. Ibid., p.11.

164. Ibid., p.18.

165. Ibid., p.18.

166. Ibid., p.10.

167. Ibid., p.19.

168. Ibid., p.10.

169. Ibid., p.68.

170. Ibid., p.5.

171. Ibid., p.14.

172. *Master Mechanic's Notebook D*, op. cit., p.62.

173. *Master Mechanic's Notebook A*, op. cit., p.82.

174. *Master Mechanic's Notebook E*, op. cit., p.73.

175. *Master Mechanic's Notebook A*, op. cit., p.83.

176. Ibid., p.13.

177. Ibid., p.81.

178. *Master Mechanic's Notebook F*, op. cit., 21.

179. Ibid., P.23.

180. *Master Mechanic's Notebook A*, op. cit., p.14.

181. *Master Mechanics Notebook E*, op. cit., p.47.

182. James Dredge, *The Pennsylvania Railroad: Its Origin, Construction and Management*, London & New York: John Wiley & Sons, 1879, p.136.

183. J. Elfreth Watkins, *History of the Pennsylvania Railroad Company 1846-1896*, Philadelphia, Pa., n.p. 1896, Vol. II, pp.24-25.

184. John H. White, Jr., *The John Bull: 150 Years a Locomotive*, Washington, D.C.: Smithsonian Institution, 1981, p.39.

185. I am not sure where Watkins came up with this date, possibly from the minutes of the Road or Finance Committees. The Watkins typescript is notorious for minor numerical errors in dates. The *Minute Books of the Board of Directors* beginning on March 30, 1847, which I consulted at the State Archives, Harrisburg, Pa., records the first mention of locomotives on October 4, 1848.

186. Watkins, op. cit., Vol. II, p.25.

187. Paul T. Warner, "Motive Power Development, Pennsylvania Railroad System," *Baldwin Locomotives*, Vol. 2, No.4, April 1924, pp. 11-12. The three article series was reprinted by the Pennsylvania Railroad as a book, *Motive Power Development on the Pennsylvania Railroad 1831-1924*, Philadelphia: Pennsylvania Railroad, 1924.

188. Ibid., p.11.

189. Ibid., p.12.

190. Charles E. Fisher, "Steam Locomotives of the Pennsylvania System," *Railway & Locomotive Historical Society, Bulletin #89*, November 1953, p.145.

191. George H. Burgess and Miles C. Kennedy, *Centennial History of the Pennsylvania Railroad Company 1846-1946*, Philadelphia, Pa., Pennsylvania Railroad Company, 1949, pp.53-54.

192. Ibid., pp.710-11.

193. *Register of Engines Made by M. W. Baldwin*, op. cit. When the book was opened to copy, the column showing the wheels (driver diameter) did not show upon the copy.

194. Benjamin F. Custer was preceded in this post by Daniel W. Caldwell (1852), and William M. McClure (1853). Reports earlier than 1852 do not show a Chief Clerk of the Motive Power Department.

195. James A. Ward, "J. Edgar Thomson and the Georgia Railroad, 1834-1847," *Railway & Locomotive Historical Society Railroad History*, #134, Spring 1976, pp.12-13.

196. Baldwin wrote to Thomson on February 26, 1848, offering to build five freight locomotives for the Georgia Railroad. Baldwin, *Letterbooks*, op. cit., MWB to JET, February 26,1848.

197. Ibid., MWB to JET, March 18, 1848.

198. Ibid.

199. bid.

200. It cost Baldwin about $2,000 for plans and patterns for a specially ordered machine. John K. Brown, *The Baldwin Locomotive Works: 1831-1915*, op. cit., p.64, also endnote #27, p.270.

201. Baldwin, *Letterbooks*, op. cit., MWB to JET, March 18, 1848.

202. Ibid., JET to MWB, June 16, 1848.

203. Ibid., MWB to JET, June 17, 1848.

204. Ibid., JET to MWB, June 18, 1848.

205. Ibid., MWB to JET, June 19, 1848.

206. Ibid., JET to MWB, June 20, 1848.

207. Ibid., MWB to JET, September 21, 1848.

208. Ibid.

209. Ibid., JET to MWB, September 26, 1848.

210. Ibid., MWB to JET, September 29, 1848.

211. Ibid.

212. Pennsylvania Railroad Company, *Board of Directors Minute Books*, op. cit., Volume I, minutes for October 4, 1849.

213. Baldwin, *Letterbooks*, op. cit., JET to MWB, October 8, 1848.

214. Pennsylvania Railroad Company, *Board of Directors Minute Books*, op. cit., Volume I, minutes for October 18, 1848.

215. Baldwin, *Letterbooks*, op. cit., JET to MWB, November 3, 1848.

216. Pennsylvania Railroad Company, *Board of Directors Minute Books*, op. cit., Volume I, minutes for November 22, 1848

217. A look at the *Register of Engines Made By M.W. Baldwin*, op. cit., is illuminating. Construction numbers 333 and 334, both with dates of November 7, 1848, are 21-ton "eight-wheel E" locomotives, *Dauphin* and *Perry*, purchased by the Pennsylvania Rail Road. The next three construction numbers are assigned to eight-wheel E locomotives purchased by the Baltimore & Ohio, the *Hector* (#335, January 16, 1849), the *Tartar* (#336, December 8, 1849) and the *Cossack* (#337, October 25, 1848). Those built for the B&O did not have the Baldwin flexible-beam truck that brought their weight into line with the B&O's specifications. The mysterious third locomotive Baldwin built cannot be identified. The correspondence clearly suggests that Baldwin had three locomotives for sale. The PRR received two of them. The correspondence also suggests that the *Westmoreland*, built to the same design, a 21-ton, eight-wheel E, was not yet put under construction in November 1848. There are two candidates for the third E engine originally built for the B&O in the *Register of Engines Made by M.W. Baldwin*: #342, sold to the Vermont Central on January 20, 1849 (which was inside connected) and #366, sold to the Mine Hill & Schuylkill Haven on August 2, 1849.

218. Baldwin, *Letterbooks*, op. cit., MWB to JET, December 8, 1848.

219. Ibid., JET to MWB, December 11, 1848.

220. Ibid., JET to MWB, January 1, 1849.

221. C.H. Caruthers, "A Baldwin Freight Engine of 1850," op. cit., pp.292-3. A drawing of the *Perry* appears in *The Railroad Gazette*, July 26, 1907, p.99.

222. Baldwin, *Letterbooks*, op. cit., JET to MWB, January 20, 1850.

223. Ibid., JET to MWB, January 26, 1850.

224. C.H. Caruthers, "A Baldwin Freight Engine of 1850," op. cit., p.293.

225. Excerpts from the Huntingdon & Broad Top Mountain Railroad & Coal Company records were supplied by Larry Williams of Saxton, Pa.

226. Watkins, op. cit., Volume II, p.24.

227. Baldwin, *Letterbooks*, op. cit., JET to MWB, June 18, 1848.

228. The first locomotive to operate on PRR's tracks may actually have been one of the Harrisburg & Lancaster's engines. JET wrote to MWB (December 11, 1848) that the contractors took the *Franklin*, an H&L Baldwin built 4-4-0, and hauled five cars loaded with passengers five miles up the road. Baldwin, *Letterbooks*, op. cit.

229. *Lewistown Gazette*, Lewistown, Pa., Saturday, August 25, 1849.

230. *Lewistown Gazette*, Saturday, September 1, 1849.

231. *Pennsylvania Telegraph*, Harrisburg, Pa., Wednesday, September 5, 1849.

232. *Lewistown Gazette*, Saturday, November 17, 1849.

233. "Engine #692, the first one turned out by Juniata Shop, was received by us about noon of 7/27/1891 and placed in charge of Jack McLellan for trial. Ran the engine seven trips assisting trains and found it to work very well. It steams well, valves are well set, and the machinery is in very good condition. After trial, engine was placed in the Middle Division Round House, subject to order of Supt. Of Motive Power." *Master Mechanics Notebook N*, op. cit., p.19, July 29, 1891.

234. The "Lovell List" shows Altoona Machine Shop #1770 as the first AMS built locomotive to have the construction number on the badge plate.

235. John H. White, *A Short History Of American Locomotive Builders In The Steam Era*, Washington, D.C.: Bass Inc., 1982, p.5.

236. Pennsylvania Railroad Company, *Tenth Annual Report*, op. cit., p.50.

237. Pennsylvania Railroad Company, *Twenty Second Annual Report*, op. cit., p.35.

238. Material in quotation marks is from J.P. Laird's report in the Pennsylvania Railroad Company, *Sixteenth Annual Report*, op. cit., p.31.

239. I have seen dates of November 1866, December 1866, and January 1867 given for #142. The "Lovell List" published by the NRHS shows December 1866. The *Locomotive Register* for February 1868 shows that a new iron firebox was applied in December 1866.

240. Pennsylvania Railroad Company, *Board of Directors Minute Books*, op. cit., Vol. 1, minutes for January 9, 1867.

241. John C. Page, *A Special Study, Pennsylvania Railroad Shops and Works, Altoona, Pennsylvania*, United States Department of the Interior, National Parks Service, May 1989, p.53.

242. J.A. Lockard to H.T. Cover, January 31, 1949, Box 486, Chief of Motive Power File, Pennsylvania Railroad Collection, Acc. #1810, Hagley Museum and Library, Wilmington, Del.

## Index of Charts & Lists